LYME DISEASE AND THE SS ELBRUS

Josef Mengele aka Henry Tolkmith?

LYME
DISEASE
AND
THE SS ELBRUS

COLLABORATION BETWEEN THE NAZIS
AND COMMUNISTS IN CHEMICAL
AND BIOLOGICAL WARFARE

RACHEL VERDON

Elderberry Press. LLC

Elderberry Press

1393 Old Homestead Drive, Second floor
Oakland, Oregon 97462—9506.
E-MAIL: editor@elderberrypress.com
TEL/FAX: 541.459.6043
http://elderberrypress.com

All Elderberry books are available from your favorite bookstore, amazon.com, or from our 24 hour order line: 1.800.431.1579

Library of Congress Control Number: 2006926404
Publisher's Catalog—in—Publication Data
Lyme Disease and the SS Elbrus/Rachel Verdon
ISBN 10: 1932762620
ISBN 13: 978-1-932762-62-4

1. Politics.
2. Lyme Disease.
3. Communism.
4. Biological Warfare.
5. Chemical Warfare.
I. Title

This book was written, printed and bound in the United States of America.

CONTENTS

ARE BIRDS OR SHIPS SPREADING LYME?

Portland

Duluth

Boston
New York
Philadelphia
80%

New Orleans
Port Arthur

FOUR FLYWAYS of North American Birds:
FOUR PORT SITES OF LYME DISEASE

Pacific Coast: Alaskan Coast, British Columbia,
California, Baja Penn., and Mexico

Central Plains: Yukon Territory, East of Continental
Divide, to Mexico

Mississippi: Central Alaska, Great Lakes, down
Miss. River, to Yucatan Penn.

East Coast: Prince Edward Is., Canada, Atlantic
Seaboard, to Florida, Cuba, Venezuela

Compare: Information from: "The Migration of Birds" by Jean Dorat,
Houghton Mifflin 1962, pg. 126, 'Flyways of North America'
to Matt Clark's "The Spread of Lyme Disease" "Newsweek"
July 27, 1987 pg. 54, map of Lyme disease areas. Canada, the
West Coast, Central Plains, Florida, Gulf of Mexico, Caribbean,
and Venezuela should be inundated, but Lyme Disease is situated
at four major port sites, with 44% all cases in New York City.

FOREWORD

The purpose of this book, in plain talk, is exposure of a potential Fascist-Communist alliance inciting world revolution and race purification, using biological warfare and the drug industry. Their objectives may very well be the destruction of democracies from within to cut the world's population in half. The history of this alleged alliance is chronologically developed from World War I through the New Millenium. Lyme Disease is merely a tracer in a barrage of diseases, its suspect origin, the Soviet fur and shipping industry, Soyuzpushnina, and some twenty-four Soviet biological warfare factories stretched across the Asian continent from the Black Sea to Eastern Siberia. The proposed strategy was simple. Hit the poor with diseases of the nervous system, and then sell them the drugs to put them out of their misery. Democracies would be put to the test, nations that professed to be ruled by law and common men, not by a race of immunologically superior geniuses, boasting Utopia. The partial evidence of this strategy appears to have been evoked during the Bolshevik Revolution, later sparking World War II. A strategy of this kind, naturally would backfire, for what goes around, comes around.

The Soviet BW factories, aided by crackpot Nazi scientists, delighted to offer their expertise, cultured a host of tick borne diseases and millions of infested rats: typhus, relapsing fever, brucellosis, tularemia, Q fever, dysentery, rickettsialpox, bubonic plague, and Lyme disease, to list a few. This is documented in our WW II intelligence files. The hoards of rats were set loose upon the unsuspecting nomadic tribesmen revolting against collectivization. Ironically, it was the poor who resisted enslavement. In a panic, the Moslems and Mongolians slaughtered all of their own livestock and wildlife: 25 million head of sheep, 15 million head of cattle, horses, ponies, camels, minks, foxes, sables, anything that walked or crawled on all fours, anything except the rats. Consequently, millions starved to death. Alexei Kosygin, head of Soyuzpushnina, and future Secretary General of the Communist Party, commanded the tons of infested furs, wool, and camel hairs be shipped to America. Loaded upon the very lend-lease ships we sent Stalin to fight Hitler, like a fleet of Flying Dutchmen, the furs and rats sailed around the globe. Soon, our cities and farms would be plagued with brand new tick borne diseases, previously not indigenous to our western hemisphere. The rats are here to this day, the furry ones and the political ones. Has our health, wealth and national security been jeopardized by an insidious medical fraud? A huge drug culture mushroomed in South America run by ODESSA, a cult of grisly Nazi double agents working for the GRU, the Soviet Union's Red Army Military Intelligence. Yes, little children, Jurassic Park is real. Guess who is the tyrannosaurus?

The Nazis have been the Communists' closest allies hiding in the Communist's closet since Kaiser Wilhelm funded the Bolshevik Revolution. Racism is the foundation of Communism; it has been all along. The Marxist's lure "Each according to his abilities, each according to his needs" is doublespeak and should be interpreted as such: "no ability, not needed." The public has been duped and doped from the start. Seeking the origin of Lyme disease has indeed opened up a can of spirochetes, just follow the furs in the wake of the SS ELBRUS. Better yet, seek an eye witness to this infamous Communist-Fascist plot inciting, riot, revolution, and race purification to bolster circumstantial evidence. Seek a witness who served Hitler, Stalin, and Truman alike. Who was Henry Tolkmith?

INTRODUCTION

Glastonbury, Connecticut is a quaint colonial town just south of Hartford, on the East side of the Connecticut River, the river running north to south, cutting the state virtually in half. And that's its problem, Glastonbury is on the east side. The town is the epitome of New England with its historic houses lining Main Street. One of the oldest operating cider mills in America ground up truck loads of apples, bees, leaves, twigs and worms, ready to drink right on the spot. Roaring Brook, now a state park, is lined with the ruins of an old textile mill, a reminder of Connecticut's once booming industry of cotton, wool and silk. Dairy farms, apple and peach orchards were replaced by bedroom town developments in the 50s and 60s, their homeowners, well educated professionals, their political persuasions swept from far right to far left.

Little Glastonbury, sporting a population if 20,000 in the 1950s became a den of intrigue. The flood plain along the Connecticut River, declared a bird sanctuary, offered rich black loam to the shade grown tobacco farmers. National corporations moved in, such as Consolidated Cigar, later purchased by Gulf and Western in 1968. Glastonbury also was home to Arbor Acres, the world's largest chicken breeding farm, each chick worth thousands of dollars. The farm was bought out by David Rockefeller in 1964, just after the Kennedy assassination. The chickens were perfectly healthy. The author asked the newest owners regarding the history of its farm, who insisted the chickens were so doped up with antibiotics that they were impervious to everything, including Lyme disease and a similar fowl parasite named Newcastle's disease. Were the birds the vector of Lyme? This theory has been disproven. But for the Rockefellers, maybe just being there was important for other reasons.

There was an old woollen textile mill in Glastonbury, first owned by the Matson family, later by the three Landry brothers, shut down since the 1950s while the New England textile industry went broke. This was only one of the many fine woolen and cotton mills which prospered on the east side of the Connecticut River. "Davidson's Textile Blue Book" indexed thousands of these small mills in the 1940s, many prospering from War Department contracts. The Landry brothers have all passed away, but the author did have an opportunity to question the youngest, in charge of the mill's machinery. They bought from New York wool auctions, and even opened an office there, but the youngest brother could offer no specifics. Old Lyme, Connecticut, where Lyme disease was first diagnosed, also ran the Old Lyme Handweavers mill. Neighboring Norwich had sported six such textile industries, also building the State's biggest insane asylum, which recently closed. Hundreds of Norwich's patients died, needlessly. Some had Lyme disease. The Pequot Indian tribe's Foxwoods gambling casino across the river made Norwich lucrative real-estate.

Glastonbury's school system was most progressive, the envy of the nation. It was first in the nation to teach Spanish and French in the primary grades, and the first to teach Russian in middle school, installing elaborate language labs. Foreign instructors flocked to Glastonbury just to teach in the prestigious public schools. There was also a NIKE site in Glastonbury, staffed by the Air Force, hidden in the back woodlands. Perhaps, that too, was drawing foreigners.

Just fifty miles north, resided the notorious White Russian, Anatase Vonsiatsky with his millionaire heiress, Marion Ream, on their Thompson golf course estate, plotting the overthrow of the Soviet Union. Vonsiatsky would prove to be a phony Fascists, with suspect ties to the KGB. He published a news journal "Fascists" with world-wide circulation, preaching the downfall of Communism. The pair globe trotted through Manchuria's White Russian community in Harbin, Nazi Germany, and the States. How much money he swindled out of his fellow refugees for his patriotic pretenses remains to be seen. Connecticut suited Vonsiatsky's personality perfectly, homeland of many other chiselers. Hartford, a safe inland port, ran a thriving spice trade in colonial days. Its seagoing merchants instructed their children to carve wooden nutmegs to mix with the real thing. "Spiced sawdust" graced the shelves of many pantries throughout New England. They don't call Connecticut the Nutmeg State for nothing. Not wanting to be named for racketeers, Connecticut changed its nickname to the "Constitution State."

Glastonbury had bigger problems. Many of its citizens had contracted Lyme disease since the 1940s. It was not a "new" disease of the 1970s as the public was led to believe. The author believes the Lyme epidemic began in the United States at the end of World War II from Soviet fur shipments and hopes the circumstantial evidence presented in this book may prompt witnesses to come forward.

The Lyme spirochete bacteria is carried by the ixodes dammini tick on the East Coast, a tick literally the size of a speck of pepper, and the ixodes pacificus tick on the West Coast. These ticks primary host on rodents. Lyme wrecks the immune and nervous system with a myriad of symptoms, very hard to diagnose without blood tests. Arthritis, heart ailments, muscle stiffness, headaches, allergies, rashes, fatigue and paralysis strike its victims. This spiral shaped microscopic worm is in the same family as syphilis and relapsing fever, eating myelin basic protein in cartilage and muscle tissue. Advanced infections reside in the blood, brain and spinal cord, one of the key components to multiple sclerosis.

The author has Lyme disease, and her twin has lupus, an autoimmune disease similar to leukemia. The author's health had been poor since childhood, and worsened after a series of passport vaccinations required for travel in 1968. Mother had been gossiping, talking of all the sick neighbors from Glastonbury having died of lupus, cancer, and suicides. Children had shot themselves in the head, others jumped out of cars into oncoming traffic, still others overdosing on narcotics. Lupus, breast cancer and brain tumors plagued the neighborhood. What was going on? After seeking a doctor for all the food and stomach allergies, suspecting the same fate as her twin, the author was diagnosed with Lyme disease, not lupus. What was Lyme, where did it come from, how long had the disease resided in Connecticut, and how many other victims were there?

Late one night, the author sought the address of the Glastonbury Health Department and called the Town Hall. Sergeant Higgins answered the phone, unbeknownst to him, his high school sweetheart, our neighbor, had died of lupus. Higgins mentioned the puzzling number of multiple sclerosis cases amongst his classmates of the 1950s. He and a fellow graduate, now a physician, approached the Farmington Medical Center to conduct a survey of our home town. They brushed him off, citing MS to be very common in Connecticut. Very true. There was a long trail of misery in the town's history going back to the 1940s. What was the source of Glastonbury's health crisis? Why did this dinky little town the size of a postage stamp have its own health department? Was this a hotbed of medical spies? Sargent Higgins was soon transferred out of his police job to another town. He became most difficult to reach. The Glastonbury Health Department could shed no light on any epidemiological evidence, only citing periodic round-ups and burnings of rats and chickens. Newcastle's disease had been a problem just after the war. There was no evidence of any chemical pollution from farms or industry in the water table or reservoirs that could have induced the cluster of Lupus or multiple sclerosis cases. Dr. Joseph Raffa, who had headed the Health Department for all those early years, had died. Nobody knew anything.

Articles regarding Lyme Disease have been published by noted scholars in the National Multiple Sclerosis Foundation, their Vice President, Byron Waksman, has gone into great detail over Lyme's involvement in the diagnosis of MS. His father, Selman Waksman, discoverer of streptomycin, a Russian immigrant of world repute, won the Nobel Prize for his research in antibiotics. Both father and son will figure heavily in the history of Lyme disease, trapped in a vice between feuding FBI and CIA.

Lyme disease was named after the town where it was first diagnosed, Old Lyme, Connecticut. In 1975, after getting a medical runaround, a group of irate mothers with arthritic children trotted over to Yale University's prestigious medical center. Old Lyme with its woolen textile mill, is situated on the east bank of the Connecticut River. Because of the tilt of the land, most of the streams feeding into the Connecticut River were on the state's east side, hence, most of the paddle wheel driven mills operated on the east side. Next to Old Lyme is the Groton Navy base, docking our nuclear subs. On the west side of the mouth of the river, is New Haven, home to Yale University, the CIA's stomping ground for new recruits, commuter distance from New York. Just a few miles further west flows another great river from north to south, the mighty Hudson, creating the border between the state of New York and Connecticut. The Hudson was part of a historical fur trader's route stretching from Montreal on the St. Lawrence Seaway down through Lake Champlain and Lake George, guarded at the portage by Fort Ticonderoga. High in the Adirondak Mountains, these lakes have long been the retreat of wealthy New York labor leaders. Crossing a second portage, the fur traders paddled down the Hudson to New Amsterdam, now, New York. Fix this geography in your mind, for these two parallel rivers, the Hudson and the Connecticut, hold a key to the distribution of Lyme disease. The fur traders and the nutmeggers have been at it for a long, long time.

Dr. Willy Burgdorfer identified Lyme's cause, a spirochete tick borne bacteria, and coined it "borrelia burgdorferi." Burgdorfer spent a lifetime collecting different species of ticks from around the globe. He still putters around his Rocky Mountain Laboratory in Montana, kind enough to take the time to answer questions from Lyme victims. His work helped differentiate the Lyme spirochete from its cousins of relapsing fever and Newcastle's disease. The medical journals first cataloged Lyme as "relapsing fever," confusing hard shelled ticks with soft shelled ticks and their spirochetes. Lyme infects humans, not chickens, and Newcastle's infects fowl, not people. Early microscopes could not distinguish between the different spirochetes. Newcastle disease had infected many Connecticut poultry farms after WW II, not originally indigenous to America. Were the Rockefellers on a wild goose chase in Glastonbury, or did they have another mission? Nothing would turn up in the "Index Medicus" under "Lyme disease" prior the 1970s.

Suspecting lupus like her twin, the author sought out a leading lupus expert in San Francisco in 1987, and found Dr. Birnbaum. When blood tests revealed Lyme, UCLA Medical Library offered excellent resources. Dr. Alan Mac Donald of Southampton Hospital on Long Island had written an article for the Manchester Gazette, a small mill town adjacent to Glastonbury where he had been raised as a child. Mac Donald recommended seeing Dr. Paul Lavoie, an old Air Force doctor and a Lyme and arthritis expert who just happened to be Birnbaum's associate in San Francisco. Lavoie treated the author for five years with antibiotics, to no avail, yet he was kind and courteous. Dr. Alan Mac Donald was more peculiar. We discussed the possible origin of Lyme disease. Dr. Mac Donald speculated that other arachnids, such as spiders could be vectors, and Plum Island may be the source. Plum Island, home to the US Department of Agriculture disease testing center, lay off the tip of Long Island, a hop skip and a jump from the Connecticut coastline. "The Birds" were suspect. Mac Donald's sister lived in Manchester, having contracted Lyme disease. He also suspected Alzheimer's disease to be caused by Lyme.

Was there any credence to the bird vector theory? Why not write the US Department of Agriculture's Animal Disease Center headquarters on Plum Island? Dr. Roger G. Breeze replied January 27th, 1988 regarding the island's history:

"In response to your questions, I can most definitely state that the USDA Agriculture Research Service does not conduct any research on spirochetes, including the agent of Lyme Disease and its anthropoid vectors, no research is planned, and none has been conducted since the Center was opened in 1953. Furthermore, no other government agency has conducted such experiments at Plum Island while this Center has been in existence."

But in contrast to this letter, maybe written a bit defensively because of local gossip, Dr. Breeze's letter had a slight contradiction to a congressional hearing conducted in 1977:

"BIOLOGICAL TESTING INVOLVING HUMAN SUBJECTS BY THE DEPARTMENT OF DEFENSE" S411-32 CIS Annual 1977 volume 1, page 971 (library ref. #3228.73 c757C) March 8 & May 23, 1977. Senators Ted Kennedy, Christopher Dodd, Orrin Hatch. Pages 77-78:

"Animal research began in 1942 and was initially concerned with developing methods for protecting our large livestock population against BW attack. This research resulted in the development of vaccines to protect against rinderpest, a deadly cattle disease and Newcastle disease, a serious poultry affliction. Research was carried out at Camp Detrick initially but when there was a need for larger scale research, a facility was established at Camp Terry on Plum Island, New York. Two field tests of potential anti-animal agents were conducted using hog cholera virus and Newcastle virus. The program at Camp Detrick was terminated in 1954. By agreement between the Secretary of Defense and the Secretary of Agriculture, the Department of Agriculture assumed responsibility for defense of our livestock against BW attack, and the Plum Island facilities were transferred to that agency."

Even though Newcastle disease is a spirochete bacteria similar to that of Lyme Disease, it is not infectious to humans, nor has it been a problem for livestock since antibiotics have preserved the poultry industry. More to the point, the research on Plum Island was defensive, not offensive, as the congressional report stressed: "concerned with developing methods for protecting our large livestock population against BW attack." The report insisted other military tests had been conducted by the CIA involving ectoparasites on birds and mammals initiated under the Kennedy Administration. It concluded:

"BIOLOGICAL TESTING INVOLVING HUMAN SUBJECTS BY THE DEPARTMENT OF DEFENSE" page 170:

"Deseret Test Center acting on the recommendations of the Deseret Test Center Medical Advisory Committee, Deseret Test Center, from its establishment in 1962 to its merger with Dugway Proving Ground in 1968, sponsored E&E effort with the Smithsonian Institute and the University of Oklahoma. These programs provided required E&E surveys in those areas outside the continental United States which had been designated for possible open-air biological warfare testing. The purpose of these studies was to determine potential reservoirs of specific infectious agents., if any and possible routes of dissemination. Studies were conducted during 1963 through 1969 on selected islands in the Central Pacific ocean from latitudes 35 degrees North to 20 degrees South and longitudes 145 degrees East to 145 degrees West (approximately from the Hawaiian Islands west to Guam and south to Samoa.) Other investigations were conducted in Alaska and the Bering Sea (i.e. Pribilof Islands,) and off the Pacific Coast. Specific objectives of this ecological program were to identify and determine the distribution of birds and mammals and their ectoparasites; to conduct biological studies on their breeding and feeding habits and migratory routes; and to ascertain the breeding and host preferences of mosquitoes and biting flies. Pelagic birds were studied more intensely in the Pacific, while in Alaska mammals were emphasized because of differences in relative abundance in the respective areas. AS AT DUGWAY, NO IMMEDIATE OR RESIDUAL ENVIRONMENT EFFECTS WERE OBSERVED DURING OR SUBSEQUENT TO COMPLETION OF TESTS ACTIVITIES AT THE TEST SITES."

The CIA and US Army would not be the only ones concluding birds were not vectors. Dr. Breeze insists there was nothing done since 1953 with any spirochete disease by the Department of Agriculture. Had anything been done prior, it would have only involved Newcastle's disease, not Lyme. Could the birds have been the vector? Hardly. The CIA's tests proved negative, and there was no offensive program on Plum Island. Dr. Breeze insisted in his letter that prior to 1953, Plum Island was used as a bombing test site - a "coastal artillery training base" stocked with "heavy guns to defend approaches to the Long Island Sound." In the early 1920s, Plum Island was owned privately by the Carnegie Foundation as a part of its Cold Spring Harbor Institute research station on Long Island and only later was it handed over the US Army. This was long before Newcastle disease or Lyme disease appeared on the American horizon after World War II. But other old intelligence agents refute this, citing John Loftus and Mark Aaron's latest publication: "The Secret War Against the Jews" (St. Martin's Press, 1994, chapter 13's note #54.) Loftus and the author have shared notes for many years debating the testimony of these "old spies - none from America" which Loftus and Aaron interviewed for their book. Communist spies have long fingered Plum Island, not particularly noted for their veracity. So much for the "old spies." Dr. Breeze was telling the truth, and had good reason to be perturbed.

Nelson Demille's "Plum Island" (Warner Books, 1997) perpetuated the mythology of Plum Island. His main character is a New York cop investigating a Long Island murder involving Plum Island scientists researching a vaccine for Lyme disease. In their free time, the scientists also sought pirate treasure buried on Plum Island, cruising its coast in their yacht,

"The Spirochete." Helicopters circled the island night and day shooting any deer that might swim ashore, stretching the liberty of the "free press." Demille gives thanks to Dr. Alfonso Torres, the new Director of the Plum Island Animal Disease Center for his "time and patience" and admits taking "a small measure of literary license here and there." Anything to make a "buck?" Let's get the facts.

The ixodes dammini tick, "the deer tick," a misnomer, is a relatively new species introduced to the United States in 1945, according to Andrew Speilman. This tick feeds primarily on rodents. The ixodes dammini tick was originally confused with the native ixodes scapularis by collectors, and only recently was the slight variation in species recognized. (1) Speilman suggests that the gaming commission after 1945 inadvertently transported the tick to Nantucket Island and Martha's Vineyard while restocking the deer population from the mainland. These two islands, just off Cape Cod, have a very high concentration of Lyme disease. Ships and rodents are well known vectors of tick borne diseases. George Schmid's "Global Distribution of Lyme Disease" lists its enormous range throughout the Middle East, Europe, and the former Soviet Union. (2) It would be easy for a "sick tick" to infest furs, travel the oceans in cargo bales and then re-infest a foreign port's warehouses full of rodents. Rodents, unlike other mammals, do not develop immunity to many tick borne diseases, perpetual vectors, passing epidemics from generation to generation. 79% of the ixodes dammini ticks on the East coast are infected with Lyme, while only 2% of the ixodes pacificus on the West coast are infected. (3) It is worth noting that both the Spielman and Schmid articles stress the close similarity between Old World and New World ixodes ticks that carry the Lyme spirochete.

Nature has a way of keeping a lid on its own epidemics through immunity and predators. The only way to initiate an epidemic on the east coast in such magnitude would be to transport either millions of infected ticks or millions of infested rats. The Russian peasants began slaughtering all their own livestock and wildlife, exporting the furs, wool and camel hairs to the West by the tons, just after WW II. Here, was a possible source of Lyme disease worth investigating. There are a wide range of deer and elk on both east and west coasts, yet we do not have herds of deer running rampant through the city of New York, which has 44% of all Lyme disease cases in America. We had herds of rats running rampant through New York City's garbage. The deer were getting a bad rap and so were the birds.

Dr. Harwood wrote in "Entomology in Human and Animal Health," that there are over 250 species of ixodes ticks, 40 known in North America. The early descriptions of Russian tick borne encephalitis carried by ixodes ricinus match the description of modern Lyme disease. Harwood also states that these ixodes tick species are big vectors of another parasite, "bovine piroplasmosia," more commonly known as brucellosis, or "bang's disease." (4) America was suffering a double whammy. It is possible for rodents and ticks to be vectors of more than one disease simultaneously. The huge presence of Lyme disease in Russia raises the question, was the Red Army using tick borne diseases as biological warfare against their own citizens? Russian doctors report big trouble with Lyme since Gorbachev's "Peristroika" (new openness.) Drs. E. I. Korenberg, S. V. Scherbakov, and V. N. Kryuchechnikiv published in "Meditainskaia Parazitologiia l Parazitarnye Bolezni" of March-April 1987 "Lyme's Disease Prevalence in the USSR" The ixodes ricinus and ixodes persulcatus ticks were its prime vectors, ranging across the whole continent from "south(ern) parts of the taiga and in coniferous/broad-leafed forests."

Russian entomologist, N. A. Filoppova sketched out an even more alarming global map of Lyme's range and the numerous ixodes subspecies in an article for UNESCO's (United Nations Educational, Scientific and Cultural Organization) Man and Biosphere program, titled "Taiga Tick: Ixodes Persulcatus Schutlze (Arcarina, Ixodiae) Morphology, Systematics, Ecology Medical Importance," Nauka Publishers, Leningrad Branch 1985. The whole of Europe, Asian continent, India, Indonesia, Korea and Japan were inhabited by the ixodes species. North Africa and the Middle East fell prey. The ixodes tick is also indigenous to all of North America and most of South America, yet Lyme is pocketed in very isolated areas.

With this vast expanse of ticks capable of carrying Lyme across the globe, bird populations with flyways north and south, deer and elk populations roaming all forty-eight states, one is awestruck by the four tight clusters of Lyme pictured in "Scientific American" July 1987 "Lyme Disease" by Gail Habricht, Beck and Benach. There is a small cluster on California's northern coast up to Portland Oregon; a second patch between Port Arthur, Texas and New Orleans in the Gulf. The third spot at Duluth, which resides on the shores of Lake Superior, is a grain shipping port for the Midwestern farm belt, fat with rats, where Lyme spreads southward along the Missouri River. The largest infestation is along the East coast between Boston, New York, and Philadelphia. A similar map graced the pages of "NEWSWEEK" July 1987, "The Spread of Lyme Disease" (page 54) by Matt Clark and Mariana Gosnell.

Gail Habricht exposed in her "Scientific American" article the role of Yale University doctors played in diagnosing the first Lyme cases. Dr. Allen Steere had just finished working with the epidemic-intelligence service of the Center for Disease Control in Atlanta Georgia prior his assignment to Yale. He and a team of doctors discovered Lyme disease to be clustered in three small towns on the East side of the Connecticut River, East Haddam, Lyme, and Old Lyme. The ixodes dammini tick was twelve times more abundant on the east side of the Connecticut River than west side and Lyme was 30 times more prevalent on the east side. According to CDC reports, 80% of all American cases resided on the Eastern seaboard between Philadelphia, New York, to Boston. And by 1988, 56% of all cases resided in the State of New York alone, 44% of all US cases resided within two New York City suburban counties, Westchester and Suffolk. (5) Ask yourself. How could eastern Connecticut and New York City be overrun with Lyme disease while the western slice of Connecticut between the Hudson and Connecticut River be void? The birds are not the vector, scratch the Plum Island theory. The deer are not the vectors, they can swim the rivers, with extra help from the gaming commission. Rats, on the other hand, don't migrate too far from their plentiful garbage dumps or grain barges without the aid of ships. "RATS" quote Charlie Brown, "RATS!"

Dr. Allen Steere, who had first diagnosed Old Lyme's children at Yale, wrote an extensive article in the "New England Journal of Medicine" noting a pattern of islands off the coast, some infected, others void, speculating implanted deer populations: "16% of 162 permanent residents of Great Island, Mass, had the illness" as the source, negating the bird vector theory. William Ziegler lives on Great Island.[6] He will resurface. Steere exposed Lyme as 30 times more prevalent on the east side of the Connecticut River, its ixodes ticks being twelve times more infected, indicating "the earliest cases that have been identified occurred on Cape Cod in 1962 and in Old Lyme in 1965." (7) Who of any consequence could have been diagnosed with Lyme disease in 1962? Who would receive such intense medical attention? Yale will figure heavily into the mystery of Lyme's origin again and again, not as a source, but as a stomping ground for ivy league sleuths tracking ticks, spies and spirochetes. Yale has a history of being the CIA and State Department's recruiting ground for agents as far back as World War II. New Haven and Yale University sit comfortably on Connecticut's west side, virtually un-infested with Lyme.

By 1988, Lyme was a hot topic. The ABC television network's "20/20" aired a program July 15th, "Lyme Disease: Danger in the Grass." Lynn Sherr interviewed Dr. Raymond Dattwyler of the Lyme Disease Clinic, University Hospital at Stonybrook on Long Island, New York. Dr. Dattwyler commented upon the similarity between Lyme and syphilis, infecting some people "virtually forever." He went on to comment that the "deer tick" (ixodes dammini) was a "misnomer," for the tick would feed upon most any animal, especially mice. The "deer were getting a bad rap," quipped Dattwyler's cohort, Dr. Edward Bosler. The medical community battled over the birds and the deer as hosts.

John F. Anderson and his colleagues investigated eighteen species of common North American birds that frequent Connecticut. (8) Half of these birds had ticks infected with the Lyme spirochete. Peterson's Field Guide to Eastern Birds (9) demonstrated that Anderson's birds had a far greater range than just New England, some covering all forty eight states, other flyways ranging from Canada's Hudson Bay down the New England coast, across Florida, to Cuba, and Venezuela. Similar flyways are diagramed in "The Migration of Birds" by Jean Dorrat, (Houghton Mifflin Company, Boston 1962, figure 48, page 126.) From Alaska down the coast of California, birds migrate to Mexico. The Atlantic coast flyway, the Mississippi flyway, the Central flyway, and the Pacific flyway are almost all void of Lyme infestations excepting the four isolated pockets at ports. It is puzzling how John Anderson concluded birds were the vector of Lyme when overlaying flyway maps on top of Lyme center maps on port infestations. Furthermore, not all ports were infested along the flyways, only selected ones involved with lend lease shipping during WW II. The medical community's doctors were not looking back far enough in history for a plausible source.

The Russians, possibly driven by politics, seemed overly anxious to finger the birds, as vectors. E. N. Pavlovskii, who once headed the Red Army's biological warfare program under Joseph Stalin, found his conscience under Nikita Khruschev's reign. Soon after publishing "The Natural Foci of Human Infections" Pavlovskii would die. This highly suggestive book would reveal the "unnatural" foci of parasitic epidemics sweeping the Soviet Union during Stalin's purges. Over 253 subspecies of ixodes ticks carrying tularemia, brucellosis, relapsing fever, encephalitis and plague are detailed in this horrid expose of "scientific missions" to the Central Asian Republics of the USSR. Pavlovskii's descriptions of encephalitis and relapsing fever mirror those of Lyme. There are over 16 species of ixodes ticks in the USSR's Central Asian Republic of Tadshik alone, including the ixodes ricinus vector of Lyme. The extent of devastation of Russia's Central Asian Republics will be revealed by escaping German POWs after the war.

According to Pavlovskii, a world renowned zoologist and parasitologist, the animal kingdom had developed a natural immune system to eliminate parasitic diseases. Larger animals, which had a longer life span, became immune to the blood parasites and created an "autosterilization" process on the infected ticks, immunizing the ticks, virtually vaccinating the animal kingdom. Other Russian doctors argued the smaller animals, birds and rodents, were chronic carriers. Pavlovskii worked at the Suchomi biological warfare test site on the Black Sea, experimenting with relapsing fever, where other Nazis and Russians, as we shall discover, worked transmitting MS to "great apes." This smacks of Lyme disease, most significance, for it was here that hundreds of Nazi scientists fled after WW II, volunteering their services, escaping prosecution as war criminals. The Israelis translated Pavlovskii's book into English for the U. S. Health Department in 1963 under the Kennedy Administration. (10) Pavlovskii book is highly suggestive, one could infer the Red Army had led BW attacks upon his own countrymen using hoards of tick infested rats. Did Pavlovskii contribute to the Soviet Union's incomprehensible purges upon its own citizens, merely to balance the budget?

Dr. Paul Lavoie, still in the Air Force Reserves speculated Lyme disease had been in America for hundreds of years. Records of infection went back as far as the history of the Hudson Bay fur traders traveling up and down the St. Lawrence Seaway. Game transportation to the East coast must be the cause, he argued. Of course, as his patient, the author argued back; this does not explain the large infestation in New York City. A few arthritic cases amongst the pioneer furriers couldn't compare to the thousands of Lyme victims on the New England coast today or the hundreds of thousands of MS cases. Furthermore, if Pavlovskii's theories were correct regarding the larger animals' immunizing the infected ticks, the disease would have been arrested a century ago while big game flourished. Lavoie was kind and dedicated, even Canadians traveling with medical vouchers ended up on his door step, their socialized medical system was in the dark on how to treat Lyme disease. Lavoie wrote about one of his patients having contracted both Lupus and Lyme, which brings to mind the unusual number of lupus cases in Glastonbury along with Lyme cases. Lavoie's patient had been diagnosed of Lyme disease while visiting Reno, Nevada, a desert environment, void of the infection and deer. (11) "Big Game Animals of North America" by Jack O'Connor, Outdoor Life, NY 1961, is fully illustrated with deer, elk, moose and mule ranges across the country. Outside of major cities, there is virtually no uninhabited land except patches of desert in Nevada and New Mexico that deer don't range. Deer have nothing to do with the spread of Lyme disease, in fact, they may be contributing to its containment. Again, overlay Jack O'Connor's game ranges with "Newsweek's" July 17th 1987 illustration of the four pocketed Lyme centers and it will become obvious deer are not the vectors.

We need look for other sources. Rodents are Lyme's prime carrier. They never develop immunity and pass infection on to their offspring, multiplying carriers. The shipping industry transports rodents around the globe. Accordingly, the whole American coastline would be open to Lyme , but it is not. Why just four isolated port sites at opposite ends of the country? How many rats would it take to hop the deck? We had ship inspectors and rat exterminators aboard each foreign vessel in American ports, but things were lax on our own liberty ships in lend-lease during WW II. Tons of grain and cattle were shipped to Russian's fur center, Vladivostok, possibly returning with infested rats, cruising up the Mississippi from New Orleans as far as Duluth on Lake Superior. But a bigger source most likely was tons of foreign furs, awaiting auction, stored in New York and Philadelphia warehouses. Follow the evidence presented as well as the evidence withheld, from the author's "FOIAs," freedom of information requests. The FBI's declassified history of New York City's Soviet fur dealers, Amtorg Trading Company, reads like Martin Cruz Smith's "Gorky Park."

One only need search the "Index Medicus" for world epidemics, including Lyme disease. Medical reports during WW II describing relapsing fever were very similar to that of Lyme, relapsing fever, more devastating of the two. Let's compare Lyme and relapsing fever definitions:

"US DEPARTMENT OF HEALTH AND HUMAN SERVICES"
'Update: Lyme Disease United States 1988'
"Lyme disease is a systemic, tick-borne illness that usually occurs during the summer. It was first recognized in 1975 in Connecticut... characterized by a distinctive skin lesion, erthema chronicum migrans (EMC), often accompanied by nonspecific constitutional symptoms, such as fever, headache, myalgias, and arthralgias... Some patients subsequently develop arthritic, neuralgic, or cardiac complications weeks to months after the initial lesion... The arthritic is intermittent and usually involves large joints. Neuralgic manifestations include Bell's palsy, meningoencephalitis, and peripheral neuritis, cardiac manifestations include myocarditis and atrioventricular conduction defects. Patients with B-cell alloantigen, DR2, often have more severe and frequent late manifestations."

"PROFESSIONAL GUIDE TO DISEASES" Third Edition Springhouse Corp.,
Springhouse, Pennsylvania:
"(Lyme Disease) having intermittent headache, fever, chills, achiness, and regional lymphadenopathy. Less common effects are menigeal irritation, mild encephalopathy, migrating musculoskeletal pain, and hepatitis..."

Lyme is disseminated through the blood and passed to essential organs, including the brain which is especially hard to treat with antibiotics, for the brain has a protective sheath around it, blocking poisons. Penicillin, made from mold, is a poison. This way, after years of chronic infection, the brain's spirochetes continually mutate, developing an immunity to anti-biotics, re-infecting the blood supply at a pace the immune system can't defeat. Lyme's close cousin, relapsing fever, is far more deadly. This spirochete has many subdivisions, and is carried by both lice and the onithodorus soft shelled tick, much larger than the tiny ixodes family.

"PROFESSIONAL GUIDE TO DISEASES" Third Edition, Spring-house Corp.,
    Springhouse, Pennsylvania:
    "(Relapsing fever)...An acute infection disease caused by spirochetes of the genus Borrelia... transmitted to humans by lice or ticks... character-ized by relapses and remissions. Rodents and other wild animals serve as the primary reservoirs... Untreated louse borne relapsing fever normally caries a mortality rate of more than 10%. However, during an epidemic, the mortality rate may rise to as high as 50%. The victims are usually indigent people who are already suffering from other infections and mal-nutrition... louse borne not found in the US since 1900... tick borne is in the western states."

This may be a mistaken reference to Rocky Mountain spotted fever, a typhus infection, not a spirochete, for the CDC refutes relapsing fever's presence. Imagine the devastation of relapsing fever in Russia while Sta-lin was in the midst of his purges, starving the Ukraine and Kazakhstan Republics to death in the 1930s. Surely the Russian historical records of relapsing fever give clues. Even the public library computer periodical search site indexed "Lyme disease" under "relapsing fever" in 1987.
    E. N. Pavlovskii, the BW (biological warfare) chief of the Soviet Unions Red Army, author of "The Natural Foci of Human Infections," chronicled the tick borne epidemics beginning in 1937 through world War II, well into the 1950s. The United Nation's Relief and Rehabilitation Adminis-tration (UNNRA) Epidemiological Studies show Russia overwhelmed by relapsing fever at the end of the First World War, then clean until 1937, as if one had switched a button on and off. In 1937, Joseph Stalin stopped all reporting of epidemics to international health organization through WW II. But the news leaked out anyway. The Soviet medical journals were translated and recorded in the "Tropical Disease Bulletin." The picture was horrifying. Russia was rotting from the inside out. With these sweeping

epidemics, one couldn't help suspect the Soviet fur and shipping industry, Soyuzpushnina, as a source of America's problems.

Were there any hints of Lyme disease here at the end of the war when normal trade resumed? Yes. The National Multiple Sclerosis Foundation and Hope Chest was founded in 1946. Multiple sclerosis, (MS), has been described by doctors as a combination of viruses and bacteria affecting the nervous system. One of the bacteria involved is the Lyme spirochete. Dr. Byron Waksman, Vice President of the National MS Society, is an immunologist of international repute, a professor at Yale University who once served in the US Army Medical Corps. He has recently published a third edition on this elusive disease for which there is no cure: "Research on Multiple Sclerosis," Demos Publications, New York, 1987, fingering Lyme disease as one of a triad of MS's culprit components.

Waksman's book is a most scholarly research, covering MS's world history. Heavy cases occurred amongst American soldiers during WW II and the Korean War, far greater in percentages than the rest of the American population. Obviously, they were infected abroad. MS was considered a "regional" problem, although the northern US latitudes held a much greater prevalence than the deep south. This was also true globally. Why would Allen Steere cite Lyme as brand new disease first occurring in the USA in 1962, while his colleague at Yale, Byron Waksman was studying it in the National MS Society in 1946? This is a very pressing point. The history of MS is the history of Lyme disease. January 6th, 1946 was the date the SS ELBRUS docked at Philadelphia with 426 tons of Russian furs, wool, and camel hairs. New York City was in the midst of a long-shoreman strike, diverting the cargo to its southern neighbor. Was this a deliberate BW attack upon the US, the beginning of the "Cold War"? Let's examine the evidence.

The Communists, as far back as 1918, plotted a world revolution, first Russia, then Europe, the Orient, and America. A recent Soviet defector, a former KGB spy, Viktor Suvorov, published a radical new history of WW II, "Icebreaker" detailing the military buildup of the Soviets in the 1930s. An intense collaboration between the German Communist Spartans emerged. According to Suvorov, the Soviet Union's Embassy in Germany was the "nerve center" for inciting a revolution within Kaiser Wilhelm's realm, figuring Germany's fall to Communism, would precipitate the fall of the rest of Europe. Joseph Unschlikht was deputy chairman of the GRU, (Red Army Intelligence) and would become the Spartan's future chief.

"ICEBREAKER" By Viktor Suvorov, Hamish Hamilton, London 1990.

Page 8: "Unschlikht was given responsibility for recruiting, equipping and organizing the armed insurrectionists detachment which would carry out the 'coup d'etat.' He was given the added responsibility of organizing a German secret police force and of exterminating the bourgeoisie and the enemies of the revolution..."

Of course, the 1923 revolution did not take place, for Germany began to recover from the disasters of World War One. But that did not dampen Lenin or Stalin's ambitions. They decided to use a new tactic: biological warfare upon the German citizens, intent on driving them mad, ripening them for a Communist revolution. This too, failed, and the Soviets created their worst enemy, the Nazis, an army of crackpots. Hitler was not the only maniac. Some of the so-called 'Nazis' were Spartans from the start. Just how does one distinguish a national socialist, a "Nazi" from an international socialist, a Communist? Hitler or Stalin couldn't tell, contributing to the downfall of both dictatorships. Viktor Suvorov exposes Stalin's treacherous usage of Hitler as an "icebreaker" to soften up Europe for a Soviet invasion. Hitler would accomplish the dirty work, Stalin would then rush in as the 'savior' and conquer Europe. Stalin needed Hitler. On the other hand, Hitler needed Stalin, for the Soviet Union offered vast resources for his war machine. So, the two monsters began courting each other in 1933. Just moments before Stalin launched his European invasion, his Mark II tanks with retractable tires poised at Poland's back door, Hitler sprung Operation Barbarossa, invading the Russian interior which lay seemingly defenseless. By the end of WW II, Stalin had only accomplished half of his goal for world conquest, Eisenhower and Roosevelt at Yalta handed over the Balkans, Poland, Czechoslovakia, Yugoslavia, Lithuania, Estonia, and Latvia under the Iron Curtain. New evidence recently declassified by the US National Archives reveals a far more dangerous scenario which nearly took place, a re-alliance of German generals with the Red Army to defeat the West using chemical and biological warfare. We came within weeks of losing the world!

"Left" from the beginning, the Nazi-Soviet collaboration was so extensive, politically, militarily, scientifically, and industrially, that all lines blur between fascism and Communism. Forget all the past political rhetoric you've ever been taught. "Nazi" is synonymous with "Communist." The world's largest military-industrial complex moved into Russia full scale just after WW I. It grew and grew, with the help of the French and America's Wall Street.

By the time Hitler came to power in 1933, the business ties between Russia and I. G. Farben were so extensive, I. G. feared arrest for treason. It had good reason to be. Interessen Gemeinschaft Farbenindustrie Aktieng-esellschaft, (I. G. Farben, A.K.) was formed during WWI by the merger of six German chemical companies in the dyestuff and coal tar industry to form "one community of interests" including Bayer, BASF (Badishce Ani-lin & Soda-Fabrik of Ludwigshafen), Hoeschst, Agfa, Casella, and Kalle. I.G. would later accumulate over 800 international subsidiaries inside the Soviet Union, Spain, France, Poland, Czechoslovakia, Great Britain, and America, including the Aniline Film Company, Dupont, and Standard Oil, all taking part in its patent booty as members of the cartel. They were the epitome of the corporate-Fascist state, ruthless businessmen.

In the beginning, I. G. Farben's founder, Carl Bosch, was rabidly anti-Hitler, pro-Communist. and remained so till his death, hiding the company's assets from Hitler's henchmen. Always aloof and one step ahead of the Nazi regime, I. G. double crossed Hitler from the day he seized power, protected by the Reich's top generals who were constantly plotting coups. I. G. Farben planned to conquer the world if Hitler failed, with their industrial octopus. WW II was a true war of the intelligensia against the world's "huddled masses" and "useless eaters." It became increasingly difficult to distinguish between the socialist robber barons and the capitalist robber barons, who were merging. John F. Kennedy, privy to I. G. Farben's treason, was murdered. Others trying to expose them, like Senator Joseph McCarthy, were destroyed. When World War II ended, the whole I. G. Farben cartel beat it to Russia to save their butts. By the early 1950s, Stalin had destroyed 84 million of his own citizens using Nazi assistance. What? Communists as racists? Oh no? Spare telling us the truth.

The American Communist Party made every effort to finger the US military and the Department of Agriculture stationed on Plum Island for the origin of Lyme disease, shielding Soyuzpushnina, the Soviet fur indus-try, from suspicion. It was easy. Prior to World War One, the American scientific community held ties to German and Soviet researchers. The Carnegie Foundation, with its founder Andrew Carnegie, an ardent racists and socialist, built many philanthropic institutions. He financed music centers, museums, paleontoligical dinosaur digs, and Cold Spring Harbor medical research center, which acquired Plum Island. Dr. T. Laanes from Cold Spring Harbor, with German and Russian scientists, co-authored "Handbuch der Biologischen Arbeitsmethoden" ("Handbook of Biological Work Methods," Urban & Schwarzenberg, Berlin, Wien, 1938) edited by Emil Abderhalden, detailing the breeding of ticks and rats. Numerous chapters include E. N. Pavlovskii's research, Russian parasitologist and Red Army BW chief. The Communist had an insider who could scapegoat Plum Island for the origin of Lyme disease; physically and ecologically, an impossibility.

Bacteriologist, Leo Szillard and his accomplice, Dr. Luria moved to Cold Spring Harbor after WW II. Luria went on to teach and research in the laboratories of the University of Indiana at Bloomington. Szillard had been one of the original European pacifists under Romain Rolland, Hans Thirring, Albert Einstein, and Georg Friedrich Nicolai's cult. Numerous left wing authors have used the University of Indiana's press, including Hans Thirring of Austria, authoring "Die Geschichte de Atombombe" (How to Build the Atom Bomb), 1946, and "Energy For Man: From Windmills to Nuclear Power" a basic blueprint to starve the Third World out of oil as an energy source.

The latest piece of Communist propaganda to fly off the University of Indiana Press was "The United States and Biological Warfare Secrets from the Early Cold War and Korea" by Stephen Endicott and Edward Hagerman, 1998. Every effort is made by this goon squad to finger America for BW attacks upon Korea in the 1950s, using of all things, the Red Communist military records, full of the most preposterous propaganda of the century, for sources. Unfortunately, the goons were not privy to newly declassified US records on the Korean War, implicating the North Koreans, Red Chinese and Soviet military collaborating in building BW factories in North Korea to incapacitate civilian resistance to revolution. Yes, let's tell it like it is, baby. The information Endicott cites as "newly declassified American files" is of defensive research, not offensive, although planning stages did exist in small research centers. This did not include Plum Island! US State Department files will show a preponderance of evidence suggesting the Soviet peasants slaughtered all of their livestock and wild life at the end of WW II to arrest epidemics; the furs, wool and camel hairs shipped via Siberian Railway to Vladivostok. Get the map. Vladivostok sits adjacent the North Korean border, its warehouses overrun with rats and diseases. Rats don't comprehend political boundaries, nor do the Communists. Were the Nazis assisting the Soviets in biological warfare? Wouldn't it be fun to uncover a witness to substantiate these theories?

To rid themselves of embarrassment, the Soviet Union exported its Nazi accomplices to the West during the Cold War, the American intelligence community welcomed them in as "dragon returnees." Just what kind of national security threat did these double agent Nazis pose to American industry and space program? What do you suppose happened to President Kennedy when he discovered these Nazi scientists camped out on America's doorstep? Many of these Nazis were specifically trained by the KGB to overthrow the West. President Truman's "100 Person Act" recruited the best Nazi brains. Debating who is more guilty of atrocities, the Communist or the Nazis, is an exercise in futility, the line between them is so blurred. Neither the Soviets nor the Americans could differentiate or identify the enemy within. Who were the Nazis really working for? Follow the wake of the SS ELBRUS.

INTRODUCTION NOTES

(1) "HUMAN BABESIOSIS ON NANTUCKET ISLAND, USA: Description of the Vector, Ixodes Dammini, and N. SP. (Arcarina: Ixodiae)" by Andrew Spielman, Carleton m. Clifford, Joseph Piesman and Melvin D. Corwin, J. Med. Entomol. vol. 15, no. 3: 218-234, March 23, 1979 "The tick implicated as the vector closely resembles published descriptions of Ixodes scapularis Say, but certain structural differences, especially in the nymphal stage, suggested that the New England population might represent an undescribed species..."

(2) "THE GLOBAL DISTRIBUTION OF LYME DISEASE" by George P. Schmid, Reviews of Infectious diseases, vol. 7, no. 1 January-February 1985
"Lyme disease first described in Sweden 1909... subsequently, cases ECM reported from at least 19 countries on three continents... Ixodes ricinus ticks principal vector ECM in Europe... This strain, (spirochete) when compared to the American isolates, is morphologically identical... I. ricinus found in North Africa, Middle East, Turkey, Egypt, Southern Europe, Southern Italy, most of the Balkan Peninsula, Spain, England, Scotland, West Germany, Romania, Moscow, Czechoslovakia, etc..."

(3) IBID.
Discussion on American subgenus of Ixodiae ticks, Ixodes. Scapularis, I. Dammini, and I. Pacificus as carriers of Lyme disease. On the East Coast, I. Dammini has 79% infection rate, where on the West Coast, only 2% of Ixodes Pacificus tick is infected.

(4) "ENTOMOLOGY IN HUMAN AND ANIMAL HEALTH" 7th edition, by Robert F. Harwood, Ph.D., Macmillan Publishing Co. Inc. New York
"Genus Ixodes. This is the largest ixodes genus, worldwide in distribution, with about 40 North American species and almost 250 species

total. In Europe Ixodes ricinus and I. persulcatus play an important role in the transmission of viruses affecting man, and the protozoa of bovine piraplasmosia. Ixodes ricinus... is more western in distribution... British Isles and Norway to... Iran through the mountains of Turkey, Bulgaria, Italy, and the Pyrenees... four diverse areas of the Soviet Union; Czechoslovakia..."

(5) "LYME DISEASE - UNITED STATES 1987" by the Center for Disease Control, JAMA Oct 27, 1989 vol. 262, no. 162209-10
"... six states in the upper northeast accounted for 80% of all cases etc...1988 NY State reported 56%... Westchester and Suffolk (NYC counties) reported 44% of all US cases... Since 1982, 13,825 cases of Lyme Disease have been reported... "

(6) "MEDICAL PROGRESS: LYME DISEASE" by Allen C. Steere, M.D., New England Journal of Medicine, August 31, 1989, pages 586-596 'Epidemiology':
"The earliest known American cases occurred only 25 years ago in residents of Cape Cod and Connecticut... (later) 35% of the 190 residents of the area adjacent the (deer) preserve (Ipswich, Mass)... In other outbreaks, 16% of 162 permanent residents of Great Island, Mass., had the illness, in most instances between 1972 and 1979; and 7.5% of 200 people ... study on Fire Island, NY"

(7) "PRINCIPLES AND PRACTICE OF INFECTIOUS DISEASES" 2nd Edition, John Wiley & Sons, Inc. New York, 1985 'Bacterial Diseases: Spirochetes: Lyme Disease' pages 1345-1349 by Allen C. Steere and Stephen E. Malawista
"The earliest cases (Lyme disease) have been identified occurred on Cape Cod in 1962 and in Lyme, Connecticut in 1965..." 'Vector Transmission' "In concomitant studies of patients and arthropods on both sides of the Connecticut River, the incidence of Lyme Disease was almost 30 times as great, and the number of Ixodes dammini on preferred hosts (mice or deer) was more than 12 times as great on the east side (where Lyme is) compared with the west side of the river... referenced in R. C. Wallis, S.E. Brown, K. O. Kloter, A.J. Main: "Erthema chronicum migrans and Lyme arthritis: Field Study of Ticks: American Journal of Epidemiology: 105: 322, 1978."

(8) "INVOLVEMENT OF BIRDS IN THE EPIDEMIOLOGY OF THE LYME DISEASE AGENT BORRELIA BURGDORFERI" by John

F. Anderson, Russell C. Johnson, Louis A. Marnarelli, and Fred W. Hyde. 'Infection and Immunity,' Feb 1986

"Table 1: Prevalence of spirochete infected I. dammini infested birds." Page 395:

(birds studied): "Blue-winged warbler, Common yellow throat, Eastern phoebe, Gray catbird, Hooded warbler, House wren, Least flycatcher, Northern cardinal, Northern water thrush, Ovenbird, Rose-breasted grosbeak, Song sparrow, Swamp sparrow, Veery, White-eyed vireo, Wood thrush, Worm-eating warbler, Yellow warbler"

(9) "PETERSON'S FIELD GUIDE TO EASTERN BIRDS" Houghton Mifflin Co. NY

re. Ranges of birds:

Hooded Warbler's rang = Eastern USA to base of Great Lakes.

Gray Catbird's range = 3/4 USA excluding Western CA, southern AZ, NM and TX

Yellow Warbler's range = Alaska, Canada, all USA except southern LA, GA, FL

Common Yellowthroat's range = Southern Canada, all USA

Eastern Phoebe's range – Canadian plains, USA east of continental divide, excluding southern coast and FL

House Wren's range = Central USA, east of Rockies, excluding deep south

Cardinal's range = TX to Great Lakes, through Eastern USA, excluding ME

Sparrow's range (includes Grosbeaks, buntings, Finches) = Rockies to Pacific coast, great plains of Canada and USA, Great Lakes region, Wash. DC through New England.

(10) "THE NATURAL FOCI OF HUMAN INFECTIONS" by E. N. Pavlovskii, Translated from Russian, Published for the National Science Foundation, Washington, D.C. and the Department of Health, Education and Welfare by the Israel Program for Scientific Translations, Jerusalem, 1963. Cosudarstvennce Izdatel'stvo Meditsinskol Literatury (Medgiz) Moskva 1960.

Page 30: 'The Virus of tick borne encephalitis' "The infection of ticks feeding on adult animals is irregular. Ticks do not become infected on immune animals and on their suckling young (A.L. Dumina, 1957)"

Page 41: "The resistance of various specimens to ENCEPHALITIS is evidently determined by acquired immunity. Species in frequent contact with ticks possibly acquire a higher degree of immunological immunity...

The immunization of host animals by the ticks may possibly be a limiting factor for the dissemination of the virus..."

Page 42: " Nonimmunized animals... mouse-like rodents, shrews, squirrels and hares, those which do not transmit passive immunity to offspring, i.e. birds..."

Page 99: 'Natural Foci of Tick-borne Relapsing Fever' "In 1942 the author, in collaboration with A. Cheskis in the Department of Parasitology of the VIEM, tried to infect suckling pigs with spirochetes isolated from O. papillipes from Fergana.... Neither manifest no latent spirochetosis resulted. Experimental infection of domestic animals was carried out at the author's suggestion in the parasitological laboratory of the Sukhumi branch of the VIEM, producing latent spirochetosis in ram and donkey, while calf proved resistant."

(11) "LYME DISEASE IN NORTHERN CALIFORNIA" by John Campagna, MD; Paul E. Lavoie, MD; and Neal S. Birnbaum, MD and Deane P. Furman, PhD. Western Journal of Medicine, Vol. 139, no. 3, Sept. 1983, pages 319-323

CHAPTER 1

DR. JEKYL AND MR. HYDE

Georg Friedrich Nicolai Meets Albert Einstein

"Making war to save the peace" became the strategy of Albert Einstein's cult of "pacifists" during World War I and World War II. No doubt, Einstein was a great physicist, but as far as his political theories went, he was no better than the next bum on the street. In fact, he was a political crackpot, a dedicated Bolshevik revolutionary, chorusing Lenin's "Religion is the opiate of the people." He joined the rank and file of his fellow atheists, abandoning his family's honorable Jewish heritage.

The history of the Communist-Fascists alliance in biological warfare begins with Albert Einstein and his best buddy, Dr. Georg Friedrich Nicolai, tooted as the "Father of German Pacifism." "Father to German Perversion" would be closer to the truth. He soon would abandon the physician's Hypocratic Oath to "Do no harm," and conceive a grandiose scheme to massacre half the world's population, cleansing the gene pool. To fill the void, he seduced one hundred and six women, siring an unknown number of bastards, in his mind, self propagating a subspecies of "geniuses." In the true German style of fastidious note taking, he catalogued each sexual conquest in a little black notebook. Even Kaiser Wilhelm's queen was under the care of this infamous rogue, and God only knows if she, too, went down on record in his little black book. (1) Einstein could not keep pace, only marrying three times, locking his offspring up in an insane asylum, "kill you, convert you, or commit you" suited his political objectives. One of the most intense biographies on Georg Friedrich Nicolai was written by a serologist and pediatrician, Wolf Zuelzer: "The Nicolai Case," Wayne State University Press, 1982. It speaks for itself.

Nicolai and Einstein co-authored "The Biology of War," in 1918. Einstein contributed the introductory "Manifesto," which had been signed by a score of German scientists, excusing Germany for starting World War I. Germany was preserving "European culture" from the "invading Negro and Mongolian hoards." Really! Has anyone witnessed a soccer game recently? Georg Nicolai, born in 1874, would spend his college days in Germany, France and Russia, researching typhus in rats under the reputed vaccine specialists, Dr. Pavlov, in Moscow. Zuelzer's biography includes one of Nicolai's illustrations of a dissected rat from his 1904 physiology manual. Infatuated with the 1906 Bloody Sunday uprising, the impassioned student changed his family name of "Lewistein" to one with a more Bolshevik flavor, "Nicolai," after Nikolai Lenin.

Finishing his Russian studies, Nicolai traveled to Paris, taking up abode with a young "damsel Emillie." Perhaps, because Nicolai was so lusty, his biographer, Zuelzer, presumed Emillie to be a passionate student of the art of l'amour. More realistically, Nicolai was learning the art of revolution from a cult of French Communists under the tutelage of pacifists Romain Rolland. Nikolai Lenin, who led the Bolshevik Revolution, also ran against Aleksandr Kerensky on this "pacifist" Menshevik ticket, according to Russian defector Alexander Solzhenitsyn's "Lenin in Zurich." Solzhenitsyn went to great length exposing the role of the German Communist Party, (the Spartans), with Kaiser Wilhelm and French "pacifist" Romain Rolland in sponsoring the Bolshevik Revolution. Other "pacifists" amongst Rolland's group of young barbarians and intellectuals were three physicists, Leo Szillard, Hans Thirring, and Albert Einstein. (2) Most likely, this is where our Dr. Jekyl met Mr. Hyde and formed a lifetime bond of friendship.

At this time in Paris, the famed biologist, Charles Nicolle, with his young assistant, Emile Roux, (a man, not a woman), also specialized researching typhus in rats. Did Nicolai join up with them in Paris after his return from his Russian studies? Had Zuelzer mistaken Nicolai's "lover" Emillie for Emile Roux? (3) It seems a logical oversight. The pacifists movement of Romain Rolland advocated the "2% Theory," postulating that only 2% of the world's population was armed back in 1918, and disarmament would create world peace. The end result would be One World Government, creating a New World Order, Utopia. This nonsense is still echoed by the United Nations today, its group of nitwit followers ready to sell humanity back into slavery and extinction in the hands of the Communists. While Einstein traveled the globe preaching peace and disarmament, the Soviet Union and Germany secretly armed themselves to the teeth, deep inside Siberia, thus breaking the newly signed Treaty of Versailles. Nicolai had already traveled extensively in Russia and China, studying their fauna and wildlife, his precise mission unknown. (4) We'll discover what kinds of new "weapons of mass destruction" Lenin and Stalin were developing with the fauna and wildlife from the Siberian tundra.

As a "pacifist" during World War I, Nicolai was in a pickle. Facing forced enlistment in the military or be arrested, he volunteered under a civil contract with the German War Ministry as a physician. His first assignment was at Templehof Hospital in a suburb of Berlin, facilitated with laboratory and library. He continued his teaching position at the University. Next he transferred to a military garrison in Graudenz working with contagious diseases. By 1915, he was vacationing in Graudenz's famed old Prussian fortress where he began writing "The Biology of War." Fritz Reuter, a well-known German novelist and patriot was imprisoned here long before. Nicolai deluded his public, taking on the same role of martyr. Many still believe he served out his war years in this "prison." This is far from the truth. His activities consisted of a much more insidious service to his king. (5)

Nicolai's movements during the next few years from 1915 through 1919 are ambiguous in Zuelzer's biography, scrambled in chronology, but enough of the picture is laid out to ring alarms. Zuelzer places Nicolai at a Russian POW camp at Tuchel Heide on the Eastern Front servicing an infirmary by order of Dr. Bottcher, Surgeon General of the Seventeenth Army. By March 17th, 1916, Nicolai was transferred to Danzig with the Seventeenth Army Corp. According to Zuelzer's biography, Nicolai's wartime associate planned to invade Russia on a secret biological warfare mission. (6) Just what "services" Nicolai performed on the Eastern Front in the typhus stricken POW camps are unknown.

"The Biology of War" hit the world market in 1918 and was formally outlawed by the German government for its pacifist stance. This ploy gave the famed physician little cover, for if anyone had read the horrid thing, it advocated ransacking the world. The strategy defined was simple: have the sick kill off the sick. The weaklings would fight to the death in a pre-arranged battle, hence, natural selection and race purification could be achieved. The geniuses would engineer the whole affair in their ivory towers and sit on the sidelines, washing their hands of any brutalities. This was Nicolai and Einstein's definition of "pacifism."

Lenin had also risen on the "pacifist" ticket. By 1918, the Bolsheviks offered Nicolai Soviet citizenship. (7) Stalin would publish "The Biology of War" in Russian text in 1926, a crisp copy of the Soviet version's dust jacket graces Zuelzer's biography on page 321 of his "Nicolai Case." It appears that the Bolsheviks were nothing less than Kaiser Wilhelm's puppets. By 1923, Raissa Golant, one of Nicolai's former lovers, was begging him to return, guaranteeing him any position he so desired in the new nation. (8) His last departure to study the fauna of the tundra was in 1931, but his fortune was short fated. As we shall see, Stalin executed his henchmen to cover his crimes against his own citizens. Zuelzer concluded had Nicolai stayed on, like many others, he would have been placed before a firing squad and executed (page 407). Undaunted, Nicolai packed up and left for Chile, later befriending President Allende. A military coup awaited Allende, while the American CIA under Allen Dulles funded Nicolai's exploits in the Chilean Congress for Cultural Freedom, organized to defeat Communist propaganda! (9) Nicolai WAS a Communist, in the purest sense. This is a prime example of the United States Government peeing our tax money down a rat hole. It would be worthwhile for Wayne State University to reprint another edition of Wolf Zuelzer's "Nicolai Case," a scholarly achievement, irregardless of Zuelzer's own taints of racism and sympathies for his subject.

The typhus epidemics of World War One were of unimaginable scope, devastating much of Europe and Russia alike. The switched on and off cycle of these typhus epidemics, closely followed by relapsing fever epidemics, were well documented in the UNRRA records, (United Nations Relief and Rehabilitation Agency), leading one to conclude they were deliberately orchestrated. They began under Lenin, and went haywire under Stalin, who then cut off any Soviet reporting of epidemiological statistics to world organizations between 1937 and 1945. The UNRRA also estimated an equal amount of relapsing fever cases following the typhus epidemics in Russia, just how many of these were actually Lyme disease, we will never know. Coupled with famine, millions more must have died. (10) Others witnessed the disaster in Russia. Hans Zinsser's book portrays the rat as the "hero" of his narrative:

"RATS LICE AND HISTORY" by Hans Zinsser, Little Brown & Company 1934-1935, page 299-300:

"In Russia alone did typhus attain its mediaeval ascendancy... There were no words to record the dreadful sufferings of the Russian people from 1917-1921. Revolution, famine, epidemics of cholera, typhoid, and dysentery helped. And from the careful and conservative calculations of Tarassewitch, it is likely that, during these years, there were no less, and probably were more that twenty five million cases of typhus in the territories controlled by the Soviet republic, with from two to one half to three million deaths."

According to Zinsser, Poland, Rumania, Lithuania, and the Near East were also stricken, the Eastern Front totally devastated, yet the German and Austrian armies were unscathed, kept clean by "extraordinary effective sanitary measures." (11) Were Eastern Europe, the Balkans and the Orient victims of the pacifists' plot for world revolution? Most likely. Zinsser's political views mellowed and then reversed as he aged, writing a bitter critique on Communism in his autobiography, "As I Remember Him: The Biography of R.S." just prior his death in 1940. This, too, deserves attention and will be reviewed later on. Remember this man, Hans Zinsser, for he was a typhus vaccine partner to Dr. Harry Plotz, an Army epidemiologist sleuth who would die in the wake of the SS ELBRUS.

Zinsser became great friends with Charles Nicolle, Nicolai's suspected accomplice in France. Zinsser and Nicolle became a cozy pair of Frankensteins. Charles Nicolle had won the Nobel Prize for his typhus vaccine research. This doesn't make Nicolle a saint, it should make the reader highly suspicious as to why and where the German dynamite tycoon, Charles Nobel, (hardly a pacifist), was directing his money. Zinsser and Nicolle had visited each other yearly, corresponding weekly, since 1915. Later, Zinsser accompanied Nicolle to the Louis Pasture Institute in Africa to study typhus. Eventually, Zinsser was accused of initiating an epidemic off the coast of Mexico. Zinsser and Maximiliano Ruiz Castaneda had sailed for Mexico in 1930 with a clutch of live typhus infected rats for research, "hidden from the captain, the crew, and the passengers." Two rats subsequently died. The rats were thrown overboard. A drunken poet, suspecting a BW attack upon the Mexican harbor, panicked, alerting the Captain. Of course, no one believed the poet's "alcoholic delirium." (12)

Infatuated with socialism in his youth, Hans Zinsser wanted to name his son "Kerensky," after the Russian Revolutionist, but his wife intervened. Having served the Red Cross in Serbia during WW I, the League of Nations invited Zinsser back to Russia as a sanitary commissioner in 1923. "Typhus and cholera were flourishing amid civil war and famine, his epidemiological efforts, he later reported, were complicated by bureaucracy, fear, hunger, and despair" cite Zinnsser's recent biographers. (13) Zinsser wrote prolifically, often quoting in Latin, flaunting his linguistic skills as well as his scientific knowledge. One of his early publications, "Infection and Resistance," smacks of the "Super Race's" theories on superior immunological resistance to diseases, electing himself as the best candidate for a new White Utopia. Ironically, Zinsser died of cancer in 1940, as did Albert Einstein later on.

Walt Disney's "Fantasia" depicts Hell on Earth, orchestrated by a rodent, the magician Mickey Mouse. The top of a dark evil mountain opened up into the shape of an enormous bat where the demons from Hell rained down till dawn. Hans Zinsser noted a similar painting by Boecklin hung in the Shack Gallery in Munich in his autobiography "As I Remember Him," referring to it as a portrait of the new Russian tyranny.

His stint in the Red Cross had changed his perspective on "Utopia." He wrote "After a month of this, I felt quite satisfied that there was no idealistic Communism, either Marxism or Leninian, in Russia. Whatever may have been the high purposes of the founders, the present state of affairs was a savagely cynical and bloody autocracy maintained by espionage and brutality, utterly inefficient... a sort of "state capitalism" with all the means of production in the hands of a ruling minority which controlled the army and the police..." Just prior his death in 1939, he began investigating a brand new typhus, "spotted fever" on Cape Cod amongst' its very prevalent tick population. (14) By 1937, America was experiencing a wave of ixodes tick borne brucellosis, considered a rarity in previous times.

Zinsser was not the only American doctor to serve in the Red Cross during WW I. Future Air Force Surgeon General, Malcolm C. Grow was persuaded by Dr. Edward Egbert in Washington, DC to head for the Russian Front. Thoroughly impassioned by the Bolshevik Revolution, he published an autobiography in 1918, "Surgeon Grow: An American in the Russian Fighting." Who had organized the International Red Cross mission to Russia? Here's a clue. Recall Zinsser's epitome of insults thrown at the new Soviet Union as "State Capitalism"? Who was he referring to? The answer can be found in James Perloff's "Shadow of Power: the Council of Foreign Relations and the American Decline" and Antony Sutton's "Wall Street and the Bolshevik Revolution." (15) Put together with a myriad of State Department files, the Rockefellers, Goulds, Morgans, Loebs, fur trader Armand Hammer and future Secretary of State, John Foster Dulles, many CFR members, poured millions of dollars into Lenin's coffers. Many members of the CFR also financed the Red Cross in Russia. The CFR's main ambition was to establish a World Bank to facilitate the One World Government, the New World Order. They partially succeeded. Zinsser had figured it out, Revolution had to be financed, and Big Business, Big Government, and Big Banks answered the call. Gorbachev was right, "socialism" is "centralized planning."

All of these "pacifists" have been paraded before us as the epitome of kindness, intelligence, sophistication, and love. Who in their right mind would marry one of these selfish, arrogant, sadistic monsters? What would they do to their own children if they perceived any weakness or political incorrectness? Lock them up in an asylum? Albert Einstein did. Murder them in the crib? Wolf Zuelzer, Nicolai's biographer, a long time member of our National Institute of Health, as a pediatrician and serologist, advocated euthanasia in "The Pediatrician and the Species," (Pediatrics, vol. 47, no. 2, February 1971). Zueler's "treatment by neglect" was the "kindest" way to cleanse the gene pool of genetic mutants! On the top of the list were

Orientals suffering thelesemia and Blacks with sickle-cell anemia, but he did not exclude whites with other afflictions. Death before reaching the reproductive age could only save humanity from itself, postulated Zuelzer and Nicolai. Genes being a fixed fate; freedom, prosperity, nutrition, in that order, had nothing to do with inheritance, rationalized these racists. These were not the arguments of scientists, but those of deluded sexual maniacs, trying to out-number what they couldn't out compete. "What's love got to do with it?"

The time has come for historians to take a serious look at these so-called "pacifists" Communists, guised as physicians. These docs are nothing but callus, high-tech cannibals, a travesty to medicine and the human race. This certainly raises the question, what are the dangers of socialized medicine? How great is the percentage of racists crackpots amongst the medical community? How many politicians would advocate euthanasia as a cheap and expedient solution to balancing the budget, guised under the alibi of "saving" humanity? It worked for Stalin, Mao and Hitler. Of what value is "human trust" between people for the survival of a society, fearing you or your children won't be sacrificed, stoned to death, as in Cynthia Jackson's "Lottery," just to make the corn grow higher?

As always in politics, the right hand did not know what the left hand was doing, and Joseph Stalin kept his bureaucracy of criminals very well compartmentalized. Most of the Russian populace had no idea of the extent of Germany's involvement in the Bolshevik Revolution, financially or biologically. By 1932, a huge network of Soviet BW factories had been completed. Stalin was planning to execute half the Soviet population to facilitate "redistribution of the wealth" amongst the remaining survivors. World revolution would follow. Who knew about this? The British, for they had their own network of spies. By the end of World War I, England fully understood Communist designs for global conquest. There was a paper trail left by the socialist spies, for this was life before TV, the free press of the West was at their disposal. They were so arrogant; presuming the general public would never read nor comprehend their least motives, that they exposed themselves before the world on paper. Little England could not invade the expanses of the Soviet Union to conquer it, but there were alternatives.

First, we can quote like hell from Nicolai's "Biology of War" since it was published nearly a century ago, and then compare the British response through Thomas Edward Lawrence's writings, a new approach to psychological warfare the world had never seen the likes of. Contrary to true pacifists' belief, Nicolai theorized that all wars were not immoral, and his book's translators quite agreed:

"THE BIOLOGY OF WAR" Georg Friedrich Nicolai, The Century Company, New York, 1918, translated by Constance A. and Julian Grande.

"Translator's Preface"

"But no one must imagine that Dr. Nicolai condemns all war of every description: revolutionary and defensive wars he would put in a category by themselves as justifiable. That wars may be prevented he urges that a society of nations should be constructed."

Page xii: Albert Einstein's "Manifesto to the Civilized World'

"But in the East the ground is soaked with the blood of women and children slain by Russian hoards, and in the West the breasts of our soldiers are lacerated with Dumdum bullets. No one has less right to pretend to be defending European civilization than those who are the allies of Russians and Serbians, and are not ashamed to incite Mongolians and Negroes to fight against white men."

According to this goon squad, Germany fought World War I as a defensive war! By the end of World War II, six million Jews had been thrown into the furnace, millions more massacred deep inside the Soviet Union. Eighty-four-million Soviet citizens have been counted as executed under Stalin's reign of terror by Gorbachev's Memoriam Commission. Surely Nicolai and Einstein could not claim to be Jews! So there you have it. As long as the weak and undesirable, technologically obsolete, "useless eaters" were being destroyed inside Russia, "revolution" was within scope of these "pacifists." The Germans hailed Lenin as a genius!

"THE BIOLOGY OF WAR" by Georg Friedrich Nicolai, The Century Company, New York, 1918: Page 87: "What a War of Extermination Means"

"There are now in the world five hundred million of us Europeans or white men originally from Europe, and a thousand million of various colored races. I believe we have even now the technical means at our disposal for exterminating these millions in the course of the next twenty years. After twenty years, however, we shall no longer be in a position to do this, as soon, that is, as China has armed her whole population, constructs her own dreadnoughts, and manufactures her own cannon and shells, as Japan is already doing...

At a time when the fate of so many men is hanging in the balance, Europeans may, perhaps must, be asked whether on careful consideration they mean to declare all colored races barbarians, and then begin a struggle for existence, in other words a war of extermination, and not a ridiculous war for power, against everything non-European. When once so terrible a conception as that of such a war is grasped, then, if anything save sense-less cruelty is to be the result, it also must be thought out to the end, and there would have to be a war "sans treve et sans relache.' "

And what was to be the weapon for this "ghastliest of wars" against the "inferior races" Disease, of course, for with diseases, one could kill even more people than with bullets, reasoned Nicolai. On page 26 of "The Biology of War" Nicolai continued on with "this theory of war.. The fit nations conquer, the unfit perish. This may be terrible... certainly regret-table, but it is the only way to sift the wheat from the chaff. ... and leads over mountains of corpses... war is profitable to mankind." "The Biology of War" laid the corner stones for both World War I and World War II. The atomic bomb had yet to be invented by the Americans, to save us from Hitler and Stalin alike. Today, the whole damned planet is armed with every conceivable weapon imaginable, ready to blow poor little Earth out of orbit. What a pathetic lot we are. It is no wonder "The Biology of War" has never been reprinted, such a disgrace to all humanity, but every race has its own crackpots paralleling the stupidity of these Communist authors. This is humanity on its lowest rung of evolution. A Soviet geolo-gist, named Velikovski, defecting to the West, wrote "Worlds In Collision" insisting cataclysms had greater effect upon evolution than Darwin's natural selection through survival of the fittest. Very possible. Maybe Christ had it right, the meek shall inherit the earth, as opposed to the university intel-ligensia calculating Armageddon from their ivory towers!

The Communists see themselves as an isolated lot of geniuses, a tiny minority, the majority of humanity as worthless consumers on a limited supply of resources, hence, "redistribution of the wealth" over "mountain of corpses" became the principle for survival. The Free-marketeers see each human as a resource, a source for building new wealth and solving problems, their contributions and ideas of great value. Every one counts. Did Nicolai and Einstein ever repent for their arrogance and sins? No. They spent a lifetime lying to their fellow men. Read "Einstein of Peace", an edited collection of his voluminous letters published through Simon & Schuster, New York, 1970. "Time" magazine selected Albert Einstein as "Man of the Century" and posted his portrait on the front cover of their 2000 edition. With his wrinkled face and wild white hair encirling his head, it was as if the devil itself was staring out from a void.

"The Biology of War" is not the only testimony to the early German-Soviet collaboration in race purification. Robert Proctor published more on this sordid alliance.

"RACIAL HYGIENE" by Robert Proctor, Harvard University Press, Cambridge, MA 1988, pages 22-23: "We now know, from a number of recent studies, that the early racial hygiene movement does not fall cleanly into Left-Right divisions. Many socialists identified eugenics with state planning and the rationalization of the means of production: many thus found the idea of a "planned genetic future" an attractive one... "

Proctor further exposed Soviet medical journals reprinting articles from the "Archiv fur Rassenund Gesellschaftsbiologie," expounding the support of the German Communist Party for sterilization of all psychiatric patients. To achieve this end, Proctor details the building of the Kaiser Wilhelm Institute for Brain Research, funded by the Rockefeller Foundation. Accordingly, "between 1931 and 1938 Germany and the Soviet Union shared a joint institute for Racial Biology," under Ludwig Aschoff and Oscar Vogt, one branch in Berlin, the other in Moscow. These men will be joined by a very mercurial group of physicians and psychiatrists, crossing political boundaries time and time again. When Oscar Vogt moved to Moscow, he was replaced by an even more infamous Nazi, Dr. Hugo Spatz in Berlin. Back in the 1980s, a weird little article appeared in one of the local San Francisco newspapers on "geniuses" regarding Oscar Vogt's ventures in Moscow. A further expose on "60 Minutes" backed up the story. The Moscow institute became a sort of macabre brain warehouse for future scientists to analyze the cell structure of Soviet "geniuses." Since when is the capacity to murder considered "genius"? Oscar Vogt had Lenin's brain pickled and preserved. Later, when microscopes became more powerful, it was discovered that Lenin and Stalin's brains were full of worms, Spirochetes!

Where did these early socialists stand regarding colonialism? Was this only a vice of the Capitalist nations? Not at all. Nicolai approved of colonialism, as did the Kaiser and his Bolshevik allies. Accordingly, all the former inhabitants were to be "exterminated to make way for the white race," ("The Biology of War," page 147). The Communist feared Great Britain the most, this sea-trading empire not only refused to exterminate its colonies' original inhabitants, it actually allowed them to flourish and prosper under "dominions" and "common markets," later repenting and granting them independence! Horrors of all horrors, cried Nicolai. Is there any wonder why the Soviet Union and Hitler alike saw England as its greatest threat? Winston Churchill was villainized since the first day he set foot in the Colonial Office in 1921. And he retaliated superbly. "Never give in, Never give in, Never give in." At Churchill's service was a young archeologist from the Syrian digs of Carchemish, an intelligence officer assigned to the Army's map making department, secretly tracking German railway expansion through the Turkish Ottoman Empire.

Enter Thomas Edward Lawrence, "Lawrence of Arabia," Stalin's nemesis and greatest nightmare.

World War I was a prime example of colonialists with the munchies. A very detailed account of the Bolsheviks' colonial aspirations and conniving for land and oil was including in Jeremy Wilson's "Lawrence of Arabia," Atheneum Press, New York, 1990. Dozens of biographies have been published on Lawrence and his younger brother, Arnold, even fictionalized by Steven Speilberg's "The Young Indiana Jones." Wilson's unabridged work is probably the most comprehensive on the history of the international political intrigue plaguing the Orient, emphasizing a secret Bolshevik and German alliance with Turkey. Up till World War I, the Turkish Ottoman Empire consisted of a vast expanse of Middle Eastern nations: what is now Yemen, Saudi Arabia, Palestine, Jordan, Syria, Kuwait, Iraq, Basra, and Armenia, all fell under the Turkish yoke. Armenia was Christian, and the Young Turks attempted to " Turkify" them, abolishing the Armenian language and faith. Eventually the Turks massacred its two million uncompromising citizens, an atrocity precursoring the crimes of Hitler's holocaust and Stalin's purges. The Arabic speaking tribes to the south fell under equal brutality, forced to abandon their dialects and customs. The whole area was ripe for revolt. German engineers offered to construct a railway throughout the Ottoman Empire, tightening Turkey's hold over its rebellious citizens. Wars would no longer be conducted in regiments of horses and camels, but by armored cars, tanks and BI-planes, troops supplied by the railroads. Kaiser Wilhelm was planning ahead.

The vast British Empire as well as the French colonialists, had their eyes on Arab oil, as did Germany and the Bolsheviks. England had already established a colony in Egypt, purchasing the Suez to build a canal, facilitating trade with India under Queen Victoria's reign. The French held interest in Syria. British Petroleum made stakes in Persia, as did Rockefeller's Standard Oil. The Russians too, moved in. All sought alliance with the Arab factors in the Ottoman Empire, plotting revolt against their Turkish masters. Turkey looked northward to Germany and the Kaiser's new found allies, the Bolsheviks for assistance, hoping to expand there Ottoman Empire across the Moslem Central Asian Republics. It was this intriguing complicated network of secret alliances between the greedy colonialists, monarchists, and Bolsheviks that sparked World War I.

King Hussein of the Heshemite tribe, a descendant of the prophet

Mohammed, was established in Mecca and recognized by many as the head of the Moslem faith. His son, Feisal, partnered with the free-wheeling archeologist and British intelligence officer, T.E. Lawrence to spark a revolt in the desert. While the greed of the British, French and Russian Czar plotted carving up the spoils in the Middle East under secrecy of the Sykes-Picot Treaty, the Turks, Germans and Bolsheviks also plotted out a new Ottoman Empire across Asia in secrecy. Once the old Czar was disposed of, Lenin moved in to carve up the Orient. Lawrence, whose sanity has been widely debated, went about putting an end to all of their colonialist ambitions, German, Turkish, British, French, Czars' and Bolsheviks, alike. The colonialists hated him, the Communists hated him, the capitalists oil tycoons hated him, and the Fascists hated him. Just whom was he working for?

Lawrence was Oxford educated, his reading were catholic in taste. His youth was spent scouring the Ashmolean Museum, tutored by David George Hogarth, his mentor and protector. The Crusades were Lawrence's passion, his knowledge of British antiquities unsurpassed. Hogarth introduced Lawrence to archeology in the Middle East. In his youth he barefooted his way through ruins of the Crusader's castles and digs at the Carchemish site, home to the Babylonian kings of ancient Syria. Under Hogarth, Lawrence became a mapmaker and spy for the British military, plotting the expansion of the German-Ottoman railway. His Arabic improved. His knowledge of the terrain and tribes was essential to the British, but his loyalty was first to the Bedouin nomads.

Lawrence was a deeply religious Christian, and traces of his beliefs in the God given dignity and rights of each individual emerge in his history of the Arab Revolt, "The Seven Pillars of Wisdom," its title taken from a reference in the Bible, the Book of Proverbs (ix. 1): "Wisdom hath builded a house; she hath hewn out her seven pillars." In the book's Third Chapter's "Abstraction," Lawrence wrote "the sea wore away ever so little of the granite on which it failed, and some day, ages yet, might roll unchecked over the place where the material world had been, and God would move upon the face of those waters" a parable on the Arab struggle against colonialism. Was the fight against the emerging global alliance of robber-barons, Fascists and Communist being secretly led by the Holy See? The Catholic Popes have played an important role fighting Communism. Perhaps Lawrence held his allegiance to a higher force than the embattled greedy socialists of the 20th Century. Crazy, or not, it was Lawrence's prolific writings that drove Lenin, Stalin, and Hitler to their wits' end, a true tit for tat. By the end of World War I, Lawrence had established an incredible network of Arab spies throughout the Orient, and his hatred for Communism was unfathomed.

In the introductory poem to "Seven Pillars," "To S. A.," Lawrence describes the colonialists' ambitions in the Middle East as "blind worms growing fat upon your substance," one of the first hints of biological warfare attacks upon the Orient by the Bolsheviks. Further reference to the sufferings of the Arabs and death of a close friend of Lawrence's, named Dahoum, was made by biographer Jeremy Wilson. Leonard Wooley had served with Lawrence at the Carshemish digs in Northern Syria prior World War I, later returning to witness the loss of many friends due to famine and typhus epidemics. Accordingly, "one half of the old Carchemish labor force had perished, and it was reported to him that almost a third of the population had died during 1916." (16)

Accoording to Jeremy Wilson, after Czar Nicholas' collusion with the French and British in the Sykes Picot Treaty, planning to carve up the Orient on the sly, the Bolsheviks joined Germany with even grander ambitions, promising the Young Turks full expansion of the Ottoman Empire across the Central Asian Republics of Russia. Once the Czar was executed, and the Romanoff monarchy toppled, Lenin planned to cash in on the Sykes-Picot spoils, "liberating" the Moslems on Russia's southern border of its oil, property, and people. Lawrence fully understood this greed for oil between East and West, and made his way to Versailles dressed in Arab garb pleading the Arab case for independence, to no avail. At this point in history, Winston Churchill had been appointed Secretary of the Colonial Office and lassoed the obstinate, freelancing, renegade Lawrence to accompany him back to the negotiating table in the Middle East. The Sykes-Picot Treaty was undone, fulfilling Britain's promise of independence and self government to the Arab nations. The Communists and Capitalists for nearly a century accused each other of being colonialists and racists, truly pot calling the kettle black.

"Seven Pillars of Wisdom" details the plight of the Arab revolt, the epidemics plaguing the nomadic tribes, their camels and livestock. With his intelligence network stretching through Russia, Lawrence must have been keenly aware of Bolshevik biological warfare used to incapacitate the resistance. What did Lawrence write that so panicked the Soviets? Here we begin one of the most interesting cases of psychological warfare in military history. Lawrence terrorized the racists Soviets. These are the words of a soldier, beaten, raped, and in the end, very much alone, having seen so many of his friends die in one of history's most senseless and barbaric wars. Lawrence had survived five plane crashes, himself perforated by bullets and shrapnel, engaging in escapades wilder than Indiana Jones for freedom's cause. He was like "Killdare," appearing everywhere, a fictitious creation, driving Stalin nuts. Good, the bastard deserved it.

Lawrence wrote prolifically for the newspapers and military journals, including the prestigious "Round Table." His brother, Arnold compiled a collection.

"ORIENTAL ASSEMBLY": by T. E. Lawrence, edited by Arnold Lawrence, Williams Norgate Ltd. London, May 1939 page 129: "The Changing East" p.72:

"None of them (the government special commissions) gave us a general survey of the new Asia: none of them describe the disease as well as the remedy. This disease is physical, material, moral, mental, all you will. It is the civilization disease, the inevitable effect of too close contact with the West. The aborigines of Australia got it when they met us, and they died of it. There were biological reasons why their frames were too weak to stand contact with the body social so different from their own. Asia is tougher, older, more numerous, and will not die of us - but indubitably we have made her very ill."

Even contemporary psychiatrist John Mack tried to analyze T. E. Lawrence in "A Prince of our Disorder," concluding Lawrence, like everyone else, had personal problems, but found a way to work them out.

Mack's frontispiece to "A Prince of Our Disorder" quoted both Lawrence and George Bernard Shaw, eulogizing the two acquaintances' opposing ideologies. Shaw insisted that all "world progress depended upon the unreasonable man" while Lawrence (presumably the unreasonable man), pooh-poohed the racism of colonialism and "their brute achievements," swept up with the new idealism of the League of Nations after the Great War. (17) Shaw, a leading Fabian Socialist, and Mack may have considered Lawrence's politics that of a madman, but history will set the record straight. Joseph Stalin would award GBS the title of "Humanists."

While the Soviet propaganda machine whipped out article after article on Western racism, Lawrence led the counter attack, fully briefed on the Bolshevik alliance with Kaiser Wilhelm.

At the end of the war, Colonel Lawrence re-enlisted in the ranks at the bottom as a private and was soon stationed at the end of the world in Karachi, India. He dropped Winston Churchill's secretary, Edwin Marsh, a little note:

"THE LETTERS OF T. E. LAWRENCE" by David Garnett, Doubleday, Doran, New York 1938, Lawrence's letter June 10, 1927 to Edward Marsh, Winston Churchill's secretary. (Churchill was then Great Britain's

Secretary of War.)

Page 521: "Winston wrote me a gorgeous letter. Called his "Crisis" a potboiler. Some pot! And probably some boil too... He alarms me a little bit, for I feel that he wants to go for Russia, and the ex-bear hasn't come into the open. It's hard to attack, for its neighbors, except Germany, aren't very good allies for us. We can only get at her, here, through Turkey, or Persia, or Afghanistan, or China, and I fancy the Red Army is probably good enough to turn any one of those into a bit of herself, as the Germans did in Rumania. Persia certainly: Turkey will be very strong, soon, and should be our ally, if common interest make for anything. China I know nothing of, but she is too huge for anyone to swallow. The most dangerous point is Afghanistan. Do you know I nearly went there last week?"

The British dailies speculated Lawrence was plotting another revolt, Lawrence of Arabia was undercover in Afghanistan inciting new revolutions against the Communists! By 1928, the American press would intensify the scandal, the "New York World" had Lawrence disguised as an Arab sheik in Peshawar making "secret agreements" with "Riza Kahn during the absence of the Soviet diplomats" and by 1929, the "Daily Herald" was citing Lawrence in Allahabad, Afghanistan "assisting rebels to cross the frontier." The official Kabul newspaper, "Amany Afghan," cited "Colonel Lawrence organized and headed the Afghan revolt." (18)

The Brits were fully briefed on Nicolai's "Biology of War" and were plotting the end of the Bolsheviks. So were the Arabs who began organizing Prometheus, a secret underground society dedicated to the overthrow of the Soviet Union. After an untimely motor-bike accident in 1935 with a mysterous vanishing black van, on his way to a secret negotiation with a Hitler aide, Lawrence died. The funeral was grand, with full military honors, and most likely faked. Lawrence was Churchill's spy. Had his cover been broken as a Fabian Socialist by his literary association with George Bernard Shaw? Shaw, also a Fabian Socialist, frequented the Soviet Union, receiving top honors as a "humanist." Steven Speilberg portrayed Lawrence as the last Crusader hiding out in the ruins of Rumm in at Petra in "The Quest for the Holy Grail." In a reversal of fate, Stalin, a truly paranoid Communist, saw Lawrence under every bed, Churchill fueling his fears:

"GREAT CONTEMPORARIES" by Winston Churchill, G. P. Putnam & Sons, 1937. "Lawrence of Arabia"

"I deem him one of the greatest beings alive in our times. I do not see his likeness elsewhere, I fear we shall never see his like again... (ha ha) I have often wondered what would have happened to Lawrence if the Great War had continued for several more years. His fame was spreading fast and with the momentum of the fabulous throughout Asia. The earth trembled with the wrath of the warring nations. All the metals were molten. Everything was in motion. No one could say what was impossible. Lawrence might have arrived at Constantinople in 1919 or 1920 with many of the tribes and races of Asia Minor and Arabia at his back...."

Doubleday published "Seven Pillars of Wisdom" in 1935. The original edition had sub-titles for its chapters on each page, its "Midnight Sermon" sent chills up Stalin's spine, "Omnipotence and the Infinite were our two worthiest foemen, indeed the only ones for a full man to meet, they being monsters of his own spirit's making; and the stoutest enemies were always of the household." And in its "Abstraction," Lawrence paralleled the Arab revolt to the "sea," "The wash of that wave, thrown back by the resistance of vested things, will provide the matter of the following wave, when in fullness of time the sea shall be raised once more." Which "sea," the ocean, or the Holy See?

Stalin was frantic. With the Russian Central Asian Republics resisting Soviet collectivization, sitting atop a wealth of oil stretching from the Baku to Kazakhstan, Stalin plotted new purges of biological warfare. Once again, he turned to Germany for assistance. The industrial-military complex between fascism and Communism intensified. The chemists and scientists from I. G. Farben and the Kaiser Wilhelm Institute for Brain Research jumped at the opportunity to destroy the hapless citizens of the Central Asian Republics. Some day the Jews and Arabs will wake up and realize they are victims of a common enemy, and the fate of this Fascist-Communism alliance be sealed once and for all.

While the West baked in the wealth of the Roaring Twenties, the East calculated crashing the world market. A coordinated run on the banks induced the Great Depression in 1929. A contemporary Jewish banker, Edwin Black, in his "Transfer Agreement" followed the money through Swiss banks and into Soviet coffers. (19) A second attempt at world revolution had begun, Stalin cozied up even closer to Hitler than Lenin had done so with the Kaiser. Clifford Barrymore, cartoonist for the "Washington Star," drew a wedding scene on October 9th, 1939, commemorating the Hitler-Stalin non-aggression pact. Arm in arm, beaming with joy, they waltzed down the isle, Hitler in a pin stripe suit, with swastikas on his lapel; Stalin in a gorgeous wedding gown and veil, necklaced in swastikas, and clutching a bouquet, dressed in drag. The caption underneath read "Wonder How Long the Wedding Will Last?" posing the $64,000 question of the century. It lasted the whole century!

CHAPTER 1: NOTES

(1) "THE NICOLAI CASE" by Wolf Zuelzer, Wayne State University Press, Detroit 1982, page 108 footnote #1 - re: Nicolai's notebook.

(2) "EINSTEIN ON PEACE" edited by Otto Nathan & Keinz Norden, Simon & Schuster, NY 1960, Page 14: August 21, 1917, Romain Rolland wrote Einstein "I have read his book..."

(3) "HOSPITAL PRACTICE" vol. 27, August 15, 1992, Page 87-116 "Hans Zinsser - Biographer of Typhus"

(4) "THE NICOLAI CASE" by wolf Zuelzer, Wayne State University Press, Detroit 1982, Pages 138-139, re: the study of fauna, 1906 with Dr. Pavlov in Arctic and Arkhangelsk.

(5) IBID.: Page 22 re: Nicolai civil contract with German War Ministry at Tempelhof; Page 26 re: Nicolai assigned to Graudenz unit for contagious diseases; Page 28 re: Nicolai authoring "Biology of War" on vacation at Graudenz prison.

(6) IBID.: Page 32: re. Tuchel Heide. Page 54: re: Nicolai colleague considers infecting Russia with germs, Page 40 re: Nicolai transferred to Danzig, March - April 1916.

(7) IBID.: Page 237: Romain Rolland diary - USSR offers Soviet citizenship to Nicolai. Page 321 re: Leningrad edition "The Biology of War" dust jacket copy, Russian text.

(8) IBID. Page 405 re: Raissa Golant's invitation, professor of physiology in Leningrad.

(9) "THE NICOLAI CASE" Wolff Zuelzer, Wayne State university Press, Detroit, 1982 Pages 439-440: Nicolai. Chili, Allende, CIA

(10) "UNITED NATIONS RELIEF & REHABILITATION ADMINISTRATION HEALTH DIVISION" "Epidemiological Information Bulletin" vol. 1, Washington, D.C. 15 Jan. 1945, #1, Page 453: "past

experience, both in North Africa and in Europe, has shown that large scale outbreaks of relapsing fever frequently accompany or shortly follow major epidemics of typhus, appearing when the incidence of typhus has passed its peak."

Page 489: Chart of relapsing fever cases 1919-1944, louse borne and tick borne, USSR & Europe. Cites 1919-1923, approximately 2,300,000 cases in USSR, then dropping to just a few cases in 1937. After 1937, all USSR cases were not reported to any world health organizations. It is noted that usually there is a statistical error of reporting cases, understating epidemics by ten fold.

(11) "RATS, LICE AND HISTORY" by Hans Zinsser, Little Brown & Company, 1934-1935, pages 298 re: typhus on Eastern Front, WW I, and in POW camps

(12) "HOSPITAL PRACTICE" vol. 27, August 15, 1992 "Hans Zinsser - Biographer of Typhus" Page 108: re: Zinsser and infected rats dumped in Mexican harbor.

(13) IBID.

(14) "AS I REMEMBER HIM" by Hans Zinsser, Little Brown & Co. Boston 1940 Page 1: Boecklin painting; Pages 283-284: Soviet "state capitalism"; Pages 210, 307-308: typhus on Cape Cod, brucellosis 1937

(15) "SURGEON GROW: AN AMERICAN IN THE RUSSIAN FIGHTING" Malcolm C. Grow, Frederick A. Stokes, NY 1918, Page 1
"THE SHADOWS OF POWER: THE COUNCIL ON FOREIGN RELATIONS AND THE AMERICAN DECLINE" James Perloff, Western Islands, Appleton WI 1988, Pages: 38-41
"WALL STREET AND THE BOLSHEVIK REVOLUTION" Anthony Sutton, Arlington House Pub., New Rochelle, NY 1974. Pages 74, 75 Malcolm Grow; Page 78, Red Cross Mission to Russia.

(16) "LAWRENCE OF ARABIA" by Jeremy Wilson, Atheneum, NY 1990 Page 544

(17) "A PRINCE OF OUR DISORDER" John Mack, Little Brown & Co., Boston 1976

(18) "THE LETTERS OF T.E. LAWRENCE" edit. David Garnett,

Doubleday NY 1939

Page 631 re: July 23, 1928. Lawrence in India, "New York World" article on TEL in Peshawar "disguised as Arab sheik." Page 632 re: "Daily Herald" Jan. 5, 1929 Afghan arrest, Page 633 re: "Daily Herald" Jan 7, 1929 re: TEL arrest unconfirmed, India sends Lawrence home. Labor Party disbelief Lawrence doing engine overhaul at Karachi.

(19) "THE TRANSFER AGREEMENT" by Edwin Black, Macmillan, NY 1984

CHAPTER 2

CONNECTICUT CADDY SHACK
&
ANATASE VONSIATSKY

Russian Fascism and Its Reverse Radishes

At this point, Utopia in Russia was Hell on Earth. The Russian royalty and peasants alike, were incapacitated with plagues, too weak to resist the advancing Red Army. The White Russians wanted out. They ran for their lives. Some went West, others to the Far East, settling in China's northern embattled province of Manchuria. Some even sailed to America. The college students in the bourgeois universities led the working proletariat in revolution, never having worked a day in their lives themselves. Sound familiar? The Bolshevik Revolution had been a joint effort of German and Russian intellectual elite. Now their collaboration intensified after WW I. First, let's focus on the conditions prompting the White Russian flight, then on their leaders in exile.

Germany had suffered a humiliating defeat in World War I and would soon descend into the same hell as the Russian peasants. The Treaty of Versailles burdened Germany with huge war reparations. Famine swept the nation. The International Red Cross and many religious organizations, such as the Quakers, sent relief packages. Even though their nation lay in ruins, their people were educated, with the capacity to rebuild quickly. Germany had both some of the largest chemical industries and universities in Europe, and became an international center for students, the arts, and businessmen. Berlin and Munich were liberal open cities, musicians, such as British born Frederic Delius conducted his Congolese Opera, based on Negro folk songs. Delius, ostracized by Londoners, was welcomed in Berlin. Impressionist artists from New York and Paris opened exhibitions. For a few years, German musicians performed their wonderful heritage of Bach, Mozart, Beethoven, Schumann and Brahms. Sadly, this would change. Their heritage could not save them from the enemy within, the German Communist Party, the Spartans, who were the biggest racists on the planet, next to Nikolai Lenin, Joseph Stalin, and Adolf Hitler.

The Spartans still dreamed of world conquest. More than the Kaiser and his Queen were in bed with Nicolai and the Bolsheviks. While Lenin sought One World Government, I. G. Farben sought One World Monopoly. Germany and the Soviets, secretly re-arming, needed oil. There were these teeny weenie little problems in the new highly factioned Soviet Union. (A) The Peace Treaty of Versailles forbade re-armament of Germany, necessitating a secret alliance with Lenin. (B) Millions of Russian peasants tenaciously held on to their two-acre farms, resisting Soviet collectivization. (C) Millions more Moslem and Mongolian tribes spanning the Central Asian Republics sat on the richest oil reserves in the world, worshiping Allah, despising the infidel Communist atheists. (D) The Jews held tightly organized towns, centered around their customs and synagogues, obeying the laws of a Higher Command, not the Commissars. What was a poor little dictator to do? Why not offer these obstinate, rebellious peasants as target practice to the Red Army, or to the NKVD (Secret Police), or better yet, to the Nazis? They would be starved, plagued, and gassed.

Testimony to this period of purges comes first from Russia's survivors, found in Alexander Solzhenitsyn's "Gulag Archipelago." Solzhenitsyn, an old "zek," survived the prison chain for decades, secretly jotting down his experiences in the rat and lice infested camps. His crime - an intercepted letter criticizing Stalin's military moves, cost him twenty years of his life. Some of his fellow zeks, so starved for meat, resorted to eating a prehistoric frozen aquatic salamander while working the Siberian Tundra. His ghoulish account of prison life was smuggled to the West for publication. Once internationally recognized, the Soviets couldn't execute him, branding him a religious fanatic akin to mental illness, and expelled him to the West. This international rabble-rouser took up residence in Vermont. There he continued writing "The First Circle," a loosely guised fictional account of a scientist who unwittingly published a medical discovery which the military deemed useful. Top technicians were then rounded up in an elite prison and ordered to create a voice decoding machine for wiretapping medical leaks. One old zek in the engineers' prison cell, going blind, surviving on a meatless diet of white and brown bread, kept asking why Stalin was killing all the horses, the only means of transportation? Russia had no automobiles. Were the horses sick from brucellosis or other tick-borne parasites?

Others began to noticed the disappearance of livestock. Victor Herman's "Coming Out of The Ice," both book and TV documentary in the late 1980s, exposed the Ford Motor Company's exploits inside Russia, and took notice of the Russian livestock massacres. Herman, an American Jew, traveled to Russia in the 1920s as a teenager with his family to build tractor factories. After the factories were built, Stalin executed all the Americans as spies, excepting Victor, who had achieved a world record in parachute jumping. Victor Herman landed in the Gulag for refusing to take Soviet citizenship, thus depriving Russia the credit. He dined on frozen rats for forty years while his prison guards ate Dinty Moore Beef Stew, Herman fearing Russia had conquered America. Nobody had meat. His autobiography of life in the disease stricken Gulag prison chain is horrifying. It was filled with brutal madmen. Herman smuggled out a letter to Madam Tolstoy in America. His cousin, a lawyer, won his release after eight years of bickering with the politburo.

Miron Dulot, who eventually escaped from the Red Army, survived Stalin's deliberately induced famine that swept the Ukraine, Northern Caucasus and Kazakhstan from 1932-1933 also noted the void of livestock. With one of the Ukraine's most bountiful harvest, all being exported to Germany, the starved citizens turned to cannibalism. Dulot published "Execution By Hunger" after escaping to the West. Its "Introduction" was drawn up by Adam Ulam, citing bizarre statistics on animal slaughter: "In 1928, the USSR had 32 million head of horses; by 1934 the figure stood at 15.5 million. In January and February 1930 alone, 14 million head of cattle were destroyed." (1) Were these animals sick with brucellosis? Future declassified WW II documents will reveal this to be the case. The disease infects meat, milk, dung, and all those who handle it or who consume it, attacking the nervous system. Brucellosis is also carried by the same ixodes tick that carries Lyme and relapsing fever.

Unlike previous famines in the Soviet Union, Stalin kept track of his dead. He hired census takers to tally the effectiveness of his purges. Once the records came in, the statisticians were executed. Stalin's purpose behind the exorbitant quotas for grain production became evident. Tons of grain were sold to Germany, along with it went tons of infested rats. Germany would decline into madness. Only until Gorbachev's arrival did the full history of Stalin's villainy come to light. Gorbachev created a special commission named Memoriam, to uncover the census taker's statistics. Eighty four million had perished, the Russians still counting. William F. Buckley's "National Review," "Stalin: Why Hitler Embraced Him Why Gorbachev Rejects Him" hit the news stands September 1st, 1989. Dulot's mother and brother survived the famine by out-foxing the Communists, hiding sacks of grain on State property adjacent their own, the officials never suspecting food to be hidden on state land. This family witnessed their whole town starve to death. It is no wonder that by the time World War II rolled around, the Ukrainians saw Hitler as their savior. Their naive hopes would soon be dashed.

Under Gorbachev, "glasnost," a "new openness," was granted, and scholars hit the archives. Roy Medvedev, one of Russia's newly liberated historians, questioned the execution of his father, a deeply committed Communist. Medvedev sought out the lists of Gulag prisoners and their "crimes" against the State. "Let History Judge" details the millions of innocent Russians victimized in Stalin's purges. Medvedev's Dad was TOO patriotic! Lenin's backers, working their way up the Politburo, were a threat to Stalin's power. Off they went to the Gulag with the rats, lice and ticks. Medvedev's own twin brother, a scientist, seeing through the hypocrisy of Communism, was locked up in an insane asylum, only later freed under Gorbachev. Keep Roy in mind, for his facts contribute to the development of Stalin's war machine and its dependency on the German chemical industry. Medically, what was happening inside of the Soviet Union?

There is second source for history buffs, awaiting exploration. Underneath the U.S. National Archives in Suitland lies a twenty-acre underground city, a maze of vaults, stuffed with old boxes of World War II intelligence files. Since the end of the second World War, only one man, John Loftus, had been granted top security clearance to mosey around down there. Loftus, formerly an Army intelligence officer, signed up as a prosecuting attorney for the newly formed Justice Department's Office of Special Investigations under the Carter Administration. Out of the kindness of his heart, he has instructed others, including this author, on how to write Freedom of Information requests for the release of these documents. Most of these records have been accessible to the public since the Freedom of Information Act was passed in 1979. Anyone could have written for the index cards to these files in the past twenty years, yet neither the old Nazis, the neo-Nazis, the Communists, nor the Justice Department were interested. Why? With the fig leaves off, thousands of politicians would have to run for cover, Right and Left, East and West. The records of the Soviet Union's collaboration with the Nazis in chemical and biological warfare from this cave shall be explored in detail in the upcoming chapters.

The third source on Stalin's purges, beyond the eyewitness accounts of fleeing peasants and POW intelligence reports, is the "Index Medicus," held in every major medical library across America. It includes an international collection of medical journals published since the turn of the 19th Century, complete with English translations housed in our National Library of Medicine and Library of Congress. Its just a matter of collating the evidence. The Russian doctors wrote profusely on the catastrophes suffered by the Soviet citizens. They also wrote of the Nazi doctors they collaborated with while conducting Stalin's biological warfare purges. We are not talking "top secret" here. They had no shame, brashly assuming the common man would never read, nor have the capacity to comprehend their exploits. The conceit of it all is flabbergasting, enough to make anyone's blood curdle. For many years, their open 'cover' relied upon public apathy.

A fourth source on the Soviet atrocities and their collaboration with the Germans also sits in every public library, "Chemical Abstracts." Here we have international catalog of scientific research, publications and patents since 1900. Even though Stalin forbade publication of Soviet discoveries, their joint research with foreigners was published by both France and Germany, greedy for patent rights.

The US Library of Congress with its "Pre-1956 National Union Catalogue" offers a gold mine of wartime intelligence files, CIOS, BIOS, JIOA, and FIAT reports. The Library of Congress holds the Department of Commerce post war index of captured German documents, "The Bibliography of Scientific and Industrial Reports" catalogued by their intelligence operation, the OSRD, Office of Scientific Research and Development, under Vaneever Bush. The war booty, including German patents, was a gift to American inventors and industrialists. Some of these files on I. G. Farben in Russia vanished long ago. Every American public library designated as a US Government Depository holds a copy of this index. Yes, the truth has been hidden in plain sight.

More files reside in the National Archives collection of OSS Reports. The State Department's WW II Office of Strategic Services was in operation till 1945, fortunately, many of these records survived. Then, the OSS was dissolved by Truman, and re-organized into the OPC, Office of Policy Coordination, whose indexes were "lost" by Allen Dulles, future director of the CIA. Imagine roaming around Suitland in its twenty acre underground city without an index. But the best witnesses to the Bolshevik's crimes came from the White Russians, themselves.

Manchuria became a haven for White Russians fleeing Stalin's purges. Amongst the destitute grew a new club of crackpots and impostors, the Russian Fascists. Two major figures emerge in the Russian Fascists movement, Konstantin Rodzaevsky, who remained in Harbin, Manchuria, and Anatase Vonsiatsky, who stationed himself in Thompson, Connecticut. By the mid 1920s, Rodzaevsky set himself up as 'Vozhd' or 'Grand Duce' of the Russian Fascist Party. Historian, John Stephan, nephew of Vonsiatsky's wife, Marion Ream, had the inside scoop on these Fascists. He paints a colorful picture of Harbin in the 1920s in his biography, "The Russian

Fascists: Tragedy and Farce in Exile, 1925-1945" (Harper & Row, NY 1978.) There were over 20,000 White Russians in Harbin carrying Soviet passports, nicknamed "radishes," "red on the outside, white on the inside." Amongst them were KGB and GRU moles, "reverse radishes," "white on the outside, red on the inside." According to Stephan, "it took a sixth sense to distinguish a real from a phony radish." (2) The significance of these reverse radishes is noted in Stephan's "Introduction" (page xxii) where he states the Soviet security organs and Red Army had seized the Russian Fascist Party files in Harbin at the end of WW II. Stephan presumes they may still be classified in Soviet archives today. Should we ask Puten to look?

The Brotherhood of Russian Truth, founded in 1923 by Don Cossack Ataman, was another operation of White Russian refugees in Europe running ruthless sabotage stints against the Communists. They merged with the Russian Fascists movement, operating out of Berlin, Paris, and Belgrade and soon became penetrated with moles. By 1927, the young Anatase Vonsiatsky joined the Brotherhood, exiled in Paris. Here, Vonsiatsky met an American millionairess, Marion Ream. Divorcing his first wife, he emigrated to America. Vonsiatsky married into enough money to finance his shenanigans the rest of his life. How much money his fellows in exile contributed to his charade we will never know.

Vonsiatsky next established himself as head of the Brotherhood of Russian Truth in America. As its chief, he became extremely irate when Standard Oil would not include him in a plot to blow up the Soviet oil pipelines. These conspirators were also on Amtorg Trading Company's payroll. Amtorg was the Soviet Union's brokerage house in New York, making most of its money from fur auctions. It was discovered that a member of the Brotherhood involved in these business ties was a member of the OGPU, the Soviet Secret Police. Vonsiatsky quit the Brotherhood just in time. The American factor of the Brotherhood was a Soviet front, exposed in the San Francisco based newspaper "Novaya Zarya" July 12, 1932 which accessed the Meunier Grand Jury Hearings on the Brotherhood's fate. (3)

Vonsiatsky's Communist affiliations were already documented by the State Department in 1921. He was first granted a three month temporary visa to visit the USA, but the day before its expiration, Marion was able to influence immigration officials to let him stay. Money talks. "Vonsiatsky's immigration dossier, filed under the heading of "Communist" is still classified" contends his biographer, John Stephan. (4) It is of great significance that Vonsiatsky, through the front of the Brotherhood, held ties to the Russian fur brokerage, Amtorg Trading Company, in New York. Amtorg would also use Rockefeller's Standard Oil tankers in 1940 to circumnavigate the British blockade at Vladivostok supplying oil to Hitler's war machine through Russia's back door. More to follow.

The newly weds, Marion and Anatase, settled in Thompson, in the north east corned of Connecticut on a large estate, including a golf course, nicknamed the "9th Hole." Anatase was Marion's toy-boy, she twenty years his senior. Picture Vonsiatsky as Rodney Dangerfield in "Caddy Shack," just as big and boisterous. The new 'Vozhd,' 'Grand Duce,' published a revolutionary rag, "Fashists," all editions cataloged in the New York Public Library. Rivaling his counterpart, Vozhd Konstantin Rodzaevsky in Manchuria, Vonsiatsky was a paper tiger. As World War II approached, Vonsiatsky taunted Thompson residents by setting loose turtles with swastikas painted on their backs, roaming the 9th Hole. The turtle, symbol of the Fabian Socialist Party, "creeping socialism," was the Communist front operation centered in England that Lawrence had tried to penetrate.

Across the Pacific, more than turtles were plaguing Harbin. General Vladimir Kosmin, prior to Rodzaevsky's takeover, had become head of the Brotherhood of Russian Truth in Manchuria. Kosmin had tried to cozy up to the occupying Japanese, but the Japanese stood their guard. The Brotherhood's Berlin leader, Boris Tedli, had been arrested by the Gestapo as a Soviet spy. (5) Japanese suspicions were well founded. As World War II approached, the Russian Fascist Union, (RFS soratniki) warlords, engaged in gang-land style battles, carving up the Manchurian territories. The Japanese police, the "Kempie," arrested them for conducting biological warfare on Manchuria:

"THE RUSSIAN FASCISTS" by John Stephan, Harper & Row, NY 1978
Page 207: "In 1940, twenty-four RFS soratniki were arrested by the Kempei at Mutanchiang, a town on the rail line between Harbin and Vladivostok... Boris Nikolaevich Shepunov, a pint-sized Pogranichnaya-based strongman who enjoyed local Kempei patronage... resented RFS men encroaching upon his 'territory' and decided to get rid of them in one stroke. He therefore denounced all local Russian Fascists to the Kempei as Soviet spies who were spreading the plague among cattle and typhus among people."

The sordid tale continues on the plight of the Manchurians, where Shepunov indicated a leading Fascist of the Central Executive Committee named Konstantin Arseniev responsible for the BW attacks. Arseniev was interrogated by the use of the Chinese water torture and finally confessed. Eventually a radio receiver and glass jars, alleged to hold germs, were produced at the trial. Arseniev and all twenty-four soratniki were executed by the Japanese Military. When Rodzaevsky protested, he was told: "It was a mistake. The act leaves a dark spot upon the uniform of the Imperial Japanese Army." (6) Vladivostok was the Soviet fur shipping center on the Pacific. With the bales of fur from the slaughtered livestock and wild-life of the Central Asian republics warehoused in Vladivostok, no doubt Manchuria suffered from its invading rats and plagues. We await the KGB archives release to reveal the complicity of their reverse radishes.

Rodzaevsky, still feigning allegiance to the Japanese and German cause, went on to recommend possible successors to the late Czar Nicholas after a Fascist victory. First, he designated himself. Next, Rodzaevsky nominated White Russian Prince "Anton Turkul, (of the) Russian National Union, United States," amongst others of royal heritage. (7) Turkul would prove to be the Soviet Union's best mole, penetrating every Western intelligence operation during and after WW II till his death in 1957. Turkul's portrait hung in the CIA headquarters' office full of dart holes. Every freedom fighter the OPC trained to liberate the Iron Curtain from Bolshevism was identified and assassinated because of Turkul. A detailed account of Turkul's exploits is exposed in Mark Aaron and John Loftus' "Unholy Trinity," (St. Martin's Press, 1991).

The Fascists lost WW II, and Konstantin Rodzaevsky beat it back to Stalin's camp. Bursting with platitudes and patriotism, Stalin had him executed, just to silence the little creep. He knew too much. This became a recurring pattern. Stephan concluded that the Russian Fascists movement was nothing but a Communist front:

"THE RUSSIAN FASCISTS" by John Stephan, Harper & Row, NY 1978

Page 373: "The Gestapo thought so. The Japanese Military Gendar-merie and Foreign Ministry half agreed. If not Soviet agents, both leaders of the Russian Fascist movement nevertheless adopted the view that Stalin was the ultimate Fascist... Therein could lie the Russian Fascist movement's significance that it patterned itself after, and wound up worshiping its archenemy."

Right on! John Stephan's book is a wonderful read, and deserves a second edition. Back at the golf course on the 9th Hole, a Caddy Shack plot of equal scale was amuck. Vonsiatsky, his role of duplicity unsus-pected by his followers, continued to distribute "Fashists," promising to raise an international army of exiles to overthrow the Soviet Empire. He began stockpiling a worthless assortment of defunct rifles, a cannon, and tear gas at the estate. Vonsiatsky became involved in organizing the Eastern European emigres on America's waterfront. Was this a weapons watch, or fur and rat watch? Surely, whatever info on epidemiology the Vozhd gathered, it not only went to Berlin, but straight to Moscow. The American waterfront, as we shall see in upcoming chapters, was alive with activity. Charles Higham, a British biographer of World War II's infamous characters, included Vonsiatsky, "the Count," in his book:

"AMERICAN SWASTIKA" by Charles Higham, Doubleday & Co. Garden City, NY 1985 Page 124: "As war approached, the Count helped the Ukrainians to set up a spy ring of White Russians, German, Lithuanian, and Estonians agents working in the factories, plants, and ship docks across the country. They were ordered to leak information in their own networks for transmission to Berlin..."

The Eastern European refugees were not the only dupes of El Duce. Vonsiatsky began to cozy up to the Connecticut State Police in 1927, first introduced to neighbor Sgt. Elton Thomas Nolan, next, to State Police Commissioner, Robert T. Hurley in 1928. Further acquaintances included Nolan's superior, and Ross B. Urquhart from the Danielson barracks. Vonsiatsky offered 35 acres of the 9th Hole to State Police Commissioner Edward J. Hickey as target practice range in 1939. Vonsiatsky even came to the CT State police department's aide donating tear gas during a labor strike at the Windham Textile Mills. He also offered financial aid in the form of personal loans to Edward Hickey. (8) Don't jump to conclusions, Vonsiatsky's police cronies did not disfavor labor, many had joined different unions to secure benefits and higher wages.

For example, another Hickey from Connecticut's police departments, took on a more significant role in State politics and labor. William Hickey of Manchester Connecticut was not only deeply involved in Connecticut's state police unions, but served as Director of the Connecticut Division of Special Revenue, overseeing the lottery and gambling casinos. Tina Lewis details the Lottery's history in "Justice Denied: Politics, Perjury and Prejudice in the Lottery," (Elderberry Press, Oakland, OR 2001). Blain Lewis, Tina's late husband, became Assistant Deputy of the Lottery in 1973, hired by John Devine, a retired FBI agent in charge of the Connecticut Division of Special Revenue. Lewis was appointed chief of the Connecticut State Lottery in 1980, making good money for the State. Profits plummeted after 1988 when General Instrument was awarded the online contract for the Lottery. Even though General Instrument came in with a lower bid for the contract, they had a poor performance record in other states. Lottery machines broke down, equipment had to be rebuilt, months of ticket sales were lost and as the odds were increased for winning, the public lost interest. Who knew where to attribute the money loss, the State of CT audited its own lottery and subsequently hired Arthur Andersen to oversee GI's CT Off Track Gaming accounts; Andersen also audited Enron! In 1989, the Governor appointed William Hickey as Executive Director of the Connecticut Division of Special Revenue. (9)

Lewis was fired by William Hickey when he refused to obey an order to present General Instrument in a positive light to the rest of the board. A lengthy lawsuit ensued, finally turned down by the Supreme Court; Lewis lost. William Hickey would die in February 2002, not long after the death of Blain Lewis, this author's godfather. Hickey had "skirted State Law that would have prevented him from working for Foxwoods for one year after he left the Division" cites Tina Lewis (10) Foxwoods is the prosperous Pequot Indian gambling casino on the west bank of the Connecticut River.

On the opposite shores of Foxwoods lies the much coveted real estate of Norwich State Insane Asylum. Anatase Vonsiatsky had also been locked up at Norwich and later transferred to a military hospital. He had been caught financing a friend's escape to Mexico after slipping secrets to the Japanese. Vonsiatsky was prosecuted in 1942 for treason; a huge show trial was orchestrated in Hartford by the Assistant Attorney General, Thomas Dodd, further facilitating Vonsiatsky's cover. The 9th Hole was portrayed as a citadel, with a roving army of turtles poised to attack Connecticut. Three and a half years later, Vonsiatsky was released. Skyrocketing to fame from grandstanding, Dodd ran for the Senate. His son, Christopher, inherited his seat.

Trial records exposed Anatase Vonsiatsky's personal secretary, Norman Watson, as having purchased the tear gas grenades from Federal Laboratories, which were offered to the Connecticut State Police for labor riot control at the Windham Textile Mills. Vonsiatsky had joined the US Chemical Warfare Service in 1930, placing himself in a position to access munitions dealers. (11) Remember Federal Laboratories. Vonsiatsky's suppliers served inside of Russia during WW II doing secret poison gas research and have an important role to play in the history of Soviet chemical warfare. Secretary, Norman Watson retired and became a independent insurance agent, the author's Father, one of his clients.

Even more interesting, Blain Lewis' first boss in 1973 during Watergate years, was John Devine, a former FBI agent. Note Stephan's biography on Vonsiatsky, "The Russian Fascists," mentions a "John Devine" as Vonsiatsky's Boston lawyer. Are they in any way related? Only the FBI can answer that. "John Devine" is a common name, but follow the pattern of events here, and wonder if there was a relationship. Soon after Lewis was hired onto the Lottery, John Devine "left rather quickly." (12) The history of Vonsiatsky, the FBI, and the police became even more entangled.

The plight of the police since World War II has been one of turmoil. Desperately in demand for national security on one hand; underpaid, picked upon and spat upon, on the other, they began to organize. Early police fraternities' constitutions forbade law enforcement to strike, but as the decade of the 60s approached, the police were fed up. The AFL-CIO muscled its way in, so did the Teamsters. A myriad of police unions evolved. They sought political support, much more than the Vozhd on the 9th Hole could offer them.

An inside glimpse of these gumshoe capers hit the press just after Watergate, "The Fraternal Order of Police 1915-1976: A History" by Justin E. Walsh, (Joseph Munson Co. Inc. Indianapolis, 1977). The FOP was shut out of America's industrial giant, Detroit, for attempting to organize during WW II, interference with war production was seen as treason in "Gotham City." (13) Lawsuits followed. In comic book styled revenge, the FOP's news journal editor and Grand Lodge Secretary, Jerry Elam, nominated "Batman" of Gotham, for a special crime fighting award in 1965. FOP National President, John J. Harrington nulled it, rightly concluding this would precipitate disaster. (14) Was there significance to Elam's hair-brained proposal? You'll have to ask the FOP. Yes, little children, there really is a Batman, and he lives inside Jurassic Park with the tyrannosaurus. You'll see.

Justin Walsh refers to the FOP 1960s history as the "Dark Ages," the "source material yet to be written." President Richard Nixon's "tough talk" on crime won FOP endorsement for his 1972 re-election. (15) By 1972, a very contested close election emerged between incumbent FOP Grand Lodge President and VP Al Hildenbrand of Miami. The big debate was over missing funds. The Fraternal Order of Police were not the only ones with missing funds, these were the years of Watergate, CREEP (the committee to re-elect the president) had bigger problems. Other charitable organizations had earlier sought the FOP's contributions, straight out of "Caddy Shack," such as Father Flanigan's "Boys Town" of Nebraska in 1949 and the Crusade for Freedom in 1950. (16) Radio Free Europe was funded by the Crusade for Freedom, an OPC Front, with "large numbers of Byelorussians and other Eastern European Nazis" running the propaganda machines and manning the air waves, according to John Loftus in "The Belarus Secret" (17). Their dossiers sanitized, thousands of Nazi collaborators, a few hiding out in Radio Free Europe, would emigrate to

America. Loftus' book goes on to expose the State Department's OPC under Frank Wisner and Allen Dulles, as horribly compromised by Fascists and Communists subversives. Surprised?

John Stephan donated his research to the Hoover Institution on War, Revolution and Peace; it is quite extensive, this author had the opportunity to view it. The Institute owns the largest collection of Russian revolutionary history in the world. Gorbachev had visited them just before his Communist opponents attempted a military coup. In 1978, before the Freedom of Information Act had been passed, Stephan only had access to Hartford court records on Vonsiatsky's trial. But plenty of information abounded, he was not limited. Relics of Vonsiatsky's Russian Fascists cult even began appearing in Hartford's antique stores in its southern Puerto Rican district. Double headed phoenix memorabilia embossed over backward swastikas, old World War II military guns and arm bands resembling loot from the 9th Hole appeared on Maple Street's corners.

New FBI files have been released to the author, October 31st, 1997, after years of waiting. As we look at them, keep in mind, the State Department immigration files catalog Vonsiatsky as a "Communist." Hoover hired Vonsiatsky for surveillance over the Eastern emigre community in America. The reverse radish would soon be dropped like a hot potato when NATO began investigating the Fascists double agents which had penetrated its own intelligence. Hoover authorized the elimination of the FBI's Vonsiatsky holdings. By 1958, a truck load of records on the Vozhd and his affiliates vanished. The name of the FBI's "SAC," Special Agent in Charge, in the New Haven Office is censored. Was the SAC who requested Hoover's approval for the destruction of the Vonsiatsky files in New Haven, the same FBI agent, John Devine of the Connecticut Division of Special Revenue, "DOSR" over the State Lottery? Was this John Devine of the FBI related to Vonsiatsky's lawyer, John Devine? Was there a tie between Lottery monies and Vonsiatsky's phony Fascists that the FBI wished covered up? We can only speculate. The author had to wait eight years for the release of these Vonsiatsky files under the Clinton Administration, (FOIA request #340,879 originally filed 10/13/90 and released 10/31/97). Only with the assistance of her Utah Congressman, Merrill Cook did she get results.

FBI file 65-1675-852 ANATASE VONSIATSKY, was ET AL ESPIONAGE CONSPIRACY G&J SECURITY MATTER -R
   TO: DIRECTOR, FBI (65-1675) Date 7-30-58
   FROM: SAC, NEW HAVEN (65-137)
   RE: New Haven letter to Bureau 4-22-46

"As the Bureau is aware, ANATASE A. VONSIATSKY, former head of the Russian National Revolutionary toilers and Worker-Peasant Fascist Party, was convicted for violation of Section 34, title 50 USC, in USDC, Hartford, Connecticut, on 6-22-42. He subsequently was sentenced to five years incarceration and on 2-26-46, he was conditionally released from Federal custody...

A review of the bulky exhibit in instant case reveals that 62 exhibits are presently contained therein. Included in this material are numerous photographs of VONSIATSKY's home at Thompson, Connecticut photographs of ADOLF HITLER, and various German soldiers, apparently obtained from magazines and newspapers, and other photographs of unidentified individuals.

In view of the status of instant case, it is requested that Bureau authority be granted for New Haven to destroy such exhibits as the above-described photographs presently being maintained by this office. Exhibits such as signed statements, photographs of subjects, subpoena duces tecum, search warrant and other pertinent material, will be retained."

SAC, New Haven (65-137) August 11, 1958
DIRECTOR, FBI (65-1675)
ANATASE A. VONSIATSKY, was, et al ESPIONAGE - CONSPIRACY G&J SECURITY MATTER -R

"Reurlet 7/30/58 requesting Bureau authority to destroy certain exhibits in instant case.

The photographs and material in reflect which were taken from subject should be returned to him and appropriate receipt obtained... subject was convicted for violation of Section 34, Title 50, USC, in Hartford Connecticut on 6/55/42 based on charges he furnished Fritz Kuhn with funds to flee U.S. after Kuhn and others affiliated with German-American Bund were charged with espionage. Subject admitted he did furnish Kuhn with money. Subject was sentenced to five years incarceration and on 2/26/46 was conditionally released from Federal custody. He served his sentence in a federal mental hospital. Material which New Haven requested authority to destroy includes numerous photographs of subject's home in Thompson, Connecticut, photographs of Adolf Hitler and various German soldiers apparently obtained from magazines and newspapers and other photographs of unidentified individuals. This material is of no value to Bureau and should be returned to subject."

The chit chat between Hoover and the New Haven SAC went on for several months and it was decided that there was virtually nothing to return to Vonsiatsky, but the tons of material left should be destroyed. We will never know just who was in the "other photographs of unidentified individuals." We are talking about a MACK TRUCK LOAD of material!

FBI file 1675-853 ANATASE A. VONSIATSKY, was et al ESPIONAGE
To: Director, FBI Date 9/3/58
From: SAC, NEW HAVEN (65-137)
RE: New Haven letter to Bureau dated 7/30/58 and Bulet to New Haven 8/11/58
"A review of the bulky exhibit in instant case reveals that New Haven is presently in possession of no material which was originally obtained from ANATASE A. VONSIATSKY and which should be returned to him.
The following New Haven exhibits in this case, however, are believed to be of no apparent value:

NH 65-137-1B8 Photographs of VONSIATSKY's home at Putnam, Connecticut, prints of which were received from (black out).

NH 65-137-1B-10-13 Photographic copies of halftone pictures which were apparently published in and copied from old issues of "Life" Magazine. These pictures are of ADOLF HITLER and various unidentified German soldiers taken during the German campaign against Poland and Russia.
(Many more numerous copies from magazines are listed, followed by):

NH 65-137-22 Photographs of a group of Russian soldiers apparently being decorated by Czar NICHOLAS II during World War I.

NH 65-437-1B-23 Photographs of a composite group of individual portraits of 16 unidentified soldiers, apparently Russian. The original picture from which the copy was made appears to have been published in an unknown publication since the original pictures were reproduced by the half-tone process.

NH 65-137-24 Photographs of a composite group of individual portraits of 35 unidentified soldiers, apparently Russian. This exhibit is similar to No. 23 above.

NH 65-137-1B-25 Letter from an unidentified individual in France to the Chief of Police, Putnam, Connecticut. This individual wrote a previous letter in an effort to locate his brother in Putnam. Letter was misdirected to VONSIATSKY and instant exhibit so states. Otherwise, there is no connection between the exhibit and instant case...

NH 65-137-1B1-2 Handwritten personal letters from VONSIATSKY to one (black out) with whom subject previously visited from time to time. Handwriting specimens of subject, other than this exhibit, are available in the exhibit section.

Since the above mentioned exhibits are believed to be of no further value in this case, they will be destroyed by New Haven after September 15, 1958, UACB. No commitments have been made to VONSIATSKY and the above information is merely passed on to the bureau for information purposes.
LLM:DB 65-137"

One might even presume Vonsiatsky was harboring White Russian refugees on his estate. The photographic records of his fellow reverse radishes serving under the Czar could have included the infamous Anton Turkul, potentially very damaging to Hoover. Earlier FBI files held on Vonsiatsky reveal his relationship to the FBI:

FBI file 65-1675-834 ANATASE VONSIATSKY was ALL RUSSIAN NATIONAL REVOLUTIONARY FASCIST PARTY INTERNAL SECURITY - G&J date 9/27/46
"It was suggested to Mr. VONSIATSKY that if at any time he had any information of value to the Bureau he should feel free to call upon the New Haven Division to furnish such information. He stated that about the only way that he could get information would be by going to foreign countries where there are large groups of White Russians. He suggested himself that he might be in a good position to get information about Communist activities if he sent to such places as South America, Paris, France, or Shanghai where there are large groups of White Russians. He suggested himself that he could pose as a disgruntled White Russian who had been imprisoned by the American Government for his anti-Communist activities.
It is noted that VONSIATSKY made this suggestion also: He said that there is considerable talk about trying to find homes for displaced persons in Europe at the present time, and that the UN will undoubtedly

take over the job of furnishing passports similar to Nausen passports for these homeless peoples. VONSIATSKY believes that these large numbers of displaced persons would offer excellent opportunities for Espionage purposes. He believes that whoever will be in charge of issuing passports for these displaced persons and whoever had any control over them will have limitless contacts among potential Espionage agents."

Just before the above correspondence, Vonsiatsky had been released from the hospital-prison in Springfield, Missouri into custody of his adoring wife, Marion Ream (FBI file 65-1675-828). A deal was struck for early release: Vonsiatsky would advise the FBI on another case involving a White Russian, Alexander Ivanovich Sipelgass (FBI file 1675-827 dated 12/19/45.) From these files, there is no doubt that Vonsiatsky was used by the FBI as an informant.

By 1952, Vonsiatsky offered his services to the FBI and hatched a plan to overthrow the Soviet Union using freedom fighters. The fighters would be dropped into the middle of the Gulag prison chain to foment revolution. Of course, the prison camps were deep inside of Siberia. More realistically the freedom fighters would become incorporated into the Gulag as prisoners themselves! The FBI passed on Vonsiatsky's suggestion to the Defense Department, FBI file (65-1675-845.) In 1956, again Vonsiatsky contacted the FBI, offering his services.

FBI file 65-1675-848 ANATASE VONSIATSKY was, et al ESPIO-NAGE

To: Director, FBI

From: SA. MIAMI (65-1068) date Dec. 12, 1956

"(Vonsiatsky) had advised the Miami Office that in January, 1946, prior to his conditional release from the United States Public Health Hospital, Springfield, Missouri, was contacted by an agent of the FBI from Washington, D.C., who tried to enlist his services as an antiCommunist."

"VONSIATSKY stated at the time he was not interested, but now, in the light of world affairs, he is interested. He stated that the Agent never presented his proposition, and that now he would like to hear it."

"VONSIATSKY indicated, however, that his former activities were more in the field of propaganda, rather than espionage, and stated that he would not be interested in activity involving domestic or foreign intelligence, because he was too well known to representatives of the present

Soviet Government."

"VONSIATSKY also stated that he intended to offer his services to the State Department, or an agency of the Department, which he felt was the Government Agency that he was best qualified to serve... It is to be noted that the Miami file indicates that VONSIATSKY in the past, and prior to his conviction, suffered "delusions of grandeur." It is also to be noted that he served his sentence in a Federal Mental Hospital."

"This is being furnished to bureau for information inasmuch as VONSIATSKY plans to make contact with the United States State Department."

"New Haven, Washington Field Office, and Kansas City will review files relative to VONSIATSKY, and will advise Miami if recontact with him is desired in connection with the alleged contact made with him by Bureau Agent in January, 1946."

The special Agent in Kansas City wrote Hoover that indeed, in 1942, Vonsiatsky while in prison, had been contacted by PITTELKOW regarding using Vonsiatsky to spy against Germany, but nothing came of it, (FBI file 65-1675-849.) Oddly, the following file concluded there were no Washington records regarding Vonsiatsky's employment:

FBI file 65-1675-850 December 28, 1956
"A Review of WFO (Washington Field Office) files fail to reflect any information which would corroborate the subject's allegation. WFO has no desire that subject be recontacted by Miami relative to this allegation."

New Haven's SAC then wrote Hoover:

FBI file 65-1675-851 ANATASE A. VONSIATSKY, was et al ESPIONAGE
To: Director, FBI
From: SAC, NEW HAVEN (65-137) date 1/9/57
"The Bureau's attention is directed to New Haven letters to the Bureau dated 7/12/46, 9/27/46 and 9/7/51. It is noted that in each of these letters subject is reported to have made an offer to be of assistance to the Bureau in its work. These offers appeared to be generally stated... No commitments were made re these offers of subject.
    The NHO has no desire that subject be recontacted by Miami relative

to his allegation or his suggested offer of assistance."

If the FBI did not take Vonsiatsky up on his offers, then, how was the deal struck to have him released early from prison? Is this discussion between the Washington Field Office and the New Haven Field Office regarding which incriminating Vonsiatsky documents to dump? Was Vonsiatsky eventually hired by the State Department? Did the State Department wish to embarrass the FBI? Was the State Department pressuring the FBI into dumping the Vonsiatsky files?

The heat of the Cold War was on in the 1950s. Allen Dulles and his OPC-CIA were given carte blanche to overthrow the nations behind the Iron Curtain. White Russian Prince, and Soviet spy, Anton Turkul, was hired on by Dulles' OPC after WW II to help smuggle Nazis out of the Soviet Union and train freedom fighters in Trieste to fight behind enemy lines. All of the freedom fighters were identified and assassinated by the Communists as soon as they set foot on their homeland. It was here that the Soviet Union returned the lend-lease SS ELBRUS to the OPC, scrubbed clean after delivering 426 tons of furs to Philadelphia. Trieste, just after WW II, a contested free state between Yugoslavia and Italy, was a hotbed of spies. Here, Anton Turkul, Vonsiatsky's boss, ran the Nazi smuggling ratlines for war criminals out of Russia.

The Hoover Institute for War, Revolution and Peace at Stanford University has the most extensive public files on Anton Turkul, his death catalogued in the Russian newspapers on September 20th, 1957. Turkul had smuggled so many Communist agents out of Russia and brought them to America that NATO was beginning to take notice. Turkul's death, in 1957 sparked a panic in the intelligence community.

"UNHOLY TRINITY: The Vatican, the Nazis, and Soviet Intelligence" by Mark Aarons & John Loftus, St. Martin's press, NY 1991

Page 270: "In 1959 the NATO intelligence services reviewed their anti-Soviet failures and concluded that support for the 'emigres' should be abandoned, as these 'exile organizations were hopelessly riddled with Communist spies.' "

Aarons and Loftus reflect on the political ramifications of Turkul's treason as a triple agent. Vice President Richard Nixon had authorized CIA chief Allen Dulles' escapades with this super spy during Eisenhower's infirmary. Exposure of CIA failures would prove extremely damaging to Nixon's run for the White House against John F. Kennedy in 1960. Aarons and Loftus spell it out:

"UNHOLY TRINITY" by Mark Aarons & John Loftus, St. Martin's Press NY 1991 Page 151: (Turkul had penetrated) "the Imperial Russian Army, the French Deuxieme Bureau, the Japanese General Staff, Mussolini's headquarters, both British Secret Services (MI5 and MI6), Ribbentrop's personal intelligence service (Bureau Jahnke), Admiral Canaris's Abwehr, Wehrmacht Intelligence on the Eastern Front (the Fermde Heer Ost or Foreign Armies East, headed by General Reinhard Gehlen), the SS Security Service (SD) and passed Soviet disinformation to virtually every nation in both Axis and Allied camps."

How many more Soviet moles entered Australia, Canada, South America and the United States, courtesy of the Prince? Turkul also penetrated Pope Pius' Black Orchestra, organized to fight the Communist who were torturing and executing priests in the Balkans. This will be covered in depth later on. The question remains, was Anatase Vonsiatsky, Turkul's subordinate, also in the employ of the State Department's OPC, as the FBI files suggest, planning a freedom fighter attack within the Gulag? Was Allen Dulles' OPC working for the Soviets? Let's lay out the evidence. You be the judge.

An enormous rift developed between the FBI and the CIA. They took to literally black-mailing each other. Did Dulles demand Hoover destroy the incriminating evidence? There were so many file cabinets on Vonsiatsky in the New Haven Bureau Office that they first considered returning them to Vonsiatsky in a moving van. Vonsiatsky notified the FBI he was not interested in their return and authorized the FBI to destroy them. All the photos and letters of Vonsiatsky's reverse radish Russian comrades in arms went up in smoke. All the photos of the Connecticut Caddy Shack and its guests went up in smoke. All the photos of the compromised German generals, went up in smoke. The career of one German general, Adolf Heusinger, is of particular significance. Why would J. Edgar Hoover destroy such incriminating evidence? He held thousands of incriminating dossiers on American subversives. How much of America's national security was Hoover willing to jeopardize to cover his own butt, literally and figuratively? What did Allen Dulles have on the FBI's greatest sleuth to force complicity?

There are other pressing questions here. Consider Vonsiatsky's affiliation with Konstantin Rodaevsky, the Manchurian Vozhd of Harbin and his involvement with Soviet biological warfare. Anatase and Marion had personally visited Harbin, their first meeting with Konstantin Rodzaevsky in April 1934 accomplished the merger of Eastern and Western exiles into an All Russian Fascist Party. What light could Vonsiatsky shed on Soviet biological warfare? Vonsiatsky's contacts with textile mills, insurance agents, police, poison gas manufactures inside Russia, and insane asylums, made him an excellent informant on the spread of Lyme disease for the FBI, OPC, and KGB. Once identified and diagnosed, what would happen to the early victims of Lyme disease in Connecticut? Had Vonsiatsky been tipping off the Soviet's whom to execute?

Did NATO discover the full extent of Turkul and Vonsiatsky's penetration? No. The stage was set for NATO's next fiasco, which almost launched World War III. President Eisenhower in his lame duck year of 1960, nominated General Adolf Heusinger to command NATO. General Heusinger had been fourth in command under Hitler, Chief of Operations (the OKH), on the Eastern Front and oversaw I. G. Farben's pesticide and poison gas munitions development. Heusinger was I. G. Farben's mentor and protector. We need to take an in depth look at I. G. Farben's treason against Germany, the transfer of its poison gas patents to Russia, and its accomplices, Allen Dulles, their patent lawyer, and Adolf Heusinger.

In the upcoming chapters we need to explore Vonsiatsky's relationship to Federal Laboratories and their poison gas research inside of Russia. We need to further explore Vonsiatsky's relationship to Anton Turkul, and the Prince's ties to Nazi war criminal, Klaus Barbie's drug cartel in South America. We need to consider the history of Soviet Union's biological warfare in Manchuria while analyzing biological warfare in the Korean War. The discovery of BW factories in Pyongyung, North Korea, staffed by the Soviets, further back John Stephan's episode with Vonsiatsky's side kick, Konstantin Rodaevsky. Vonsiatsky died 1965 in St. Petersburg, Florida, saving Richard Nixon, Allen Dulles, and J. Edgar Hoover from the embarrassment of another inquisition. The deaths of Dulles and Hoover would soon follow, Nixon facing impeachment. While Vonsiatsky organized a Communist front under phony fascism in America, I. G. Farben did likewise in Nazi Germany. To cover I. G. Farben and Heusinger's treason against Germany and NATO, Dulles would have to cover up the voyages of the SS ELBRUS. Once again, don't get confused, trying to sort out who's on whose side. The Communists and the Nazis are virtually one in the same people.

CHAPTER 2: NOTES

(1) "EXECUTION BY HUNGER: The Hidden Holocaust" by Miron Dulot, W. W. Norton & Co. NY, London 1985 Page vii and ix: 'Introduction' by Adam Ulam; peasants slaughter livestock.

(2) "THE RUSSIAN FASCISTS: Tragedy and Farce in Exile 1925-1945" by John Stephan, Harper & Row, Publishers, New York, 1978 Page 45, on radishes.

(3) IBID. Page 121: Brotherhood of Russian Truth and Amtorg.

(4) IBID. Page 100: Immigration dossier

(5) IBID. Pages 118 and 317: Konstantin Rodzaevsky, Communist agent

(6) IBID. Page 207: arrest of 24 soratniki

(7) IBID. Pages 260-261: "suitable candidates for the National Government"

(8) IBID. Page 118: CT St. Police Commissioner Robert T. Hurley. Pages 215, 216, 366: Police Commissioner Edward J. Hickey.

(9) "JUSTICE DENIED: Politics, Perjury and Prejudice in the Lottery" by Tina Lewis, Elderberry Press, Oakland, OR 2001. Page 72: William Hickey, General Instrument, Arthur Andersen.

(10) IBID. Page 67: William Hickey, gambling regulator, Foxwoods

(11) "THE RUSSIAN FASCISTS: Tragedy and Farce in Exile 1925-1945" by John Stephan, Harper & Row Publishing, NY 1978 Page 119 Norman Watson buys Federal Laboratories tear gas

(12) "JUSTICE DENIED: Politics, Perjury and Prejudice in the Lottery" by Tina Lewis, Elderberry Press, Oakland, OR 2001. Page 15: John Devine heads DOSR & hires J. B. Lewis.

"THE RUSSIAN FASCISTS" by John Stephan Harper & Row Publishers, NY 1978.

Page 250: John Devine, Boston Lawyer for Vonsiatsky.

(13) "THE FRATERNAL ORDER OF POLICE 1915-1976: A HISTORY" by Justin Walsh, Joseph Munson Co., Indianapolis, IN 1977. Pages 183-185: Howard Heine's efforts to organize FOP in Detroit fail, case reaches Supreme Court and turned down.

(14) IBID. Page 239: Jerry Elam nominates "Batman" for FOP crime fighting award.

(15) IBID. Page 289: FOP endorses Richard Nixon's re-election 1972

(16) IBID. Pages 217-222: Boys Town Nebraska seeks charitable contributions, Korean War interferes. Pages 240-245: Crusade for Freedom seeks FOP contributions.

(17) "THE BELARUS SECRET" by John Loftus, Alfred Knopf, Boston 1982.

Page 118: Crusade for Freedom, Radio Free Europe, Radio Liberty, OPC funded.

CHAPTER 3

FLUBBER BY I. G. FARBEN

Schrader, Ipatieff and the Waffen Pruf 9

To seek the origin of Lyme disease, we must go back to World War I. The history of Soviet biological warfare offers a substantial possibility. It is entwined around the development of German pesticides and poison gases. The poison gas industry became entwined with the synthetic rubber industry, "buna." Biological warfare begot pesticides, pesticides were strengthened and became poison gases, and poison gases were incorporated into the manufacturing of buna as a softener. The relationship of these three industries, biological warfare, poison gases, and synthetic rubber can be investigated by simply doing a little homework in the public library

The Soviet Union had over twenty-four chemical warfare "CW" and biological warfare "BW" sites. The demand for more rats, ticks and lice made the demand for new pesticides to contain them even greater. The Communists were suffering from delusions. The rats had different ideas. They did not sneak from house to house, asking each neighbor, are you a Capitalist or are you a Communists? The Germans were working on pesticides developed by the I. G. Farben cartel. I. G. Farben, originally in the textile dye industry, needed pesticides to destroy vermin in wool, especially ixodes ticks. With the political ties already sewn between the Bolsheviks and the Kaiser, the industrial giants followed suit. The scientific collusion between these two nations was far greater than publicly acknowledged.

By the end of WW II, when the Americans interrogated Nazi scientists, a puzzling story emerged. The Russians had the Nazis' most secret poison gas technology. Two different versions of how this happened were postulated. First we shall look at the story through the Nazi poison gas specialists' eyes, desperately trying to cover their butts for treason. Next, we shall look at the Russian's alibi on how they acquired the Nazi poison gases and how they desperately tried to cover their butts for treason. The

Nazis insisted the secrets had already been publicized in pesticide patents years before the war. The Russians tooted their own geniuses as the inventors. Both sides were lying.

Russia needed rubber for tires and tank treads, secretly amassing the biggest military buildup in history in 1930. Their partner in crime, Germany, needed both oil and rubber for its own military ambitions. The US Patent Office can do little to track down Soviet patents between WW I and WW II, Stalin forbade all publications. But I. G. Farben's subsidiaries inside of Russia gave Germany joint claim to patent rights, as did their interests in France. Russian research appears indexed in "Chemical Abstracts" under I. G. Farben. Here, geography plays an important role. By 1941, Japan had captured 90% of the world's crude rubber supply in Indonesia. Lawrence and the Arab Revolt put an end to German designs on the Ottoman Empire for cheap oil, but Alsace-Lorraine was rich in coal. From coal tar, 'coke,' arose the acetylene chemical industry of synthetic fuels, plastics, and rubber. This process of cracking coke for derivatives, butadiene and nitrium, (hence buna) was developed by Dr. Walter Reppe, director of research at I. G. Farben, Ludwigshafen, often referred to as the "Reppe Process." (1) Reppe was not particularly sympathetic to the Reich, nor was the rest of I. G. Farben, well hidden from historians.

Stalin took his top chemist, Serge Vasilevich Lebedev, and introduced him to the German and French synthetic rubber specialists, assigning him the impossible task of constructing ten buna factories. The Soviet Union was experimenting with a new economic system of "volevoi" or (willful) Five Year Plans, which had many failures. Only three buna factories were completed, according to Stalin's biographer, Roy Medvedev, in "Let History Judge." (2) In the early 1920s, Russia was still a backward nation, having suffered revolution, famine, typhus and relapsing fever epidemics, with 80% of its population still engaged in agriculture. These were tough times for everyone and constructing ten new factories was out of the question. Imagine what kind of war Stalin was planning, and who was the "enemy" in his backward nation?

Serge Lebedev died in 1934, but the German and French patents making reference to Lebedev's work appear in "Chemical Abstracts" under "vinyl rubber." (3) Early attempts at manufacturing buna bounced like a brick. It needed a softener, which I. G. Farben supplied from its pesticide-poison gas industry. Lebedev's biographer, A. E. Arbuzov, conveniently, , would later receive the Stalin Prize for development of the G-2 poison gas series. American intelligence experts familiar with Arbuzov's limited background suspected a cover-up. Remember both Lebedev and Arbuzov, they figure heavily in Stalin's deception. (4)

Russia, battling over 23 million cases of typhus and relapsing fever, offered a profitable market to I. G. Farben's pesticide industry. Dr. Gerhard Schrader of the I. G. Elberfeld Works developed a pesticide to kill leaf insects and aphids on roses, later, its stronger derivatives killed ticks. Suffering temporary blindness in his lab from the new product, the military pressed him into concocting more deadly compounds. Once captured after WW II by the British, he was forced to write a history of his poison gas research. Half of the truth came out. These reports have been partially declassified under Freedom of Information Act requests, "FOIAs," but their relevance will not make sense until we understand the nature of the ticks these pesticides were originally designed to destroy. Ticks, mites and spiders are not true insects, but of the arachnid family, with their skeletal structure on the outside. Tick borne typhus and relapsing fever can not be fought by conventional means using DDT. Theodore Savory explains in his "Arachnida" the necessity for a stronger pesticide:

"A considerable proportion of the exoskeleton of an arachnid has been believed to consist of chitin, a resistant material that is unaffected by air or water and is insoluble in caustic alkalis. It is dissolved by stronger sulfuric or hydrochloric acid, forming a solution from which dilution or neutralization causes it to be deposited in a changed form as a white precipitate."(5)

We need a pesticide with a sulfur and chlorine base to dissolve their shells and kill the little beasties. From this, Schrader cooked up a "pesticide" that not only killed aphids, and ticks, but rats, dogs, horses, and "large apes," needing only a milligram on skin contact to make every living creature on Earth drop dead. (6) It was named TABUN, later derivatives SARIN and SOMAN, became the most deadly war gases of its time, both Hitler's and Stalin's super weapons. Together, the two crackpots made enough poison gas to take out the planet ten fold. (7) Fortunately, America developed the "bomb." We have never given enough credit to Julius Robert Oppenheimer for ending the war. Of course, there was bias, he was a Jew.

Gerhard Schrader's interrogation report claims he handed over the new pesticides to the German High Command for Operations, the (OKH), headed by General Adolf Heusinger, fourth in command under Hitler. Heusinger, in turn, gave the new weapon to the OKW, High Command of German Forces CW and BW Unit, the Waffen Pruf 9 under Walter Hirsch. Captured after the war, Gerhard Schrader testified:

"Since the OKH demanded the utmost secrecy in the field of latest discoveries, the I. G. works at Elberfeld was limited to the minimum number of experts... The head of I. G. Works at Elberfeld (Prof. Hoerlein), could only entrust one physiologist (hygienic specialist Prof. Gross) with the substance tests. A chemist (Dr. Hollrung) and a physician (Dr. Bock) were at the disposal of Prof. Gross as scientific experts. For my experiments I had the cooperation of a biologist Dr. Koekenthal of Leverkusen and an analyst, Dr. Tetteiler of Elberfeld...

'The Wa. Pruf 9'

Dr. Von de Linde permitted all interested parties in the OKH to work independently on the substances that I had produced. He or rather OKW Abt. Wa/Pruf 9 had at its disposal at the Citadel in Berlin-Spandau a large technical and scientific research station equipped with all the latest contrivances. An extensive stretch of open land near Munsterlager (Lueneburger Heath) was also available to Wa Pruf 9 for practical experiments in firing the new substances. Animals were used for testing their efficiency... In 1944 Prof. Richard Kuhn of KA, without my knowledge, became acquainted with my work. R. Kuhn was the first to apply a single biological test (unclear) and thereby able to synthesize new substances. In the course or his work, Kuhn produced SOMAN." (8)

Here, it is important to make a mental note of Dr. Bernhard Von Bock working with Gerhard Schrader's little gang at I. G. Elberfeld. Bock will resurface inside of Russia after the war with more a more infamous suspect. General Adolf Heusinger will also resurface as head of NATO. Walter Hirsch and his Wafen Pruf 9 are the central characters in the Soviet-Nazi collaboration in BW and CW. It began in 1928 at the Tomka Proving grounds, just outside of Volsk on the Volga River with the NKVD (Soviet Secret Police). By the outbreak of WW II, Hirsch had over 300 German scientists working under him, including members of I. G. Farben's poison gas specialists, the Kliewie BW laboratories, and Wolfgang Wirth and Adjutant Mengele in the gas and smoke weapons toxicology unit. "Adjutant Mengele" had actually been interviewed by British intelligence, but there were numerous "Mengeles" serving the 3rd Reich. This one, in the company of Hirsch's cut-throats, certainly fits the bill of the future infamous Death Angel of Auschwitz. (9)

Greater detail on Wolfgang Wirth's role as a "toxicologist", Group VII Waffen Pruf 9, appears in the OACSI files, MIS 206481 "Interrogation of German Chemical Warfare Personnel" Alsos Mission MIS WD c/o G-2, Hq USFET (Rear) APO 887 dated 26 Sept. 1945. He ran the toxicology labs at Spandau, experimenting on animals only, insisting his ignorance of the gas chambers at Dachau, Meidernich and Auschwitz. Still Stalin's ally in 1940, the Waffen Pruf 9 moved inside of Russia for "decontamination missions." What or whom was being "decontaminated" at this point in history - the Poles? We will explore the significance of NKVD chief, Beria's poison gas testing on the Poles at the Katyn Forest Massacre site in the upcoming chapters.

The chronological history of the German Army's Waffen Pruf 9, beginning at Tomka in 1928, is nicely documented in a CIOS (Combined Intelligence Objectives Subcommittee) report "Investigation of Chemical Warfare Installations in the Munsterlager Area Including Raubkammer" by A. K. Mills, held at the National Library of Medicine, Bethesda, MD. It was indexed in the Library of Congress' Pre 1956 National Union Catalog under "Allied Forces Supreme Headquarters: CIOS" listings, not by title, but by its subtitle under "CW Item #8." Some years later, the author wrote the National Archives for the declassification of its index to German CW reports in the OACSI collection, Office of the Army Chief of Staff for Intelligence, and discovered this same A. K. Mills report to be listed as "DESTROYED." There it sat all these years, hidden in plain sight at Bethesda. Nervous, the author made numerous copies and circulated them amongst the intelligence agencies. Let'em catch each other. A librarian later mentioned to the author that the FBI had posted letters to the public libraries requesting they immediately alert them of any classified material.

What was going on at the Tomka Proving Grounds with the Waffen Pruf 9, far out of reach from Treaty of Versailles inspectors? Sweden captured a Russian Army report on their gas buildup and forwarded it to America. In the style of Soviet journalism's misnomers, such as "Provda" (Truth), the captured report was titled "Gas Defense" instead of "Gas Offense." Its introduction was authored by J. Fischmann, chief of the Military Chemical Department of the Red Army, April 1931. Fearful of "the increasing preparations being made by the capitalists for an attack upon the USSR" gas masks were being developed in massive quantities. But the rest of the report was devoted to offensive new phosgene gases and methods for dispersal. America was not developing these new sophisticated gases, and Germany was the Soviet's ally. Who was "the enemy"? Clues arise from the Swedes' report:

Page 26: "Incendiary bombs are used against buildings, growing crops, and camouflage materials. The picture in the lower right hand corner represents the explosion of a 50-kg phosphorous bomb. 'Apparatus with a compressed air container': From low heights this apparatus is used for contaminating important terrain areas, and from great heights it is used for attacks against towns and villages and large troop concentration positions." (10)

Just whose "towns and villages" were to be attacked? Their own! The Moslems, the Jews, and the Christians posed the greatest threat. "Organized religion," organized Anything, was a threat to Soviet dictatorship.

Let's view this history of Soviet-Nazi collaboration through "The Hirsch Report" first, stressing the German Army had pulled out of Russia by 1934, only 'private' businessmen remaining. Two different translations remain, the Nalbandian translation includes only Chapter 1, housed in the Carl Isle Military History Institute. The second translation by the US Chemical Warfare Service (CWS) contains three chapters, slightly altered, held at both the National Archives and Pentagon Plans and Operations Department. Hirsch intended nine chapters, but he mysteriously died while writing them. The intrigue surrounding his death deserves a whole chapter. By reading the report, it becomes increasingly evident that Serge Lebedev acquired his gas and buna technology through the I. G. Farben Works. Understand, phosgene gas is the precursor to TABUN:

"SOVIET BW AND CW PREPARATIONS & CAPABILITIES" also known as "The Hirsch Report" by Walter Hirsch, Chapter 1, Nalbandian translation:

Pages i-ii: 'Introduction' "The joint German-Russian collaboration years from 1928-1935, Japanese intelligence reports on Siberia and the Far East, and German technicians and chemists who worked as civilian employees in Russia during 1930-1937."

Page 45: "Fishman, the former chief of the Chemical Warfare Division of the Red Army, had already hinted in some of his publications to current activities on 'burning gases' which had a severe effect on the human skin. (footnoted 'Gas Warfare' by J. Fishman, Moscow 1925) Further information on this appeared in the Polish technical journals. (footnoted Major Sypnisvaki, 'Chemical Warfare in Russia; in Przeglad Piechoty' Warsaw, August 1937.)"

Page 46: "Phosgene Oxime being new and very secret war gases, were allegedly in large quantities in two factories in the neighborhood of Moscow, namely at Stalingorsk (50 km east of Tula). For purposes of better preservation, the gas was kept in glass ampoules 50 cm long and 10.15 mm in diameter. It was stable for 1/2 to 1 year."

Page 47: "It lends itself only for attacking living targets, and is unsuitable for ground contamination. Neither Russian nor the German gas masks afford protection against its effects; it penetrates the protective garments."

Page 133: "In 1928-1931, a German experimentation party carried out a series of experiments in a small proving ground which at the time bore the name of "Tomka." The experiments started on a small scale by a party of 30 men, then called "Battalion S" of the Army Ordnance Department. In years that followed up to 1931, the program and the personnel were almost doubled. The agents in these experiments were made either in the laboratories of the "Auer" company or were produced in the factories at Samara and Tomka (probably Shishany), as they claimed. In 1932, the detachment was recalled prematurely, and a subsequent order in 1933 wound up the activities of Tomka, putting an end to the German-Russian cooperation in the CW field. Experiments were carried out yearly from May to the end of November."

Page 109: "From 1922 to 1937 there were many foreign experts who took active part in the Russian industry and research to make up, i.e. some extent for the lack of indigenous ability. Most of these were dismissed in 1937 and had to leave the country It is obvious from this time on, the Russians decided to obstruct any peering into their preparations... for a future war against the imperialist countries."

The Hirsch Report continues on page 33 of the Nalbandian text, citing there would be more material on Tomka in an upcoming chapter, which prompted to author to write the Pentagon, hoping to obtain the full text. Out of nine chapters, only three remained, some 681 pages, translated for a second time, by the US Army CWS. It is important to differentiate between the two translations of the first chapter, for the CWS edited out significant lines. Hirsch continued on page 33 of the Nalbandian text, citing the Soviets had attended the Waffen Pruf 9 experiments at Tomka, involving mustard and lewisite gases, and "pushed these experiments forward to find an improved product." The "civilian employees" were those of I. G. Farben and they would soon be caught a pickle. With Hirsch dead, and the last six chapters vanishing, their history vanished.

I. G. Farben's acetylene chemist, Otto Ambros, interrogated after WW II, gave a startling account of Soviet-Nazi collaboration in the 1930s planning Auschwitz.

"I. G. FARBENINDUSTRIE: A.G. AUSCHWITZ, UPPER SILE-SIA" reported by Walter Hirshkind CWS, 22 August 1945, CIOS Item 22, Library of Congress PB 9703. Page 4: 'Section 2: the Auschwitz Project'

"It was the obvious the object to divide the vital Buna production into four geographically separate zones, each of which must, because of the high energy consumption of Buna, in the immediate vicinity of coal fields... It must be emphasized that at that time, no indications of a possible German-Russian war were on the horizon. On the contrary, intensive and very friendly negotiations with the Russians were in progress for the purpose of erecting rubber plants within the Russian territory itself. Taking into consideration the threat of bombing attacks from the West, it could be safely assumed that the works of Schkopau (in Saxony) and the new project in Upper Silesia would be able to operate undisturbed for German wartime needs.

It was at one time considered to create new industrial areas in Southeastern Europe on the Danube near Vienna, Hungary or Rumania, but the raw material considerations always prevailed over those stressing the proximity to the markets. Moreover, a canal from the Odor to the Vistula was projected and one from the Odor to the Danube had already been started. These shipping routes would assure Auschwitz of the cheap transportation to Russia as well as to the Balkans.

The fact that Eastern and Southeastern Europe is, in its technical development, far behind Central and Western Europe, would make the erection of a large chemical plant of the most modern type highly desirable for the economic penetration of Russia and the Balkans. Although the primary purpose of Auschwitz was a plant for Buna production, it was contemplated from the beginning to UTILIZE APPLICATIONS OF THE ENTIRE FIELD OF ACETYLENE AND ETHYLENE CHEMISTRY INVOLVED IN THE BUNA PROCESS..." [Including a softener shared with the Soviets? Let's see.]

Not only was Ambros planning on "cheap transportation" to Russia, he was planning on cheap labor from Russia, with Stalin's compliance. Victor Suvorov, a recent KGB defector in London, in his "Icebreaker," (Hamilton Hamish, London, 1990,), records these canal systems to "nowhere" dug by Gulag zeks through miles and miles of muck, most dying in the bug infested swamps. No wonder the Russians were so anxious to "liberate" Auschwitz at the end of the war and destroy any incriminating evidence of collaboration. The US Army CWS filed similar intelligence reports, the role of German "civilians" conflicted with those cited by Walter Hirsch:

OACSI File: MIS 167845 record group 165 'p' file chemical warfare, National Archives, "Intelligence Division Report No. 3875" Headquarters European Theater of Operations US Army CWS June 6, 1945, source 21 Army Group Chemical Warfare Intelligence, Report No. 1

Page 1: "In 1925 the German General Staff established Pruf S, with a staff of ten men, for research on chemical warfare. From 1929 to 1933 a delegation of Germans in civilian clothes went to Tomka, Russia, each summer to carry out field experiments. This scheme became progressively unsatisfactory to the Russians and the Germans, until 1934. Wa Pruf 9 was organized at Berlin to handle chemical warfare research and development. It was at this time that the Raubkammer installation and the Spandau installation commenced operations. Work on the first gas factories was begun in 1935 and by the autumn of 1944 the staffs of Wa Pruf 9, Spandau and Raubkammer comprised 1,600 people."

Page 2: "They were very interested in phosgene-oxime because they knew the Russians were making it but had great difficulty in stabilizing it for use in weapons. Oberst Hirsch, head of Wa Pruf 9 went so far as to say that if phosgene-oxime could be manufactured in large quantities and stabilized, it would probably be the best war gas ever developed... Because the Russian interest in HCN (hydrocyanic acid) the Germans had also carried out trials with it and planned to use it as an aircraft spray... They considered HCN spray to be only a winter weapon and that it would be valueless at temperatures over 20 degrees Centigrade."

Make a mental note, the Germans began building their own poison gas factories in 1935, long before the concentration camps with gas exterminations had be built. The compounds above are found in TABUN. The Soviet-German phosgene-oxime research intensified at Tomka after 1933. As WW II progressed, German intelligence noted Soviet development of a brand new war gas named "Lebedan or Lebeda":

"The Hirsch Report" Nalbandian Translation, Carl Isle Barracks Historical Inst.
Page 106: "According to repeated and well-confirmed reports, the depot [had] undergone a ten-fold expansion. The Pricharasvakaya railroad station, serving this depot, has an extensive loading annex and a railroad yard. Tracks extend from it like a harp through the woods into isolated and well-camouflaged depots. In the principal depot there are large storage rooms for gas shells and bombs..."

"The Hirsch Report" 2nd translation by US CWS, Pentagon Plans & Operations
Page 40: 'Lebeda or Lebedan'
"In the fall of 1941, for the first time a Russian prisoner of war mentioned an entirely new, very toxic war gas called "Lebeda" or Leb-

edan," subsequently, to the end of 1944, this name was again and again mentioned by prisoners of war who had technical training or belonged to the intelligence service and who allegedly had been told at the chemical warfare schools or in gas courses that by this name was meant a new and very effective and toxic war gas."

The "Hirsch Report" continued describing "Lebedan" as a HNC compound, a "reddish-brown liquid smelling like rotten pears," toxic to the skin but "quicker in action" than mustard, of phosgene-oxime base, "vapors highly toxic even in 140 degrees Centigrade" dispersible by aircraft. They suspected a methyl and ethyl dichlorasine base. Supplemented to this intelligence data was 'Other alleged New War Gases' on Page 41, speaking of such toxic agents that gas masks offered no protection, "the charcoal in the mask's canister actually set afire by the agent." Here the Germans suspected Russian use of "fluorine compounds of the type CIF3..." concluding "these allegations appear to be of no practicable military significance." Ha! Ask yourself why, in the upcoming chapters, the US CWS (also stationed in Russia) would make such a remark? This description smacks of TABUN in the hands of Serge Lebedev. The stability problem of TABUN caused the Nazis to alter the compound and create SARIN. The I. G. scientists were squirming. So was the US CWS. In 1935, Hitler had passed a law forcing all German industry to hand over new weapon technology to the Reich, keeping patents secret. One of Gerhard Schrader's TABUN partners testified after capture:

"INTERROGATION SUMMARY No. 1505 of HEINRICH HOERLEIN" OACSI file 360340, National Archives, record group 319 declassified 6/27/91

"According to subject, KLENK... before and after 1939 Ordnance requested him to sign the usual statement that he would treat all classified documents as confidential. To give information to any person who was not entitled to it was considered high treason... Owing to the revolution in 1933, subject himself was in an embarrassing situation. There was the fight in connection with the destruction of plant parasites where toxic agents were looked for. There was the danger that if informant had found such an agent and had not reported it, he might be considered a traitor. The first anti-parasitic agent for plants was developed in 1910... he ran the risk of making himself liable to prosecution for high treason. One of the substances developed before GELAN [another name for TABUN] was Fluoracthyl alcohol... A regulation of 1935 forced subject to submit the matter to Ordnance before he could apply for patents."

One of Klenk's OACSI interrogation files vanished altogether prior their accession to the National Archives. The Nazis did not want to confess treason and fudged further on TABUN's date, pushing it further and further ahead. "GELAN" the early term for TABUN, was a derivative of Schrader's pesticide Gehla, "Gewerbehygensches I. G. Labor." No-one would give a straight story:

"INTERROGATION OF PHILIP HEINRICH HOERLEIN, PROFESSOR, I.G. CHEMIST" Interrogated by Mr. Von Halle, 11 March 1947, Nuremberg, Office of US Chief of Counsel of War Crimes PO 696 Evidence Division Interrogation Branch, Interrogation Summary No. 1536 Microfilm roll #26, #1019 Nuremberg Pretrial Testimony, Index #902:

"Summary: Hoerlein asserts that Gelen (TABUN) was invented by Dr. Schrader in Leverkausen towards the end of 1936. Then, Professor Gross, in examining this new production, found that it was toxic to a very high degree so that it could not be used without proper precautions... thereupon the Army Ordnance Department took over the work.... In 1939 subject states that Ministerialdirektor Zahu declared that the Army had decided to construct a Gelan factory. After the factory had been completed, some of the IG chemists who had been engaged by AMBROS there were sent to SCHRADER in order to study the production of Gelan in the laboratory of this new factory."

GERHARD SCHRADER files, U.S. Army Intelligence & Security Command, Fort George Meade, MD. FOIA request declassified 2/7/90

"(I) discovered TABUN at the I. G. Works, Leverkusen in 1937 in the course of many years of comprehensive investigation into poison gas. Further technical research in the development of this class of chemicals took place at the I. G. Works at Elberfeld. It was there that I discovered SARIN in 1938."

Further testimony to Hitler's patent proclamation and the conflicting dates of TABUN's invention come from US Army intelligence records:

"THE DEVELOPMENT OF NEW INSECTICIDES & CHEMICAL WARFARE AGENTS" OACSI file 329097

Page 27: "Since the year 1935 an order has been in force to examine each Patent registered, in order to keep secret anything which might be of interest in the country's defense."

But on page 25 of this same report, Gerhard Schrader admits organic fluorine compounds in pesticides began in 1925 and that I. G. Farben had a patent exchange with all of its subsidiaries. That would include Russia. Refusing to admit collusion with the Russians, Gerhard Schrader cited every pesticide patent on the market available to the public to his British interrogators. The British were most skeptical. How could Germany invest so much money in the development of an untried poison gas? Wolfgang Wirth, (the Waffen Pruf 9 toxicologist from the Russian decontamination mission of 1940), with Dr. Flury, gave further details on Schrader's pesticides to the British, raising suspicion. When and where had TABUN been tested?:

"INTERROGATION OF PROFESSOR FERDINAND FLURY AND DR. WOLFGANG WIRTH ON THE TOXICOLOGY OF CHEMICAL WARFARE AGENTS" BIOS trip 160 Target C8/127,C8/169 OACSI file MIS 349321 record group 319 box 394, National Archives

"It is not clear how Schrader came to be interested in these phosphorus compounds in the first place. His work started with the general objective of finding a non-flammable insecticide to replace ethylene oxide, and it had apparently already been determined that the first attack should involve the preparation of compounds containing fluorine... When this step was taken... is not clear. (footnoted: Compare the I. G. patent 326,127 on insecticides...) Evidently, however, the I. G. felt they had struck a profitable line in the phosphorus compounds... patented in the names of Schrader and Bauer in several countries (German patent 664,438; British patent 477,534; French patent 807,769; US patent 2,148,356; all in 1938-1939.)

Page 7-8: Most of the SS operations involving the killing of inmates of concentration camps, institutions for incurables or the insane, etc., under various euphonious titles, seem to have started well after the outbreak of the war, and it therefore seems more than likely that the original Wa Pruf 9 recommendation in favour of TABUN was not supported by quantitative experiments on humans... It does seem to be a matter for serious doubt whether the higher party organizations would have agreed to the diversion of considerable effort, in difficult circumstances, to the production of a chemical warfare agent which had not been shown unequivocally to be capable of killing men. It will be realized that this point carries the more weight in that TABUN was not being offered to the services as a 'Harassing' agent, but as a quick-acting lethal agent."

Schrader insisted his early fluorine-sulfur compounds were patented in "Germany, America, England, and Switzerland." He and his partner at Elberfeld, Dr. Kukenthal, had been publishing pesticides for years. But in this very slippery interrogation, Schrader let the "rat" out of the bag, a second early use for TABUN's compounds was exposed.

"DEVELOPMENT OF NEW INSECTICIDES AND CHEMICAL WARFARE AGENTS" OACSI file 329097 National Archives MRB
page 23: "Development of Tabun"
" For a year, attempts to improve the weak insecticidal action of the substance (III) by the introduction of a new substitute were made... the testing of insecticidal properties of this ester by my co-worker, Dr. Kukenthal, in the biological institute, Leverkusen, gave a negative result. Further testing of the material in the Central Rubber Laboratory, Leverkusen, showed that the ester (IV) possessed a certain interests as a softener for buna and buna special products."

The huge buna factories of Serge Lebedev must have acquired these buna softeners, but how? Was the new deadly poison gas described in the Hirsch Report as "Lebedan or Lebeda" named after Lebedev? How did the Nazis know enough in advance to invest millions of dollars into the development of TABUN by 1935 without conducting any human tests, as noted in the above OACSI file MIS 165847 "Intelligence Division Report # 3875"? Prof. Hoerlein cited Schrader's discovery in 1936 and construction of the TABUN gas (Gelan) factory in 1939. Despite the confusion over construction dates in the 1930s, the Nazis knew TABUN was lethal enough to kill millions of people, enough to conquer the world, prior the gassings in concentration camps of the 1940s. Who had made the tests? The answer is in "The Hirsch Report." The use of Chlorpicrin by the Soviets for 'vermin control' and HCN as an offensive weapon, is first documented on pages 5, 14, 15 and 16\). Further along, the targeting of their own citizens evolves:

"THE HIRSCH REPORT" Nalbandian translation, Carl Isle Barracks
Page 74: "The manufacture of C. W. agents was carried on under the strict supervision of the NKVD and in unlimited quantities. Chemical warfare agents were tried on the political prisoners in the most inhumane way without any consideration whatsoever."

Did the "international civilians" of I. G. Farben inside of Russia till

1937 witness these executions? Yes. Stalin made the tests for Hitler. Serge Lebedev was already building his buna factories in 1929, with Schrader's buna softener, TABUN. Next, Schrader moved the construction date of the Tabun gas factory up to 1939. Keep in mind, its construction was under the full approval of Hitler. One milligram could "kill an ape":

"DEVELOPMENT OF NEW INSECTICIDES & CHEMICAL WARFARE AGENTS" by Gerhard Schrader, OACSI file 329097

Page 28: "In the year of 1939, the H.W.Z. built its own plant for production of substance 83 at Munsterlager... At the end of 1939, Herr Director Ambros received the order from the High Command to establish a special factory for the large-scale production of substance 83. As a site for the new establishment a place near Dyhernfurth Odor (about 40 km NW of Breslau) was chosen. The building of the new works began in Autumn 1940, and April 1942, the Anorgana concern began the production of substance 83, which was then termed Trilon 83, later T.83 and finally TABUN up to the end of 1944 which produced in all about 15,000 tons of TABUN." [How much - 15,000 tons? And one milligram kills an "ape"?]

Otto Ambros, running Dyhernfurth, had also collaborated with the Soviets in the expansion plans of "I. G. Farbenindustrie, A.G. Auschwitz, Upper Silesia." Had Ambros access to Soviet TABUN tests? Confronted by the US Army, Ambros wormed his way out of his predicament, citing Hitler opposed the deployment of gases:

"INTERROGATION OF DR. AMBROS" Report No. R3796-45, OACSI file MIS 179560, July 7, 1945, from M. A. London. National Archives

"In the spring - April of 1943, Adolf Hitler called him to his headquarters, which were then on the Eastern front, so that he could discuss the subject of chemical warfare and the potentialities of the I. G. Farben Industries in case gas warfare broke out. Hitler, at the start of the conversation said that he did not want to initiate the use of gas. In fact, he would want to do all within his power to prevent its use. He recalled his own experience with gas in the last war when he was partially blinded by it. He also said that the senior officers of the high command were opposed to the initiation of gas warfare, although there were some junior officers who had recommended it being employed."

This was a flat out and out lie. Ambros did admit Hitler was aware of

Soviet gas buildup, a gas mask had been discovered. That was as far as he would go, implicating Russia and Hitler's collaboration. Further pre-trial testimony at Nuremberg exposed Ambros and Adolf Heusinger of the OKH collaborating with TABUN at Dyhernfurth:

"INTERROGATION SUMMARY NO. 3287" Office of U.S. Chief of Counsel for War Crimes APO 696-A Evidence Division Interrogation Branch, National Archives Film #3. 1019 'Interrogation of Otto Ambros, Member of I. G. Farben Vorstand Inces No. 1062 D' Interrogated by Mr. Von Halle, 21 April 1947, Nuremberg

Pages 1-3: "Ambros remembered that at the beginning of October 1939, the first discussion with the OKH in Berlin took place about the production of TABUN. The I. G. was notified on 15 September 1939 to produce 1,000 tons per month... On 30 December 1939, the decision was made to erect the plant in Dyhernfurth. The project was financed by advance payments from the government..."

"TRIALS OF WAR CRIMINALS BEFORE THE NUERENBERG MILITARY TRIBUNALS" volume 7, case 6, US vs. Carl Krauch 'Extract from the Testimony of Defendant Ambros' Pages 1043-1044:

"Question: Did you have the impression Hitler wanted to use the poison gas?

Answer: No, Hitler himself did not, but around him there were people who did.

Question: Well, go ahead, please; describe to us what happened at this conference.

Answer: He discussed the main types, always with a point of view of "How does it look on the other side?" and I reported objectively... I know that Tabun had been publicized as early as 1902, that Sarin was patented, and that these appeared in patents... I am convinced that other countries, in case the German side might use these gases, would very shortly not only be able to imitate these special gases, but even produce them in much larger quantities."

Such an elaborate effort to protect the Russians! Ambros, serving 2 years of his sentence, went to work for the Grace Chemical Company, released by John J. McCloy, High Commissioner to Germany, ("New York Times" 3/5/82 sec. IV pg. 2).

Let's look at the development of pesticides, poison gases and buna from the Soviet side. A very comprehensive study in a commerce journal "Industrial and Engineering Chemistry" appeared in their November 1926 edition, (no. 11, vol. 18, page 1174), "Synthetic Rubber" by Richard Well, crediting Bayer at Elberfeld for discovery of synthetic rubber in 1909. Bayer would soon join the I. G. Farben 'community of interests'. Wells noted a "small scale" manufacture of synthetic rubber going on in Russia and "no further details are known." In the same journal, {page 1176), 'Disadvantages of Synthetic Rubber' were discussed as "Lack of Plasticity" and "Lack of Elasticity." All this would change. Different by-products of acetylene were experimented with, butadiene and chloroprene, for the creation of synthetic rubber. Derivatives of butadiene were isoprene and methyl isoprene; all three termed "diolefins." (11) These were improvements, but did not entirely solve the problem. Both Germany and the USSR began secret works to improve buna's bounce, which lead to the early usage of TABUN's compounds.

By 1936, Western businessmen sounded alarms over a massive buildup in Russian synthetic rubber industry. A backward nation, with no automobiles, what was the need?:

"INDUSTRIAL AND ENGINEERING CHEMISTRY" vol. 28, no. 4, 1936

Page 394-398: "The synthetic rubber industry is being developed in Russian and in America under economic conditions that are diametrically opposite to each other..." (and quoting from) 'Kriegswirtschaft' (War Industry):

"cost of synthetic rubber remains excessive. However, this does not seem to be a matter of concern to the Soviet Government... reorganization of its entire tractor industry toward production of caterpillar tread tractors... is primarily a part of the armament program."

Natural rubber then cost 15 cents a pound on the international market, buna $3.00 per pound. That's 20 times the cost, folks! Slave labor was cheap, the West did not comprehend Gulag economics. Eventually, "Industrial and Engineering Chemistry" November 1933, (volume 25, no. 11, pages 12204-1211) began an extensive two part series on the buna industry, noting "substantial improvements in the production of synthetic rubber by 1929" and a "rapid stream of patents" coming forth from I. G. Farben. The Russian work under Lebedev took a far more expansive direction, for "tons of (buna) were in production, and the new tires had a range of 27,000 kilometers." Weird, since there were virtually no paved roads in Russia to drive upon. A new factory had been built at Yarsolav, this information came by way of the French who had shared in Russian diolefin research. Further collaboration between the Soviets and the Germans in diolefin research was again documented in "Industrial and Engineering Chemistry" (12)

KGB defector, Victor Suvorov also noted the huge Soviet tank buildup in his "Icebreaker", Hamish Hamilton, London 1990 (pg. 14), and blamed Stalin for the initiation of WW II. "In 1933, Colonel Heinz Guderian visited a Soviet locomotive engineering works at Kharkov... the yard was producing tanks as a side product...at the rate of 22 a day." (22 x 365 = an average of 8030 per year.) The tank was the Mark BT, meaning "high speed" with retractable rubber tires to be replaced by tractor treads, according to terrain. It was primarily designed for conquest on European roads. That's a lot of buna, baby. Stalin's tanks were poised on Europe's border just days prior to Hitler's invasion of Russia in 1941, Operation Barbarrosa.

The French connection in diolefins was Joseph Frossard, first fingered in "The Crime and Punishment of I. G. Farben" by Joseph Borkin, (The Free Press, 1978.) Borkin was hired by the US Senate Special Committee to Investigate the Munitions Industry in 1934. I. G. Farben, headed by Carl Bosch, was engaged in "cut throat competition" and racketeering. They made a fortune in the manufacture of synthetic nitrates for gun powder during WW I. After the war, I. G. argued that nitrates were a peacetime industry, badly needed in fertilizers, saving the company from shut down. This nonsense suited Romain Rolland pacifist movement just fine, and the French swallowed it hook, line and sinker. I. G. Farben's international exploits continued under the Treaty of Versailles disarmament program, overseen by Joseph Frossard. I. G. Farben had merged with the French Compagnie National des Matieres Colorantes et des Produits Chemiques, which Joseph Frossard headed, and surrendered its patents. During WW I, Frossard had been assigned to the French Chemical Warfare Service. His previous experience had been inside Russia while employed in the textile industry. Eventually, mergers arose between the French Compagnie National des Maiteres Colrantes, Kuhlmann and I. G. Farben in the mid 1920s. By the time Hitler arrived on the scene, Frossard and Kuhlman partnered with Polish dyestuff companies. (13)

Despite the fact that Carl Bosch was rabidly anti Nazi, he realized Hitler needed I. G. Farben for armaments and purged the Jewish members of the board. It must be considered that "Jews" by Hitler's definition were a race, not a faith. All the members of I. G. Farben had long lost their scruples, budding atheists, ignoring their Christian and Jewish heritage of love and law. Joseph Borkin quotes a peculiar incident with Frossard at the end of World War II, taken from records of the Nuremberg Trials, (TWC VIII, page 104, NI-68839). Accordingly, in "The Crime and Punishment of I. G. Farben" (The Free Press, 1978, page 101), Frossard "who was then in unoccupied France with the rest of the directors of Kuhlmann, told the I. G. people that he could not enter the German occupied zone because he would have to expect trouble as a German deserter." A deserter?

The mystery was cleared by Dr. Vladimir Ipatieff, chief of Soviet chemical warfare. Close personal friends with Joseph Frossard, Ipatieff defected to America in 1930, running for his life. Once again, Stalin began to execute his own accomplices with Germany in chemical and biological warfare. Safe and sound in America, Ipatieff went to work for the oil industry, publishing two autobiographies. They have to be read in conjunction to understand his collaboration with Frossard and I. G. Farben, in the acquisition of TABUN secrets for Lebedev's buna industry. Ipateiff's first book "Catalytic Reactions at High Temperatures" published in 1936, details his development of a high pressure gas combustion chamber. With its silver lining acting as a catalyst, most of the compounds no longer were lost as a precipitate. (14) This was a big advancement in chemical warfare technology, something the Germans greatly coveted. The author was directed to the attention of Ipatieff by members of the United Jewish Appeal in Washington, DC, citing a January 26, 1996 edition of "Novoye Russkoye Slovo" featuring a January 1927 reprint of front page headlines on Vladimir Ipatieff "Chemical Warfare Chief of the Soviet Union" collaborating with the Germans in "strangulating gases."

Ipatieff's second autobiography, "The Life of A Chemist," (Stanford University Press, 1946, [pages 122-123]) details his research in the acetylene chemical industry, passing on his successes in diolefins to Serge Lebedev, advancing Russia's buna industry. Stalin had used Ipatieff, a loyal Communist, to gain access to the German poison gas research of I. G. Farben through the assistance of Joseph Frossard. The trade became evident, the new gas chamber for the buna softener, TABUN. Both parties, true patriots, exchanged no money, just patents, for the good of the State.

Joseph and his brother, Louis Frossard were originally members of the French Commission for the Preparation of Explosives during WW I according to Ipatieff, "The Life of A Chemist" (page 200). Even during WW I, German chemical companies conducted business as usual inside of Russia while their governments waged war. When the Revolution arrived, Ipatieff and Joseph Frossard joined in. After the war, Frossard made arrangements for Ipatieff to work at I. G. Farbenindustrie while under the Kuhlmann Company's control. Ipatieff exposed just how fast the French dye industry advanced while under Frossard's control, gaining access to the I. G. patents. The new Soviet Union also advanced, allied with Germany and France.

Ipatieff worked with the Russian Commission for the Preparation of Explosives and received his assignments from the Central War-Industries Committee, the "C.A.A." (15) He had a view from the top. Frossard, under Ipatieff, was assigned to the Moscow Bureau of the C.A.A. Frossard began arranging Ipatieff's numerous visits to I. G. Farben plants in Germany, writing letters of introduction. (16) Ipatieff was assigned a contract with the Bayerische Stricstoff Werke in 1927 involving his high pressure and catalysis research. He made six separate trips to Germany, ("The Life of A Chemist" pages 438-460). In 1946, Vladimir Ipatieff wrote of earlier encounters with I. G. scientists at Leverkusen, Ludwigshafen, and Frank-fort, raising grave suspicions. Was he insinuating he had bartered his catalytic gas chamber design for I. G.'s buna softening TABUN patent? Was he warning America of a pending security threat if we hired these Communist Nazis?:

"THE LIFE OF A CHEMIST" Vladimir Ipatieff, Stanford Univ. Press 1946

Pages 351-352: "While I had asked Frossard to get me permission to visit certain German chemical plants,... Dr. Mattach, whom I was meeting for the first time, told me that they were then testing out the thousandth catalyst for this particular synthesis. His cordiality made me feel that I, too, had contributed something to this colossal undertaking through my pioneer work in the application of high pressure and temperatures to catalytic reactions... at the Badische Anilinfabriken and the Farbenwerke I was often shown processes which they said were operated "nach Ipatieff." Before the Revolution my friends had often criticized me for not taking out patents. My philosophical attitude probably cost me some millions while others patented my discoveries in foreign countries. It was common knowledge that the cheapest and one of the best research workers in the I. G. was a man by the name Ipatieff who did his work for nothing!"

Nevertheless, with Ipatieff's apparent confession on public record, we began the Nazi smuggling ratlines out of the USSR. Frossard, facilitating the exchange of TABUN gas patents to Stalin through Ipatieff, would have indeed "committed treason" against Germany and France, his fear to enter the German occupied zone well justified. By 1926, Trotsky was put in charge of the newly organized Scientific Technical Administration, the "NTU" governing the German-Soviet gas collaboration, Ipatieff serving as vice chairman. (17) Stalin got rid of Trotsky. Ipatieff's close subordinate, Sysoev faced Stalin's execution squad for having served abroad, and eventually committed suicide. (18) Stalin pushed his scientists into industrial espionage, milking them for all their worth in the name of patriotism, and then executed them for treason, "conspiring with foreigners." Ipatieff made a final visit to his German poison gas accomplice, Professor Haber and then broke for America in 1930. (19) The US Army Intelligence and Security Command at Fort George Meade has no records on Ipatieff. Astounding! If there once were records, did they disappeared under Eisenhower's CIA director, Allen Dulles?

Carl Bosch died, his successor Carl Krauch ran I. G. Farben during WW II, with draconian ambitions to take over the world, "in case Hitler failed." A curious CIOS report on I.G.'s mania sits in the Hoover Institute for War, Revolution and Peace:

"I. G. FARBENINDUSTRIE, AG. OFFICE BUILDING: FRANK-FURT/MAIN" by Colonel K. Gordon, Lt. Col. O.F. Thompson, on behalf of British Ministry of Fuel & Power and U.S. Technical Industrial Intelligence Committee; CIOS Target Number 30/4.17 Fuels and Lubricants, Item #30, File No. XXIII-15.

Page 16: "Relations with the Government"

"The ramifications of the I. G. Farben are the subject of a special study group under the Financial Section of G-5 SHAEF and in conjunction with the Department of Justice and the British Treasury... Schmitz, Ilgner, and probably Krauch, should have played a leading part in the original dealings with the Party..."

Page 19: 'Arrangements where the I.G. cooperated with the Government plants'

"I. G. rented the plant from the government... ran it with its own management and personnel... I. G. rented the plant from the government allowed to make an agreed profit... I.G. owned and operated the plant... assisted by a government grant. Various companies were formed on the basis of these arrangements. A number of them were engaged in the manufacture of poison gases and the names given these companies not only helped conceal the nature of their operations, but also helped do disassociate the I.G. from activities of which they did not whole-heartedly approve... [Really!] The Nazi party was dependent upon the benefices of the I. G. and likewise the extent to which the I. G. used the Party as an instrument for the purpose of attaining objectives no less wide-reaching than those of the Nazis.

"Espionage & Post War Plans"

"Their world-wide ramifications, and especially the technicians that supervised manufacturing processes in many countries, provided a ready-made intelligence gathering organization, the value of which evidently went beyond that of commercial fact finding. The direction of these activities came from the Wirtschaftspolitische Abteilung in Berlin, a prominent part in the direction of which was played by Dr. Max Ilgner. In the early stages of the war, the I. G. took such steps as they were able to safeguard their interests in the event of the German defeat. One of these measures was the sale, for a nominal sum, of all their patent interests to a patent attorney (a brother of one of the directors) in New York, this transaction taking place some time before America entered the war."

Here it is, the New World Order in a nut shell, under direction of I. G. Farben's own goon squad, hatching a plot to take over the world if Hitler failed. According to Joseph Borkin's "Crime and Punishment of I.G. Farben," they were guilty of "price cutting, protracted patent litigation, kickbacks to customers, and bribery to gain technical secrets..." and might we add, assassinations, drug smuggling, money laundering, all going into the coffers of the KGB. There is a fine line between Corporate Fascism and Communism, so fine, both Germany and Russia couldn't identify the enemy within. Once I. G. Farben was allied with the Soviet Union and Allen Dulles, (their American patent lawyer in New York) as referred to above, the world was doomed for decades. First, Dulles would work for President Roosevelt under Colonel William J. Donovan, the "Coordinator of Intelligence" in 1941, then join the OSS (Office of Strategic Services) run by Roosevelt's State Department in 1942, joining the OPC (Office of Policy Coordination) in the Truman Administration in 1946, and appointed Director of the CIA by Eisenhower in 1953. (20) We had a mole working for the Soviet Union, (code name "ALES - in the Venona files), "ALlen dullES."

CHAPTER 3 NOTES

(1) "SIMON & SCHUSTER ENCYCLOPEDIA OF WORLD WAR II" Simon & Schuster, New York, 1978, edited by Thomas Parrish. "Buna"

(2) "LET HISTORY JUDGE: The Origins and Consequences of Stalinism" by Roy Medvedev, Alfred Knopf, New York 1972. Page 108 on Serge Lebedev - buna.

(3) "CHEMICAL ABSTRACTS" Edited by e. J. Crane, Am. Chem.

Soc., OH St. Univ., Columbus, OH Vol. 24, 1930: page 1390: "Diolefins" Serge V. Lebedev, French patent 665,917, Dec. 15, 1928.

Vol. 28, 1934: page 481: "Diolefins" "Serge V. Lebedev, German patent 577,630, June 3, 1933. [This patent was published by the Deutsche Reich in 1933, but was written on December 29, 1928." [The full patent, in German text, is available throughout the British Library Patent Express in London.]

"CHEMICAL WARFARE ACTIVITIES OF FOREIGN COUNTRIES DURING WW II" Project 4693, record Group 319 National Archives,

FIRST QUARTER August 1949: 'USSR' "Stalin Prize, 1st Class, awarded to Academician Alexander Arbuzov, Ju. 1947 for "Investigations in the sphere of phosphorus-organic combinations. The latter possibly the G agents."

SECOND QUARTER, September 9, 1949: 'USSR,' "Soviet continued interest in compounds related to nerve gases - Stalin Prize awarded to J. L. Knunyantz in 1948."

THIRD QUARTER, October 1949: 'USSR' "Some useful suggestions concerning... A. E. Arbuzov... at Kazan Chemical Technical Institute... obtained from a naturalized US citizen who fled from Russia in 1918... now Associate professor of chemistry at Alabama Polytechnic Institute - expressed view Prof. Arbuzov has received his Stalin Awards for unpublished research possibly related to the G agents since his published works are not of the distinction and quality that would merit the awards received."

(4) "CHEMICAL ABSTRACTS" Vol. 39, 1945, Am Chem. Soc. OH St. Univ., Columbus, OH, page 1579- 2: 'General And Physical Chemistry'.

"Sergei Vasilevich Lebedev, 1874-1934. Tenth Anniversary of His Death" by A. E. Arbuzov "Uspeki Khim" 13,253-64 (1944). "Special emphasis is given to the development of the industrial production of synthetic rubber."

(5) "ARACHNIDA" Second Edition, by Theodore Savory, Academic Press, New York 1977, page 282, chapter 33 'Chemical Arachnology' definition of 'Chitin.'

(6) "THE DEVELOPMENT OF NEW INSECTICIDES AND CHEMICAL WARFARE AGENTS" by Gerhard Schrader, OACSI file 329097, National Archives

Page 2: 'Preface' "In August-September 1945, an investigating team interviewed amongst others at Kransberg-dustbin, Dr. Gerhard Schrader, research chemist I. G. Works Elberfeld. - a brief account was obtained on fluorine and phosphorus compounds, embracing discovery of nerve gases Tabun and Sarin... Dr. Schrader has been handicapped in writing these (fuller accounts) by destruction or inaccessibility of his records and notes, so that there are certain gaps, especially in the insecticidal data and the preparative methods..."

"CHEMICAL ABSTRACTS" Vol. 32 Part 2, June-October, 1938 column 4697 & 4698, Patents of I. G. Farben's Gerhard Schrader: 'Vermin-destroying preparations' I. G. Farbenindustrie A. G. Brit. 478,350, Jan. 12, 1938.

"Combating vermin such as insects or rats and mice" Gerhard Schrader, Otto Bayer and Hans Kukenthal (to Winthrop Chemical Co.) US 2,114,577, April 19.

(7) "THE DEVELOPMENT OF NEW INSECTICIDES AND CHEMICAL WARFARE AGENTS" OACSI File 329097

Page 25: [Gerhard Schrader] "My stopping work on the substance (VII) for many days, the symptoms vanished, proving that the strange physiological action was due to the new cyanide, caused strong irritation of the cornea, and a very strong feeling of oppression in the chest... I dispatched a sample of (VII) to Prof. Gross Elberfeld on 5-2-37. Dr. Kukenthal in March placed this new series under patent protection (J57 029 Iva/541). The patent claimed as pest eradication agents."

(8) "GERHARD SCHRADER FILES" Fort George Meade US Army Intelligence & Security Command. Report written by Gerhard Schrader; From Commandant, "dustbin" to Major Wilson EPS G-2 FIAT dated

5/10/45. and OACSI file 234732 "Reports Written by Dr. Gerhardt Schrader"

(9) "INVESTIGATION OF CHEMICAL WARFARE INSTALLATIONS IN THE MUNSTERLAGER AREA INCLUDING RAUBKAMMER" by Wing Commander A. K. Mills, Ministry of Aircraft Production, British CIOS Item 8 Chemical Warfare, Combined Intelligence Objectives Sub-Committee, G-2 Division, SHAEF (Rear) APO 413, National Library of Medicine, Bethesda, MD.

Page 7: " 'Organization of German Chemical Warfare Development' 'Oberst Dr. Walter Hirsch' In 1938 posted to the Waffenamt, Berlin where he was first a Referent in Group VI and then Head of Group VI, Waffen Pruf 9. In December 1940 sent to Russian front in charge of a

Decontamination Mission Battery

Page 12: 'History of German CW Development' 1928 Trials at Tomka - 1933

Page 27: 'Table 1 Waffen Pruf 9' Head-Oberst Hirsch, Group VI: Min. Rat. Weinberg* and Adjutant Mengele* - Gas & Smoke Weapons. Group VII: Oberstrabartz Prof. Dr. Wolfgang Wirth. Group VIII: Hygiene & Bacteriology Prof. Kliewe, Oberstabartz.

Page 6: The important witnesses interrogated are marked in Tables I, II, and III with asterisk, but in addition to these, a number of subordinate grades were also questioned. These are referred to where necessary in the body of the report."

(10) "GAS DEFENSE" OACSI file 440744, record group 319 National Archives 'Information of or from: Swedish, subject: chemical warfare, dated 1932/Moscow-Leningrad'

(11) "INDUSTRIAL AND ENGINEERING CHEMISTRY" April 1926, vol. 18, pg. 404 'Is Commercial Synthetic Rubber Probable' by L. E. Weber.

(12) "INDUSTRIAL AND ENGINEERING CHEMISTRY" vol. 25, no. 12 Dec 1933 'Synthetic Rubber Concluded' by G. S. Whitby and M. Katz, National Research Council of Canada, Ottawa. Pages 1338-1348: "... the butadiene is being made by a method developed by Lebedeff (footnoted: #126a: Lebedeff, French Patent 665,917 (1928): British patent 331,482 (1930)"

(13) "THE CRIME AND PUNISHMENT OF I. G. FARBEN" by Joseph Borkin, The Free Press, New York, 1978, Page 32 - Carl Bosch. Page 97: Frossard, Kuhlman, Poland.

(14) "CATALYTIC REACTIONS AT HIGH PRESSURES AND TEMPERATURES" by Vladimir N. Ipatieff, Macmillan, New York 1936

"THE LIFE OF A CHEMIST: The Memoirs of Vladimir N. Ipatieff" by Vladimir N. Ipatieff, Stanford University Press, Stanford University, CA 1946.

"DICTIONARY OF SCIENTIFIC BIOGRAPHY" Charles Scribner & Sons, NY 1973

'Ipatiev, Vladimir Nikolaevich' "... member of the Presidium of the Supreme Soviet of the National Economy, exerting leadership over the

chemical industry and scientific research. From 1926 he was simultaneously a consultant to many chemical enterprises in Germany... From 1930
director of Catalytic High Pressure Laboratory at Northwestern University,
... established new means for synthesis of unsaturated hydrocarbons and
obtained isoprene... basic monomeric component of natural rubber..."

(15) "THE LIFE OF A CHEMIST" by Vladimir Ipatieff, Stanford
University Press, CA 1946, Page 262 on the C.A.A. Page 220-221 on
Joseph Frossard in Moscow dye plants.

(16) IBID. Page 344 & 351: Frossard arranges Ipatieff trips to Ger-
many & France, I. G. Farbenwerke in Leverkusen, Badiche Anilin un
Sodafabriken in Ludwigshafen, Farbenwerke of Frankfort, lunch with Dr.
Duisberg... Page 352: friendship with Haber, and Dr. Villiger of Badishe
Aniline, F.G. Ludwigshafen.

(17) IBID. Page 413 Russian-German Commission on the production of poison gases, Haber is consultant to German government on CW.
Trotsky chairman N.T.U.

(18) IBID. Page 425 Sysoev commits suicide.

(19) IBID. Page 407: Ipatieff goes to Germany seeing Dr. Stolzenberg's
demos of gases. Page 426: Ipatieff visits Prof. Haber on preparation of
poison gases.

(20) "THE SECRET WAR AGAINST THE JEWS" John Loftus
& Mark Aarons, St. Martin's Press, New York, 1994, Pages 56-57: Allen
Dulles is I.G.Farben patent lawyer and brother John Foster Dulles is "a
director of I.G.Farben
"HISTORICAL BACKGROUND OF THE CIA" Prepared by the
Office of General Counsel of the CIA" Page 1: "World War II" 'Coordi-
nator of Information'

CHAPTER 4

A SOLDIER'S TALE

The Hirsch Report

Only six-hundred-eighty-one pages exist of the tell-all Hirsch Report, "Soviet BW and CW Preparations and Capabilities." Had it been completed, or its contents fathomed during WW II, the Russians, and the Nazis would have been exposed in their insidious collaboration. Roosevelt would have been booted out of the White House for the cover-up, our State Department arrested for treason, Stalin overthrown, and Hitler executed by his own generals. We wish! Of the intended nine chapters, only the first three survive. Stalin, a staunch supporter of the NPG (Negative Population Growth Society), executed half of his country's citizens, ridding the nation of its "technically obsolete labor force." With a combination of biological warfare, gassing, and Gulag prison chains, the death toll exceeded 84 million. Oberst Walter Hirsch, of the German Army Waffen Pruf 9 Chemical and Biological Warfare Unit was captured and put under control of the US Army Counter Intelligence Corps and ordered to write a "FIAT" report (Field Information Agency Technical). He soon died, Dulles' OPC had an aversion to truth. Others had tried earlier to expose the Nazi-Soviet alliance in gas warfare; they too, were silenced.

In the 1930s, America once again took the "isolationist" stance, Charles Lindbergh's wife, Anne Morrow Lindbergh, led the charge with her open letter to the President, "The Wave of the Future," insisting the alliance between Hitler and Stalin would bring Utopia to all humanity. By 1939, the Hitler-Stalin non-aggression pact had been publicly signed, secretly plotting to carve up Poland, World War II loomed on the horizon. As Hitler's blitzkrieg swept over Europe, Britain declared war; America subsidized her with armaments. Hitler launched Operation Barbarossa into Russia; Japan attacked Pearl Harbor; America was at war. Stalin conveniently switched sides.

The American Commission of Engineers and Chemists was sent to the USSR after British-American-Soviet negotiations towards the end of 1942. Federal Laboratories (Anatase Vonsiasky's weapons supplier from the 9th Hole), Dupont, the Hydrogen Engineering Company, Lake Erie Chemical Company, Westvaco Chlorine Products Company, and the US Army Chemical Warfare Service rushed overseas to help our new ally. New plants were erected at Akmolinsk and Sverdlovsk. (1) The Americans were in for a rude awakening. Stalin had new gases unknown to the West. Sounding the alarm, many of these firms protested waves of sabotage at home. Hoover and the FBI turned a deaf ear. More significant, Hirsch and the Waffen Pruf 9 knew the Americans knew.

"SOVIET BW AND CW PREPARATIONS AND CAPABILITIES" by Walter Hirsch, 2nd Translation, US Army CWS, Pentagon Plans & Operations Dept.

Page 41: "March 1944, the German Intelligence Service obtained through a trustworthy informant... that no gases whatsoever... arrived from the USA or England, because the Soviets had no need for them... American chemists, among others those of the Westvaco Chlorine Products, allegedly reported to Washington that the Russians possessed war gases that were unknown even in the USA."

Page 47: "Word was received, on 3 July 1943. by the German Intelligence Service, that a special commission had arrived in Moscow in order to gather information on CW preparations. Members of this commission were chemists and engineers of the Hydrogen Engineering Company, of Westvaco Chlorine Products Company and the Dupont Interests. Military members of the commission were a brigadier general and two representatives of the CWS - E.P. Palmer and Robert Survis...

About the end of 1943, it became known that the CW supplies of the USSR were unusually large. The experience of a decade of production and extensive researches had brought a high degree of performance. The manufacture of CW agents was carried on under strict supervision of the NKVD and in unlimited quantities. Chemical warfare agents were tried on political prisoners in most inhumane ways without any consideration whatsoever. In 1944, continuous information was coming also about the foundation of a trans-Uralian chemical industry on a grand scale."

At some point, the Americans realized the "enemy" of the Soviet Union was its own citizens! The author was unable to locate any correspondence between these American CW firms and the US Government voicing their concerns over the huge Soviet gas buildup with "unknown weapons," although German intelligence made note. But the FBI files on these firms document a bizarre pattern of apparent sabotage attacks. Sabotage was considered treason during the war. American industry, long anticipating entrance to the war, began early preparations despite Roosevelt's rhetoric of non-involvement. Westvaco Chlorine called the FBI's West Virginia Office October 9th 1940 asking for FBI surveillance of its factories. Letters followed into the war years, their plight becoming increasingly desperate:

"WESTVACO CHLORINE PRODUCTS COMPANY: SABO-TAGE"
FBI file 99-1105: October 21, 1940: Westvaco to Hoover:
"As we are engaged in the manufacture of chemicals... we request that you have the proper trained operator visit us and go over our property... to guard against any hazards from possible sabotage."

Hoover replied November 2, 1940 that although the FBI did make some industrial surveys, it was primarily the War and Navy Department's responsibility for munitions manufacturers. Some of Westvaco's files were under joint custody of both FBI and the Army at Fort Meade's Intelligence and Security Command, revealing increased difficulties in 1942. Westvaco got a "FAIR" to "GOOD" overall rating in their "Plant Protection Survey Report" of February 6, 1942, its president, William Thom, planned further upgrades, (FBI file 99-5444433-1). His efforts were not only in vain, but the subsequent events went completely unheeded by the FBI:

"WESTVACO CHLORINE PRODUCTS COMPANY: SABO-TAGE"
FBI file HQ98-13106 Teletype Sep 18 1942 FBI Newark 4-30PM
"FIRE AT CARTARET PLANT OF WESTVACO CHLORINE PRODUCTS CORP... THE FIRE WAS COMPLETELY OUT OF CONTROL BEFORE THE LOCAL FIRE DEPARTMENT ARRIVED. THE BUILDING WAS A TOTAL LOSS. NO FURTHER INVESTIGATION CONTEMPLATED."

The FBI file continued with a "synopsis of facts" concluding the fire started because of "overheating of exposed wooden ceiling from furnace immediately below. No evidence of any sabotage... barium nitrate was being produced... US Coast Guard called into assist in fighting the fire."

Three months later, a dynamite fuse was found in Westvaco's Newark California parking lot, again, sabotage suspected, the FBI finding nothing unusual, fuses were frequently used in Westvaco's mining operations. (2) By April 1943, Westvaco's South Charleston research laboratory went up in smoke:

"WESTVACO CHLORINE PRODUCTS COMPANY: SABOTAGE"
FBI file HQ98-19161 Teletype FBI Huntington 4-10-43 5-05 PM
"FIRE IN RESEARCH LABORATORY, WESTVACO CHLORINE PRODUCTS CORPORATION, SOUTH CHARLESTON, WEST VIRGINIA. APRIL 10 1943, SABOTAGE DAMAGE ESTIMATED 5000 DOLLARS CONFINED TO RESEARCH LABORATORY WHICH IS ONE STORY CONCRETE BLOCK, WOOD ROOFED AND TIMBERED ADDITION TO OTHERWISE FIREPROOF STRUCTURE. THIS LABORATORY NOT A PRODUCTION OPERATION AND NOT A LOGICAL OBJECTIVE FOR SABOTAGE. NO EVIDENCE OF SABOTAGE. NO INVESTIGATION BEING CONDUCTED. NO INVESTIGATIVE REPORT BEING SUBMITTED."

More trouble! Right in the middle of war production, the company faced a strike, which should have brought out the National Guard. Instead, the FBI dropped the ball:

"WESTVACO CHLORINE COMPANY: SABOTAGE" FBI file 98-32055
Teletype July 9, 1944 FBI Communications Section, FBI Huntington
"KANAWHA PLANT CWS OWNED BY THE GOVERNMENT AND OPERATED BY WESTVACO CHLORINE PRODUCTS CORPORATION ON A CONTRACT BASIS IN MANUFACTURING OF (blackout) AN INGREDIENT USED IN MANUFACTURING SMOKE USED TO SCREEN (blackout) LANDINGS, WESTVACO CHLORINE PRODUCTS CORPORATION ALSO CONTRACTS WITH THE ARMY AND NAVY FOR MANUFACTURING OF CHEMICALS... OPERATION EMPLOYEES OF KANAWHA PLANT CWS OWNED BY US GOVERNMENT DID NOT REPORT FOR WORK ELEVEN PM JULY TEN LAST AND SEVEN AM JULY ELEVEN FORTYFOUR. PLANT IDLE WITH 100% LOSS IN PRODUCTION UNTIL APPROXIMATELY TWELVE THIRTY PM THIS DATE WHEN OPERATORS RETURNED TO WORK FOLLOWING

MEETING OF LOCAL 12625 UMW DISTRICT NUMBER (blackout) 50. EXPECTED TO RETURN TO NORMAL PRODUCTION JULY TWELVE FORTYFOUR. NO FURTHER ACTION BEING TAKEN UNLESS ADVISED TO CONTRARY BY BUREAU."

Westvaco had signed a contract with the Union May 24, 1940, and there had been no previous disputes. The trouble originated with six disgruntled employees, argued the Huntington FBI SAC, not "subversives." And, as always, "No further inquiry is being made in this matter." But Hoover was not finished with Westvaco. He went after them in the courts with anti-trust violations. The charges were felonious. Instead of indicting American industries in partnership with the I. G. Farben cartel for violation of the anti-trust laws, he applied these charges to I. G. Farben's competitors!

"WESTVACO CHLORINE PRODUCTS INC." US Department of Justice Criminal Division. FBI file 60-Q-28, Number 346, Confidential report on the International Alkali Cartel December 5th, 1944 submitted by Harold J. Carter, Economic Warfare Section, War division.
"... the alkali cartel is a close-knit, well managed organization whose members support agreed upon policies through a series of agreements... the cartel has come to regard the entire world as its economic sphere of influence..."

Of the seventeen companies indicted, only a few were charged, like I. G. Farben, out of reach of American law. The stock of its few subsidiaries were ceased, yet most of the noise was political posturing, an enormous waste of time and money. Roosevelt's Justice Department was virtually attacking the war munitions industry we so desperately needed to fight Hitler. DowChemical would soon be dragged in. There is a telling letter from the FBI SAC in San Francisco to Hoover giving him the facts of life on American commerce laws, dismissing Westvaco and twelve other companies in the anti-trust suit:

"WESTVACO CHLORINE PRODUCTS, INC." FBI file 60-5981-5

Letter to Director FBI, from FBI San Francisco Office, July 7, 1944
RE: Soda Ash Industry Antitrust
"In the defendant's motion to dismiss the charges, "it was noted that

the brief discusses thoroughly the Webb-Pomerene Act together with the other Acts related to the Sherman Act such as the Interstate Commerce Act, Capper-Volstead Act, Agricultural Marketing Agreement Act, Fisheries Cooperative marketing Act, and Bituminous Coal Act of 1937. This information is being submitted as being of possible interest to the Bureau, and this case is being closed in the San Francisco Office. Very Truly Yours, Special Agent in Charge, M. J. Pieper."

By the end of the war, Westvaco Chlorine was in financial straits. The "New York Times" 'Obituaries' October 7, 1964 for CEO William Burton Thom, detailed the 1948 sale of Westvaco to Food Machinery Corporation. FMC today is a multi-national corporation, manufacturing tanks, combat vehicles and of course, food machinery. One might surmise that Westvaco Chlorine had been under poor management from the start, yet the evidence suggests something more sinister. Many of the other CW firms accompanying Westvaco to the USSR would suffer likewise.

In the mean time, Westvaco Chlorine kept up its end of government contracts, fulfilling its duty to the war effort. The origin of Westvaco's troubles may have arisen from its meetings with the State Department's Foreign Intelligence Group. Other members of this select cult of economic sleuths included Wall Street banker, Lt. Frank G. Wisner, future head of the OPC, Allen Dulles' partner. After the war, when Frank Wisner learned the OPC was so hopelessly penetrated by Soviet moles and all of the Freedom Fighters they trained to overthrow the Iron Curtain were identified and assassinated, he went mad and shot himself in the head.(3) Murder by madness. What else could anyone expect, Wisner's subordinate, Dulles, I. G. Farben's patent lawyer, was a Soviet mole.

The other American chemical warfare munitions companies would soon follow in its fate. In august 1942, Dupont de Nemours plant in Arlington New Jersey suffered sabotage, their machinery broken, inducing work stoppage. The Dupont estate was burned down twice in January 1942, the source of the fires, unknown. (4) Federal Laboratories, Vonsiatsky's old munitions supplier, had an even more peculiar sequence of events. To start with, they were not owned or operated by the government, as their name implies. Their FBI files are extensive, covering attempts to arm the Mexican Revolution in 1924. By WW II, the firm was exporting armaments to Argentina under the State Department's export neutrality act. (5) Nothing in the FBI's report suggest these arms went outside of Argentina. The State Department files, which were denied to the author, were accompanied by a letter from Frank Machak, of the FOIA Office, reassuring that Federal Laboratory was not involved in exporting weapons to Germany or Russia. (6) By April 10th, 1945, Federal Laboratories was also reporting sabotage. Attempts were made at the hand grenade factory at Tunnelton, Pennsylvania, where fuses for the Army's weapons were being improperly assembled, the plant nearly blown to bits:

"FEDERAL LABORATORIES" FBI file 98-35858
TELETYPE 3/22/45 PITTSBURGH to DIRECTOR, URGENT
"FEDERAL LABORATORIES, PLANT NO. THREE, TUN-
NELTON, PA TAMPERING WITH (blackout) HAND GRENADES
MARCH TWENTY TWO FORTYFIVE, SABOTAGE.
(blackout) ADVISED FOR PAST WEEK SOME ONE HAS BEEN
TAMPERING WITH HAND GRENADES AND OTHER EXPLO-
SIVES BEING MANUFACTURED FOR U.S. ARMY ORDNANCE.
NO DAMAGE, (blackout) CAUSED SINCE TAMPERING DISCOV-
ERED BY INSPECTIONS, COMPANY OFFICIALS BELIEVE ACTS
ARE DELIBERATE SINCE MANUFACTURE AND, INSPECTIONS
HAVE BEEN CAREFULLY CHECKED. GRENADES WHICH HAVE
BEEN TAMPERED WITH WOULD CAUSE SERIOUS DAMAGE
IF NOT DETECTED BY INSPECTION, INVESTIGATION CON-
TINUING."

Again, the report concluded, 4/4/45 that the "abnormal number of straight pull pins discovered on fuses" "attributed to sabotage" were the result of "recently hired employees and carelessness of employees and visitors." "The plant had no labor troubles, and that the union and management cooperated 100 percent." The US Navy took a dim view of industrial sabotage and had previously instructed Federal Laboratories to report any such attempts to the FBI. They had advised Federal Laboratories to enhance security in 1942. (7) Unfortunately, Undersecretary of the Navy, James Forrestal, didn't realize J. Edgar Hoover was a fraud.

The case of Lake Erie Chemical is more complex. Organized just after WW I with many ex-U.S. Army CWS veterans, they were the leading CW experts of the time. (8) The history of this firm involved Chemical Warfare chief, Claude Ernest Brigham. Investigations had been launched into the firm's acquisition of Army poison gas formulas, specifically phosgene, and their marketing these patents along with US Navy bomb secrets in the 1930s. Eventually, nobody was charged because the patents were public. According to the FBI files, by World War II, the War Department had written Lake Erie Chemical off as disreputable, but when the FBI questioned Brigham on the firm's integrity, J. Edgar Hoover vouched for Lake Erie 100%. General Brigham was next investigated for his own integrity in an internal security report, (FBI file 62-32760-3) on Lake Erie Chemical, crossed referenced with "CLAUDE ERNEST BRIGHAM," October 25, 1942, subtitled "ESPIONAGE: SALE OF PLANS AND SPECIFICA-TIONS FROM GOVERNMENT ARSENALS." And in return, Hoover vouched for Brigham as beyond reproach. (9) Roosevelt's Attorney General brushed off the whole affair:

"CLAUDE ERNEST BRIGHAM" FBI file 65-57899-199 cross refer-ence #2 LAKE ERIE CHEMICAL" Subject ESPIONAGE file 65-2698
To: Director, FBI, From SAC, Cleveland
"By memorandum dated May 20, 1937, the Department of Justice advised that prosecution in the Lake Erie Chemical case was not warranted and authorized the submission of the information gathered in that case to the War Department for such administrative action as it might desire to take."

Much of the documentation is blacked out in these FBI files, whole pages are withheld concerning General Claude Ernest Brigham. The FOIA request was appealed, and denied. Later, more would surface. Brigadier General William C. Kabrich took over the CWS in 1942, (possibly the general cited in the Hirsch Report), winning many service awards as the war closed. He died a relatively young man, three weeks into January, 1947, while his predecessor, Brigham lived to a ripe old age of 90, dying in 1968. William Karbrich's records from the National Personnel Records Center in St. Louis, went up in smoke with many other war veteran's files July 12, 1973 in the middle of Watergate. (10) Richard Nixon had collated Navy intelligence files just after the war. Was there a connection? Kabrich's death was to follow that of another US Army official, Dr. Harry Plotz, Chief of the US Army's Typhus Commission on January 6, 1947. This was exceedingly inconvenient, for both men were very knowledgeable sources on Russian BW and CW warfare. The Russian piloted lend-lease tanker, the SS ELBRUS had docked just one year earlier to the day in Philadelphia January 6th, 1946, with 426 tons of furs, wools and camel hairs.

J. Edgar Hoover's impotence in resolving the suspect sabotage plights of the American CW firms serving inside of Russia may revolve around his personal life. His ties to the Mafia and their gay lawyer, Roy Cohn, and the OSS's discovery of Hoover's homosexuality through Mafia godfather, Meyer Lansky, is detailed in Anthony Summers' biography, "Official and Confidential: The Secret Life of J. Edgar Hoover." The State Department's OSS had hired Meyer Lansky's crooks to guard the waterfront! (11) Dono-van and the Dulles gang could blackmail Hoover into silence. Our whole national security had been compromised.

On September 25, 1990, the author placed a FOIA request to the FBI on Lake Erie Chemical Corporation, case #340,437. FBI Lake Erie file #65-33943 was released October 27, 2000 and received November 2nd, 2000, ten years later. Out of 361 pages, 285 were released, many solidly blacked out, others remained with different government agencies. This mini monopoly with its American and foreign subsidiaries, included characters close to the author's former home in Connecticut.

Lt. Col. Byron Goss began Lake Erie Chemical as a WW I veteran of the US Chemical Warfare Service. The company expanded, purchasing U. S. Ordnance Engineering, its former president, Alva Foote Spring, became Lake Erie Chemical's vice president. Spring, had also served in the US Army CWS. The new team, Goss and Spring, began acquiring new enterprises, the Burgess Company, Cleveland Screw Products Company, Anakin Company, Protex Corporation, and abroad, Sigmund Pumps of Czechoslovakia and Siamec in Nevers, France. They facilitated countries such as France, Czechoslovakia, Holland, Rumania, Algiers, and England with armaments, all apprehensive over Hitler's increasing menace.

Hoover put Lake Erie Chemical on his "Espionage" watch and tapped into their bank accounts with the Cleveland Trust Company, Chase National Bank, Marine Trust Company, Guarantee Trust Company, and National City Bank. Inquiries of credit stability were received from National Tube Company and in March 1940, Banca Romaneasca, at Bucharest, Romania, in November 1937. Business transactions with Holland dealt with bombs, and one transaction was endorsed to Brown Brothers and Harriman and Company by the Netherlands Company, Inc. cleared through Chase National Banks in New York. Large transactions over $10,000 were noted, many between Atlas Powder Company, and one with Joseph Kennedy and the Cleveland Clearing House. The "Hirsch Report" noted that "in the beginning of November [1942] several chemists of the Federal Laboratories, and of the Lake Erie Chemical Corporation were to be sent to Russia to study, apparently the state of the Russian Chemical Warfare preparations" (page 47, CWS version).

Lake Erie was in a peculiar position with an international view of the munitions industry. One of its later acquisitions, Sigmund Pumps, and its subsidiary, Siamec, brought two unusual Czechoslovakian refugees to America, inventor Frantisek Sigmund, AKA 'Frank' Sigmund, and his broker, Robert Kratschmer, a wealthy Czech aristocrat. As they departed from their homeland a few steps ahead of the Nazis, Sigmund's family vanished. Although Catholic, the FBI presumed Sigmund's family Jewish, imprisoned in a Nazi concentration camp. Safe in America under the employ of Byron Goss, Sigmund worked as an advisor, offering his sub-pump patents to the US Navy.

Robert Kratschmer became Lake Erie Chemical's broker, and after the war, moved in with famed Czechoslovakian sculptor, Mario Korbell, first in New York City, then on the Great Island estate of multi millionaire, William Ziegler, heir to the Royal Baking Soda fortune. This is the same Great Island off the Coast of Massachusetts and Connecticut, over run by Lyme disease, mentioned in Dr. Allen Steere's study "Medical Progress: Lyme disease" (The New England Journal of Medicine, 8/31/89). By 1989, at least 16% of its 162 permanent residents were infected. (See note #6, 'Introduction.') Korbell achieved international recognition for his portraits, fetching many thousands of dollars in the art world. Robert Kratschmer assisted Korbell in his studio. Accordingly, once on the island, Kratschmer's character took a turn for the worse, becoming "shrewd, unscrupulous, self grandising, ruthless, and bombastic." Sigmund and Kratschmer split, squabbling over lost properties in France. Kratschmer continued his career as an international broker for many American based firms. In those days, he would have been required by law to be vaccinated to travel abroad, including smallpox, yellow fever, polio, DPT (Diphtheria, Pertusis, Tetanus). The reactions to these vaccines while infected with spirochetes will be discussed in upcoming chapters. Was Kratschmer another attempted case of "murder by madness"?

The FBI had a knack for tailing and "turning" State Department recruits into their own informants. They went after Byron Goss. In 1944, he was nabbed at the border on one of his return trips from Mexico, grilled rudely and aggressively about his armaments deals with foreign countries. Finally Goss played his ace, he was a former consultant to the Office of Strategic Services (OSS) in the employ of the Donovan -Dulles gang (FBI file 65-33943-40 with subfile 100-5456). The FBI "Lake Erie Chemical - Espionage" file #65-33943-41, was closed. The author could find no records of "sabotage" complaints from Lake Erie Chemical while it served inside of Russia during the war years.

Kratschmer and Korbell's mentor and protector, William Ziegler, supposedly a staunch conservative Republican, headed numerous philanthropic ventures, including the Boys Club. His house guests were described as being on both ends of the political spectrum, avidly anti-Communists, to "pro-Russia." Kratschmer became a broker for Ziegler's business deals, and later brokered international deals for Trans American Mercantile Corporation under Jan Stadler, this firm on the Confidential Consignor Watch List (FBI file 65-33943-51, subfile 100-9123). Kratschmer became the broker for the International Office Appliances under Joseph Rubenstein, and the Manufacturers Mercantile Corporation under Leo Kahn, the Atlantic Export Industrial Company, the North American Machine Tool Company, and the Sardik Food Products Corporation, later known as the Maryland Export Corp (FBI file 1009123) These firms had business ties to Turkey, Italy, Belgium, Luxembourg, Holland, Brazil, Columbia, and other Latin American countries. A whole fleet of obsolete DC-8s was purchased from Peru. After an eleven month world tour, Kratschmer was finally apprehended and interrogated (FBI file 65-33943-57, subfile 100-9123, April 7, 1953). Most of the text is solidly blacked out, Kratschmer's few sentences pleading he was not a Communist.

What shenanigans were these old Catholic Czechs up to? We can only speculate. Arms for Israel had been brokered through Czechoslovakia, circumnavigating the British blockade upon the fledgling nation in 1948. An inside intelligence scoop was published by John Loftus and Mark Aaron's "Secret War Against the Jews." (12) Oscar Schindler was not the only Catholic Czech allied with the Jewish underground fighting both Nazis and Communists. Certainly Lake Erie Chemical Company must have observed the "brand new gases" of I. G. Farben inside Russia that Westvaco Chlorine described in the Hirsch Report, fully comprehending the significance of this Communist-Fascists alliance. Were they obliged to help Israel after WW II?

Let's return to the Hirsch Report and follow the Nazi-Soviet development of biological warfare. By World War II, a huge range of BW and CW factories had been assembled from the Atlantic to the Pacific, but who was the "enemy"?. An additional paragraph in the Hirsch Report tipped off the intelligence community, which decided to sit back in silence and watch the Soviet Union self destruct:

"SOVIET BW & CW PREPARATIONS AND CAPABILITIES" by Walter Hirsch, US Army CWS translation, Pentagon Plans & Operations

Page 78: 'Desert Regions of the USSR'

"In uninhabited regions of the USSR... islands in large seas, steppes, deserts and Taiga, etc. are carried out large scale experiments in CW and BW to which nomadic tribes are often unconscionably sacrificed as victims. Ghastly experiments, it is said, have also been performed on human targets... political deportees, Mongolian and Chinese prisoners of war - in Siberian tundras. The number of those whose lives were forfeit in this manner is reckoned in many thousands. However, there is no documentary evidence, since it is only natural that these experiments would be carried out under specially strict surveillance of the NKVD."

Thank God for the downfall of Communism. The bulk of the text in the Hirsch Report dealt with gas attacks upon military and civilian targets, and the full scope of the human tragedy revealed. Hitler didn't need to test TABUN, the NKVD had done it for him. In fact, he didn't even need to invade the Soviet Union, the Red Army and NKVD was his closest ally. By the end of WW II, I. G. Farben scientists were in a position to blackmail all who knew of the Communist-Fascist alliance. But the Soviets were not only testing chemical warfare upon their own citizens, refusing to succumb to the yoke of Communism, they were attacked with hoards of infested rats. Walter Hirsch revealed Soviet innovations on dispersing plagues upon the populace, some of the preparations concocted at Tomka, "Shishany":

""SOVIET BW & CW PREPARATIONS AND CAPABILITIES" by Walter Hirsch, US Army CWS translation 'Russian Activities from 1933-1937'

Page 101: "[Interview] from a POW captured 1942 who had worked from the spring of 1933 to the end of 1937 as a bacteriologist in various bacteriological institutes of the Red Army... He entered, in the spring of 1933, the Scientific Medical Institute of the Red Army in Moscow... in the fall of 1934, the Institute received BW assignments from the higher Soviet and party authorities. It was put under the jurisdiction of the CWS of the Red Army with the name of "Bio-chemical Institute of the Red Army." Part of the assigned personnel were professors and bacteriologists who were the prisoners of the NKVD, the remaining were mostly younger engineers, chemists and technicians who had graduated from the Military Chemical Academy... Practical trials were made at the "Volsk Polygon" at Shishany on the Volga."

Page 192, from the Nalbandian translation, Carl Isle Barracks, PN
""STARI SHISHANI Here is located the main CW Proving Ground of the Red Army... Oldest proving ground of the USSR... Enlarged in 1937/38, whereby 4 large towns were evacuated entirely. In 1941/42, it grew to 1000 square kilometers size. In 1940, there were in this station large laboratories (at least 9-10 large buildings), workshops, garages, stalls for animals, barracks for experimental details, building for the station commandant and the personnel stationed there, an airfield with hangers, a gas school with spacious instruction halls, a military hospital and building for the manufacture of the after mentioned CW agents... In 1938, a German experimentation party carried out a series of experiments in small proving

ground which at the time bore the name of "Tomka." The experiments started on a small scale by a party of 30 men, then called "Battalion 3" of the Army Ordnance Department... In the years that followed till 1931, the program and the personnel were almost doubled... The Russians were very backward in the technique and the evaluation of experiments; but they proved themselves good, teachable pupils and copied successfully a great deal from their German instructors in the course of 4 years."

Included amongst these dirty dozens of CW and BW factories were those at Suchomi on the Black Sea and Beketovka, eight miles south of Stalingrad. These two sites were of great significance after the war. Other numerous installations sat upon islands in central Siberian lakes. A center to study leprosy, plague and foot-and-mouth disease was established in the Fall of 1935 near Ostashkov, on the island of Gorodomlia in the Seliger Lake. According to Walter Hirsch, the institute was later "dissolved and transferred to a new branch bearing the name of "Velikonovski Institute," code designation No. v/2-1094." The institute was run under the strictest surveillance by Professor Velikonov and his assistant, Professor Nikanorov. Velikonov made a special "Foreign Study Travel" to Japan in 1936 and later joined the Red Cross delegation under Rakovsky. His wife, Sonya Ivanovna Mikhailova, went to France for further study, "the couple wrote under the pseudonym of Jacques Eiffel and Sonya Orska in a popular brochure entitled 'The Bacteriological Warfare.' " (13) Germany and Russia were not the only spawning grounds for socialists crackpots. Eventually, like all the other witnesses to the Fascist-Communist collaboration, Stalin had them destroyed. Hirsch went on to reveal the list of tick borne diseases, including relapsing fever spirochetes, that were to be dispersed amongst the Soviet population:

"THE HIRSCH REPORT" US Army CWS translation
Page 101: "It was further claimed that infected rats could be dropped from unmanned balloons... It was alleged that successful experiments with carriers of relapsing fever... of spotted typhus... and meningitis were carried out abroad... the Soviet Union must be able to strike back with telling effect..."
Page 103: "The experiments with the dangerous disease-producing agents could not be carried out at the "Volsk Polygon" Proving Grounds, as the risk of infection and difficulties of secrecy were too great there. On this account, a tract of land of some 10,000 square kilometers extent on the isle of Vozrozhdeniya is in the Aral Sea was allotted for the exclusive use of the Institute v/2-1094, after driving away the Kulaks who were banished

there... In the fall of 1936 the Institute was renamed the "Biotechnical Institute of the Red Army..." However, in June of 1937, the Velikonovs, the engineer Busanov and several other leading specialists were, all of a sudden put under arrest charged with "pernicious activity," "sabotage and squandering of government property" (Footnoted: this seems to be the fate of most scientists in Russia...) In 1937, the informant left the Institute in strict secrecy. Up to his departure, the following microbes had undergone a close theoretical and practical test: plague, tularemia, leprosy, hoof-and-mouth-disease, cholera, dysentery, typhus, paratyphus, pyemia and tetanus... release of microbes in the form of bacterial emulsions were effected in two ways... mist, darts, dropped from aircraft."

After pages of details on "prepared bacteria for contaminating wells and food products," "extensive plague attacks on the combats in Mongolia" and "employment by agents in the hinterland, mainly in Warsaw... zones of communications such as Kiev and Minsk," Hirsch concluded "This practice reached its climax in the Summer of 1943." Further methods of dispersal were detailed, "A. Bacterial pestis, B. Bacterial anthrax, C. Vibrio cholerae asiaticae, and typhoid".

"THE HIRSCH REPORT" US Army CWS translation
Page 104-105: "the carriers of group "A" were in the form of a bacteria emulsion that could be sprayed from aircraft or be carried by rat fleas, rats infested with them could be dropped from parachute cages into the combat area... Group "B" was in the form of dust... Group "C" was to be used for infecting reservoirs, springs and rivers."
Page 106: "Dropping Infected Rats and Mice in Parachute Cages"
"Experiments have established that the big, gray biting stain of rats bred by special, strict selection are the best contagion carriers; they are capable of holding their own and are not bitten out of existence by the rats living in the area where they are let loose. Rats infested with infected fleas transmit the contagion to other rodents of the locality, where from it is carried over to men by means of fleas. The rats are dropped in parachute cages. This experiment was repeated by the informant many times and the performance of the cages observed; the rats came down to ground always alive and unhurt. Principal targets for such an attack are: large railroad stations, large villages and cities, food supply depots, etc. and to a lesser degree, masses of men. No results are to be expected before the lapse of a certain period of time necessary for the infection to spread among the local rats and their fleas. Once that has taken place the fight against the rampant plague epidemic becomes extremely difficult."

Page 110: "Further Plans and Experiments"

"The escape of a prisoner infected with bubonic plague started a great plague epidemic... during which some 3-5,000 Mongol met their deaths... Other thorough experiments have been made with highly effective infection producing agents, e.g. with germs that cause encephalitis, by using ticks... Also various sorts of Tularemia carriers and infected rodents were tried."

Page 113: Chapter 2: 'Biological Warfare'

"Here is how he (the POW informant) stated the Russian point of view about the Bacterial Warfare: 'Stalin will not initiate BW so long as it is not absolutely necessary. Only as a last resort in case the German troops penetrate deep into the country and an anti-Soviet revolution breaks out in the land, will he order the use of the BW agents, alleging, for propaganda purposes as an excuse that it was first started by the Germans... Humanity or solicitude for their own people play no part at all, must needs be. He is convinced that the Soviet Union is undoubtedly in a position to wage a long-term BW. Presumably all prerequisites are provided, and all preparations are made.' "

Russian Red Army BW chief, E. N. Pavlovskii further confirms the Soviet effort to eliminate their 'counter-revolutionaries' in "The Natural Foci of Human Infections." He detailed 20 years of expeditions to the Central Asian Republics, investigating "new public health problems, brain infections in the Far East, encephalitis, and other diseases." These trips were organized by the Ministry of Public Health of the USSR, the former VIEM, Department of General Biology and Parasitology of the Military Medical Academy, the Department of Parasitology of the Zoological Institute, and the Academy of Sciences of the USSR, the Department of Parasitology of VIEM, the Department of Medical Zoology and Parasitology, of the Institute of Epidemiology and Microbiology. Accordingly, "a calendar of infection by ticks was compiled" and the progress of attacks by ticks on cattle in pasture, and the manner in which this cattle was utilized by man... all this was done for the study of the Ixodes ricinus, the specific vector of piroplasmosis babesiosis (brucellosis) in cattle."

"The Natural Foci of Human Infections" cites further work on tick spread encephalitis and relapsing fever conducted between 1937 and 1941. Thousands of infected wild animals were rounded up, "the entire work was carried out as if on a conveyor-belt... together with a parallel inspection of domestic animals.." Sixteen species of ixodes ticks were discovered to be the culprits. Further details on 'Keeping and Feeding Live Ixodidae' up to eight years required three full pages of instructions. His chapter on

'Methods of Collection of Ixodid Tick' included the inspection of "shorn wool of sheep." (14) It became exceedingly obvious that there was nothing 'natural' at all about the spread of these tick-borne diseases from the testimony of returning POWs escaping Russia. The sudden arrival of brand new tick borne diseases after the war, previously unknown to America, would heighten suspicions. Had these epidemics been a long range plan of Stalin's. Pavlovskii's early research published in the "Handbook of Biological Work Methods" would certainly imply this, as noted previously.

Pavlovskii further wrote in 1960 in "The Natural Foci of Human Infections" that "No vaccines against some of these infections exist" and that "apparatus for treating the area with gas, smoke and insecticides" was deployed (pages 15-19). Pavlovskii boldly published in 1939, article after article appeared in "The Tropical Disease Bulletin" with English translations. The medical community was keeping track:

"A Register of the Spirochetes of Tick Strains of Relapsing Fever in the USSR and Neighboring Countries" F. N. Pavlovskii, Tropical Disease Bulletin, v. 42 No. 7, July 1945, summary from Rev. of Applied Entom. Ser. B. 1945, Feb. v. 33, Part 2, 17-18 from "Probl. Region. Parasit.." Moscow, 1939, v. 3, 19-35

"Laboratories in the Russian Union have maintained a number of strains of spirochetes of tick-borne relapsing fever for years by keeping them in live examples... strains isolated from ticks in the Russian Union and adjacent countries in places where relapsing fever is prevalent... particulars are given to ten strains of relapsing fever spirochaetes isolated from O. tholozani in Tadzhikistan and southern Kirghizia..."

"Tick-borne Relapsing Fever in Southern Kirghizia" E. N. Pavlovskii, Probl. Region. Paraist. Moscow. 1939, v. 3, 72-98. "Tropical Disease Bulletin" 1945

"South Western Part of Kirghiz Republic in July and August 1935, many... onithodorus (ticks) were found... in which grain was stored or sheep were kept in winter... Experiments with several strains of relapsing fever spirochetes from various parts of Central Asia showed that they could not be differentiated by the character of the disease they produced in guinea pigs or, with any reliability by cross-immunity tests." [Hence, the confusion over Lyme and relapsing fever.]

The FBI furnished a short biography on Pavlovskii, in "List of Members of Academy of Sciences of the USSR" file 100-641759-23, which they released under joint jurisdiction of the State Department. He was described as a prominent zoologist and parasitologist, having received the Stalin Prize, a member of the Academy of Medical Sciences of the USSR, heading the Red Army 's BW Academy. But more interesting, Pavlovskii joined international zoological societies in London, France, Algiers, and Iran. Was he there to keep track of Stalin's rats? Had he tipped off the Iranians?:

E.N. PAVLOVSKII, FBI FOIA 303125, 8/4/55, forwarded to CIA, response 7/8/94 case #31-0103 CIA letter to J. Edgar Hoover, 2 April 1952: 85494 'SOVIET PROFILES' (blackout) Page 184: 13 March 1952 E.N. PAVLOVSKII

"described as one source as not a Communist, and in fact opposed to the Party, Pavlovskii is elsewhere reported as a believer in the ideals of the USSR 'One of those Russian scientist who realize early in the revolution that science was one of the means by which the revolution could succeed.' (blackout)"

The plight of the Russian populace was further noted in the medical journals. The Hirsch Report noted Soviet usage of the gas, Chlopicrine as a pesticide to fight vermin, coupled with induced famine in these Republics, thousands must have died:

"Experiments on the Application of Carbon Disulfide, Chlopicrine, K. Soap, and other Insecticides for Destroying and Repelling the Ticks" by N. V. Troitsky 'Med. Pariasi. & Parasitic Dis.' Moscow, 1945, v. 14, No. 3 75-9, summarized in "Tropical Disease Bulletin." under subject 'relapsing fever' and 'typhus'

"The author notes the importance of Ornithodorus papillipes, as a vector of tick-borne relapsing fever in Middle Asia, where up to 100 percent of the population in endemic areas is affected."

One hundred percent infected in endemic areas? This was a catastrophe. Worse, Stalin was using the Nazis as patsies for his own crimes. Soviet journals began publishing reports of brucellosis, or 'Bangs disease' inside 'occupied territories' as the results of Nazi attacks. Further emphasis was made regarding brucellosis raging inside of Germany and Great Britain. Why would the Germans attack their own country, or were the Spartans at hand? Brucellosis is easily passed through livestock, their dung, milk, and meat, causing cattle to abort, and in humans, causing intestinal disorders and neurological problems. (15) What was the real source of Germany's brucellosis? Viktor Suvorov in his "Icebreaker" exposed the truth. By

June 21, 1941, a day prior to the German invasion of Russia, Operation Barbarossa, some hundreds of thousands of heads of cattle and sheep and Soviet troops were relocated and poised on the border to attack Germany. The animals were infected. The troops were then removed. Soviet spies kept exacting files on the German sheep consumption and livestock market prices. (16) The epidemics spread.

There were others tallying the increasing cases of madness in Germany. A psychiatrist from Austria, Dr. Leo Alexander, continued his research on racial hygiene in America. After attending the University of Vienna and the University of Frankfurt, he moved to Peiping, China, where the Rockefeller Foundation ran a hospital, the city a hotbed of Communist spies. Here the infamous Duchess of Windsor, Wally Simpson, learned the oriental arts of seducing, which were applied towards capturing the heart of Prince Edward. Here, author Graham Greene and Ian Fleming's brother met with British spies, Kim Philby and Roger Hollis of MI6. From there, Alexander immigrated to America, renouncing his Austrian citizenship December 19, 1933. (17)

By 1936, Alexander was well established, publishing prolifically, including "Eugenical Sterilization," with a host of co-authors. Financed by a grant from the Carnegie Foundation, this text gave a summary of Western sterilization laws with the intent of eradicating a long list of genetic disorders, including encephalitis, spread by insect vectors. Alexander wrote: "The only cultural country from which good statistics are obtainable and which that a marked increase in the admission rate (to asylums) is in Germany, where the rate has gone up from 25 per 100,000 in 1923 to 36 in 1929." Were Stalin and his Spartans trying to incite a Communist revolution through disease and madness? Praising Hitler's efforts in sterilization, Alexander gave credit to earlier German psychiatrist for cleansing the gene pool. (18) He next served the U.S. Army Medical Corps as an intelligence officer, reporting to the famed ALSOS Mission, investigating the concentration camps and writing numerous CIOS reports, which will be studied in detail in upcoming chapters. (19) His discoveries on Nazi research in the Kaiser Wilhelm Institute for Brain Research Spirochete and Serology Labs are most revealing. Eventually, after the war, Alexander would be sent as a consultant to the Nuremberg Medical Trials, "US vs. Karl Brandt" in a face-off with his old classmates.

The US Naval Technical Mission to Europe interviewed Professor Kliewe, who had previously accompanied Walter Hirsch and the Waffen Pruf 9 on the 1940 'Decontamination Mission s to Russia' (CIOS report, "Investigation of Chemical Warfare Installations in the Munsterlager Area, Including Raubkammer" by A. K. Mills), the "Hirsch Report" reciting a similar tale dropping rats from parachutes like Kliewe:

"NAVAL ASPECTS OF BIOLOGICAL WARFARE" August 5, 1947 CD 23-1-4 by the Navel Technical Mission to Europe, National Archives, record group 350, Office of the Secretary of Defense, Chief of Naval Intelligence.

Page 60: "Research in biological warfare in Germany during WW II was under the direction of Prof. Heinrich KLIEWE whose title was "Director of German Bacteriological Warfare Research in the Office of the Surgeon General of the Wehrmacht." Biological warfare research in Germany was, in general, limited to extent and inadequate in experimental tests... because:

(1) The Fuehrer prohibited all biological warfare investigation of an offensive nature, defensive methods, however, were supported.

 (2) KLIEWE was constantly being called away from his work

(3) Dissension existed in the COMMITTEE ON BIOLOGICAL WARFARE (Blitzarbeiten) as to methods of study and procedure.

German biological warfare activities can be classified as Offensive and Defensive. The actual work was grouped into four sections, i.e., Human Section, Veterinary Section, Agriculture Section, and Ordnance Section."

Kliewe didn't need a huge laboratory for offensive research, the Soviet Union was annihilating its own population for the Nazis. Kliewe had five little rooms to complete all his research at Giessen, the former residence of the Institute for General and Military Hygiene in Berlin, eventually evacuated because of allied bombing. Forced to talk, Kliewe revealed the same apparatus for dropping infected rats that Hirsch attributed to the Russians. There was also a Nesselstedt Project, Posen, under Dr. Kurt Blome, for cancer research. Blome was barbaric, and prosecuted at Nuremberg. His facility was captured by the Russians. (20)

The CIA was watching the Soviet Union rot from the inside out. By 1950, Pavlovskii was named head of the Red Army Military Medical Academy and his predecessor, Lebedinsky was edged out in a wild scientific purge. A front page article in "The Red Star" November 30th, 1950 boasts that the "Russian Military medical services are unsurpassed elsewhere, but that the teachings of the great Russian physiologist I. P. Pavlov (Georg Friedrich Nicolai's typhus and rat instructor) are insufficiently applied." (21) As recently as August 28, 1994, "60 Minutes" Sunday night rehashed the 1950s nuclear holocaust upon Kadzhakistan, one of the USSR's Central Asian Republics victimized under Pavlovskii's "expeditions." The racists Communist were still trying to kill off the surviving ticks, rats and tribesmen with above-ground nuclear testing. Horrid deformities of fetuses pickled in formaldehyde in KGB medical museums were revealed in this "60 Minutes" report. Did the bomb cover up old BW atrocities? The reign of Communism has been that of pure insanity, beyond basic greed. The lust for power far exceeded "redistribution of the wealth." If Communism isn't racism, what is? Thank God for the fall of the "The Evil Empire."

As World War II progressed, Stalin, fearing a coup, executed his own troops with the help of the NKVD. Let's explore the nitty gritty battles deep inside the Caucasus that historians refuse to cover, brushing over them in great vagueness, or avoiding them all together. Get your maps out to draw up the battle plans for Operation Nalchik and Ordzhonikidze at the base of Mount Elbrus.

CHAPTER 4 NOTES

(1) "SOVIET BW & CW PREPARATIONS AND CAPABILITIES" US Army CWS translation, National Archives MRB and Pentagon Plans & Operations by Walter Hirsch
Page 47: list of US companies sent to USSR for CW research

(2) "WESTVACO CHLORINE PRODUCTS INC: SABOTAGE" FBI file HQ98 14870 Newark, CA 11/13/42

(3) "WESTVACO CHLORINE PRODUCTS INC." FBI file 06-102-38-95, originated through the US Army Intelligence & Security Command, Ft. George Meade, MD
Page 1: 'Minutes of the Foreign Intelligence Group' 10 August 1943. Meeting held at the District Intelligence Office, 3ND, 50 Church St, NY, NY. includes Lt. F.G. Wisner.
Page 2: 'Director of Intelligence Second Service Command, ASF' Interview Report - New York Office, M.I.S. for week of 5 August 1943, includes Employee of Westvaco Chlorine Products Inc. Source transmitted recent information on Tata chemical plants at Mithapur, India.
"THE BELARUS SECRET" John Loftus, Alfred Knopf, New York 1982 Pages 115-116

(4) "NEW YORK TIMES" August 13, 1942, page 7, col. 1 "Acts of Sabotage laid to 2 in Jersey" Du Pont de Nemours, Arlington, NJ, conveyer system
"NEW YORK TIMES" January 7, 1942, page 17, col. 5

'Second fire on Du Pont Estate Wilmington, Del. Jan. 6'

(5) "FEDERAL LABORATORIES, INC. PITTSBURGH, PA" FBI file 64-0-460, Jan 11, 1924. "NINETY FOUR BOXES POLICE GAS GRENADES MARKED TEAR GAS... SHIPMENT TO MEXICAN REVOLUTIONARY FACTION REPLY..."

"FEDERAL LABORATORIES Mexican Revolutionary Activities (de la heurta Faction)" FBI file 64-0-1487, June 13, 1924

"FEDERAL LABORATORIES, INC." FBI file 64-0-464 Just Dpt. Tel., 1/10/24

"FEDERAL LABORATORIES, INC." FBI file 62-20117

"FEDERAL LABORATORIES" FBI file 2-262 letter to Director, Hoover, 3/11/43 NY

Re: International Forwarding Co., Inc, NY City, Federal Laboratories, Inc. Pittsburgh, PA, Neutrality Act - Exporting Control.

(6) US Dept. State letter to Rachel Verdon, 7/6/94: Case #9400281 from Frank Machak, Director FOIA/Privacy & Classification Review.

(7) "FEDERAL LABORATORIES" FBI file 99-4933-1 Letters from Commandant, Fourth Naval District, to Assistant Secretary of the Navy Security Division, Internal Security and Passive Defense Survey Reports, 3/14 & 5/22/42

(8) "FEDERAL LABORATORIES" FBI file 62-20117

(9) "WHO'S WHO IN AMERICA" vol. 22, 1942-43 BRIGHAM, Claude Ernest

SS Death Index 1988 Edition BRIGHAM, CLAUDE b. 4/14/1878, d. Jul 1968

"CLAUDE ERNEST BRIGHAM" FBI file 62-32760-31, cross ref. file 62-3230' "LAKE ERIE CHEMICAL COMPANY: ESPIONAGE" 'Sale of Plans and Specifications From Government Arsenals' 3/21/36

"CLAUDE ERNEST BRIGHAM" FBI file 100-335075-118, Cross Ref. #3 FBI case originated at Newark, NJ, file 100-24689, made at San Francisco, 5/18/45 'Internal Security' (pages 2-9 withheld entirely)

"CLAUDE ERNEST BRIGHAM" FBI file 65-57899-199, Cross ref. #2 LAKE ERIE CHEMICAL COMPANY. Office Memorandum 'Espionage-R' (Bureau file 65-57899)

(10) WILLIAM C. KABRICH X091995, FOIA request 11/15/92 to

National Personnel Records Center St. Louis. Reply: "The record needed to answer your inquiry is not in our files. If the report were here on July 12, 1973, it would have been in the area that suffered the most damage in the fire on that date and may have been destroyed. (Extract from 1946 Army Register.) Enclosed page from "Who Was Who In America" 1943-1950 v.. II. "Brigadier General William Camillus Kabrich b. 9/19/1895, d. 1/27/47. chief CWS and commanding general CWS Technical Command, Edgewood Arsenal, MD 1942-1945'"

(11) "OFFICIAL AND CONFIDENTIAL: The Secret Life of J. Edgar Hoover" Anthony Summers, G. P. Putnam's Sons, NY 1993. Page 240: Mafia/ Hoover's homosexuality. Page 242: Meyer Lansky photos/Hoover & Clyde Tolson in bed. Page 245: OSS hires Mafia guard waterfront. Pages 251-255 Roy Cohn, Mafia lawyer, orgies with Hoover.

(12) "THE SECRET WAR AGAINST THE JEWS" John Loftus & Mark Aarons, St. Martin's Press, NY 1994, Chapter 9 'Robert Maxwell's Czech Guns'

(13) "SOVIET BW & CW PREPARATIONS AND CAPABILITIES" Walter Hirsch, US Army CWS translation, National Archives & Pentagon Plans & Operations. Page 102 Re: Velikonovski Institute, code V/2 1094.

(14) "THE NATURAL FOCI OF HUMAN INFECTIONS" E. N. Pavlovskii, Gosudarstvennoe Izdatel'stvo Meditsinskoi Literatury, Moskva, 1960, Translated from Russian, Published for the National Science Foundation, Washington, DC and the Department of Health, Education and Welfare, by the Israel Program for Scientific Translations, Jerusalem, 1963. Pages: 7, 9-10: Expeditions to Central Asian Republics in 1930s. Pages 72-74: Shorn wool carries infested ticks, Collection & feeding ixode ticks.

(15) "ANTI BRUCELLOSIS WORK IN THE LIVESTOCK INDUSTRY of the USSR"
OACSI file MIS 555217 National Archives MRB, Moscow, USSR, April 29, 1949 Restricted: No. 247; 861.622/4-2949. US State Dept. translation of "Veterinary Science" No. 4, April 1949. 'To Eradicate the Livestock Disease Brucellosis' April 29, 1949
"... the capitalist countries brucellosis is widespread. According to data of British scientists, more than 40% of the livestock on large dairy farms

in England are seriously affected by brucellosis... in the United States where brucellosis is especially common among cattle, hogs and sheep. The sterility (failure) of German veterinary science is demonstrated particularly well in the large increase of brucellosis in Germany. During the war, Germany introduced brucellosis into the temporarily occupied territories."

"SCIENTIFIC INFORMATION REPORT: Organization and Administration of Soviet Science" summary No. 5111, 18 Oct. 1963, FBI file 100-341759-61 released by joint custody of CIA June 1997. (FBI FOIA request 3/5/92) 'Section IV' "Awards"

Page 14: M. M. Rementsova, special recognition for "Brucellosis in Wild Animals'" states the necessity for liquidating possible carriers and transmitters of Brucella pathogen (rodents, insects, and ticks) on animal-raising farms."

(16) "ICEBREAKER: Who Started the Second World War?" Victor Suvorov, Hamish Hamilton, London, 1990 Pages: 320-322.

(17) LEO ALEXANDER, FOIA request CO 891267 on 4/10/89 to Immigration & Naturalization Service. b. Vienna, Austria, 10/11/05; d. 7/20/85 pneumonia.
Certificate of citizenship No. 4377175, 4/18/38. Naturalization #183483 4/14/34 "My last foreign residence was Peiping, China, I emigrated to the United States of America from Yokohama, Japan... lawful entry US at Seattle 12/29/33, renounces Austrian citizenship"

(18) "EUGENICAL STERILIZATION: The Committee of the American Neurological Association for the Investigation of Eugenical Sterilization" by Abraham Nyerson, James Ayer, Tracy J. Putnam, Clyde E. Keeler, Leo Alexander. Macmillan Co. 1936 reprint by Arno Press, New York Times Co., NY 1980. 'Forward': grant financed by Carnegie Foundation. Page 36: German admittees to asylums increase late 1920s.
"NEW YORK TIMES" 7/24/85 'Obituaries -Leo Alexander' re: psychiatrist and neurologist writes Nuremberg code, moral ethical and legal principles for experiments on humans.

(19) "ALSOS" Samuel Goudsmit, Henry Schuman, Inc. Manufactured in USA by H. Wolff, NY 1947. Page 207: re: Ahnenerbe division for 'Applied War Research' experimentation on humans, Major Leo Alexander US Army Medical Corps makes reports available to A Mission.

(20) "NAVAL ASPECTS OF BIOLOGICAL WARFARE" August 5, 1947 CD 23/1/4 by the Naval Technical Mission to Europe, Office of Secretary of Defense Chief of Naval Intelligence, National Archives MRB. Pages: 62, 65, 89.

(21) "PURGES IN SOVIET MILITARY MEDICAL ACADEMY" OACSI file 744587, 12/20/50, National Archives MRB re. firing of Prof Lebedinskiy, replaced by E. N. Pavlovskii, head of Military Medical Academy.

CHAPTER 5

A NIGHT ON BALD MOUNTAIN

Kleist in the Caucasus, the Legacy of Mount Elbrus

Hitler's foreign minister, Joachim Von Ribbentrop, approached Stalin's foreign minister, Vyacheslav Molotov, with the deal of the century, carve up Poland and split the spoils. On September 1st, 1939, Hitler invaded Poland. Russia followed. England declared war and sought to cut German supply lines. Historians are more familiar with England's blockade in the Atlantic, not the Pacific. As discussed previously, Anatase Vonsiatsky's Brotherhood of Russian Truth, along with Rockefeller's Standard Oil, a subsidiary of I. G. Farben, was making plans to blow up oil fields in the Caucasus. This was merely a bluff, for this cult of reverse radishes (white on the outside, red on the inside) sold oil to Russia's broker, Amtorg Trading Company in New York. Amtorg in turn, contracted Rockefeller's Standard Oil to sail for Valdivostok, Russia's back door on the Pacific to Hitler's supply lines. Standard Oil, if not a 'reverse radish' certainly was a worm in the garden. The British were furious and threatened to sink American ships in the Pacific. Standard Oil, unable to deliver, was sued by Amtorg; the District Court of New York favoring the plaintiff! The "Denial Digest" is full of Amtorg's law suits.

More trouble was brewing in the Middle East, Russia's underbelly. Just to the north lay the Caucasus oil fields of Grozny, Maikop, and the Baku. The British, with the help of the French, were going to stir the pot and cut off more of Hitler's oil sources. The old Arab family secret societies from WW I, a network of spies organized by T. E. Lawrence, extended through the Middle East, north into the Caucasus and Central Asian Republics. The Arab underground, calling themselves Prometheus after the Greek god of fire, allied with the Polish underground. They were going to bomb the Baku.

Nikolai Tolstoy, the grandson of the famous Russian author, Leo Tolstoy, paints a bizarre picture of this Arab-Polish alliance. Everything Winston Churchill forecast with Lawrence was materializing under French General Wegand and Caucasian tribesman Said Shamyl in Beirut. "Contacts were made with Prometheus, an organization based at Paris and Constantinople, representing Turkoman resistance movements in Soviet Azerbaijan, Crimea, Turkestan and Kazan." Wegan had 60,000 poorly trained troops under his command in Lebanon. Stalin, received stretched intelligence reports from British NKVD agent, Konni Zilliacus, estimating "half a million troops, accompanied by thousands of tanks and hundreds of airplanes." In response, "entire nations" of the Asian Republics were sent to the Gulag. The British learned of the Polish-Prometheus alliance through the Polish embassy in London, arrangements were made to facilitate them via Colonel Colin Gubbins. Gubbins later ran SOE, British Special Operations Executive, specializing in guerrilla warfare. To counter the subversion, the Russian Army on February 10th, 1940, raided "thousands of Polish homes, to lop off what popular leadership in Poland surviving the massive deportations that followed the Soviet invasion in September 1939." (1)

What followed became known as the Katyn Forest massacre, where 15,000 Polish officers and civic leaders were taken to three secret prison camps inside the Soviet Union, Ostashkov, Kozielsk, and Starobielsk. The town of Ostashkov was located on the Seliger Lake, part of the Gorodomiya BW test complex, "Section V/2-1094" under Professor Velkonovski, described the Hirsch Report. From there, they were transported to the Katyn Forest and murdered. (2) When the advancing German army pressed forward on the Eastern Front invading Byelorussia, they entered the Katyn Forest with its huge sunken pits planted over with rows of tiny pine trees. The German soldiers were ordered to dig. The history of this monstrous crime is partially documented in one of the most extensive US Congressional investigations in history, 7000 pages of testimony from Germans, Poles, and American POWs, just prior General Eisenhower's bid for the Presidency. Its incriminating files are still classified. Author Allen Paul ran into a brick wall while writing "Katyn, the Untold Story of Stalin's Polish Massacre." (3) The current author had no better luck, the National Archives Center for Legislative Archives wrote Katyn's files must remain closed for fifty years. (4) Time's almost up, boys. Who today would benefit from keeping parts of these hearings classified, I. G. Farben's collaborators?

The first issue raised was "who done it." The Nazis and the Soviets accused each other. The Russians insisted the Nazis captured the Poles while on a road construction job in the summer of 1942. The invading Nazis suspected the NKVD in 1940, with good reason, the Poles were dressed in brand new winter woolen uniforms and heavy boots, exhibiting no toil. The US War Department silenced the press, not to jeopardize our fragile alliance with Russia. Who would believe the protesting Nazis?

Was there another reason for the cover-up? How were the Poles executed? Lavrenty Beria, chief of the Soviet Secret Police, the NKVD, was put in charge of the execution. The NKVD had been conducting CW and BW tests upon its own citizens since the days of Tomka. Was the Katyn Massacre a "TABUN-Lebedan" test conducted by Beria? Was the massacre witnessed by the Waffen Pruf 9 on Hirsch's Decontamination Mission described in the 'destroyed' OACSI files, "Investigation of Chemical Warfare Installations in the Munsterlager Area Including Raubkammer" by A. K. Mills found by the author at the National Library of Medicine? Hirsch was accompanied by Professor Kliewe, toxicologist Wolfgang Wirth and Smoke and Gas specialist Adjutant Mengele. After all, Dyhernfurth's TABUN gas factory was not built on a whim.

The Nazi soldiers in 1942, unaware of Hirsch's Decontamination Missions, insisted upon German innocence. They brought in foreign POWs to witness the excavations. They unanimously concluded the Soviets were responsible, even thought the British, Polish, and American POWs hated the Nazis. Lieutenant Colonel John Van Vliet was captured by the Germans in Tunisia, February 1943, and with a group of 350 British and 125 American POWs, sent to Rotenburg, Germany. Ten from this group were singled out and taken to Katyn to serve as witnesses. As the war closed, Van Vliet made it to the American lines near Duben and sought out G-2 Army Intelligence of the 144th Division. He handed over his long kept photographs of the massacre, the military was greatly concerned. From there he went to Leipzig, to see General "Lightning Joe" Collins of the 7th Army Corps. Again Van Vliet told his tale. General Collins sent him to Lieutenant Colonel William C. Lantaff, Assistant Chief of Staff, G-2 War Department in the Pentagon, arriving May 17, 1945. From here, Van Vliet was instructed to report in person to Major General Clayton Bissell, Assistant Chief of Staff for Intelligence under General George C. Marshall. Bissell ordered Van Vliet to dictate his report, which subsequently vanished. General Bissell insisted it had been passed along to the dubious State Department! According to author Allen Paul, "An independent investigation by the Army Inspector General in 1950 concluded that the report had been "compromised" and that there was no evidence to indicate that it ever left Army G-2. Bissell admitted that had the Van Vliet report been made public in 1945, its impact would have been explosive."

(5) Congress, so concerned over the missing Van Vliet report, brought in "three high ranking army officers" from G-2 Intelligence to testify in secret session, February 26, 1952.

Congress demanded Van Vliet write a second report. It conflicted with testimony of Polish POWS supplied through the British. Van Vliet testified the Polish soldiers were stacked in huge pits, like corrugated cardboard, all shot in the back of the head. The Polish POWs saw other pits with huge tangled piles of corpses, some seemingly buried alive, no bullets holes. Some had hideous frozen screams upon their faces, others mouths were stuffed with sawdust. More had coats hooded over their heads with ropes around their necks, according to testimony of Mr. Rowinski.(6) Were these crude attempts at gas masks? Did Eisenhower, as Commander in Chief, know about Katyn, and when? Eisenhower, as Roosevelt's hand picked General to lead the Allied Forces, had handed over half of Europe to the Soviet Union. Republicans in Congress were rightly concerned over having this guy on their ticket. They grilled Van Vliet over and over:

"Katyn Forest, Soviet Union Polish Military Officer Execution in Katyn Forest Investigation" House Select committee, Resolutions 390 & 539

Page 41: "Mr. Mitchell: Were any moving pictures or still pictures taken of your group?

Col. Van Vliet: Yes, sir. German photographers took still pictures and motion pictures of the party climbing in and out of the graves... later each given copies of the still pictures.

Page 46: Col. Van Vliet: I went to Eisenhower's headquarters at Reims where I didn't report to anyone except the billeting officer and told him I wanted transportation to Paris...

Mr. O'Konski: You didn't get to see General Eisenhower himself?

Col Van Vliet: I had no occasion to see anyone there at all, sir. I just passed through."

"Just passing through!" How'd ya like that? That would have cost Ike the election! The whole history of I. G. Farben's patent exchange with Ipatieff would have been blown open with Allen Dulles, their patent lawyer and the State Department on the hot seat. The whole Roosevelt Administration would have collapsed. The "New York Times" (October 15th, 1992, page 1 and 7) ran a lengthy article on Gorbachev handing KGB Katyn Forest Massacre files over to newly elected Polish President, Lech Walesa, the former Solidarity Labor leader who orchestrated the collapse of Communism. The files, citing the execution of more than

20,000 prisoners by firing squad, made no reference to poison gas. The KGB, too, was on the hot seat. To help instruct Poland on the virtues of democracy, Ronald Reagan sent Teamster chief Lane Kirkland to Poland as an advisor to Walesa. Paralleled with a new Polish Pope, John Paul II in the Vatican, the Soviet Union became frozen in fear. "National Review" (9/1/89), "Stalin: Why Hitler Embraced Him, Why Gorbachev Rejects Him" (page 52) "The Unquiet Ghosts of Stalin's Victims" by Eugene H. Methvin cited the execution of 84 million, concluding: "A full-scale hearing on the Stalin era would mirror nothing less than the 1946 Nuremberg trials of Nazi war criminals."

Just before the Nazi invasion, Operation Barbarossa of 1941, Stalin executed 90% of his top generals, including the famed Mikhail Niko-layevich Tukhachevsky, leaving Russia virtually defenseless. Tukhachevsky was as sharp as a tack, and he and his wife, both music lovers, befriended the young brash composer, Dmitri Shostakovich. His music was radical and western, and Stalin hated it. Only by wit, intrigue and blackmail was Shostakovich able to out-survive Stalin's reign of terror. Towards his death in 1975, the internationally famed composer published "Testimony," dictated to the musicologist, Solomon Volkov, damning Stalin's execution of the only general who could have defended Russia against Hitler. Sleeping with a pistol under his pillow every night, Shostakovich was wracked in fear while his beloved friends vanished into the Gulag. As an old man, Shostakovich reminisced:

"TESTIMONY" Dmitri Shostakovich, Harper & Row, New York, 1979
Pages 96-99: "It was the first and last time that I was friends with a leader of the country, and the friendship was broken tragically... Now it's well known that Tukhachevsky was destroyed through the joint action of Stalin and Hitler. But one musn't exaggerate the role of German espionage in this matter. If there hadn't been those faked documents that "exposed" Tukhachevsky, Stalin would have got rid of him anyway."

World War II progressed, minus Tukhachevsky's military genius; the Nazis besieged Leningrad. Supply lines were cut, the citizens starved. Fires raged throughout the city. Shostakovich took up the defense. "Time" magazine's cover of July 20th 1942 featured a portrait of Dmitri Shostakovich in a fireman's helmet, battling the blazes of Leningrad. His symphonies and operas had already won international acclaim. For his acts of patriotism, Stalin advanced Shostakovich's name to the top of the execution list. His music, "too decadent, too modern," was ordered destroyed. Ah, art under socialism! When listening to Shostakovich's 11th Symphony, "Bloody Sunday," the battle themes for revolution repeat themselves more times than history would allow. The finale is rung out in church bells. Had he joined Pope Pius' Black Orchestra like Oscar Schindler to overthrow Communism? The 13th Symphony, "Babi Yar" on the Nazi and Soviet execution of Jews at Kiev, nearly landed Shostakovich in the Gulag again. Were the Christian and Jewish underground connected inside the Soviet Union? Were they allied with Prometheus? Stalin's paranoia intensified, his purges unparalleled in human history.

Enter Lavrenti Pavlovich Beria, chief of the NKVD (Secret Police). Born in the Republic of Georgia, he rose to power in 1938 heading the Soviet State Defense Committee. He was murdered in 1953, soon after Joseph Stalin's death. Beria made two trips to the Caucasus, August 1942, and March 1943. Katyn was just the beginning. While Hitler secretly amassed one army in the 1930s, Stalin openly amassed two armies. Hitler's public adored him, Stalin's hated him, and they were both nuts. After The Great Purge of the 1930s, NKVD chief, Kokolai Yezhov was removed. To balance the possibility of a military coup, Lavrenty Beria replaced him, fortifying the NKVD.

Viktor Suvorov, KGB defector, exposed the inside history of the NKVD-KGB World War II operations in "Icebreaker." Six new independent chief directorates were created under the NKVD, taking over military responsibilities under the command of Lieutenant General I. I. Maslennikov. One of these new troop responsibilities was the "retreat-blocking service." The Red Army soldiers were caught in a vice. In front of them lay the barbaric Nazis advancing over their homelands, and behind them was the NKVD, with "burst of machine guns at the backs of their heads," forcing them into the meat grinder. This would certainly help account for the 34 million Russians lost in the war. Beria had TABUN. Far worse was to follow.

With the launching of Operation Barbarossa and the blitzkrieg, Hitler figured it would be a matter of weeks before Russia fell, not anticipating the millions of troops Stalin concealed for sacrifice. Perhaps he had bad intelligence? At first, the going was easy, the Germans were lured in deeper. The same fate that trapped Napoleon awaited the Nazis, the Russian winter. Leningrad and Moscow held out by the skin of their teeth, while Hitler's ambitions became bloated with overconfidence. Sidetracked, he turned his lust towards the industrial riches of Stalingrad and the oilfields of the Baku. He literally bit off more than he could chew, costing the Nazis the war.

The Volga River stretches from the north of Moscow south eastward to the Caspian Sea, bordering Persia. It is the commercial artery connecting the Soviet Capital to Central Asia. Stalingrad, situated on the Volga's southern course, was an industrial giant. Not only was it home to the Red Army's tank assembly lines, it housed one of the largest chemical warfare complexes in the Soviet empire, Beketovka. The battle for Stalingrad was the turning point of the war, and an unnecessary loss for the Nazis. Not only had Hitler spread his army too thin, his top general, Field Marshal Freidrich Von Paulus, was a Communist! This would surface in the recently declassified OACSI files.

In 1942, Field Marshal Von Paulus and Army Group 6 were sent on a mission impossible. Accompanying him were General Ewald Von Kleist and Field Marshal Sigmund Wilhelm List, commanding Army Group I. Overconfident, hoping to capture the oil fields of the Caucasus, Grozny, Maikop, and Baku, Hitler separated Kleist and List from Army Group 6, sending them southward. Kleist and List were expected to proceed to Iran, cutting off British petrol supplies. These unrealistic plans fell short. Millions of Russian troops were amassing around Stalingrad. Even more lay hidden in the Caucasus mountain passes. It was a trap. Von Paulus needed Kleist with his tank division at Stalingrad. By the winter of 1942, the Nazis and Russians were engaged in hand to hand combat, house to house, at Stalingrad. Victory was gained or lost, one block at a time. The Luftwaffe could only drop in enough supplies in the dead of the Russian winter to fend off starvation.(7)

Stalin had millions of troops in reserve, but deliberately dribbled them in to inflict the greatest losses upon his own army. William Shire's "Rise and Fall of the Third Reich" cites the Nazis entering Stalingrad with 285,000 troops and 20,000 extra Rumanians. After Von Paulus' surrender, 91,000 troops were left. Of the captured POWs marched off to Siberian prison camps, 5,000 returned to their homeland, Germany. Many had died of typhus. (8) As future intelligence reports will reveal, the returning German POW medics reported armies of rats enveloping Soviet towns. Field Marshal Von Paulus lived on in luxury, heading the "Free German Movement," the German Communist Party.

A young reporter for the 'New York Herald Tribune,' Walter Kerr, naively ventured into Russia, intending to bolster the Allies' morale with his journalism. Baffled by what he discovered, he published "The Russian Army" in 1944. Horrible typhus epidemics were sweeping the land, Stalin and his Generals refused British and American help, protecting Russian sovereignty by keeping foreigners out. Older and wiser, Walter Kerr went back to Russia in the 1970s, under the Brezhnev regime for his second book "The Secret of Stalingrad." This is indeed, one weird little book. Brezhnev granted Kerr the first opportunity since the end of WW II to view Soviet classified battle plans of Stalingrad, maps the Russian generals had never seen—the military so compartmentalized, each general only knew the position of his own unit. Kerr came to a startling conclusion. Stalin had millions of troops available in the wings to defeat Von Paulus quickly and swiftly, but chose not to do so, drawing the battle out piecemeal, month by month, deliberately feeding one unit at a time into Hitler's war machine. Stalin's own troops constituted the "enemy" as much as Hitler's. (9)

Much attention has been focused on the battle of Stalingrad, but next to nothing on General Ewald Von Kleist in the Caucasus. Hitler's lust for oil was noted in Albert Seaton's "The Russo-German War," one of the better attempts to record the Nazi penetration eastwards. He writes "Directive Number 41, which the 'Fuhrer' himself had drafted, was an untidy disarray of disconnected thoughts... [its] main aim of the operations was seizing the Caucasus oil fields and the passes through the mountain range, which opened Turkey and Iran." Post war explorations in the Upper Volga discovered even richer oil fields. (10) The Germans were meticulous record keepers, but most of the Directive Number 41 war diaries were destroyed. By whom, and why? General Adolf Heusinger, headed the OKH (Operations) on the Eastern Front and also oversaw I. G. Farben's poison gas facility at Dyhernfurth. How could Heusinger explain to Hitler, Beria had I. G. Farben's TABUN and was operating in the Caucasus? Heusinger certainly had motive. The US Army compiled a 3 volume series on WW II; noting the void in records for the Caucasus:

"MOSCOW TO STALINGRAD: DECISION IN THE EAST" Army Historical Series, by Karl F. Ziemke and Hagna E. Bauer, Center of Military History, US Army, Washington, DC 1987

Page 520: "The OKH was the central staff for the conduct of the war against the Soviet Union, and after September 1942 the Eastern Front was its exclusive and sole responsibility. The OKH records that have survived, though substantial in bulk, are fragmentary..."

Page 521: "In accordance with German practice, the army group and other field commands each kept an Ia ("operations") war diary in which were recorded the incoming and outgoing orders, summaries of reports and conferences... Only the December 1941 segment of the Ia war diary and scattered 'Anlagen' survive from Army Group Center, and from Army Group South (B), only a very few 'Anlagen.'"

What happened to Kleist in the Caucasus? Kleist was interviewed by British historian, Liddell Hart in 1946 as a POW. Hart was a biographer and personal friend of T. E. Lawrence, both well schooled in military strategy. Kleist was first captured by the Americans, interrogated by G-2 and handed over to the Brits for further interrogation. Next, Kleist was extradited to the Yugoslavs, wanted for war crimes. In turn, they forwarded him to the Russians to face prosecution at Nuremberg. He never arrived.

What did Liddell Hart pry out of Kleist in "The German Generals Talk," a first hand account of Hitler's quest for the Baku? (11) Kleist and List separated from Von Paulus' assault on Stalingrad, August 9th, 1942. First marching on Maikop, his 17th Army center and left columns fanned out southwards to the foothills of the Caucasus Mountains. Within six weeks, Kleist had captured the most westerly of the oil fields, then ran out of fuel! Kleist insisted this was not the ultimate reason for his failure, for his troops were being drawn away "bit by bit to help the attack at Stalingrad." The Red Army sent 800 bombers southward, stopping Kleist's advance on Grozny and the Baku, setting the Caucasus ablaze. Further follies weakened Kleist. Field Marshal List separated and ventured eastward along the coast of the Black Sea, intending to meet up with Kleist in Turkey. Kleist ran into far more serious trouble.

To escape Soviet bombers, Kleist fled into the "densely wooded" terrain of the Caucasus Mountains. Russian reserves brought in from the Southern Caucasus and Siberia awaited Kleist in ambush. Crossing the turbulent Terek River, Kleist headed for the mountain passes near the base of Mount Elbrus, the highest peak in the range. Unable to break through, they passed Mozdok and Nalchik, converging his troops at Ordzhonikidze and Prokhladnaya. Kleist described his maneuvers to Hart by tracing them over a map as "a very elegant battle." "Weather held him up, and after a short interval the Russians counter attacked... suffering a sudden collapse, a stalemate set in." What are these euphemisms "elegant battle," and "weather" inducing "a sudden collapse"? It will all come to light. Supply lines cut, out of fuel, and unscathed, Kleist retreated westward to Rostov on the Crimea. Biographer Hart made an odd little quip, comparing Kleist's lack of fuel, referring to "petro lorries" "brought forward on camels - an ironical revival of the traditional ship of the desert." The Soviets would later rename one of our lend-lease oil tankers after this exact location, the SS ELBRUS, a place of great military significance, and stack it full of camel hairs, wool and furs, destined for New York. Coincidently, new unknown epidemics would soon be spawned across America's East Coast. The CIA will neither "confirm nor deny" they hold files on Liddell Hart.

The US Army paints a more detailed account of Kleist and List. Just before the battle of Ordzhonikidze, the Nazi Mountain Corp XXXXIX and Italian climbers scaled Mount Elbrus, the highest peak in the Caucasus range, planting the Reich's flag with its spider swastika atop, on August 21, 1942. This stupendous event occurred only days after the Fascist mountaineers battled Soviet troops at Klukhorskiy Pass. The Army historians forecasted, "If the mountain troops reached the coast near Sukhumi, they would undermine the entire Soviet defense north to Novorossiysk." (12) This was an understatement. Sukhumi was a BW and CW plant, engaged in gas toxicology research. What followed next is vague, but knowing Beria had TABUN, we can fit the pieces together.

The US Army historians continued, citing the Soviets were "shocked" at the advance of Kleist's panzers, more afraid of an internal revolt than the advancing Nazis. At this point, the Moslems considered Hitler their savior, oblivious of the fact that I. G. Farben had armed Beria, their executioner. Beria entered the scene from the south with 4,000 Russo-Turkish troops, taking command of the mountain defenses, suppressing all local opposition "thoroughly and ruthlessly." General Kleist picked up a few Moslem troops made out of POWs under the command of General Der Flieger Helmut Felmy, prompting Beria's panic. The additional handful of Rumanian troops that had accompanied Kleist into the Caucasus, closed river crossings to the south and east. Soon, Kleist's panzers would become completely surrounded by 7,000 troops as the Russians advanced from both north and south. Caught in a vice, Kleist's "very elegant battle" began November 2nd 1942 when, according to US Army historians: "Panzer Division took Gizel, five miles west of Ordzhonikidze", and by November 9th, "the Nalchik operation ended when 13th Panzer Division broke out of Gizel to the west. By then, as in the Taupse area, weather was bring both sides to a stop." (13)

Bad weather again, possibly "dense fog"? Kleist beat it back to Rostov, virtually unscathed, the only German General to be promoted to Field Marshal by Hitler for a retreat. What happened? A clue lies tucked away in our National Archives OSS Research and Analysis collection. Dr. Kerschbaum, an old British CW annalist, filed a report. This information was forwarded through British intelligence's Russian division, headed by Kim Philby, one of the 20th Century's most infamous Communist moles, the truth slightly twisted:

"GERMAN USE OF POISONOUS FOG" OSS Report 110, R&A 698, 1/28/43

"Numerous reports, some of them highly reliable, have reached us concerning the use of a poisonous 'smoke bomb' by the Germans... They are used only as a last resort on positions that must be taken, which are occupied immediately. They are shot from a distance of three kilometers or less. They are presumably shot in high concentration from mortar or projectors. In one report the shell was said to be in the shape of a torpedo 40 centimeters long; caliber 10 centimeters. They are most useful in wooded regions. They give out great amounts of smoke. The smoke lifts quickly. They are highly toxic so that all people in the area are killed instantly. The effects are not persistent, since no anti-gas precautions are taken while the enemy occupy the area attacked."

Kerschbaum continued his analysis of this 'smoke bomb' guessing it might be some kind of a Clark II French invention from the First World War. He cited descriptions from Augustin M. Prentiss' "Chemicals in War," (McGraw-Hill, New York 1937). It was worth looking up this reference, since the Clark I and Clark II weapons volatility concentrations as "irritants" were a thousand times weaker than the lethal dose necessary to kill a human. (14) Things didn't add up. Had the Nazis deployed gas warfare during WW II, both Churchill and Roosevelt promised to respond in kind. This attack would have been plastered over the front pages of the "New York Times." Historically, nothing of the kind took place.

How powerful was Kerschbaum's gas, where were the forest it was deployed in, and whose gas was it anyways? The report was located by accident while researching Russian shipping files in the National Archives, and its date, January 28, 1943 prompted the author to seek a WW II battle of unknown consequence, far removed from the front lines of Europe. Once again, the British and Americans could not risk exposing their ally for committing atrocities against their own troops, allowing Kleist and List to retreat westward to Rostov on the Crimea. Neither the Germans nor the Russians ratted upon each other for the debacle at Ordzhonikidze. The Hirsch Report offers an explanation; there was a gentlemen's agreement on not reporting 'accidents,' only 'premeditated' attacks were considered offensive. (15) Gorbachev's Memorium should start digging at Ordzhonikidze.

Beria was not alone in the Caucasus fighting List and Kleist. Leonid Brezhnev was cited in "The Battle for the Caucasus" by a Soviet historian, Andrei Grechko, as having served in the 18th Army as a political officer. Army Group 18 was primarily made up of natives of the Central Caucasus. (16) Here, a similar battle at Taupse took place, a few miles east of Suchomi, the Black Sea resort town and BW/CW toxicology test center for the NKVD. Newly declassified OACSI files on Suchomi deserve full attention in the upcoming chapters. Grechko's work was relied upon by both the US Army Historical Series and Reporter Walter Kerr in "The Secret of Stalingrad" for the defense of Taupse. Grechko was brought in as a reserve general for the Russian 18th Army Group at Taupse to block Field Marshal List's advance. Presumably, witnessing the full calamity, his historical account was somewhat 'edited'? Once again, "bad weather" set in, a stalemate incurred, the Russian troops retreated into the mountains, "lost in the fog"? By mid October, 1942, List also beat it back to Rostov, another honorable retreat, the enemy mysteriously defeated without having fired a shot. Brezhnev, "several months later was on a trawler that hit a mine in the Black Sea... hurled overboard and later rescued unconscious from the water," Walter Kerr citing Russian Historian Grechko. (17) That's a fine alibi for being gassed by Beria's NKVD! Leonid Brezhnev later became Secretary General of the Communist Party, ousting Nikita Khruschev after the assassination of President Kennedy.

It was Brezhnev who ordered the occupation of Afghanistan in the late 1970s. One would think the inhabitants of the Central Asian Republics today would rejoice in the downfall of Communism and work diligently to build their new democracy. The Chetnya rebels and Osama Bin Laden's operations smack of Communist subterfuge. Since CIA director Bill Casey planted Bin Laden inside the Mujahadeen, like a bad seed, this poor little oil tycoon suffering the embarrassment of riches, has turned to the Red Chinese for support. Weigh this against the possibility that Casey too, was a Soviet mole, earlier assigned to the OPC under the Dulles gang. Casey's untimely death in Iran Contra will be covered later.

The National Archives housed a collection of "Captured German Documents" including "Operation Nalchik" and the battle of Ordzhoni-kidze for November 9th 1942. Brief mention is made of OKH commander Adolf Heusinger's awareness of the arrival of 4,000 Russo-Turkish troops under Beria's command. (18) The US Army Intelligence and Security Command insisted its files on Heusinger in the Caucasus must remain classified. The author FOIAed the FBI for the Heusinger files 2/24/90. They responded:

ADOLF HEUSINGER FOIA request #331,071, 5/24/90
"Dear Ms. Verdon: We have located documents which may pertain to your request and we will assign them for processing soon... Sincerely Emil P. Marchello, Chief Freedom of Information -Privacy Acts Section"
    [They did not arrive]
FBI letter to author September 1991: "Dear Ms. Verdon: Reference is made to our letter to you dated January 9, 1991. We are still unable to locate the file pertaining to Mr. Heusinger. Although our efforts to locate this file for processing are continuing, these efforts have been unsuccessful for the last several months. According if and when the responsive file is

located, we will so advise you. Sincerely Yours, J. Kevin O'Brien, Chief FOIA/Section."

Was this hocus pocus, or bungling bureaucrats? Heusinger was not prosecuted at Nuremberg, surely there was no incriminating evidence against the OKH on the Eastern Front? Instead, President Eisenhower nominated him to head NATO in 1960. The Russians made a big stink at the UN, protesting their own man for heading the new "Fourth Reich." These files were eventually forwarded to the author by the FBI. But were they the originals? (19) Keep Heusinger, I. G. Farben's mentor and protector, in mind as our history on Lyme progresses.

What became of Field Marshal Ewald Von Kleist? Historical encyclopedias cite Kleist being captured by the British Army in 1945, extradited to the Yugoslavs for war crimes and sentenced to 15 years in prison, and then transferred to the Soviets, dying in prison November 5, 1954. (20) Ft. Meade's Intelligence & Security Command have two separate holdings, offering a more curious biography:

"EWALD VON KLEIST: Field Marshal" FOIA 11/19/89, case 1937F-89
Page 13: "'Arrest Report' Nuremberg, Germany, 31st May 1946, US I.N.F. DIV."
"Reason for arrest: War Crimes...Subject has been cleared through all interested sections of G-2 Division, and this Headquarters has no further interest nor objections to extradition, For the Chief, CIC.... Headquarters Counter Intelligence Corps, US forces European Theater (Main)"

"Von KLEIST, Ewald, Field Marshal" 27, Oct. 1954 leader Army Group A, later S. Ukraine. APO 757, US Army, 10 July 1946
Page 3: "British give Von Kleist to Yugoslavs for Trial"
Page 6: "21 October 54 Von Kleist, Ewald, Field Marshal - Ref: D-377654, ltr G-2, dtd 18 June 54, file GID 64 4692, Subject: German Officers in USSR, Microfilm was illegible unbearable read os-Klekner, WB Form 195, 30 Mar 54."
Page 15: "Kress, Von Maj. Gen. Subject is identified as a member of the PAULUS Group, now said to be cooperating in the training of the Soviet Army. Ref. D. 137892, National Komite Freie Deutschland, Memo 20 Oct. 1947. Happiness/2. Reg. VIXX."

Future files will further expose Von Paulus' subversion running the German Communist Party while detained in the USSR. Was General

Ewald Von Kleist in the PAULUS Group too? Who was Kress? With Kleist, Paulus, List and Heusinger covering for I. G. Farben, it is no wonder Germany lost the war. Soon after the author received these files, the Berlin Wall came down.

As the handful of German survivors straggled back to their homeland, bizarre reports began to surface on conditions inside of the Soviet Union. The full extent of Beria's purges using biological warfare began to unfold. Keep in mind, that typhus epidemics would be followed by relapsing fever epidemics, louse and tick borne:

"MOSCOW AREA RYASAN AREA" OACSI file 692771, National Archives, MRB, record group 319, Foreign Service of the USA, Scientific Intelligence Report (SIR 45/4), Dept Secret Instruction No. 27, 1/13/50.

'Medical Information Concerning Moscow'

Page 3: "Typhus occurred endemically in Moscow from 7/1948 to 12/1949. during the winter of 1947/48 there was a widespread typhus epidemic in the Ryazan Oblast. A severe epidemic of bacillary disentery (type Flexner) occurred in Ryazan in 7/46 - 8/46. This disease has an extremely high mortality rate.

Page 4: Plague was absent in the Moscow area, but it was said to still be present in Middle Asia and Uzbek SSR."

Page 5: "Immense numbers of the anopheles mosquito were found in the Volga River swamp area May -August. No prophylactic measures were noted.

Page 12: Typhus... in Ryazan... no control system known of..."

"USSR, CITIES & TOWNS, HEALTH & SANITATION" OACSI file MIS 911514, National Archives MRB record group 319, Intelligence Division Office of Naval Operations, From: Assistant Naval Attaché at Kuibyshev, USSR, 1/21/43.

Page 3: "Encephalitis occurs sporadically throughout the USSR. this type is tick borne... Many types of rodents act as reservoirs for the disease."

The Naval report continues: "Typhus epidemics were rampant, Murmansk was suffering starvation. Tick borne spotted fever swept Poland, Latvia, and Estonia." More appeared in South West Germany. "Eastern front reinforcements are plane-carried to avoid passing through these areas, about 1000 planes being used for this."

"STALINGRAD" OACSI file 685310, noted malaria, tuberculosis, typhoid fever, dysentery, Bangs disease (brucellosis), malaria, and influenza were flourishing epidemics. Accordingly, "During the war practically 100% of the population was infested with lice, now improving with housing conditions... Rats, mice and squirrels are present in large numbers..." The reports poured in, one on the Ukraine was extremely dismal, filed by the Military Intelligence Service on the Eastern Front, July 20th, 1942:

"PUBLIC HEALTH & SANITARY CONDITIONS IN THE UKRAINE" OACSI file 911513, National Archives MRB record group 319

"Bovine tuberculosis and Bang's disease are frequent in cattle, and Malta Fever... are not uncommon in sheep and goats. Dairy products are not protected by pasteurization or bacteriological control measures... There are few facilities for their inspection of meats and proper storage of perishables. The fungus ergot not infrequently contaminates grain crops.... Ticks capable of transmitting fievre boutonneuse (tick typhus) are found in the western part of this area... Among the native people, tuberculosis, trachoma, leprosy, deficiency disease and ergotism are not uncommon. Certain animal borne diseases are epidemic in this area. Undulant fever... anthrax, rabies, and tetanus, tularemia... Recently the tick, Ixodes persulcatus, the carrier of the causative organisms of spring summer encephalitis, has been found in this regions..."

POW Dr. Gunther Pfeifer's shrewd observations were forwarded to the High Commissioner of Germany, hundreds of pages of similar testimony would follow:

"MEDICAL INTERROGATION REPORT ON CITY OF ASBEST" OACSI file 689166, record group 319, Foreign Service of the US Government SIR 28/1 from HICOG, Frankfurt 7/19/50.

Page 5: "Vector of diseases" "There are many flies in the area. Mosquitoes are widespread and include the anopheles... Lice are common. Rats are present in tremendous numbers... Among the PWs, which he believes was cholera, although no bacteriological diagnosis was made. The history of the disease picture were highly suggestive."

Page 9: "The public health activity in Asbest is either ineffectual or disinterested."

Not only was the Soviet health authorities "disinterested," they were racially biased, postulating that some humans were capable of "self healing," initiating a treatment by neglect approach, a new game of Social

Darwinism, survival of the fittest.

"MEDICAL GROUP DISCUSSES PROBLEMS OF BRUCELLO-SIS CONTROL" OACSI file 5755157, National Archives MRB record group 319

"Source: "Meditsinskiy Rabotnik," No. 24, 1949 by Prof V. Troits-ki

Page 1: "Recently the Department of Hygiene, Microbiology, and Epidemiology, Academy of Medical Sciences USSR, convened in special session at Alma-Ata to discuss various aspects of brucellosis and methods for its control... well attended by scientific workers of Kazakh SSR... and middle Asiatic cities."

Page 2: "Pavlovskii contends that many domestic as well as wild animals are responsible for the spread of brucellosis in nature.. goats and sheep are the chief... transmitting agents... Immunity from brucellosis can now be studied from a new viewpoint because of knowledge concerning the dynamics of infection and common characteristics of the self-healing of the man or beast afflicted with brucellosis... the possibilities of self-healing and postinfection immunization, there is also the problem of live vaccine to prevent infection from the disease."

The report continued on with noting a vaccine had been created through experimentation. "Dr. M. Kh. Farizova reported on the clinical aspects of nerve disorders brought about by brucellosis infection... N. D. Beklemishev... described the significance of allergy in the treatment of brucelloisi." God only knows how many political prisoners died in the Gulag from these experiments. One must learn to read between the lines like an old zek, as Alexander Solzehnitzyn might have done. If one had a strong immunological system and a full plate, one recuperated. Were the Communists deliberately brainwashing their nomadic populations into submission through disease and deprivation, offering "redistribution of the wealth" as the only antidote? Communism, itself, is the disease.

What was the origin of these these tick and louse borne epidemics? The Suchomi BW/CW toxicology test site was just a few miles from Taupse, where Leonid Brezhnev nearly met his fate under Beria's "retreat blocking services." Eventually, the whole Kaiser Wilhelm Institute for Brain Research, experts in multiple sclerosis and Lyme disease spirochetes, would flee to Suchomi. The OACSI file below is cataloged under the National Archives 'BID' designation of 'biological warfare':

"SUKHUMI BIOLOGICAL RESEARCH STATION" OACSI file

MIS 209351, Report #2365, 9 Oct. 1945 Military Intelligence Division, W.D.G.S. Military Attaché Report Russia, National Archives MRB

Page 2: "An extensive program of research is being conducted at the Monkey Nursery in Sukhumi on the coast of the Black Sea, by the Sukhumi Biological Station of the Academy of Medical Science. G. A. Levitina is the director of the station. Nursery has 180 animals. They are being used for research on diseases affecting human beings and research in acclimatization. The station has laboratories in biology, physiology, experiment of cancer and epidemiology. The station's activities will be expanded next year. 100 to 150 new animals including chimpanzees will be acquired."

Dr. G. A. Levintina would move to Beketovka, a larger BW/CW research site, at the southern end of Stalingrad. He would be eventually replaced by I. G. Farben's doctor Berhnard Von Bock from Dyhernfurth to run Beketovka in 1948. This episode in Russia's CW history will be covered more fully in the upcoming chapter, re. OACSI file "Chemical Warfare Activities of Foreign Countries, Project 4693." It is significant to note here that Field Marshal Von Paulus never attacked Beketovka, instead concentrating his forces on the northern sector of Stalingrad where the tank factories were situated. Just eight miles to south of Stalingrad, completely neglected, Beketovka was making TABUN. Did OKH General Heusinger order Von Paulus, "hands off"? Had Von Paulus captured Beketovka with its poison gases, it could have defeated the Red Army and Beria's NKVD troops simultaneously. Every effort was made to protect I. G. Farben's secret. Surely, the loyalty of Von Paulus' commander, Adolf Heusinger, head of Operations on the Eastern Front, comes into question.

The living conditions inside Russia were simply awful. Let's look at the plight of a naive American mother and her brucellosis infected baby, wife to a Foreign Service officer stationed in Moscow. She finally made it to the American Embassy filing a long, rambling complaint over how her baby faired in the hands of Soviet physicians, her report classified for nearly half a century:

"REPORT ON TREATMENT RECEIVED IN SOVIET HOSPITAL" OACSI file MIS 358560, National Archives MRB, record group 319, American Embassy Moscow 3/21/47

"It was impossible to take notes during the hospitalization, since all objects which could not be fumigated had to be left at the hospital for burning... The hospital in which the baby was placed is considered by Russians to be the best hospital in the Soviet Union..."

Page 11: "As I remember the label on the bottle, this medicine was put up by Merck and was a combination of penicillin and sodium... The baby's lack of appetite for food and liquids was our chief problem... but it still refused fresh milk. I finally gave him a mixture of half fresh and half powdered skim milk and gradually reduced the proportion of the latter. The doctor was triumphant when she saw him relishing the "Good Russian Milk."

Was the Merck Pharmaceutical Company supplying Soviet hospitals with penicillin? State Department files contradict this notion. Why should this need classification? Russia was our ally. Had our ally attacked America? Keep this in mind as our story progresses. George Merck, Chief of the War Department's BW defense program, was a true patriot. Amtorg made numerous approaches to American firms to build penicillin factories inside Russia after the war, Merck politely declining, but close associate Selman Waksman, discoverer of streptomycin, made numerous trips.

The clincher, the most detailed and conclusive evidence of Stalin's biological warfare against his own people, came from a Czechoslovakian defector, a chemist named Moudry. He had invented a new disinfectant from colloidal silver, far exceeding the efficiency of chlorine, to be used for pasteurization of milk against brucellosis, food preservation, and reservoirs, for protection against typhoid, cholera and dysentery. The Red Army had different designs for Moudry's disinfectant, demanding he manufacture a dried, more compact, portable version of the solution, "movidyn," to protect their own troops in combat. World War II had come to an end. Who was the "enemy"? Moudry figured it out. Moudry fled to the West and filed a report, but no formulas were offered. Instead, he cited a strange story, the Red Army had offered the formula to Western intelligence, discussing it's composition, with General Schneider. "Schneider," according to Army intelligence officer, John Loftus, was the American code name for General Gehlen, Abwehr (intelligence) chief during WW II, who was placed in American service after the armistice. The Nazis hadn't made the BW attacks against Russia, they didn't have Movidyn. Marching across the Eastern Front, the Nazis encountered polluted wells:

"REPORT ON MOUVIDYN" OACSI file MIS 549086, Lt. Col. Williamson/3596/ra, to: CSGID, ATTN: ID-4 Section C National Archives MRB

Page 13: "During World War II, the German Wehrmacht in Ukraine and Russia were dealing with almost catastrophically infection of wells, and applied on a large scale, KATADYN, with satisfactory results. After WW II Katadyn produced in Germany became unobtainable in Czechoslovakia.

The chemical company MOUDRY a spol, was summoned by the Ministry of Industry at the urgent request of Ministry of Public Health to develop the manufacture of a similar product, badly needed at the time. By extensive laboratory research based on a different approach, Mr. Moudry developed a new product called MOUVIDYN. The efficiency of this product was at least 3,000 times greater than that of Katadyn."

Page 14: "At this time General Schneider of the USA Forces investigated and discussed the eventual possibilities with Mr. Ing. VACLAVICK of the use of Movidyn and the manufacture of this product in the USA. The Institute of Public Health suggested a large scale preventative campaign for disinfection of all wells in typical areas endangered almost every year by typhoid... In April 1947, Mr. Adenek Moudry was appointed by the Ministry of Public Health in charge of these operations.. sanitary disinfection achieved 99%.. Meanwhile, the Ministry of Public Health.. informed the Ministry of National Defense about the outstanding properties of MOUVIDYN. The Military Bacteriological Research Institute... soon realized that MOUVIDYN is a very important weapon in dealing with bacteriological warfare... the MOVA WORKS was set under permanent confidential personal control by Major Ing. F. of the Ministry of Defense, who has figured since as a civilian..."

The military began experimenting with the effectiveness of Movidyn, deliberately infecting "102 wells in 15 communities." By September 1947, a "joint secret meeting of civilian and military representatives of the Ministry of National Defense, Ministry of Public Health, the Soviet Army and Bulgarian Biological Research Institute... revealed that during this unique campaign a solution of Movidyn was applied 79,000 times for 6 successive treatments of approximately 13,170 wells..." The "resistance" had used biological warfare against the invading Germans, explaining the infected wells in Russia. The Red Army took Movidyn away from the public health authorities and classified it as TOP SECRET, leaving the populace defenseless. Moudry refused to concoct a "powder" form of Movidyn to further facilitate the Red Army, and fled Czechoslovakia.

The American Embassy in Moscow was planning construction, and requested information on sanitary conditions of local water supplies. The records were out of reach. The US Foreign Service filed a complaint to the Military Intelligence Division of the War Department, February 4th, 1947, explaining their dilemma constructing a new building:

"SANITARY CONDITIONS IN THE USSR" OACSI file MIS 356679, Foreign Service of the USA, National Archives MRB record group 319

"To: Director of Intelligence War Department General Staff, The Pentagon

Extensive search has failed to disclose the information desired concerning the unsanitary water supply of certain cities of the USSR and sanitary requirements for the construction of new buildings, etc... The chief consultant of the reference department of the Lenin Library stated that the memoranda being sought were probably intra-ministry publications which are not available to the library..."

In the mean time, captured Field Marshal Von Paulus was doing everything possible to convert his fellow German POWs to Communism; after all, the Communists had achieved everything the Nazis dreamed of. Just how many Nazi doctors and technicians remained in Russia after the war as "research assistants"? Thousands. Historians wish to portray these scientists as "kidnapped" and "enslaved." The truth is, most beat it to the other side on their own volition, fearing prosecution from their own country, particularly the personnel from I. G. Farben and the Kaiser Wilhelm Institute for Brain Research. In an attempt to incite a Communist revolution amongst their own German citizens, they defamed a once great and humane nation for generations to come. It is difficult to discern whether Frankenstein originated in Bavaria or Beketovka.

CHAPTER 5 NOTES

(1) "STALIN'S SECRET WAR" Nikolai Tolstoy, Holt Rinehart & Winston, NY 1979

Pages 104 & 16: General Wegan's' troops in Beirut

Pages 105 & 107: Stalin's paranoia, exaggerated intelligence reports

Pages 174-175: Polish Embassy & Prometheus, NKVD raids Polish homes

(2) IBID. Page 177: Katyn

"SOVIET BW & CW PREPARATIONS & CAPABILITIES" Walter Hirsch

Page 102: "1935 - create a branch for specially dangerous work - transfer it to the island of Gordomiya in the Seliger Lake - Ostashkov... Velikonovski Institute No. V/2-1094..."

Page 82: GORDOMIYA BW research

(3) "KATYN: THE UNTOLD STORY OF STALIN'S POLISH MASSACRE" Allen Paul, Charles Scribner's & Sons, NY 1991; Page 116: Poles executed by Beria NKVD

(4) IBID. Page 313: Testimony withheld from Allen Paul.
National Archives Center for Legislative Archives, Robert Coren letter to RV 12/6/91, Katyn testimony classified 50 years, House rule 36, records of executive session proceedings 'unavailable for public inspection'

(5) IBID. Page 308: Van Vliet "whisked to Leipzig..."

(6) "THE KATYN FOREST MASSACRE FINAL REPORT OF THE SELECT COMMITTEE TO CONDUCT AN INVESTIGA-TION AND STUDY OF THE FACTS, EVIDENCE, AND CIRCUM-STANCES OF THE KATYN FOREST MASSACRE": House Resolution 390 & 539, 12/22/52, totaling over 7,000 pages.
Page 30: "Some Victims Buried Alive"; Pages 692-693: Rowinsky testimony.
Pages 21: "Berlin broadcasts 4/13/43, secret mass executions of the Bolsheviks"; Page 29: "American Army Officers Visit Katyn" (Part 1 hearings: Van Vliet testimony)

(7) "STALIN, TRIUMPH & TRAGEDY" Dmitri Volkogonov, Grove Weidenfeld, NY 1991, Page 334

(8) "THE RISE AND FALL OF THE THIRD REICH" William Shire, Simon & Schuster, NY 1960, Page 932

(9) "THE RUSSIAN ARMY: ITS MEN, ITS LEADERS AND ITS BATTLES" Walter Kerr, Alfred A. Knopf, NY 1944; Pages 232-233: Spring 1943, Russia denies typhus. "SECRET OF STALINGRAD" Walter Kerr, Doubleday, Garden City, NY 1978

(10) "THE RUSSO-GERMAN WAR" Albert Seaton, Barker Publishing, London 1971
Pages 266-267: Hitler Directive 41, oil in upper Volga and Kama, E. of Caspian.

(11) "THE GERMAN GENERALS TALK" Liddell Hart, Quill, NY 1979. Page 201 Kleist's troops siphoned off to Stalingrad, Page 203, Ordzhnikidze, petrol on camels

(12) "MOSCOW TO STALINGRAD: DECISION IN THE EAST" Army Historical Series, Karl F. Ziemke, Hagna E. Bauer, Center of Military History, US Army, Washington, DC 1987; Pages 370-373: on Suchomi - Taupse

(13) IBID. Pages 370-373, Taupse, List; Pages 453-454: Operation Felmy, Nalchik

(14) "CHEMICALS IN WAR: a Treatise on Chemical Warfare" Augustin M. Prentiss, CWS, US Army, McGraw Hill Book Co., Inc NY & London, 1937
Pages 204, 208, 165, chart 363.

(15) "SOVIET BW & CW PREPARATIONS & CAPABILITIES" Walter Hirsch, Nalbandian translation, US Army Historical Institute, Carlisle Barracks, PA
Page 5: Nazi/Soviet "gas accidents"

(16) "ICEBREAKER" Viktor Suvorov, Hamish Hamilton, London 1990
Page 62: NKVD retreat blocking services. Pages 153 & 157, makeup of 18th Army

(17) "SECRET OF STALINGRAD" Walter Kerr, Doubleday, Garden City, NY 1978
Page 100: Beria in Caucasus, police forces in Mozdok, Ordzhonikidze, Baku.
Page 190: Taupse, Brezhnev as political advisor to 18th Army in Caucasus, "hurled overboard" citing Grechko, p 255)

(18) Captured German Document files at National Archives MRB, "O.Kdo. H.GR. A, Zustands-u. Erfahrungs-Berichte uber eingesetzte Turk-Btle." "Detailed studies and reports from the winter of 1942/43. Organization and training of such units. September 1942-April 1943." National Archives Guide Microcopy T311, item No. 751266/5: Roll 152, frame 7199906 Ia O.Ido. H.Gr. A, Kriegstagebuch, band 1, Teil 5, Nov. 1-30, 1942 Page 66: (November 9, 1942) Der 1, Gen. St. Offz. Unermittelt um 11,40 Uhr der Op. Abt. (Gen, Major Heusinger) den Antreg der 1, pz. Armes suf baldige Entscheidung tiber die in der Macht voralegte Absicht betr. Die Fortfuhrung de Operationan bei der 1, Pz Armes . Gen Major Heusinger erwidert, dieselbe sell noch heute dem Fuhrer vorge-

tragen werden. (Wegen schlechter Verstundigung muste das Gespruch unvollemdet abgebrochen werden)... die gereits befohlene Abgave von 4,000 Turk-Gefangenon einstweilen suzsusstzen."

(19) ADOLF HEUSINGER FBI files #162-107579-1 'Embassy of the Union of Soviet Socialist Republics' Press Department: 1706 18th Street, N. W. Washington, 9 DC No. 231, 12/15/61. Page 5: "Communique by State Extraordinary Commission for Investigation and Establishment of Atrocities Perpetrated by German Fascist Invaders"

(20) "SIMON & SCHUSTER ENCYCLOPEDIA OF WW II" Simon & Schuster, NY 1978, "KLEIST, Paul Ludwig Ewald Von (1881-1954)"

CHAPTER 6

DOW, DYHERNFURTH & BEKETOVKA

Batman and Alfred the Butler

While Beria gassed Russia's Army to death, leaving his country defenseless, President Roosevelt was sabotaging our strategic industries at home necessary to defeat the Nazis. Senator Harry Truman, grandstanding in the limelight, lead the Congressional investigations into the alkali munitions 'monopoly' in collusion with the enemy, I. G. Farben. Soon, Roosevelt would drop Vice President Wallace, a Communist, and place Truman on his ticket, greatly impressed by the senator's charade. The "Investigation of the National Defense Program" began March 6th, 1944, fingering Dow Chemical Company for price fixing, just like Westvaco. By May 25th, the "New York Times" cited the War Production Board was poised to shut down DOW. Just like Westvaco, Dow was innocent. DOW's magnesium, the new light metal used in the manufacture of aircraft, was credited for winning the war. Willard Henry Dow fought back, addressing Congress personally in his own defense, his testimony precise and eloquent. He detailed I. G. Farben's early attempt to destroy his father's bromine business through cutthroat competition, dumping, and price fixing on the international market, prompting Congress to pass new tariffs. Dow and I. G. Farben had remained arch enemies.

In a dispute with the aluminum giant ALCOA, Dow in 1933 was granted access to some of its shared patents with I.G. Farben which Dow dropped when war broke out. By 1943, Dow had constructed three major magnesium seawater distillation plants, a revolutionary innovative process for obtaining the rare metal, at Ludwinton, Maryville, and Freeport, at a cost of one-half cent per pound for the Defense Department. Dow became the largest magnesium producer by default, producing 91.2% of all US magnesium for the war effort. American air power won the war. Pratt &

Whitney Aircraft cranked out 100 bombers a day on its assembly lines. Willard Henry Dow called Truman's charges "utterly baseless" at New York's US District Court in Foley Square. Towards the close of the war, Dow had won the American Chemist Industry's Medal for War Contributions. (1) Once again, Roosevelt and Truman had tried to facilitate I. G. Farben and its secret ally, the Soviet Union, by destroying its American competitors. As a member of the US Army Chemical Warfare Board, Dow sought to hire legitiamte German Scientists after the war.

Albert Einstein approached President Roosevelt with concerns that the Nazis had the atom bomb. In a race against time, Roosevelt ordered General Leslie Groves to construct the Manhattan Project, its Los Alamos test site placed under command of physicist Julius Robert Oppenheimer. In his youth, Oppenheimer, a product of UC Berkeley, was a left wing dingbat, "probably having joined every Communist Front organization in America," later testifying in Congressional hearings. As he matured, he became increasingly conservative, fully aware of the Nazi-Soviet alliance, later heading the Atomic Energy Commission. Army intelligence officer, Boris Pash, would be assigned to spy on Oppenheimer, impeding the war effort further. To get Pash out of his hair, General Groves created the ALSOS Mission ("alsos" being Greek for olive grove, not particularly discreet) putting Pash in charge of finding the Nazi's A-bomb. Guess what? The Nazis didn't have 'The Bomb,' so ALSOS investigated Nazi BW and CW sites.

Pash was the precursor to Rambo. Oddly, he chose leftwing physicist Samuel Goudsmit from the University of Michigan as lead scientist for ALSOS. Goudsmit had entertained Albert Einstein and physicist Werner Heisenberg at the University of Michigan in the 1930s. By his own admission in "The ALSOS Mission," Goudsmit was nearly left behind, his Communist affiliations interfering with military clearance.

August 16th, 1944, the US Army forwarded a report to the CWS "Possible German Use of Chemical Warfare" concluding "While there is evidence that the Germans are prepared for both offensive and defensive CW, we have no reliable indications that they intend to use chemicals at the present time or in the immediate future." (2) Only after German surrender, did the British zero in on Dyhernfurth, and the ALSOS Mission would follow. The Brits arrived at I.G. Frankfurt/Main after most of the scientists had fled. The stragglers were most uncooperative, only making slight reference to the existence of Dyhernfurth. Otto Ambros, head of the I. G. Farben acetylene and buna industry at Auschwitz, was pulled away by OKH chief, Adolf Heusinger, to head an "unknown assignment" along with Dr. Kranz, Kleinhans, Herr Begel, Gerhard Cramer, Kaup,

Danz, Von Boch, and Tolkmith. (3) They will resurface in Beketovka, south of Stalingrad.

On September 26th, 1945, a few days after the arrival of the British at I.G. Frankfurt/Main, the ALSOS boys filed a report suggesting something was up at Dyhernfurth, again, fingering Ambros' crew. ALSOS estimated Dyhernfurth had already manufactured 15,000 tons of TABUN, but it was nowhere in sight. (4) The British and Americans were getting the run-a-round. Most of the Germans knew nothing of Dyhernfurth. General Blumentritt, interrogated October 24, 1945 regarding the OKW at Raubkammer, (the robbers' lair) insisted gas testing was purely defensive. (5) He knew nothing of Dyhernfurth, General Heusinger's OKH is going to incredible lengths to conceal its existence. According to historian, John Loftus, "The Nuremberg Trials were a farce," most of the ALSOS Mission reports were never presented as evidence.

Dr. Wolfgang Wirth, Hirsch's toxicologist from the 1940 'decontamination missions' was apprehended by the 970th US Army CIC (Counter Intelligence Corps) Region II on July 25th, 1945, charged with being a security suspect. Next he was passed over to Internment Camp Number 9 on July 8th, 1946, only to be interrogated and released! CIC 970th Unit Region II will prove very significant, other witnesses to the Russian mission will turn up here. Make a mental note of this. "To constitute a security threat subject would have had to commit an overt act, offense, or crimes for which he can be tried. He has not, and therefore should be released…" Signed: Richard Lehr, 1st Lt. TC CIC, Screening Team. Worse, Wolfgang Wirth held a second position in the Militarzliche Akademi of Berlin from 1938 through 1945 under biological warfare specialist, Dr. Walter Schreiber. (6) Schreiber's academy in Berlin later moved into Dr. Kliewe's BW facility because of Allied bombing during the war. Soon, Schreiber would flee to Moscow, hiding out in luxury, figuring heavily in the history of Lyme disease.

Back at I. G. Farben office Frankfurt/Main, the gas scientists played a game of cat and mouse with their interrogators. Dr. Walter Flotho was cornered and shaken up. He had written a "little black book" of chemical codes to be used in disguising railroad shipments of chemicals to Dyhernfurth. His interrogators sent the book on to "T-Force Headquarters, Wisebaden on 6 May, 1945 for removal to the UK Base." Other documents in the bag arrived safe and sound, but the I. G. Farben chemical code book was gone. What happened to Flotho's little black book? It's probably at the bottom of the Danube with Van Vliet's report. Other OACSI files on Nazi chemical warfare vanished later, including the interrogation of I. G.'s Tabun expert, Jurgen Von Klenck. (7) These OACSI files were formally accessioned to the National Archives in 1967, four years after the assassination of President Kennedy, dropped down the rabbit hole to vanish into Suitland's underground city. Many are cited as "MISSING" or "DESTROYED." Withdrawal slips are required to be kept in place on a borrowed file for three years for 'secret' and four years for 'top secret' classification. Now, no-one knows who borrowed the files. Had Kennedy seen them? Tuck this under your bonnet.

Where were the 15,000 tons of TABUN, that ALSOS had rumored? Russia raced ahead and captured Dyhernfurth, lock, stock, and glass ampoule, followed by most of its 3,000 technicians and research files. The adjacent plant at Falkenhagen was also dismantled brick by brick and taken to Beketovka. The Russians knew their exact locations. Ike let 'em have it all.

"GERMANY/USSR GASES" Issued by the Intelligence Division Office of Chief of Naval Operations Navy department Serial 414-S-49 at APO 742 NY, NY 10/8/49; OACSI file 615458 record group 319 National Archives, MRB

"The manufacturing plants were at Dyhernfurth/Silesia (South of Breslau) and at Falkenhagen 25 km NE of Frankfurt/Oder). Falkenhagen had large subterranean plants and - according to reliable information - fell into the hands of the Russians quite undamaged and with about 1,000 tons of TABUN. Recent reports (unconfirmed) say that the Russians are at present producing hydrofluoric acid there. This is an important processing agency for the production of atomic bombs.

The most important chemist of I. G. Farben and perhaps of all Germany is Prof. Dr. Reppe, who rejoined the I. G. Farben at Ludwigshafen (French Zone). Since he was badly treated during his interrogation by the Americans, in particular at Oberursel, he is inclined to withhold information.

Dr. Von Klenck, a chemist who is living at Frankfurt/Main, will be able to give some information on persons who took a conspicuous part in the development of TABUN and SARIN.

'Interrogation of Hans Hoyer' reported by Mr. Weldon, Australian Chemical Warfare Military Intelligence division, W.D.G.S. from M.A. London, report #R301-26, Date 19 August 1946"

This is a brief outline of interrogation of Hans Hoyer whose office was concerned with the Dyhernfurth Sarin plant... It is in the opinion of certain personnel that the Russians must have been able to acquire full working details of Tabun and Sarin manufacture since plant, personnel and portable documents were left at Dyhernfurth on evacuation...' "

The Navy had no clue about Ipatieff , I. G. Farben and the NKVD at Tomka a decade earlier, but they began to catch on:

"INFORMATION ON A NEW GROUP OF TOXIC WAR GASES" Army Intelligence Document files, Headquarters European Theater of Operations US Army CWS Intelligence Division Report No. 3709, 28 April 1945, source CIOS; OACSI file MIS 148565, record group 319, National Archives MRB.

Page 2: "Before the area was taken by the Russians the key members of the staff were evacuated to Ludwigshafen. These included Dr. Albert Palm, in charge of the Dyhernfurth plant, Dr. Kleinhaus, Dr. Tolkmith and Herr Vegel, pharmacologist. Dr. Palm had been head of the Alizarin dye department of I. G. Ludwigshafen, which had given him experience in production on a large scale.

The rapid advance of the Russian armies prevented the demolition of the factory before it was evacuated. It was believed that the Allies knew nothing of the existence of the plant; at any rate, it was never bombed by them. In order to destroy the plant after the general area had been occupied by the Russians, the Luftwaffe was sent in to bomb it. Schrader considers the job was completed."

Pay attention to Dr. Henry Tolkmith. We want him. P. S. The Luftwaffe didn't hit Dyhernfurth. What happened to Dr. Walter Reppe after his rough interrogation? He certainly wasn't going to offer his services to the West:

"GERMAN SCIENTISTS EMPLOYED BY THE RUSSIANS AND FRENCH" Office of Naval Intelligence of Washington, DC date 7 February 1949, source: Interrogation of German Paperclip Scientists; OACSI file MIS 533903, National Archives MRB record group 319

"Dr Walter Reppe, Address Unknown." "Dr. REPPE was director of the main laboratory of the I. G. Farben Industrie at LUDWIGSHAFEN. G101, a chemist and physicist... received information in a recent letter from his son that Dr. REPPE was either killed or disappeared at the time of the recent explosion at the I. G. FARBENINDUSTRIE. The letter stated that the explosion was no accident and intimated that REPPE may have taken this opportunity to escape."

TA TA! POOF! Did Reppe bring other Dyhernfurth technicians, Von Bock and Tolkmith to Beketovka? They soon followed. The dates are very important here:

"CHEMICAL WARFARE ACTIVITIES OF FOREIGN COUN-TRIES DURING WORLD WAR II" 4th Quarter, B. USSR" OACSI files Project 4693, 1 February 1949-January 1950; National Archives MRB

"Information relating to the Soviet CW installations at Beketovka continues to come in from PW's who worked in the area. The evidence strongly indicates that the German equipment from Dyhernfurth/Silesia for the plant production of GA (Tabun, capacity approx 1000 MT/mo) and GB (sarin, pilot plant capacity approx. 25 to 50 MT/mo) had been installed in newly constructed buildings on the southeastern edge of the chemical combine area at Beketovka. If the Soviets acquired and have installed the Falkenhagen plant (see paragraph D. Germany) at Beketovka also, they should have an additional capacity of at least 6000 MT per year. Recent reports support earlier PW reports that equipment marked Dyhernfurth arrived at Beketovka and was unloaded at the chemical combine area. These reports also indicate the presence of German Scientists, believed to be Dr. Von Bock, who appears to have some supervisory responsibility for the new installation and construction*. (footnoted: see CW intelligence - First and Third Quarter, 1949)"

'First Quarter' February 1949: "USSR AGENTS"

Page 6: "Recent reports have confirmed the location of Dr. Bernhard Von Bock, outstanding I. G. Farben chemist at Beketovka (E4430-E4840), about 10 km south of Stalingrad. The reports indicate that equipment from the I. G. Farben Synthetic Rubber Plant at Schkopau and the war gas plant at Dyhernfurth had been transferred to Beketovka. It appears possible that the Soviets have located the Dyhernfurth Tabun plant here and possibly are operating it now but no confirmation is available on these points.

A report from (EUCOM, RI-475-48, 29 October 48) indicated that Dr. Von Bock's assistant, Dr. Tolkmit, has gone to the USSR and that he worked on technical details of the Sarin process. As yet no indications have been received as to his whereabouts in the USSR, possibly he has joined Von Bock."

[Tolkmith could have easily taken off with Reppe after the Ludwigshafen explosion? Note the date of the above EUCOM is October 29, 1948.]

'Third Quarter' October 1949, "USSR AGENTS"

"Beketovka continues to be an intelligence target of much interest. Interrogation of returning PW's from the USSR reaffirm the views that production of CW agents is in progress here. It is believed to be one of the principal centers of Soviet work on one (GA) and possible two (GB) of the G agents. More complete reporting on this center should be possible in the near future as indicated from information being received now.

Dr. Tolkmit, former assistant to Dr. Von Bock, and thought to have gone to the USSR last year has been employed by the Dow Chemical Company in the US and is now in the process of giving some valuable information to the Chemical Corps. A primary report from Dr. Tolkmit on his knowledge of the nerve gases is in process of reproduction for dissemination to interested agencies."

Mention is also made regarding the poison gas ampoules brought back from Dyhernfurth being unmarked, allowing for confusion. The Russians remedied the situation by painting red, black and green circles around the canisters to avoid future explosions. As Tolkmith, Von Bock, and Reppe fled to Russia, 800 documented others followed in exile. With the Cold War emerging, Great Britain's super spies, Kim Philby and Donald McLean of MI6 would establish Nazi smuggling ratlines, Operations Dustbin and Paperclip, relieving Russia of further embarrassment from its infamous residents. With these Nazi double agents, American national security was compromised for decades to come. The State Department with Allen Dulles and the re-organized OSS, now the OPC, went gun-ho smuggling "dragon returnees." Congress passed the "100 Persons Act," for "nuclear physics, guided missiles, electronics to include radar, infra-red and heat homing, proximity fuzes, television, chemical and biological warfare, aerodynamics, metallurgy, physical organic chemistry, ordnance, especially torpedoes, and advanced ordnance." (8) The Nazi scientists' dossiers were "sanitized" of any war crimes.

Henry Tolkmith and Bernhard Von Bock came out from the cold. But when? Tolkmith is the real mystery. In the above OACSI file Project 4963 "Chemical Warfare Activities of Foreign Countries", Tolkmith was reported at Beketovka as early as October 29, 1948 in the "EUCOM, RI-475-48" in its 'First Quarter' and by October 1949, at Dow Chemical, cited in the 'Third Quarter.'. Hoping to find out more on Beketovka, the author wrote the US Army Intelligence & Security Command at Fort Meade in 1988. Out of 366 pages, 144 were released, the files later transferred to the National Archives, the rest declassified after Tolkmith's death in 1995. The Army files cite Tolkmith arriving in America on April 16th, 1948 on page 121. How could this be, when he was cited in the "EUCOM, RI-

475-48" report on October 29, 1948 at Beketovka? How could he be in two places at once? There were two different conflicting physical descriptions of Tolkmith in the Army files. They were similar, but not identical. Eventually, the author asked that the thumbnail photos on his identity card be enlarged. Instead, the National Archives forwarded the negatives. Two different head shots appeared, arrogant, sly, almost cocky, making the author's blood curdle. Was this Josef Mengele?

"HENRY TOLKMITH" files, National Archives, MRB

Page 121: "Biographical & Professional Data German and Austrian Scientists and Technicians and their Dependents"

"Date of Arrival in US: April 16, 1948

Description: Age 40, Height 5' 10"; Weight 163 lbs; Eyes gray-brown; Hair dark partly gray, complexion fair; Sex male.

Distinguishing Marks: Scars on left cheek, temple, ear.

Physical Condition: Unobjectionable (good)

Personal Data: Born February 10, 1910; Place Berlin; Citizenship German; Religion Christian; Marital Status married.

Dependents: Valentine Tolkmith, wife, Midland Michigan, age 36; Peter Tolkmith, son, Midland Michigan age 11; Valentine Tolkmith, daughter, Midland Michigan, age 8.

Special Fellows, or research participation: 1933-1935, study in chemical warfare agents at the Gas Institute of the Technical University, Berlin (Prof. Dr. K. A. Hofmann.)"

The files continued, citing Tolkmith's residence at Dyhernfurth from January 1943 till January 1945, and at Gendorf Germany from April 1945 to December 1945, and at Goslar, Germany, January 1946 till March 1948 "self employed," arriving in Midland, Michigan at DOW, April 1948. No mention of work at Beketovka with Von Bock! Were his files sanitized too? His secret war gas patents were turned over to the OKW. His employment with I. G. Farben, Frankfurt began 1937-1940, and move to Dyhernfurth, Anorgana in 1941-1945. He insists he ended his employment in 1945 with the intention to go to the USA. On Page 333 of the Army files, Tolkmith is described as having never joined the Nazi Party, his wife "a Russian Half Jewess... Owing to his dismissal from his position as lecturer at the Berlin Technical Highschool in 1937, Nuremberg laws." It was here that Tolkmith met Valentine. After Tolkmith's arrival in New York, April 16th, 1948, Dow Chemical employee, Dr. L. R. Drake, took him under his wing, reporting to military intelligence every day for the next year. The following pages from Fort Meade's files, now residing at the National Archives, reveal a man of contrasts, see Appendix:

Page 212: 'Civil Finger Print Card' of Henry Tolkmith with two photos, front & side views, physical description typed in underneath: "Name Henry Tolkmith; Height 5' 8"; Build medium; Weight 158 lbs; Complexion sallow; Eyes gray; Hair dark; Scars and marks none; Date of birth 13 February 1912."

What? Back up. One Tolkmith is fair skinned with very prominent scars, the other with 'sallow' complexion and no scars; the first with brown eyes, the other gray eyed; the first with graying hair, the second with dark hair; the first born February 10, 1910, the later born February 13, 1912; the first Tolkmith is 5' 10" and the later two inches shorter? Whose files are we looking at? Are there TWO Tolkmith's? The photos, even though old and spotty, show the scars. We have a few too many discrepancies. Sneaking Tolkmith into America on April 16th, 1948, caused a legal scandal for the military with Truman's passage of the "100 Person's Act." As a poison gas specialist, he may have been a suspect war criminal. To comply with the law, it was arranged for him to leave America and return through Canada in 1950, making his entry 'legal.' Page 69 of his Army files cites him re-entering at Niagara Falls, April 3rd, 1950, German NP Visa #1050. The "monthly reports" filed by Dr. Drake were "no longer necessary." .

What happened to other prominent associates of Tolkmith and Von Bock? Richard Kuhn, creator of SOMAN gas, the third in the G-2 series of TABUN and SARIN, continued on at the Kaiser Wilhelm Institute at Heidelberg after the war. The Americans watched him like a hawk, fearing the Communists would kidnap him. Still an ardent Nazi, he refused all services to the West, concentrating on vitamin research. Soon, the US Army Air Force would establish the Aero-Medical Research Center at KWI Heidelberg, ordering the Luftwaffe doctors to collate their research under one roof, Hubertus Strughold editing out the human experiments. (9) Richard Kuhn's research is of particular interest, for it involved experiments with animal eye tissue. Eye tissue is similar to tissue found inside of the spinal cord, but much easier to access and more abundant for testing toxicities of poisons. Kuhn was well read in his profession, keeping abreast of international research in his field. Upon his capture and interrogation, Kuhn began reciting the vitamin B12 research of an American biochemist, Dr. F. M. Snell. (10) Snell would eventually team up with another Luftwaffe immigrant from the Heidelberg Aero Medical Research Center, Dr. Werner K. Noell, Strughold's old Luftwaffe associate.

Werner K. Noell spent most of his war effort at the Kaiser Wilhelm

Institute for Brain Research, a laboratory of high-tech cannibals, under Lufftwaffe contract. After the war, Noell moved to the University of Buffalo, New York, with his immigration files 'sanitized' on a new six month US Air Force contract. He stayed. By 1962, Noell and Snell compiled and edited a series of lectures given by the American Physiology Society on cell osmosis of nutrition and toxins. Noell cited a previous series of experiments by a 'W. Kuhne' in Heidelberg on human eye tissue and retina responses to different stimuli, including poisons, "(the phenomena) can be recorded with case and in a comparable manner from all vertebrates including the conscious man and are subject to intriguing species variations; (the phenomena) are modified in a definite but complex fashion by various pharmacological agents and metabolic poisons." Noell concluded the information could be used for "retinal diseases" "applicable on an imperical basis" on patients. (11) His statements must have made the hair stand up on the backs of the other researchers' necks. Was Knoell alluding to something more insidious?

Beria tested TABUN for the Nazis on his own citizens, but who made the SARIN and SOMAN tests for Richard Kuhn? Josef Mengele. His laboratory at Auschwitz conducted gas toxicology tests on human eyes "with intriguing species variations" and "metabolic poisons." ALSOS interrogated toxicologist, Wolfgang Wirth, who insisted the poison gas tests were made by "injecting subcutaneous compounds into mice" and by applying "toxic compound(s) to the eyes of rabbits." The 'Action of Tabun' subchapter in the ALSOS report stated that "studies by Dr. Schrader and R. Kuhn... indicate in the animal, Tabun stimulates the entire nervous system and 'uncoordinated' cramps result." Of course, no one would admit to human testing, that was a death warrant. The chemists insisted there were no known human experiments using poison gas, but they weren't certain about the Waffen SS activities. "Mere mention of the name SS-Waffenamt caused an 'allergic reaction' among the members of the regular Heereswaffenamt." (12) The survivors of Auschwitz would shed light on Mengele's gruesome collection of poisoned eyes, gouged out from his gas chamber victims:

"MENGELE: The Complete Story" Gerald Posner & John Ware, McGraw Hill Book Co., New York 1986

Page 34: "I went to the gypsy camp in Birkenau. I saw a wooden table. On it were samples of eyes. They each had a number and a letter. The eyes were very pale yellow to bright blue, brown, and violet. Another witness, Vera Kriegel, said she saw a wall covered with eyes in one of Mengele's laboratories. "They were pinned up like butterflies," she said. "I thought I was dead and already living in hell." The eyes were dispatched to Professor Von Verschuer's Institute in Berlin."

"Verschuer's Institute" would be the KWI for Brain Research in Berlin, its affiliate, the KWI in Heidelberg, Kuhn's establishment. As a trained geneticist under Professor Von Verschuer, Josef Mengele took an intense interest in the different racial reactions "species variations" to chemical and biological warfare. The absurdity of analyzing which race was more susceptible to gassing by SOMAN was like asking who was more susceptible to the atom bomb. This was truly science gone mad. Certainly, Josef Mengele's expertise was in high demand, both East and West. Did Josef Mengele flee to Russia with the other Nazi gas specialists? Had Josef Mengele switched identities with Henry Tolkmith at Beketovka, taking his wife, Valentine, to facilitate his escape?

Josef was the oldest of the three Mengele brothers, born March 16, 1911. Karl, Jr. was only 16 months his younger, often mistaken for Josef's twin. Alois, the baby, stayed at home to run the family farm under Karl, Senior, which evolved into manufacturing farm equipment. The Mengele family was known to treat their employees generously and justly, becoming prominent members of their Gunzburg community. Karl Mengele, Senior, was appointed ambassador to Rumania by Hitler. Karl, Jr., mysteriously died of illness December 1949 while Josef disappeared somewhere "in the east." A peculiar incident involving the two older Mengele brothers is cited in Posner and Ware's biography, "Mengele: The Complete Story." Occupied Germany was divided into four zones of influence, American, British, French, and Russian. Josef, so anxious to retrieve his Auschwitz experimental data, now in the Russian Zone, sent look-alike Karl as a decoy on trial runs. Karl's route passed through the American Zone before reaching the Russian Zone. The French document a 'Mengele' detained by the Americans on November 29, 1946, later released for unknown reasons. (13) They had the wrong man.

Further documentation on "switching" exist at the US Army Intelligence & Security Command. Later, this same material would surface in the US. Justice Department publication "In the Matter of Josef Mengele" a report to the Attorney General, October 1992. On February 7, 1979, "Josef Mengele" supposedly drowned on a Brazilian beach. By June 1985, "Josef" Mengele's body had been exhumed in Sao Paulo, Brazil, prompting an enormous international investigation, the US intelligence community anxious to prove no connection to this infamous war criminal.

On file is a 'Denazification Card' for Karl Mengele, Jr. by the War Department's Defense Detachment "DD 25" in the CIC Unit #970, the same unit in which Wolfgang Wirth had been detained and freed. According to former OSI attorney and military intelligence officer, John Loftus, the War Department's DD, "Defense Detachment" Unit, was another anachronism for Donovan and Dulles's dissolved OSS, under the State Department. The War Department Detachment Unit, 'WDD' would, soon become the War Department Strategic Services Unit, 'SSU' to later emerge as the Document Disposal Unit, 'DDU.' "Dulles's chameleons went under various names" even though under jurisdiction of the War Department, were still paid by the State Department. Eventually, the War Department settled upon the title Office of Policy Coordination, 'OPC' for this predecessor to the Central Intelligence Agency. (14) Under this myriad of acronyms, the Dulles gang was granted carte blanche to overthrow the Soviet Union. As I. G. Farben's patent lawyer, this was like hiring the fox to guard the chicken coop. The 1992 Justice Department report made no acknowledgement whatsoever regarding the "DD-25" marcations on Karl Mengele's denazification card, only citing the fact that the card was undated. Reference to Karl's brother, Josef is made on this card, listing an incorrect birth date, of March 16, 1912, not 1911. Just a typo, or was the CIC 970th DD 25 Unit in the process of switching Josef and Karl's identities? (15) Karl Mengele was in the hands of the Dulles gang.

After gaining employment in the Institute for Heredity, Biology and Racial Purity, Josef Mengele joined the staff of Professor Otmar Von Verschuer, to study twins. The German Research Council (Deutsche Forschungsgemeinschaft, "DFG") funded Von Verschuer's twin projects through his stay at the University of Frankfurt, and later, the KWI for Anthropology, formerly headed by Eugene Fischer. The original "Fischer Foundation" had been funded by the Rockefeller Institute. The DFG, headed by Kurt Blome, radiology and cancer specialist, also funded Otto Reche's work on criminal biology and racial biology, and psychopaths. Von Verschuer had Mengele posted to Auschwitz as an SS officer, where Mengele continued to send his twin research back to his mentor. Mengele was seeking evidence of immunological failures to establish patterns of social deviance amongst different racial types.(16) The doctor was madder than his patients. The whole of Germany was infected with brain disorders. The Nazis postulated human behavior was locked into a DNA genetically coded cast system. The flaw in this pseudo-scientific research was the establishment of theory before the collation of data, dumping any contradictions that might alter conclusions. How could they explain away the many healthy psychopaths and their crippled saints? As the German troops confronted Stalin's plagues on the Eastern Front, Hitler demanded the Reich manufacture new vaccines. The work was assigned to Dr. Josef

Mengele at Auschwitz along with gas toxicology. Further reference to Mengele's Auschwitz experiments arose at Fort Meade:

JOSEF MENGELE files, US Army Intelligence & Security Command, Ft Meade Page 62: 'The SS Hygienic Institutes' "only activity that has emerged was an effort made to combat bacteriological warfare in which the Polish underground movement were expert. The SS who were not very efficient had to call in the aid of an Army bacteriologist, Prof. Kliewe..."
'Miscellaneous Evidence Not at Present Involving the SS'
"This came from Prof. Karl Kisskalt, Munich U (in no way involved in the sinister business) ALSOS report BC/148. Dr. SCHUSTER and Dr. KLEIN. The last in a POW camp, and the information came through Sz. Ldr. JWR Thompson, RCAF, 84 Group RAF. "The summary is that experiments went on at AUSCHWITZ (or OSWRIG) and were then evacuated to DACHAU and BELSEN. At all these places prisoners were used. A professor CLAUBERG stated to be the leading German authority on diphtheria was in charge of all the bacteriological work at Auschwitz; according to Klein he experimented on women. Dr. Klein - a very nasty piece of work - a Rumanian, was at the same place. His war work was to select prisoners for the gas chamber and he was assisted by two thugs named MANGERLAY and LERNIG (name also stated as MENGLE and KOENIG)... In another bacteriological laboratory at Auschwitz were VATTER and ENTRES working on typhoid and dysentery, and WIRTHS working on cancer using female prisoners and perhaps X-rays."

For controlled medical experiments, thousands of pairs of twins were selected. Only several hundred survived. Spirochetes, typhus, and diphtheria were the priorities. Combinations were attempted to induce multiple sclerosis. The following chapter will describe the medical state of Germany more fully. Of the remaining survivors, Eva Moses Kor and her twin, Mariam, organized CANDLES (Children of Auschwitz Nazi Deadly Laboratory Experiments Survivors). Eva lives in Terre Haute, Indiana, interviewed on Oprah's TV show with Steven Spielberg, she spoke out against the Nazis with many, including the author. She does not recognize the photos of Henry Tolkmith, but she was much too young to recall, yet insists the public photos could not be him.

Eva Kor had acquired her medical experimentation records from Auschwitz, her twin, and others suffering from multiple sclerosis, MS. The disease listed by Mengele on her records was named "Takata-ara" which she could not identify. The author was able to identify this term as a blood test in "Chemical Abstracts," first used to diagnose tuberculosis and later spirochetes in the blood and spinal chord. (17) Today, we know from MS vice president Byron Waksman's publications that the Lyme spirochete is one of the components of MS. Eva's sister has since died from MS. Did the OPC need Mengele's "expertise" to help combat a Lyme epidemic in America? Seeking other Auschwitz witnesses, the author forwarded the Tolkmith photos to Auschwitz POW pharmacist Sig Halbrich. Too old to recall much of anything, he insisted he had seen Mengele in a marimba band in Los Angeles.

The author also approached the Washington DC Holocaust Museum and the Simon Weisenthal Center in Los Angeles, as well as its branch in Tel Aviv, to no avail. "Case Closed." "Not interested" cited the Americans. Israel's response was guarded, they were considering my request. The author wrote the Berlin Document Center requesting any available material on Tolkmith, with no reply. The author also approached Russian National Security chief Urinov for Tolkmith files, her letter returned unopened. The author sent rough drafts of her book to both President and Mrs. Clinton, receiving a post card of acknowledgement from the President and a brief letter from Hillary's secretary citing she could not facilitate any publishing ambitions, something the author had not requested, returning the manuscript. The author sent rough drafts to the CIA and the FBI and letters to Janet Reno's Justice Department to facilitate investigation of Tolkmith, to no avail. Instead, the IRS landed upon the author's doorstep with several thousands of dollars owed in back taxes, the book's research could not be claimed as a business expense prior publication, even though other authors do this. the author was making $6.30/hour at this stage. Despite a very frugal life style, it has been exceedingly difficult to continue research and publish the manuscript with this extra tax burden, setting the author back several years in purchasing a computer. All this aggravation and stonewalling went on while Soviet mole, FBI counterintelligence officer Robert Hansen, went undetected. Was there a connection?

Still hot on the trail, the author located Henry Tolkmith in the phone book, retired from Dow in sunny Lake Marry, Florida on Peppertree Road. Hoping to match Army photos with a driver's license, the author called the Seminol County DMV, who refused to release his picture. For assistance, the author called Sgt. Ron Gilbert of the Seminol Police. Being a history buff, he asked for the photos and volunteered with his partner to pay Tolkmith a visit off duty, asking the suspect about his war time service under Hitler. Did Tolkmith recognize the Army photos? "No!" Tolkmith insisted they were not of himself! Surprised, Gilbert asked Tolkmith for other wartime photos of himself. Tolkmith replied that the photo albums were kept by his wife in the attic, and she was shopping at the mall. Gilbert's partner spotted her down the hallway, peering around the corner. Tolkmith then took his toes and pushed an album under a stack of newspapers on the living room floor. He had scars on his face, too. Sgt. Gilbert, his suspicions aroused, called the Salt Lake Police to locate the author at work, "please phone him immediately" and send him everything on "Tolkmith." But of course! With this encounter, the author approached the Justice Department's OSI, hoping for further investigation. "CASE CLOSED!" Would the FBI declassify their "Tolkmith" holdings? No. He was still alive! Gilbert became silent. The author was unable to locate Tolkmith's two children.

It was necessary to pick up the paper trail again, for the 'eye witness' accounts were proving unreliable. In the summer of 1994, a newly declassified OACSI file MIS 924453 arrived on "German Scientists Employed USSR" This had been one of the classified reports withheld from FOIA requests, pending review. Here were over 800 German scientists, doctors, and technicians employed in the Soviet Union. Amongst them was a Professor Wollmann, one of the aliases of Josef Mengele, taken to "Kalag, AG, Strassfurt, taken to Russia." Additional reference to "Ulman," "Henrie Hollman" and "Henrique Wollman" with Mengele's ID card swaps is made by his biographers, Eva Kor, Gerald Posner, John Ware, and the US Justice Department. How apropos, a "wool man" and his ticks hiding out at Beketovka and Suchomi. (18) Had Josef Mengele gone to Russia with his fellow Kaiser Wilhelm Institute scientists? Apparently so.

US Army Medical Corps intelligence officer, Leo Alexander, reporting to the ALSOS Mission, uncovered the KWI for Brain Research Department of Serology, Experimental Therapy and Spirochaetal Research labs. Once run by his eugenical sterilization hero, Ernst Rudin, who fled with the approaching Americans, Franz Jahnel took over. Alexander filed this CIOS report #359, "Neuropathology and Neurophysiology, Including Electro-encephalography, In Wartime Germany" for ETOUSA, on public record, at the State University of Iowa since 1947, and National Library of Medicine, Bethesda, for all to read. The whole KWI for Brain Research and Mengele's co-horts were shipped off to Russia:

"GERMAN SCIENTISTS EMPLOYED USSR" OACSI file MIS 95443, Nat. Arch. MRB

Page 55: 'Industrial and Scientific Enterprises, Under Control of USSR, Which Employ German Scientists'

"Atomic Research in Russia April 1947 Under the Direction of the Russian Generals Sawiniaki and Krawtschenko. Composed of the following Groups":

"Collective group SUCHOMI, Black Sea, divided into:"
"Group Prof. Hertz
Group Manfred v. Ardene
Group Prof. Thiessen
Group Prof. Bweilogua
Collective group ATOMGRAD, East of the Urals, under Prof. Pose.
Collective group Taschkent/Turkestan under Dr. Patzschke.
Mining of uranium ore.
Elektrostal Uranium plant near Moscow under Dr. Riehl.
A group under the nuclear physicist Prof. Doepel in Moscow or Leningrad was not yet assigned in April 1947."
Page 58: "KWI for Brain Research, Buch was near Berlin, was completely dismantled and shipped to Russia with its Director Tiomofejeff-Ressovski."

Oscar Vogt's little gang was safe and sound at the Suchomi BW experimental station to practice on larger apes with MS where Brezhnev's 18th Army met its fate earlier under Beria's retreat blocking squads. Peter Thiessen had been director of the KWI for Physical Chemistry in Berlin-Dahlem. He was assigned chief of one of the Nuclear Physics groups at Suchomi, as noted on page 47 of the above OACSI file MIS 954453. On Page 55 of the same file, the biography of KWI for Brain Research geneticist director Timofejeff-Ressovski appears, who must have received all of Mengele's twin research experiments along with Professor Von Verschuer, and Rudin's and Jahnel's spirochete and serology lab. We will go into depth of Alexander's report on the KWI for Brain Research in the next chapter, for it is important to understand just what was happening to Europe under the Soviet Union's BW attacks. In turn, when the authorities came for Mengele's mentor, Von Verschuer, he too fled, taking with him the entire library of the KWI Anthropology Research Center, including Mengele's twin papers that had been forwarded from Auschwitz. (19) Other KWI branches, the Physical Chemistry Lab and the Experimental Therapy lab of Berlin-Dahlem, and the Animal Culture Lab of Muenchenberg beat it to Russia. Here lies the end result of the Rockefeller Foundation's funding. David Rockefeller purchased Glastonbury's Arbor Acres chicken farm in 1964. Did he have a reason to watch the Newcastle epidemics in Connecticut. What was their source? Most likely, Lyme would have arrived via the textile industries' wool and fur trade with Amtorg, not through chickens, but science couldn't differentiate between spirochetes back then.

Soon, Stalin would boot the KWI doctors out of Russia via Dulles's OPC ratlines. The politicians were starting to squirm like spirochetes. Dr. Gustav Hertz, a nuclear physicist from the Siemens Werke, Berlin was also carted off to Suchomi, his biography on page 21 of the above report, "German Scientists Employed USSR." His name also appears on OACSI file 749586, "Dr. Hertz and Others" and OACSI file 800647 "Gustav Hertz BW Suchomi." both under the BID category for biological warfare. Both reports have been entirely withheld. Wouldn't you like to know who the "others" are, possibly "Wollman"? Had "Wollman" traded ID's with Tolkmith? Many gas specialists were dying at the carelessly operated gas factory at Beketovka, and it is most likely the real Henry Tolkmith, Von Bock's partner, perished in Soviet service with 200 others:

BERNHARD VON BOCK files, Ft. George Meade, US Army Intelligence & Security Command, FOIA request 869-90

Page 29: "Letter from the Foreign Service of the United States of America, Office of the Army Attaché American Embassy, London England, October 7, 1954. To: Assistant chief of Staff, G-2, Department of the Army, Washington 25 DC"

1. "Bernhard Von Bock formerly design engineer of the Tabun plant DYHERNFURTH has returned to the Eastern Zone of Germany through the exit camp at RUBIZHNOV (blackout) Russians at BEKETOVKA, USSR, he is now employed at the Leuna Werke, SCHKOPAU, Eastern Zone, Germany."

The report continued citing how difficult it would be to lure Von Bock to the West, employed in the East with "good salary and pension." Eventually, a deal was struck, Bock simply drove across the border with his wife and daughters. When interrogated, he was evasive regarding Beketovka, admitting when the Soviets hired him, "the Soviet interrogators knew almost as much as he did of Tabun..." "Upon arrival at Beketovka he was put to work writing reports on the manufacture of Tabun... Soviet colonel actually knew the whole process before he came. Beketovka POWs show Von Bock was responsible for Uffland's removal" the CW plant's former director (page 10). The US Army concluded "It is very difficult to evaluate Von Bock. Test questions given to him were not answered satisfactorily... His powers of observation are seriously lacking for a man of his education and experience," his testimony "rehearsed" (page 13). The real conditions at Beketovka surfaced in the OACSI files, Von Bock in Russia since 1927:

"CHEMICAL COMPLEX AT BEKETOVKA" To the Department of State, from HICOG, Frankfurt 1231, June 28, 1950. State Department file listing 961.715/6-2850; OACSI file 682922, National Archives MRB

Page 2: "In March 1948 a German chemist arrived at the chemical plant. His name was Dr. Von Bock. He was a Doctor of Chemistry. Source said that he was an important man for the Russians because he had been in Russia in 1927-1930, and spoke fluent Russian... The wife said ironically that they were forced "on their own free will" to sign a contract with the Russians... Bon Bock became the official director of the whole chemistry complex."

Page 3: "There was a severe conflict between Von Bock and the Russian director of the plant... the Russian director left... PWs had to relocate the laboratories at Von Bock's direction... the high tension cables in the plant had to be repaired and new ones installed..."

Page 4: 'Poisonous Roots'

"In the summer of 1946 a series of poisoning cases among the German PWs began. Every four to six weeks a new case or two would appear. This continued all during the source's stay until he left the district in September 1948... The source was certain that the cause of this poisoning was the eating of certain kind of roots which were brought to the chemical plant in RR cars. See Annex for a sketch of these roots... When the roots were unloaded a few would fall to the ground. PWs would pick these up and eat them which was the cause of the poisoning cases... According to the source, all these symptoms excite secretion from the mouth and are typical of atropine intoxication. Scapalamine will also cause the same effects..."

POW Dr. Helmut Becker further described to the High Commissioner to Germany (HICOG) how the Beketovka chemical plant #91 used a very high grade of silver and stored phosgene gas in dark green glass bottles, handling by German PWs later assigned to the Russians, (page 5). Numerous other reports began to surface on the use of atropine as an antidote for Tabun and Sarin gases. Apparently, under the former Beketovka director, Dr. Uffland, over 200 poisoning casualties had occurred. Atropine roots were very much in demand. Certainly, Mengele's toxicological gas tests at Auschwitz would have come into high demand at Beketovka:

"PHYSICAL PROPERTIES OF THE WAR GASES TABUN, SARIN, SOMAN and EXCELSIOR" Headquarters, 7707 European Command Intelligence Center APO 757 US Army march 28, 1949. OACSI file SD 924162, Nat. Arch. MRB

Page 2: "The effectiveness of Tabun is based on the blocking of the cholinesterases, the antidote is atropine, especially in combination with lobelin... An area gassed by Tabun therefore cannot be entered for a considerable length of time and the tactical advantages produced can not be exploited... Sarin and Soman are poisons with characteristics similar to Tabun. They are appreciably more toxic than Tabun... Upon detonation of the shell, the gas is completely vaporized. The gas clears rapidly from the contaminated areas and the area can be occupied by troops within about fifteen minutes after shelling. Both gases are therefore considered to be ideal for chemical warfare agents for offensive operations..."

Reflect back to the OSS report #110, R&A 698, "German Use of Poisonous Fog" where people dropped dead instantly in the forest, and troops were able to occupy soon after. Did Beria use Sarin instead of Tabun? How much had I. G. Farben given to Stalin? Surely had Kleist and List been carrying poison gas in the Caucasus, the Soviets would have reported it to the world, retaliating in kind. Adolf Heusinger, head of OKH on the Eastern Front and in charge of the I. G. Farben gas site at Dyhernfurth, was fully aware of the Soviet possession of Sarin when Eisenhower appointed him to NATO in 1960. ALSOS was also reporting usage of atropine in Tabun poisonings. (20)

But more than poison gas was going on at Beketovka, biological warfare experiments using brucellosis, "Bangs" disease, inflicting tuberculosis in cattle and humans was placed under Professor Yachontov. Once again, Josef Mengele would have fit in perfectly. According to the source "The BW implications of this site were quite striking," the High Commissioner to Germany reported beck the US State Department. Even penicillin was present. (21) HICOG was John J. McCloy, former President of Rockefeller's Chase-Manhattan Bank. The Army's G-2 Intelligence (USFA) was sending reports back to Washington on a new BW facility located in the Urals, "harboring 25,000 to 30,000 persons engaged in bacteriological research... constructed along the lines of Marie Antoinette's palace in Paris...with high powered microscopes and high speed centrifuges" reported in OACSI file 676278 "Soviet Biological Warfare Research Center," June 12, 1950. The name of the subject interrogated was censored, but the report was signed: "Lewis E. Perry, Colonel GSC Deputy Assistant Chief of Staff, G-2." Remember Perry, heavily tied to the death of Walter Hirsch, (BW/CW chief of the Waffen Pruf 9).

An even more curious report on Bernhard Von Bock's escapades inside Beketovka came from the National Archives, 1/5/95, heavily censored, citing serious accidents:

"VON BOCK" 7 Sept 1950, Prepared by Miles A. Cowles, Colonel, GSC, Army Attaché. OACSI file 716489 National Archives MRB record group 319

'Production of Nerve Gases, Special Handling - American Eyes Only'

"Source stated his contacts with (blackout) were a (blackout) and a German living in the U.S. Zone, a relative by marriage of the source. Neither has heard from (blackout) during the past year...

Source stated quite positively that, after sustaining 200 casualties, the Russians used (blackout) as the director and moved all the Dyhernfurth equipment intact to near Stalingrad (not Moscow as reported in N-129-50) along with stocks of gases. Source could give no information as to Dyhernfurth plant capacity, or quantity of stocks taken over, nor to the Falkenhagen am Oder Sarin plant... Distribution by Originatory, DI, EUCOM."

The Army, and the CIA, rather rudderless in 1995, released the Tolkmith files held in joint custody on Tolkmith's birthday, February 13, 1995, the original request filed in 1988. Soon, the author would forward these files to the OSI. By December 13th, 1995, Henry Tolkmith was dead. Valentine would die March 17, 1997. Not hearing from any of the intelligence agencies regarding his death, awaiting further declassification of documents, the author presumed both were alive. The FBI continued to sit on its files. Tolkmith, employed at Dow, was under suspicion for spying for the Russians:

"MEMORANDUM FOR THE CHIEF, CHEMICAL CORPS JULY 14, 1950"

Attention: Lt. Col. William E. Williamson, Subject: Dr. Henry TOLKMITH and Bertold G. W. ROAXER.

1. "The following information concerning the above subjects has been furnished us by CIC and is forwarded to you as of possible interest and for any action you may care to take.

2. In 1948 information came to the attention of CIC to this effect that one Dr. Henry TOLKMITH, (blackout) (blackout) a German chemist in the employ of Dow Chemical Corporation might be engaged in espionage for a foreign power. It was believed that TOLKMITH was in touch with the Soviets via one Dr. Engels in Brazil.

3. From April 1945 to April 1948 TOLKMITH lived at Gozlar in the British zone of Germany and later in Heidelberg, U.S. Zone of Germany. During this time he was allegedly in contact with one Bertold ROAXER

in Ziegelhausen, near Heidelberg. ROAXER reportedly is communicating information concerning his chemical experiments to one Dr. Wilhelm Engels in South America.

4. The records of CIC indicate that Bertold Georg Wilhelm ROAXER, a former member of the Nazi Party, was formerly associated with the I. G. Farben Chemical Industries, Ludwigshafen. ROAXER is said to consider Dr. Henry TOLKMITH and Dr. Wilhelm Engels as associates. Dr. Engels, a chemist, specializes in research for rubber industry in Sao Paulo, Brazil.

5. ROAXER, a specialist on phosphorus gas, desires to emigrate to Brazil which he has a visa to enter. He is now awaiting his exit permit from Germany.

6. It would be appreciated if you would furnish this agency with any information which you may have on the individuals mentioned herein."

FOR THE DIRECTOR OF CENTRAL INTELLIGENCE: Robert X Sceow

SO DE-28496, Distribution: The Director, FBI, The Secretary of State

Stop and think. I. G. Farben had been in the Soviet Union's pocket since World War I. Was "Dr. Engels" (add a 'M') Karl Mengele in Sao Paulo, Brazil? Was this Josef Mengele communicating with his brother in Brazil, in turn, working for the Soviets? The Army Attaché in Sao Paulo made a feeble attempt to locate "Dr. Engels" to no avail. The case was dropped. (22) The author even wrote to Henry Tolkmith in Lake Mary in 1996, unaware of his death, pressing him to come forward with the history of Beketovka. The FBI finally forwarded the author its Tolkmith files in 2001, after receiving a copy of the 1988 Social Security Death Index listings. The new FBI files greatly strengthened the author's suspicions that Tolkmith was Mengele.

Back in 1950, the CIC requested the FBI's assistance, Tolkmith's legal residency pending. FBI agents interrogated Tolkmith's friends, and associates, of course, all affirming his patriotism. Tolkmith's guard had been forwarding his outgoing mail for censorship to "the Officer in Charge, Fifth Army Regional Office, 464 Federal Building, Detroit, Michigan" for years. Although incoming mail was intercepted, outgoing got through. Suddenly, Valentine began reminiscing over her old friends in Germany and Russia, triggering a flood of syrupy correspondence, apparently from Roaxer:

HENRY TOLKMITH FBI file 105-11134-17

Page 2: "At the time instant letter was presented by TOLKMITH to (blackout) the former explained that one evening during the early part of May 1950 he (blackout) were discussing friends in Germany and conjecturing about their whereabouts and activities. As a result, within a day or so, (blackout) wrote a letter to the (blackout) family requesting such information. This outgoing letter was not presented to (blackout) consequently, he had no knowledge of it until subject presented him with the reply."

"As noted previously, instant letter is written in German. According to (blackout) the first part of the letter sets out the following information which may be of pertinence: (blackout)

1. (Blackout) is working on acetylene dyestuffs. According to (blackout) is a German chemist who is renown in the field of Acetylene Chemistry and has written several books.

2. (Blackout) is no longer a company executive at Ludwigshafen...

3. (Solid paragraph blacked out)

4. (Blackout) is no longer employed at Ludwigshafen due to his sympathy with the "White Russians." This person is unknown to (blackout).

5. Mr. SCHOLL F died of stomach cancer. (This person is unknown to (Blackout.)"

[The FBI translated the incoming letter]:

"Ziegelhausen, 5/23/50"

"Dear family Dr. TOLKMITH:

At first we wish to thank you very much for the received letter, it has been a very long time indeed, however, in the meantime, diverse loathsome and unpleasant things happened with us, but it is useless to write about it in detail. Thank God, everything has passed over us without leaving scars behind.

[What, leave old scarface behind?]

I was really glad that you had not forgotten my birthday and I thank you for the congratulation very much. We were very glad about the enclosed picture; it is a very beautiful photo, the faces have become less restrained and show less anxiety, and (blackout) already makes the impression of a young gentleman. Very often we have talked about you and it was correct indeed that you left... I have heard nothing new from LU (blackout) is said to have attained good successes with his newly-invented carbide dyestuffs. (Blackout) has completely disappeared, about three quarters of a year ago he received mail from (blackout) from Stalingrad. Since the end of the war, (blackout) has no longer been employed in LU, he is said to have belonged politically to the White Russians. Master SCHOLL died of cancer of intestine. Another item of interest: the sprayings of the fruit trees are no longer done with Z605, apparently it has not become a great success for LEV, reason: poisonousness and no permanent storing capacity.

This will be my last letter from Germany because I have received the papers for my departure today. I am really glad that I can leave this hopeless soil now. If you have anything which could aid my journey, I should be glad to hear from you concerning this. Wishing you continued good fortune, I remain with the heartiest greetings. Yours (blackout)"

[Enclosed was a second letter.]

"Dear (Blackout)

Well, finally the time has arrived to thank you for your dear letter and the pretty picture, but as already stated, diverse things happened with us, and we are also very much occupied to earn our livelihood... We have established a good soap trade with some good customers who spend so much that I can live well to some extent. but how everything will later be, one cannot say as yet for the sky is rather dark again. Well, I want to see how (blackout) will be in the future; it was rather difficult to get all the papers. The many things they wanted to know! but now he has succeeded. Well, I always have some peculiar feeling; when I think that (blackout) will journey too far. It is not quite certain whether I shall go over there; it entirely depends upon the conditions. I am glad that you are all right and well accustomed to America... Today we have some heat, almost as in Brazil, but May makes good that which April neglected, for it was cold and rainy, and thus beautiful. May makes us feel twice as good.... It is certain that the children like it very much. Well (blackout) has always been just like papi, now he looks more like Mami... The main point is that they are healthy and obedient. I wish all the good things to you and to your dear family and remain with many hearty regards. Yours, (blackout)"

Oh, such sweet family chit-chat, "leaving the loathsome details" behind. Valentine's real husband, Henry Tolkmith never made it out of Stalingrad's Beketovka because of a gas accident with the "poisonous fruit tree pesticide Z605," probably a derivative of the I. G. Farben Zyklon B gas used at Auschwitz. In the meantime, (blackout), most likely Dr. Roaxer, is telling Valentine and the impostor Henry that his family and kids are "healthy and obedient," Roaxer on his way to Brazil, hoping for a rendezvous with Dr. Engels. Here's the tip. TOLKMITH FBI file 11-11134-8 entitled "Memorandum March 10, 1950" to D. M. Ladd, from H. Belmont, had a censor boo boo, the "Subject" of the memo is listed as: "HENRY TOLKMITH, ENGELS, ROKAHR" exposing Valentine's contact. Valentine's beloved husband was dead, worse, was this Russian Jewess forced to legitimately wed his impostor in Midland? Similar tales of Josef

Mengele divorcing his first wife, Irene, and remarrying Karl's wife, Martha, in Brazil appear in the Posner-Ware biography. Perhaps Karl kept Martha, and Josef remarried Valentine. In the end, the FBI closed the espionage investigation on Tolkmith, concluding he was an avowed patriot.

The last source upon the mystery of Tolkmith resides within the Justice Department's own report, "In the Matter of Josef Mengele" 1992. It is full of pot holes, using Mengele's SS files in possession of the Berlin Document Center, originally under control of the US State Department, mixing the two brother's identities. How could anyone rely upon State Department files when its OPC was in the business of Nazi smuggling and sanitizing dossiers? The skull in the Brazilian grave had so much dental work, it was virtually unidentifiable, the OSI postulated the old boy had suffered migrating molars to conform with SS X-rays. The head's diameter seemed small, but the OSI rationalized away the centimeters. A childhood attack of osteomyelitis mysteriously migrated from Mengele's lower femur to his hip. Prior to ratlining it over to Brazil on a Red Cross ID card, the OSI placed Josef in a potato patch on the Sedlmeier's farm just down the road from his Gunzburg home! CANDLES was skeptical, but in the end, Israel, Germany, and the US passed judgement. "Case closed." Once we discover who were Mengele's drug partners in South America, arming every terrorist on the planet, left and right, alarms will go off. Surely there must be something terribly wrong with all these intelligence agencies.

While the Army's CIC 970th Unit was hunting Nazi war criminals, the CIC 430th Unit was hiring them. The State Department's Dulles gang, camouflaged inside the CIC's 430th Unit under Colonel Lewis Perry, must have had a hand in switching the two brother's identities; recall Karl Mengele's 'denazification card.' More on Perry's role in Dulles's rogue CIC Units at Salzburg, training Iron Curtain freedom fighters and running Nazi rat lines appears in Aaron's and Loftus' "Unholy Trinity." (23) Mengele's biographers, Posner and Ware also report an incident where Josef was supposedly retained by the 430th CIC Unit in charge of Vienna. In December 1946, a CIC agent named Benjamin J. Gorby of the 970th CIC heard Mengele had been captured by Allied Forces, assuming "the 430th CIC Unit to have made the arrest." This coincides with the French report showing Mengele released by American authorities November 19, 1946. (24) Was it Josef, or was it look-a-like Karl in the clutches of Lewis Perry's rogue 430th CIC Unit?

The Justice Department waited a decade after Mengele's death to collect DNA from obstinate family members for positive identification of the Brazilian corpse.

"IN THE MATTER OF JOSEF MENGELE" US Justice Department, Neal Sher, Director OSI, & Eli Rosenbaum, Deputy Assistant OSI. 1992

Page 191: "The scientific analysis performed on the three samples established that 'the skeletal DNA has a consistent genotype compatible with the father of Rolf, and that (more than) 99.9% of Caucasians unrelated to Rolf would be excluded from paternity by this analysis."

Hold it folks, stop right there. Do the math. "99.9% of Caucasians UNRELATED to Rolf (Josef and Irene's son) would be excluded from paternity." Therefore, 0.1% of all Caucasians ARE RELATED. Presume, for simplicity's sake, one billion of the 6 billion people on earth are Caucasian. A tenth of one percent of a billion is a million. The body in the Sao Palo grave could be related to ONE MILLION people, most likely, one being his brother. If Karl, Jr.'s Gunzburg grave had been dug up, we would have discovered the corpse of a great ape? Yes, you figured it out, and you're not a graduate of Princeton's Institute of Advanced Studies. Switched at birth, switched at death.

In short, Willard Henry Dow was probably horrified when he discovered his I. G. Farben coup had flopped. The prospect of having the wrong Tolkmith on his doorstep, the infamous Angel of Death from Auschwitz, must have caused a panic. On March 31st, 1949, Willard Henry Dow, with his wife and business partner, Calvin Campbell, boarded their private plane in Michigan for a trip to the Massachusetts Institute of Technology where their son Herbert, was attending Winston Churchill's lecture. Was Dow Senior attempting to contact Churchill personally, warning MI6's Paperclip and Dustbin Nazi smuggling operations were run by two Soviet moles, Philby and McClean? The plane crashed outside London, Canada, on direct route between Midland and Massachusetts. All aboard were killed, excluding Campbell, the company lawyer. Pilot A. J. Bowie, a 38 year veteran and co-pilot, Fred Clements also perished. Was this sabotage? On April Fools' Day, the "New York Times" reported the deaths of three prominent Americans, two from Truman's Congressional investigation, "George Clapp, Alcoa founder and Willard Henry Dow, the Third, William Bell, was Chief Fish & Wildlife, Department of the Interior, will play a major roll in combating New York's epidemics. The Dow fortune was divided equally between brother and sister, an estimated $8,000,000. (25)

Suddenly the artistic imagination of the author took over. Was Detroit the industrial giant, Gotham City? Picture Herbert Dow, MIT's technical wizard now orphaned as Batman; the "Penguin" as Harry Truman and J.

Edgar Hoover, dressed in drag, with an affinity for April Fools pranks, as the "Joker." (26) Henry Tolkmith was "Alfred, the Butler." Was Batman's Butler, Alfred, really dead, or was he engineering another escape? Perhaps we can track him in the batmobile? Just push the on star button!

More mysterious deaths would follow on April Fools' Day. Hoover hounded G-2 Intelligence Assistant Chief of Staff, Hoyt Vandenberg with malicious false charges of bribery until his death from stomach cancer. The FBI opened a huge "BRIBERY" file against Vandenberg. Vandenberg was supposedly having his miltary suits tailored for free, the mischievous tailor had even made the same service available to President Harry Truman! Air Force Intelligence investigated and found the charges baseless and ludicrous. After entering the Walter Reed Army Medical Center, November 4, 1953, Hoyte Vandenberg died in the night, pronounced dead April 2, 1954; the Joker had struck again. Hoover's condolences to Vandenberg's wife dripped with sympathy and sarcasm. Truman nominated Vandenberg for the new Central Intelligence Group in 1946, a forerunner to the CIA. Vandenberg declined, so Truman appointed Wild Bill Donovan, Dulles' OSS superior. When Hoover congratulated Vandenberg on the nomination, G-2 chief replied "Please accept my heartfelt thanks for your kind note to me. I am under no illusions concerning the difficulties that confront an organization of this type. However, I feel certain they can be surmounted if we put our backs to the job." (27) Crudely put, they hated each other. More to the point, the OSS network of Donovan, Dulles and Vandenberg knew Hoover was gay.

Had Beketovka and Dyhernfurth escaped attack to facilitate a future Nazi-Soviet re-alliance against the West once Hitler was out of the way? Germany surrendered just two weeks prior Dyhernfurth's capability to deliver poison gas via V2 rockets. Had the Spartans taken over the Third Reich? Who would save the West?

CHAPTER 6 NOTES

(1) "INVESTIGATION OF THE NATIONAL DEFENSE PROGRAM" Part 24, March 6, May 22-26, June 19, 1944. Cong. Session 78-2, SODOC: YA.N 21/6:D36/pt.24

"NEW YORK TIMES" 5/7/44 p. 1 "Dow Denies Link to German Cartel"

(2) "POSSIBLE GERMAN USE OF CHEMICAL WARFARE"

OACSI file Project 425-A, Publications file 1946-51 NND765081 MID 907, 16 August 1944; To Chief CWS, Army Service Forces, War Dept. Wa. DC. Nat. Arch. MRB, record group 319

(3) "I. G. FARBENINDUSTRIE A.G. OFFICE BUILDING: FRANKFURT/MAIN CHEMICAL WARFARE" by Irvin H. Jones, US Bureau of Mines on behalf of British Ministry of Fuel & Power and US Technical Industrial Intelligence Com. CIOS Target 8/59a, August 220, 1945. OACSI file MIS 42365, Nat. Arch. MRB record group 319

(4) "INTERROGATION OF GERMAN CHEMICALWARFARE PERSONNEL" ALSOS Mission MIS c/o G-2, Ha USFET (rear) APO 887, 9/26/45. Source: C. A. Baumann & R. W. Helmkump, Expert consultants. OACSI file MID 206481, Nat. Arch. record group 319; Page: 10.

(5) "INTERROGATION ON GAS WARFARE" (German) General I. g. NO 2802.0600 from M. A. London, Report No. R5545-45, 10/24/45, source: War Office MID W.D.G.S.
OACSI file MIS 214196, Nat. Arch.. MRB record group 319 box 1408: Gen. Blumentritt.

(6) "INTERROGATION OF PROFESSOR FERDINAND FLURY AND DR. WOLFGANG WIRTH ON THE TOXICOLOGY OF CHEMICAL WARFARE AGENTS" by Mr. L.T.D. Williams, Ministry of Supply, BIOS Trip 1610 Item 8. OACSI file 349321, Nat. Arch. MRB record group 319.
"Wolfgang Wirth, head of Group VII of Wa. Pruf 9 and Sanitits Inspektion, as well as being head of the Toxicological and Therapeutical Section of the Military Academy in Berlin. Page 6: 'Details of Arrest'; Page 15: 'Chronological Record of Full Time Employment and Military Service.'

(7) "I.G. FARBEN INDUSTRIE OFFICE BUILDING FRANK-FURT/MAIN CHEMICAL WARFARE" by Irving H. Jones, US Bureau of Mines, on the behalf of the British Ministry of Fuel and Power and US Technical and Industrial Intelligence Committee, CIOS report #8/59a, August 20, 1945, G-2 Division, SHAEF (rear) APO 413; OACSI file MIS 42365, Na. Arch. MRB record group 319. Page 3: Flotho
"CHEMICAL WARFARE (Germany) REPORT BASED ON IN-TERROGATION AND WRITTEN REPORTS OF JURGEN E. VON KLENCK" OACSI file S.D. (sensitive Document) 17847. Nat. Arch MRB

record group 319. Listed as "DESTROYED" prior to accession to Na. Arch. letter to Rachel Verdon, 8/17/87.

(8) "PRIORITY FIELDS FOR DENIAL OF GERMAN AND AUSTRIAN SCIENTISTS TO THE USSR" OACSI file MIS S.D. 8894, Nat. Arch. MRB, record group 319. To: Chief Intelligence Group; From: Scientific Branch, 6/17/46 Major C. D. Fisher/74738/eeg.

(9) RICHARD KUHN file, US Army Intelligence & Security Command, Ft. G. Meade
"Prof. of Philosophy and biochemistry... Did valuable research for Nazi Government... internationally known and brilliant scholar in field of organic and physical chemistry... outspoken Nazi sympathizer... director of KWI, (Medical Research at Heidelberg) excluded by directive from all activities and subject internment... Winner of Noble Prize 1938 in chemistry, declined a US War Department invitation... vitamin research in US."

(10) "INVESTIGATION BY PROFESSOR KUHN KAISER WIL-HELM INSTITUT FUR MEDIZINISCHE FORSCHUNG" CIOS Report Item 24, no. XXIV-13 Target number 24/17 Medical. Page 4: "Vitamin B6 has also received attention... Kuhn isolated and characterized it... Kuhn stated that he had been informed that Snell at Wisconsin had independently made the same observation."

(11) WERNER KARL O. H. NOELL files US Army Intelligence & Security Command, Ft. G. Meade. Pages 25-26: "His last rank was 'Oberarzt' of the 'Lufftwaffe' but through whole war... engaged in research work. April 1943 he started work as research assistant at the KWI in Berlin-Buch under Prof. Kornmuller and from Easter 1945 on he worked in Gottingen at the Brain Institute with the same Professor... On the occasion of a visit at the institute by the American authorities he received an invitation to co-operate and work also in Heidelberg at the AAF Aero Medical Center KWI... offered a contract to work for 6 months in USA"
"TRANSCELLULAR MEMBRANE POTENTIALS AND IONIC FLUXES" Edited by Fred M. Snell and Werner K. Noell, State University of NY at Buffalo, NY. 'Proceedings of the 14th Annual Fall Meeting sponsored by the American Physiological Society Univ. of Buffalo,' August 28-31, 1962. Gordon & Breach, Science Publishers, NY. Page 92: 'Transretinal Currents and Ion Fluxes' by W. K. Noell D.R. Crapper, and C. V. Paganelli, Dept. of Physiology, St Univ. of NY at Buffalo.

(12) "INTERROGATION OF GERMAN CW PERSONNEL" ALSOS Mission 265, OACSI file MIS 206481, Nat. Arch. MRB record group 319, Page 27: 'Section III' "Dr. Straus denied having any knowledge of tests on inmates of concentration camps..."

(13) "MENGELE: THE COMPLETE STORY" Gerald Posner & John Ware, McGraw Book Co., NY 1986. Pages 4-6: childhood. Page 109: Death of Karl Jr. December 1949.

Page 66: Josef retrieves Auschwitz logs. Page 74: Karl's trial runs. Page 84: Americans detain Mengele 11/19/46. Page 55: Josef lost 'somewhere in the East'

(14) "UNHOLY TRINITY" Mark Aarons & John Loftus, St. Martin's Press, NY 1991

Pages 233-234. OSS, SSU, WDD, DDU, DAD.

(15) "IN THE MATTER OF JOSEF MENGELE" Report to the Attorney General of the United States October 1992. Prepared by the Office of Special Investigations Criminal Division, Neal M. Sher, Director, Eli M. Rosenbaum, Principal Deputy Director. Page 95

(16) "RACIAL HYGIENE" Robert Proctor, Harvard University Press, Cambridge, MA 1988. Pages 43-44 Von Verschuer's DFG, Mengele, Blome, twins. Page 349: (note 115) Fischer Foundation funded by Rockefeller Foundation.

(17) "CHEMICAL ABSTRACTS" vol. 35, 1941, page 4091 "'The Diagnostic Value of the Takata-Ara reaction in the cerebrospinal fluid." by Paul B. Szanto and Samuel Burack. Journal Lab. Clin. Med. 26, 1079-84, 1941.

"From the examination of 314 patients including 167 treated cases of peresis, the conclusion is made that the Takata-Ara reaction in cerebrospinal fluid is of great value in the diagnosis of syphilis of the central nervous system." [The syphilis spirochete, suspected of originating from sheep intestines, is a cousin to the Lyme spirochete.]

"CHEMICAL ABSTRACTS" vol. 39, 1945, page 5314 "Changes of the cerebrospinal fluid and blood in closed traumas of the central nervous system" I. Study of the cerebrospinal fluid and blood pressures. A. B. Mandelbolm, Bull. Eksptl. Biol. Med. 17, No. 1-2, 22-6 (1944). (Uses of Takata-ara reaction)

"CHILDREN OF THE FLAMES" Lucette Lagnado & Sheila Dekel, William Morrow & co., NY 1991 Page 62: EVA MOSES KOR testimony: "the blood tests were the most basic component of Mengele's program. Virtually all the twins were subjected to daily withdrawals of blood. Page 70: "Mengele would plunder a twin's body, sometimes removing organs and limbs. He injected the children with lethal germs, including typhus and tuberculosis, to see how quickly they succumbed to the diseases. Many became infected and died..."

(18) "GERMAN SCIENTISTS EMPLOYED USSR" OACSI file MIS 924453, Nat. Arch. MRB, Page 53. Professor Wollmann

"MENGELE: The Complete Story" Gerald Posner & John Ware, McGraw-Hill, NY 1986.

page 301: Mengele alias Henrique Wollman, CIA 1972 reports

"CHILDREN OF THE FLAMES" Lucette Lagnado & Sheila Dekel, William Morrow & Co. NY 1991. Page 22: Mengele alias - Fritz Hollmann, Fritz Ullman in POW camp. Page 103: Friend Fritz Ullman had two ID cards, gives one to Mengele, "Ulman" changed to "Hollman" to become "Henric Hollman."

(19) "CHILDREN OF THE FLAMES" Lucette Lagnado & Sheila Dekel, William Morrow, NY 1991; Page 118: Von Verschuer flees with Mengele files

(20) "INTERROGATION OF GERMAN CW PERSONNEL" ALSOS Mission OACSI file 206481, Nat. Arch. MRB Page 15: 'Action of Tabun' "On several cases of poisoning in the war gas factory at Dyhernfurth... For this reason it is possible by use of artificial respiration and atropine to revive a person poisoned in this way."

(21) "STALINGRAD-BEKETOVKA" OACSI file 689320, "Medical Information Concerning Stalingrad" State Department file 861-55/7-1450; to Department of State, source, Dr. Helmut Becker'; Na. Arch MRB

Page 7: 'Item 16': 'Pathological Anatomy Institute' "This institute is in Beketovka... Professor Yachontov, described above, an alleged internist and epidemiologist..."

"STALINGRAD" OACSI file 685310 "Medical Information Concerning Stalingrad" source Dr. Hans Girbensohn, pathologist, PW. State Department file 861.55/7-750, from HICOG, Frankfurt 1370 July 7, 1950; Nat. Arch MRB; Page 6: 'Item 17' 'Medical Research' "Footnote #1: Professor Yachontov... the medical institute at Stalingrad should perhaps be watched... antibiotic preparation said to be like penicillin but the exact nature of which source does not know was tested clinically at the institute..."

(22) "INFORMATION REGARDING ACTIVITIES OF DR. ENGELS" OACSI file MIS 785362 (BW bid #7501) Nat. Arch. MRB declassified 3/17/98

From Army Attaché, reference Control No. CW-753 9/26/50, Evaluation: A-1, date of information 4/24/51, report prepared by Colonel B. C. Andrus, G-C; Source, American Consulate Sao Paulo, Report #R-138-51 BRAZIL 4/30/51

1. "Source was informed by Major General Henrique Baptise Duffles Teixeira Lott, commander of the 2nd Military Region of the 2nd Infantry Division, SAO PAULO, that he did not know a "DR. ENGELS" but stated he would inquire. Inquires by General LOTT did not so - much reveal the name of "DR. ENGELS" within the military establishment, and further, GENERAL LOTT informed that there are no military laboratories in SAO PAULO or in the second Region..."

(23) "UNHOLY TRINITY" Mark Aarons & John Loftus, St. Martin's Press, NY 1991 Pages 240, 241, 243, 245, 246, 257. Lewis Perry CIC Unit 430, rogue unit Allen Dulles.

(24) "MENGELE: The Complete Story" Gerald Posner & John Ware McGraw-Hill Book Co. NY 1986, Page 83: 430th CIC Unit/Mengele, 1946; Page 84: French files.

(25) "NEW YORK TIMES" April 1, 1949, Page 25 and 26 'Obituaries' "George Clapp, 90 an Alcoa Founder" "Dr. William B. Bell, Wildlife Authority" "W. H. Dow Killed in Plane Crash"

(26) "OFFICIAL AND CONFIDENTIAL: The Secret Life of J. Edgar Hoover" Anthony Summers, G. P. Putnam, NY 1993, Page 19: "Edgar's childhood dossier on Edgar... 'Fooled lots of people' he noted with glee on April Fools' Day."

(27) HOYTE VANDENBERG, FBI file 62-81003-2 letters 6/7/46 Hoover to Vandenberg, and 6/10/46 Vandenberg to Hoover.

FBI file 62-81003-1 "confidential informant of unknown reliability" - bribery charges.

FBI file 62-81003-24 AF Intelligence clears Vandenberg of all charges.

FBI file 62-81003-28 Vandenberg's death, Walter Reed Army Hospital.

FBI file 62-81003-30 Hoover condolences to Mrs Vandenberg.

CHAPTER 7

FRANKENSTEIN

The Nazi Doctors in Soviet Service

Recall that famous line in the cartoon strip "Pogo," "I see the enemy and he is us!" It is worth following the careers of the Kaiser Wilhelm Institute's doctors before, during, and after World War II to present to the public the risks of State orchestrated health care. It will become increasingly apparent that the Nazi doctors considered their own citizens the "enemy," deliberately creating an army of madmen. With good reason, they beat it back to Beketovka and Suchomi. While the epidemics ran rampant on the Eastern Front, the Nazi doctors were summoned to crate vaccines for the German troops, the same doctors that had instructed the Soviets in the art of BW sabotage under the Waffen Pruf 9, including Professor Kliewe, Wolfgang Wirth, and "Adjutant Mengele." Little blurbs would appear in the "New York Times" regarding Hitler's troops confronting tick borne typhus, "spotted fever" and an epidemic "Plague of Eastern Europe" causing "violent attacks of fever accompanied by severe pains in the legs and head," smacking of relapsing fever and Lyme. (1) Further articles in the medical journals were more specific, blood samples drawn from the returning troops on the Russian Front finding spirochetes:

"LATENT RELAPSING FEVER INFECTIONS WITH RHEU-MATOID MANIFESTATIONS" "Die Latent Rekurrensinfektion und das Rekurrensrheumatoid" A.. Boeger, ('Tropical Disease Bulletin' 2/45, v. 42, #2)

Page 130: "The author mentions that in South Russia and the Caucasus, where the disease is endemic, many cases of relapsing fever occurred amongst the German troops... The method of transmission is said to be usually the body louse, but the author considers that the bed bug may also be a carrier. The main object of the paper, however, is to call attention to the rheumatoid manifestations that may accompany latent infections of the disease, and the necessity for careful blood examination for spirochaetes in all doubtful cases."

The American military was also leery regarding conditions throughout Europe, tracking relapsing fever and typhus, both tick and louse borne, calling upon Dr. Harry Plotz and the American Cyanamid Corporation to manufacture vaccines for the troops. (2) The medical community, Communist and Socialist, had not been able to create a spirochete vaccine, so they wrote their patients off as "incurables." The epidemics surging out of Russia spread across its southern borders, Pavlovskii's rats infecting Iraq and Iran, finally sweeping through Palestine and North Africa. By 1939, reports of a brand new tick borne relapsing fever surfaced in Babylon. (3) Eventually, the Balkans and the Orient would be inundated with typhus, brucellosis, relapsing fever and Lyme, its citizens still malnourished and raging mad today.

The Communist doctors inside of Russia were sporting two theories of thought on immunology at the time, Neo-Mendelism, based on heredity, and Lysenkoism, based on environment. As a result of this split in philosophies, as so eloquently written in Julian Huxley's "Heredity East and West: Lysenko and World Science," the Nazis roasted their own children deemed genetic mutants in the gas chambers and the Communists starved them to death. While the Nazis hoped to rid the world of its genetic mutants, the Communists played upon human insecurity, brainwashing their victims with such ploys as 'redistribution of the wealth' hoping to spark world revolution. No one was building and creating the wealth, and food simply ran out. The 'useless eaters' were exterminated, both philosophies of Neo-Mendelism and Lysenkoism driven by simple greed.

Dr. Fredric Wertham straddled both sides of the fence when it came to immunological and environmental deficiencies in behavioral psychiatry. His early years were spent under the tutelage of Franz Jahnel at the KWI for Brain Research Serology and Spirochete Laboratory. Jahnel, in our previous chapter, took over the serology and spirochete lab under Ernst Rudin when Dr. Leo Alexander of the Army Medical Corps arrived to investigate war crimes, Rudin fleeing prosecution as the rest of KWI skipped off to Suchomi. Back in the 1930s while psychiatrist Leo Alexander was tabulating the increased cases of mental illness in Germany in his "Eugenical Sterilization," Frederic Wertham and Franz Jahnel were studying spirochetes at the KWI in Munich.(4)

Jahnel, with his underling Wertham, began publishing new material in the 1930s from the KWI branch in Moscow on spirochetes in chicken brains and Russian peasant women, Newcastle disease of chickens undistinguishable from Lyme at the time. Wertham then emigrated to America, his voluminous writings included an ardent protest against violence in the mass media in his "A Sign for Cain, an Exploration of Human Violence," fingering cartoonist's Bob Cane's "Batman" as the epitome of barbarism. With 44% of all Lyme cases cited by the CDC in New York City (see 'Introduction'), Wertham went about building an insane asylum in Harlem, lecturing Congress on the necessity of school bussing and forecasting America's race riots. (5) Wertham is worth following. The situation in New York deserves a whole chapter.

The doctors at the KWI for Brain Research were a mixed bag of tricks, some Neo Mendelists, others Lysenkoists. The institute was turned over to the German Army and Luftwaffe Medical Corps for research. It is important to comprehend that these doctors were all socialists, willing to follow both Hitler and Stalin over the edge of the world. The horrors of the KWI's medical experiments and its killing centers, the concentration camp experiments, are neatly catalogued in their own diaries. The Nuremberg medical trials, US vs. Karl Brandt, documents medicine at its lowest point in human history. The Jews, Gypsies of Eastern Europe, and the Slavs were brutally tortured to death for the 'advancement of science.' The macabre experiments came straight out of Frankenstein's laboratories.

Psychiatrist Dr. Leo Alexander, once emigrating to America through China, would be assigned to the US Army Medical Corps, for the investigation of his old classmates in the "Applied War Research Department" of the Ahnenerbe. Section H was stationed at Strasbourg, where Professor August Hirt and Dr. Eugene Von Haagen experimented with viruses and typhus upon thousands of prisoners from Naztweiler. Von Haagen fled to the Russian Front as ALSOS took over his apartment for their headquarters. Haagen had previously researched at the Rockefeller Institute in New York, returning to Germany when war broke out. Section R of the Applied War Research Department was conducted at Dachau, where Dr. Rascher's Luftwaffe exposure to cold experiments took place.

Alexander's reports were turned over to Boris Pash's ALSOS Mission, such as "Treatment of Shock From Extreme Exposure to Cold," "Measures Concerning Public Mental Health Practices in Germany: Sterilization and Execution of Patients Suffering From Nervous or Mental Disease," "German Military Neuropsychiatry and Neurosurgery," "Miscellaneous Aviation Medical Matters," "Methods for Influencing International Scientific Meetings as Laid Down by German Scientific Organizations," and "Neuropathology and Neurophysiology Including Electro-encephalography in Wartime Germany." All have been public record for over fifty years.

(6) Yet there remain mysteries, the National Library of Medicine holds "Methods for Influencing International Scientific Meetings," on page 3, Alexander cites he "scrutinized Ernst Rudin's confidential files," but where are they today? Ironically, many of these reports testify to the Nazis doctors' atrocities against their own non-Jewish citizens. For anyone suffering Lyme disease, the most chilling of Alexander's CIOS reports discern the Nazi treatment of patients, many children, suffering from multiple sclerosis and encephalitis. Even though they suffered tick borne diseases, they were termed 'mentally ill' and exterminated by the thousands. Alexander details the Nazi doctors' history when Hugo Spatz took over the KWI for Brain Institute after Oscar Vogt was transferred to its Moscow branch:

"NEUROPATHOLOGY & NEUROPHYSIOLOGY INCLUDING ELECTRO-ENCEPHALOGRAPHY IN WARTIME GERMANY" Leo Alexander, Major MC, AUS Hq. ETOUSA 20 July, 1945 CIOS team 94, report 359 G-2 Division SHAEF (Rear) APO 413, National Library of Medicine, Bethesda, MD, originally released to the State University of Iowa Library, 1947.

Page 41: 'The Department of Serology, Experimental Therapy and Spirochaetal Research of the Deutsche Forschungsanstalt fur Psychiatrie, Kaiser Wilhelm Institute, in Munich, headed by Dr. F. Jahnel.'

"Dr. Jahnel is now, in addition to his other duties, director of the entire Forschungsanstalt, as Dr. Rudin fled on the arrival of the Americans... as to his routine work, Dr. Jahnel carried out serologic examinations for military and civilian hospitals, including examinations of blood and spinal fluid. The annual turnover of his examinations varied somewhat but the period from 1 April 1944 to 1 April 1945 appears representative. During this period examinations of 7,750 cases were performed, of which 5,000 were members of the armed forces, 170 prisoners of war, and the remainder civilians..."

[Multiply those figures times ten years under the Reich, 80,000 citizens?]

"Of scientific investigations Dr. Jahnel was particularly interested in the non-specific positive syphilis reactions occurring in non-syphilitic illnesses, the so called "false-positives" which occurred, for instance, after injection with horse serum, immunization for diphtheria, in and after malaria, and in other conditions (Nos. 1-5, Appendix 9)... Another confidential report concerns immunological and serological studies of relapsing fever. In these studies he transmitted seven different strains of North African relapsing fever through mice and cultures. they came from seven cases which occurred in the African Corps. These cases had originally been mistaken for malaria, but blood tests revealed Spirochaeta recurrens. He found that several of these strains were highly neurotropic. (Unpublished paper. appendix 9, No. 9)."

"In concluding the interview, certain general problems of psychiatric interest were discussed with Dr. Jahnel (who had been a general neuropsychiatrist before he specialized in serology). Regarding the handling of neurosis problems, Dr. Jahnel feels that in the First World War one had confronted this problem in a helpless manner. He feels this problem has now been solved by means of suggestive treatment with the aid of painful electric currents, as well as by the policy of not letting the patients attain the goals which the illness served. In the last war, the patients definitely felt that they could attain things by their illness, while this war they could not."

'The Genealogical Section of the Deutsche Forschungsanstalt fur Psychiatrie, Kaiser Wilhelm Institute in Munich, formerly headed by Dr. E. Rudin'

"On visiting Dr. Rudin's department I found that he had fled, presumably because of the part that he had played in the program of killing the insane. He felt that some of the relatives of the killed patients might exact retribution from him because in the course of this (blank line), but also patients suffering from remedial illnesses, such as depressions or brain tumors. Spot-checking of Dr. Rudin's files failed to produce any of the material on the organization of the killing centers. I was told that he had destroyed all of the damaging evidence..."

Page 14: 'The Anatomical and General Pathology Section of Dr. Hugo Spatz, of the Kaiser Wilhelm Institut for Hirnforschung.'

"As for brains from the killing centers of the insane, Dr. Spatz denied that he or any other member of his Institute ever had received any. He added that the killing of the insane was done in deep secret, that nobody was supposed to know about it except SS personnel although of course it did leak out, that consequently no scientists or scientific institutions could be contacted in order to undertake neuropathological studies, and that thus invaluable pathologic material was lost and remained unutilized... This statement was later revealed to be in part inaccurate when Dr. Hallervorden who was a section chief right in Dr. Spatz's own institute, admitted having received and examined 500 brains from the killing centers of the insane."

Page 17: "A curious case is one in which the brain of a patient who died from endocarditis showed, in addition to small abscesses and shortenings, another single lesion which exhibited all the characteristics of a focus of multiple sclerosis. In view of his rejection of the vascular theory of multiple sclerosis, Dr. Hallervorden comes to the conclusion that this must have been a rare case of single isolated lesion of multiple sclerosis, thus postulating that two diseases co-existed in the patient."

Page 20: "Dr. Hallervorden had obtained 500 brains from the killing centers for the insane. These patients had been killed in various institutions with carbon monoxide gas. Dr. Hallervorden himself initiated this collaboration. As he put it: 'I heard that they were going to do this, and so I went up to them and told them Look here now, boys, if you are going to kill all these people, at least take the brains out so that the material could be utilized.' 'There was wonderful material among those brains, beautiful mental defectives, mal-formations and early infantile diseases. I accepted those brains of course. Where they came from and how they came to me was really none of my business.' Dr. Hallervorden went on to say 'This thing was a beautiful mess.' "

The items listed in Alexander's report in 'Appendix 9' regarding relapsing fever spirochetes were not to be found amongst the National Library of Medicine's miscellaneous holdings on Franz Jahnel. Jahnel's research in chicken brain spirochetes and "non-syphilitic illnesses" with "false positives" from reactions to diphtheria vaccine remain a mystery. Can anyone locate Alexander's collection of Rudin's files? There seems an unusual void in vaccine reaction material on spirochete infected patients from the WW II vintage. The syphilis spirochete is a cousin to the Lyme and relapsing fever spirochetes. Just imagine the fate of the German troops on the Russian Front as they were vaccinated by their own Nazi doctors for diphtheria. Was this a form of medical sabotage? Just a little race purification of soldiers with weak human constitutions? Their neurological condition of madness intensified. The library tower at the Hoover Institute for War, Peace, and Revolution holds a curious little CIOS report filed by the British on Hugo Spatz's KWI research. Here, Spatz testified that he had received only brains from dead German soldiers on the Russian Front. His interrogator naively presumed Spatz completely honest and up front, withholding nothing, just two weeks after the Nazi surrender, May 7, 1945, concluding:

""OBERFELDARZT PROFESSOR HUGO SPATZ THE DEPARTMENT OF BRAIN RESEARCH KAISER WILHELM INSTITUTE" item No. 24, file no. XXVII-96, CIOS trip 277. May 27, 28 1945. Hoover Institute, Stanford Univ.

"The impression we gained was that the Kaiser Wilhelm Institute, or at least that part of it concerned with brain research and neuropathology, had spent the whole war collecting brains, and that they had in fact achieved nothing. In any event, the material collected has probably been lost forever. Their work in general seems to have been based on rather old-fashioned morbid anatomy and will probably be sterile."

By this time, diphtheria was running rampant throughout Europe, vaccinated or not, the population went nuts. To justify the compassion in the killing of the insane, the Reich made a documentary of a MS patient's sufferings, Jack Kavorkian style, and presented it to their fellow colleagues. We will never know if Mengele's SARIN and SOMAN tests from Auschwitz were amongst Spatz's collection, but it would be a good bet and reason enough to destroy the evidence. Here, Luftwaffe doctor and eyeball specialist, Werner K. Noell researched toxins inducing neurologic seizures. (7)

Germany was not particularly secretive with its early war research sharing tests with the Chinese, Japanese and Russians. Noell's Luftwaffe supervisor, Dr. Hubertus Strughold, had been captured and interrogated after the war by the Naval Technical Mission to Europe. Accordingly, Dr. Chang Tusute spent three years with the Luftwaffe and left in 1939 to later head General Chiang Kai Shek's Aviation Medicine. "Russian visitors to the aviation medical laboratories were frequent and the German workers were instructed to cooperate completely and to show their work in all details." Dr. Miura from Japan was also "free to travel throughout Germany" but was later killed while returning to Japan on a U-boat. Strughold insisted the Nazis didn't like the Russian or Japanese doctors, slyly choosing sides before his interrogators. (8) Strughold would later move to America and head the US Air Force Medical Research Center. He collated his colleagues' Luftwaffe research at the AAR Medical Center in Heidelberg in "German Aviation Medicine," editing out the concentration camp experiments, the full text later discovered in the US National Archives. By then, Dr. Malcolm C. Grow from the WW I Red Cross typhus mission in Russia had become the first Air Force Surgeon General, overseeing Strughold's literary achievements. Grow's 1918 publication "Surgeon Grow: An American in the Russian Fighting" celebrated the Bolshevik Revolution. (9)

Grow's choice of Strughold to head Randolph Air Force Base's Aero-Space Medical Research Center may have laid the foundation for another intelligence fiasco. As we shall see, the Mafia and the American Communist Party now had a patsy to blame their own atrocities upon. Congress's Frank Church Report on MKULTRA and the MONARCH Program with Nazi Paperclip scientists using mind control experiments and hallucinatory drugs like LSD would lay the foundation for Hollywood's "Conspiracy

Theory" and years of nonsense to follow. Leo Alexander partnered with the CIA's future psychedelic drug idiot, Timothy Leary, to investigate poisons in 1941. (10) Mistakenly, Noreen Gosh would attribute the kidnapping of her son to MKULTRA brainwashing operation run by Nazi scientists for the US Air Force, while he may actually be a victim of a Mafia run international pedophile and drug-money laundering ring with ties to the old KGB. But that's down the road a piece. "Why Johnny Can't Come Home" is a tragic tale indeed, yet personal distrust for the US Government may have clouded the mother's judgement and limited the depth of her research. Nevertheless, she finally found him after years of anguish and determination, a testimony to her perseverance. Noreen Gosh would ask for the assistance of Nebraska Senator, John Decamp, author of the "Franklin Cover-up" in tracking down an international ring of pedophiles and child kidnappings.

Also assigned to the Heidelberg Aero Medical Center was a young Texan, Colonel William Randolph Lovelace, II. His uncle established the Lovelace Foundation, a highly regarded hospital and research facility. The young Lovelace, assigned to the Air Technical Intelligence of the US Army Air Force, would crank out his share of CIOS reports on the Nazi Luftwaffe doctors, like Dr. Leo Alexander reporting to ALSOS. (11) Lovelace would become John F. Kennedy's physician. Fully briefed on Heidelberg, Richard Kuhn's Soman Gas and I. G. Farben's duplicitous role, Lovelace would vanish after the assassination. The FBI holds extensive background checks on Lovelace.

Further documentation of the Nazi doctor's atrocities upon their own citizens arose from Leo Alexander's CIOS reports. Admittance is made to the fact that "insanity" was not inherited, but induced by environment and disease. Nevertheless, the doctors continued to execute their own non-Jewish citizens at an alarming rate, eliminating the "useless eaters," be they rich or poor, in an air of intelligensia arrogance:

"PUBLIC MENTAL HEALTH PRACTICES IN GERMANY" Leo Alexander, CIOS report item no. 24, file no. XXVIII-50. National Library of Medicine
Page 3: "Despite exaggerated hopes concerning the eugenic effects of compulsory sterilization, which were constantly kept alive by the agitation of Dr. Rudin and his associates, the practice of sterilization nevertheless fell gradually into disuse in Nazi Germany... it had been realized that shortly before the war that most insane do not descend from other insane, and that therefore, according to studies by Essen-Mueller, only 3% of the insane in the next generation could be eliminated by sterilizing the insane of the

present... This was exactly the view taken several years before, namely in 1935 by a committee of the American Neurological Association of which I was a member."

Page 6: 'Execution of Patients Suffering from Nervous or Mental Disease':

"Dr. Braunmuhl stated that between January 1940 and June 1941, 1857 patients were taken away to be killed. When these figures were checked with the lists included in the documents, it turned out that this figure did not include the special transport of Jewish victims dispatched on 30 September 1940 to Lubin, Poland, of which no figures remained available in the files... all but one of the 1857 victims, whose names and other data are available in the salvage lists, were non-Jews."

Page 10: "The killings of children were carried out in a special section of the children's department at Eglifing. The most popular substance used for the killing was 'modiscop,' which was a preparation manufactured in Vienna, and widely used as an anesthetic in Vienna..."

"As an illustration of the great secrecy in which the killings were carried out, Dr. Von Braunmuhl pointed to the fact that even county officials and mayors of towns whenever they inquired about one of the killed patients were merely told that the patient had been transferred to an institution of unknown location..."

Page 11: "Looking over these documents one finds that no direct reference to killing was ever made; that the matter in general was veiled with an air of secrecy... frequently referred to as "treatment," "intensive treatment" or "treatment with all means of medical science." Equally non-committal were the killing of the mentally sick..."

Page 29: "Professor Bumke stated on 7 June 1945, that the practice of killing the mentally ill which had been instituted by the Nazis, was supposed to be a deep secret, but the secret soon leaked out. 'While no-body was supposed to talk about it, the sparrows were whistling it from the rooftops.' Professor Bumke stated that for more than one reason it was a tragic crime. The mistrust of the public against psychiatrists had been gradually stilled through faithful public service... extending over 100 years, but this policy of killing the mentally ill had stirred up all that old mistrust again."

"Mistrust"? That would be an understatement! "The sparrows were whistling it from the rooftops"? Soviet biological warfare, coupled with the famine of war, induced madness amongst the German citizens, yet into the furnace they went, minus their heads, of course, handed over to Spatz. This was a war of Socialist doctors against Capitalist patients. These psychiatrists should have been extradited to the astroid belt so that the rest of humanity could achieve peace on earth and some semblance of civilization. Leo Alexander attended the Nuremberg Trials as a counselor, writing the Nuremberg code of ethics, while 99% of the Nazi doctors walked scot free due to lack of evidence. Of course, the majority were hiding out at Suchomi and Beketovka.

In flamboyant prose, Alexander contributed to the Introduction of "Doctors of Infamy" by Alexander Mitscherlich, "This Nazi infamy was not merely the infamy of a few crazed, psychologically twisted practitioners. It appears that fewer than two hundred German physicians participated directly in the medical war crimes; however, it is clear that several hundred more were aware of what was going on." (12) In particular, Leo Alexander singled out Dr. Georg Schaltenbrand in the 'Introduction' for publishing a book on transferring MS from monkeys to humans with no conscience whatsoever, titled "Die Multiple Sclerose des Menschen." Schaltenbrand attributes the cause of MS to a "bakterian," a "spirochaeten" and a "virus" with vaccines inducing an allergic reaction. In an about face, Alexander would then volunteer his assistance to the newly founded National Multiple Sclerosis Society under Byron Waksman, and consult Schaltenbrand for the largest MS survey in the history of the United States. (13)

Schaltenbrand had been captured at the end of the war and politely asked to compile a FIAT report (Field Intelligence Agency Technical) for the Allies comprising Nazi medical research, "FIAT Review of German Science 1939-1946: NEUROLOGY" which covered Franz Jahnel's serology and spirochete laboratory, Hugo Spatz and Hallervorden's typhus brains, and a dozen more KWI Brain Research doctors investigations into multiple sclerosis and spirochetes. Were all of these German citizens merely executed because they were living proof of the Nazi-Soviet collaboration in biological warfare to induce a Communist revolution in Germany, an experiment that backfired, producing Russia's worst enemy? This was a case of socialist crackpot verses Communist crackpot. It will be Leo Alexander's implicating America-Nazi collaboration as responsible for BW attacks upon North Korea, instead of Nazi collaboration with the Soviets, that raises this author's deep suspicions. Was Leo Alexander another Communist agent working for Eisenhower, just like Allen Dulles? This, too, needs further exploration in the upcoming chapters.

Other intelligence reports cited tick borne relapsing fever amongst the German troops in North Africa. Surely the Nazis were not dispersing epidemics amongst their own troops. By the end of the war, the Arab nations were devastated. (14) Following these epidemics since the 1930s was a team of Russian, German, and American scholars at the

Rockefeller Institute in New York conducting similar research to that of Schaltenbrand's vaccines and spirochetes stimulating allergic reactions in the brain, inducing MS. Amongst these doctors was Natzweiler's virus and typhus expert, Eugene Von Haagen, partnered with Dr. Thomas Rivers, future head of the Institute's Hospital in New York. (15) When the British finally caught up with Eugene Von Haagen in 1946, they arrested him for working in a Soviet biological warfare laboratory, something Samuel Gousdsmit failed to mention in "ALSOS," even having resided in Von Haagen's apartment! Surely, our country was betrayed at Nuremberg by our own representatives.

The ALSOS Mission's leftwing bias at Nuremberg, withholding incriminating evidence against the Nazi doctors' crimes and whereabouts further helped the Soviets commit mass murder amongst their own citizens. Goudsmit is documented in a US Army Intelligence report from Fort Meade, "Scientist's Committee on Loyalty Problems (SCOLP)" May 17, 1949, implicating him as a Communist agent. But this was during the McCarthy era, and no one paid attention. According to US National Archives war criminal files, Eugene Von Haagen had actually been captured by US forces in April 1945, prior to Germany's surrender and held in the Hersbruch POW Camp near Nuremberg until June 1946, then released. He returned to his home in Saalfeld Thuringia, but afterwards, his whereabouts became vague. Next he was offered a position at the KWI for Medicine and Biology, Berlin-Buch. Was it then that he vanished across the Eastern Front with the rest of the KWI scientists? The war crimes file continues:

"EUGENE VON HAAGEN" files, National Archives MRB Collection of WW II War Crimes, RG 258, ID No. 677592, Date of Information: May 1950, Date of Report: 31 May 1950.

Page 2: "On 16 November 1946 HAAGEN was arrested in BERLIN-ZEHLENDORF (U. S. Sector) by a sergeant of the British Intelligence Service on suspicion of conducting research in a Soviet Institute for bacteriological warfare... HAAGEN was first placed in the MP jail in BERLIN-WESTEND and then taken to MINDEN (Westphalia), where he was kept in solitary confinement at the so-called War Criminals' Center. Here, according to HAAGEN, he was ill-treated and was not permitted to communicate with his relatives or to use the services of a lawyer.

On 31 January 1947 HAAGEN was taken to a French jail in BADEN-Baden, where at the end of February he was presented an arrest warrant, sighed by a French military government office, charging him with murder, being accessory to murder, mistreatment, etc. In late February he was taken to the military police jail in STRASBOURG and during the next two months was interrogated a few times by a French judge. On 16 May he was brought to NURNBERG as a witness at the Nazi physicians trial... Since 26 January 1948 he has been staying at the maison d'Arrest in METZ.

In December 1947 and March 1948 HAAGEN was frequently interrogated about his activities at the SCHIRMECK and NATZWEILER concentration camps, where he was charged with having tested his antityphus vaccine on gypsies. Subsequently, he was again charged with murder and mistreatment. According to the latest information Prof. HAAGEN is still confined in METZ."

The Rockefeller Institute must have been squirming at this point. Suchomi and Beketovka were revolving doors for the Nazi doctors. This War Crimes report indexed seventy-five of Von Haagen's medical articles, including his collaborations with Ralf Muckenfuss and Thomas Rivers at the Rockefeller Institute. Other German war correspondence between Von Haagen and the SS's Dr. Hirt using humans for spotted fever vaccines made it into the appendix. Further requests by Haagen for lab rats and mice from Walter Schreiber's Military Medical Academy are indexed. God only knows what Haagen was doing with Schreiber's rats, letting them loose upon the camps, or the German populace. Recall that Schreiber's underling, Wolfgang Wirth accompanied "Adjutant Mengele" on the Waffen Pruf 9's "decontamination mission" to Russia in 1940. Walter Schreiber, too, would defect to Moscow, sharing abode with Field Marshal Von Paulus, defeated at Stalingrad, father of the National Komite Freie Deutschland. Whose side were these Nazi doctors on? Or, were Germany and Russia secret allies all along? Would Nelson Rockefeller's former bank president, John J. McCloy, now High Commissioner to Germany, be able to keep a lid upon the Von Haagen affair?

Dr. Walter Schreiber was one of the slimiest characters to have every crawled out from under a rock. Not only did he "instantly" become a Communist, he offered his services to the Soviets as a 'witness for the prosecution' against his fellow Nazi doctors in the Nuremberg War Trials. No one could pin anything on this schmuck once in the hands of the Russians, who protected him and tutored him. After his training by the KGB in espionage and political sabotage, he was whisked across the border to West Germany. In a rush to save the world, America snapped him up, depriving the Soviets of Schreiber's further services? Schreiber had "very interesting" company in Moscow, including BW and CW experts from I. G. Farben:

"INDIVIDUALS IN SOVIET PW SPECIALISTS CAMPS" From: ID EUCOM reference: ECIC RT-634-49(SI-451): ECIC RT-1121-49(SI-467) date of information Sept. 1949, date of Report 14 March 1950. OACSI file MIS 661866, Nat. Arch. MRB.

Page 1: "A German technician who was held in the USSR from November 1945 to September 1949 has furnished an extensive list of Germans and other nationals held in PW specialists' camps in the Soviet Union.... Camp No. 7027/2 In Krasnogorsk, Moskva Oblast..."

Page 3: "... Interrelated comments made by Source B: are from Dr. Walter P. Schreiber, who was in the USSR from April 1945 to October 1948. b-2 information supplied by Schreiber has been included in ECIC reports RT-634-49 and RT-1121-49."

Page 6: "In the Winter of 1946-1947 when Source B (Walter Schreiber) was living in the same house as PAULUS in Timilino, several scientific trade papers and magazines in Russian and other languages were misrouted by the post office and arrived at the house by mistake."

Additional doctors of consequence in the Specialists Camps were listed as Helmut Grauer, I. G. Farben representative, having spent six years inside Russia during World War One; and Dr. Hohorst, parasitologist, "working at an unknown location in the USSR"; and Professor Jung, "formerly with the Chemical Warfare Laboratory at the Citadel in Berlin- Spandau... After the capitulation of Germany, Jung voluntarily went to the USSR where he headed a group of German chemical warfare experts... later for some unknown reason, Jung was deported to Siberia." Also listed amongst the elite POWs were Field Marshal Friedrich Von Paulus and Prince Radziwill of Poland in camp 7027/I with his family, (page 15). Eventually, one of the Radziwill princes would marry Jacquelyn Kennedy's sister and become an I. G. Farben consultant. Walter Schreiber, himself is described as "former surgeon general, left the USSR to participate as a witness at the Nuremberg Trials. Upon his return to Moscow, Schreiber spent a long time in a camp under agreeable circumstances where he held the position of "Starshina" (elder in the military, corresponding to M/Sgt.) with the NKFD." Other POWs "wondered about his attitude." "Schreiber has settled in one of the Western Zones of Germany" concluded the OACSI file. He was on special assignment for the KGB. The American Embassy in London tipped off the FBI on its possible new arrival from "Russia with love."

WALTER P. SCHREIBER FBI file 64-32655-66
To the director, FBI Washington DC, August 11, 1949. From: J. A.

Zimmerman, Legal Attaché, American Embassy, London, W. 1.

"For the information of the Bureau, there are quoted below the contents of a letter received by me from (blackout) dated at Wuerzburg, Germany, August 8, 1949":

"...attached is a [magazine] clipping which reads as follows:

'The Soviet Secret Police has the intention to expand activities into West Berlin and into the Western Zones. So reports the "Sozialdemokrat" British licensed Berlin paper. For assignment in those areas will be chiefly selected former members of the Gestapo. According to the paper, the decision was made at meeting of the NKWD in Karlshorst where the following persons were present...'

A second clipping reports: 'Former German Diplomats in the USSR'

'At first they were unknown men who had exposed themselves not too far through activities with the National Committee, but who had won the confidence of the Russians by graduation in Russian Antifa-Polit-Schools (Anti-Fascist-Political-Schools). They all appeared as members of the Socialist Unity Party... but did not appear in any conspicuous leading positions. Later they infiltrated also into the first ranks of the DCU (Christian Democratic Union, one of the strongest parties in the West-zone, but also represented in the East-zone)... The officer, created in their organization in the USSR and directed by occupation authorities, occupied slowly key positions in the East zone. Their names were never mentioned and only the Russian propaganda for the so-called 'National Front' exposed this corps to the eyes of the public. More so, because since the Summer 1948 more and more of the members of this former National Committee appeared in the East zone and took over responsible positions with the volks-polizei and with the National Bolshevist National-Democratic Party. The men of the former National Committee occupied a large part of the country-director and police chief positions.' "

Following these clippings was a list of seventeen German secret agents trained by the Soviets to overthrow the West by infiltration. Last on the list was Walter P. Schreiber. The Berlin Wall had not yet been erected, and it was easy for these agent provocateurs to infiltrate the Western Zones. What did Schreiber, a NKVD secret police agent, do as head of the East German Medical Corps? Incapacitate his fellow Germans with disease, facilitating a Communist takeover? The conditions inside East Germany were simply appalling. In contrast, the West launched an aggressive campaign to stamp out epidemics and clean up, far beyond the financial aid of the Marshall Plan. One in every three carcasses of meat was infected with brucellosis. The milk was equally bad. The Americans brought in doctors for the German citizens and veterinarians for livestock inspections, who in turn, trained thousands of Germans into a medical work force. Medical station check points were set up, citizens weighed to measure mal-nutrition, insurance companies established for financing health costs.

In contrast, the Russian zone perpetrated the misery, actually refusing to let doctors report epidemiological statistics and deaths. Millions of East Germans died along with millions more Soviet citizens. Again, we return to the OACSI files for a vivid picture inside the Eastern and Western Zones:

"MILITARY GOVERNMENT OF GERMANY: PUBLIC HEALTH AND MEDICAL AFFAIRS" Monthly report of Military Governor US Zone, 20 February 1946, No. 7. OACSI file 241822, Nat. Arch. MRB

Page 7: 'Meat and Dairy Products'

"There are 171 veterinarians and 44,134 lay inspectors engaged in meat inspection in the US Zone. The latter are being selected and given training in the handling and disposing of inspected meats to supplement available veterinary personnel... During the month 92,623 carcasses were examined, 1,190 metric tons of examined meat being passed and 386 metric tons being rejected because of disease. These figures are exclusive of Wuerttenberg-Baden, from which no reports were received. Milk surveys made by German veterinarians show that the larger, well equipped dairies are satisfactorily pasteurizing the milk they receive. Owing to a lack of equipment and fuel shortages, the small dairies heat the milk either to insufficient temperatures or not at all... there were 383 dairies employing 4,786 personnel reported in the Zone..."

Keep in mind that the same ixodes tick that carries brucellosis infecting the livestock and milk also carried typhus and Lyme. In contrast, how were the East Germans coping with the post war situation? OACSI file MIS 647595 "Public Health Measures and Epidemics in the Soviet Zone Germany" cited "Illegal border crossers who were interrogated by the 66th CIC Detachment have given the following information concerning public health measures and epidemics in the Soviet Zone of Germany." Typhoid epidemics were rampant with "an undetermined number of fatalities." School children were vaccinated against diphtheria, and tuberculosis and venereal diseases were "prevalent in Rostok," the Soviet soldiers "especially susceptible to tuberculosis." Were the vaccinated children actually protected against diphtheria, or further weakened in resistance to other diseases? Think back to the vaccination reactions of the German soldiers at Jahnel's spirochete and serology lab.

This was just a hint of interior troubles. East Germany was a disaster:

"Vital Statistics and Health in the Soviet Zone of Germany," OACSI file MIS 491620 "The number of abortions equaled the number of live births in the Russian Zone... Vital statistics as well as the population data, were among the most closely guarded fields of information in the Central German Administration for the Soviet Zone... an especially high death rate... due primarily to tuberculosis and undernourishment, the Soviet Military government has recently prohibited the registration of these cases on medical certificates... All records were destroyed on diseases of former prisoners of war. The number of TB cases rose from 2,000 in 1944 to 25,000 in the spring of 1948... The Welfare Offices, to which were available only two doctors and ten nurses, had been visited in 1947 by 44,000 persons..."

Reports on Russian attacks with Flexner's dysentery surfaced, where 40 thousand cases had been reported in Finish hospitals. American intelligence actually received this information during the war, the Finns had captured the Russians red handed, with flasks of the bacteria culture in 1944, American intelligence filing the report six years later in 1950. Once again, the dirty work of America's "ally" was suppressed to enhance the war effort in OACSI file MIS 705856 "Transmittal Samples of Flexner Bacillus." Recall the Red Army had confiscated the Czechoslovakian Movidyn factory to immunize itself while poisoning its own wells and water supplies. Were they deploying Flexner's Bacillus?

There was mounting evidence that something was amuck in West Germany, too. Diphtheria began to emerge in the non-vaccinated civilian population. The nation was already inundated with typhus and relapsing fever. Reflect back to Leo Alexander's "Neuropathology and Neurophysiology" report on Franz Jahnel's Serology and Spirochete laboratory at the KWI. This is where Jahnel began investigating the neurological reactions of German troops infected with the combination of typhus, relapsing fever spirochetes, and diphtheria vaccines, driving the victims mad. The following pattern of epidemiological statistics in the city of Hamburg, located in the British Zone, reflect the same scenario as Jahnel's laboratories. Here, Dr. Rudolf Degkwitz of the Hamburg Health Department, had been assigned chief of the Committee to Combat Tuberculosis, soon to resign. Eventually, our State Department got hold of an interview of Dr. Degkwitz through the American Consulate General in Hamburg on March 17, 1947 and painted a not too rosy picture of its condition. Obviously, Dr. Walter Schreiber was not alone in his efforts to destroy Germany from the inside out:

"COMMENTS BY DR. RUDOLF DEGKWITZ ON HAMBURG HEALTH CONDITIONS" OACSI file 358868, National Archives MRB record group 319, RB/BW Bid # 7502 & 5302.

Confidential: American Consulate General, Hamburg, Germany, March 17, 1947 To: The Honorable Secretary of State, Washington.

"To the people of Hamburg Degkwitz is a controversial figure. According to many of them, verified by British Intelligence, he was one of the original members of the NSDAP, [Nazi Party] was in fact a member of the Munich Putsch. However, he became disaffected early but in 1937 applied for re-admission to the party, which was refused. In 1943 he wrote a letter to his son, serving as an officer on the Russian Front, advising him not to continue with the senseless war which the Allies would win. The letter fell into the hands of the Nazis and the Doctor was put into a concentration camp, where he remained to the capitulation. He is classified by the British as officially, an anti nazi... He tells the following story to illustrate the de Nazification program in the British Zone. One farmer tells another that he is de-Nazifying his turnips. The other farmer asks him to explain. 'I am pulling up the little ones, but leaving the big ones, is the answer.'

MEDICAL One hears about the shortage of medicines, particularly from the Germans, many of them report that it is impossible to get the most common items, such asaspirin... 260 mega units of penicillin were confiscated on the Black Market. It was the biggest boon to Hamburg's penicillin supply yet. It is commonly stated that the source of supply of Black Market drugs in the UNRRA (United Nations Relief & Rehabilitation Association).

TUBERCULOSIS The most alarming aspect of public health in Hamburg, as in all the British Zone is tuberculosis... during the recent cold wave and resultant coal crisis, the milk pasteurization process broke down. An estimated 25% of the cows have tuberculosis..." [this is brucellosis]

MISCELLANEOUS There were a few cases of typhus in Hamburg in 1945, none since Control based on two rather separate operations. One is a regular program for rat-catching. This formerly included each year an extensive extermination program through the use of poisoned cereals. Now, since there are no cereals for such purposes, the program is limited to what a team of rat-catchers can do. Those who cross the border of the British Zone legally are de-loused at the border. Those who cross the border "back" are forced to report themselves for food cards and then de-loused. There had been no immunization against typhus. There was a small epidemic of diphtheria in Hamburg this winter... confined to adults and easily controlled."

The Brits retired Degkwitz. Edward M. Groth of the American Consul General in London concluded that "On the whole the retiring director of Public Health in Hamburg points a more optimistic picture of health here than one might expect." This reads like another case of treatment by neglect to incite revolution amongst the destitute. The beginning of this report stated that the returning Nazi doctors from Russian were being kept off Hamburg's Health Department payroll, leaving one doctor per 800 citizens. Once the Nuremberg Trials began, the Nazi doctors became hot potatoes, too hot for their Soviet sponsors to hold on to. No wonder the British were skeptical. Were these revolving door docs from Suchomi and Beketovka armed with the same intentions as Walter Schreiber? Keep in mind that rat borne typhus epidemics were usually followed by relapsing fever epidemics; mixed with diphtheria, the population was ripe for re-volt. Coupled with brucellosis, "tuberculosis in cattle," another disease of the nervous system, the veterinarians also had their hands full. Estimates between 100,000 and a million starving residents in Hamburg were cited by the British under Degkwirtz's control. Was Degkwitz a "big turnip" or a "reverse radish"? It was a most perplexing state of affairs.

While the British were arresting Nazi doctors like Eugene Von Haagen, and firing suspicious incompetents like Degkwitz, our American CIC 430th Unit was either releasing Nazis like Wirth and Mengele, facilitat-ing their escape to Russia, or hiring them, fresh out of Beketovka and Suchomi. By the end of the war, President Truman had a problem in his State Department, replacing James Byrnes with George C. Marshall, only to be followed by Dean Acheson, all left wing deviants who would lead America into disaster at home. Truman's State Department had planted reverse radishes, big turnips, and hot potatoes in its garden, leaving America virtually defenseless against a potential Soviet biological warfare attack. Leading a fleet of Flying Dutchmen out of Vladivostok, the SS ELBRUS silently encroached upon the port of Philadelphia with its cargo of furs, the hammer and sickle furled atop its mast.

CHAPTER 7 NOTES

(1) "EPIDEMIC EXPERTS AID HITLER" "New York Times" 7/25/42 p. 3 c. 4

"PLAGUE HITS NAZI ARMY: REICH RADIO TELLS OF EPI-DEMICS OF STRANGE DISEASE IN RUSSIA" "New York Times" 2/16/43 p. 4

(2) "Mass Production of Vaccine Against Typhus Fever of European Type" Hans Zinsser, Harry Plotz, J. F. Enders, "Science" v. 91, p. 51-52, 1/12/40.

"Geographic Distribution of Certain Diseases" War Department, Number 8-6, 6/16/44, US Gov. Print. Of. Wash. DC, Lib. of Cong. PB 15166, by order of Secretary of War, G. C. Marshall. Page 9 "'Relaps-ing Fever' Louse & Tick Borne; Page 12: 'Typhus Fever' Louse & Tick Borne."

"HOOVER'S HANDBOOK" edited by Gary Hoover, Alta Campbell, Patrick J. Spain. Reference Press of Publishers Group West, Emeryville, CA 1991. Page 72: 'American Cyanamid Company' "leading US supplier of biologicals (vaccines)... leading supplier of DPT (diphtheria-pertussis-tetanus) vaccine for US children since the 1940s... During WW II the company supplied US troops with typhus vaccine..."

(3) "Une Nouvelle Fievre Recurrente Humaine Discoverte Dans la Region de Babylone Iraak" by M. Emile Brumpt, comptets Rendus Hebdomadaires des Seances de l'Academie des Sciences, 6/19/39. Pages 2029-2031.

(4) "Ueber das Vorkommen Positive Wassermann - und Flockung-sreaktionen im Serum anscheinend Gesunder Hammel" by Professor Dr. Franz Jahnel of the Deutschen Forschungsanstalt fur Psychiatrie in Munchen "Aeitschrift Fur Immunitiatsforschung Und Experimentelle Therapie" 4/24/40, v. 98, pages 306-314.

(5) "A SIGN FOR CAIN: an Exploration of Human Violence" Fred-ric Wertham, MD, Macmillan Company, NY 1966, Dust Jacket: "Dr. Wertham received his medical training in Germany and England and did postgraduate studies in France, England, and Austria."

"Are the Histological Lesions of Dementia Paralytica Specific?" Am. J. Psychiat.v. 89 part 2, 1932, Pages 811-815: "In the course of experimental studies on the reaction of the central nervous system... I stumbled upon a hitherto undescribed spontaneous disease of the brain in chickens..."

"THE BRAIN AS AN ORGAN" Fredric Wertham, Macmillan Co., NY 1934

Pages 452-453: "Since the discovery of spirochaetes in dementia paralytica by Noguchi... Spatz has evolved a theory that in brain syphilis the spirochetes enter by way of the spinal fluid, in dementia paralytica through the blood vessels..."

"Psychotherapy in Disorders of Gastro Intestinal Tract" Fredric Wertham, Rev. Gastroenterol. 20: 573-578. Aug. 1953

"Uber das Vorkommen Positiver Wassermann - und Flockungsreaktionen im Serum Anscheinend Gasunder Hammel" by Professor Dr. F. Jahnel, Eingegangen bei der Schfiftleitung am 24 April 1940. Page 312: cites Jahnel's research with Fredric Wertham on spirochetes back in the early 1930s at the KWI for Brain Research in Germany.

(6) "ALSOS" Samuel A. Goudsmit, Henry Schuman, Inc. NY 1947. Page 66-67, ALSOS take over Haagen residence. Page 207: cites Ahnenerbe and Eugene Von Haagen, Alexander reports. Pages 73-75: cites Haagen Natzweiler experiments.

(7) "Neuropathology & Neurophysiology Including Electro-encephlography in Wartime Germany" Leo Alexander, Nat. Lib. Medicine, Bethesda, MD. Pages 25 & 27.

(8) "AVIATION MEDICINE: ORGANIZATION OF THE LUFTWAFFE" CIOS Item no. 24, file no. XXIII-10, by Lieut. A. H. Andrews, U.S.N.R., NavTechMisEu; CIOS, G-2, Division, SHAEF (Rear) APO 413. Nat. Arch. MRB. Pages 2 & 5.

"THE NAZI CONNECTION" "Frontline" #505, 2/24/87 broadcast on PBS, copyright 1987 WGBH Educational Foundation. Pages 17 and 18.

(9) "SURGEON GROW: An American in the Russian Fighting" Malcolm C. Grow, Formerly Lieut. Colonel Imperial Russian Army Medical Corps; Frederick A. Stokes Co. Publishers NY 1918. Pages xi - xii: 'Forward'

"GERMAN AVIATION MEDICINE" vol. I, prepared under the auspices of the Surgeon General, US Air Force, Major General Malcolm C. Grow, Department of the Air Force, US Government Printing Office 1950, Randolph Air Force Base, School of Aviation Medicine. Page 111: "German scientists come to USA from KWI Heidelberg." Page V: 'Table of Contents' Part I: "Development and Organization by Hubertus Strughold. Part IV: "High Altitude Physiological Fundamentals" by Werner K. Noell & others."

(10) "Deaths From Poisonings Incidents in Massachusetts" by L. Alexander, M. Moore, and T. Leary; J. Crim Psychopath. 3: 100-111, 1941

"Foreign & Military Intelligence, Book I, Final Report of the Select Committee to Study Governmental Operations with Respect to Intelligence Activities" US Senate, 94th Congress, 2nd Session, April 26, 1976. Pages 384-393, 402-405.

(11) "RESEARCH IN AVIATION MEDICINE FOR THE GERMAN AIR FORCE" by Colonel William Randolph Lovelace II, M.C. US Army Air Force; CIOS Item no.. 24 file no. XXVI-56; National Library of Medicine, Bethesda, MD. Page 4.

(12) "DOCTORS OF INFAMY: THE STORY OF THE NAZI MEDICAL CRIMES" by Alexander Mitscherlich, head of the German Medical Commission to Military Tribunal No. 1, Nuremberg and Fred Mielke. Henry Schuman, NY 1949. With statements by Andrew C. Ivy, MD; Telford Taylor, Brigadier General, and Leo Alexander, MD. Pages x & xxxi.

(13) "DIE MULTIPLE SKLEROSE DES MENSCHEN" Georg Schaltenbrand, Georg Thieme, Verlag, Leipzig 1943, Chapter II 'Theorien uber die Urschen der Multiplen Sklerose' Page 32. citing cause of MS

"MULTIPLE SCLEROSIS PROGNOSIS AND TREATMENT" by Leo Alexander, Charles C. Thomas Publisher, Springfield, Illinois. Page xi: expense... ten year project were defrayed by... 1948-1950 National Multiple Sclerosis Society... 1951-1953 Massachusetts Chapter of the National Multiple Sclerosis Society...1960," Pages 157-159, 'bibliography' #56 & #57 Georg Schaltenbrand, "personal communication 1957."

(14) "TROPICAL MEDICINES AND OTHER MEDICAL SUBJECTS IN GERMANY" CIOS report item # 24, file XXIX-35 by J. B. Rice, US Civilian, T.I.I.C.; Nat. Arch. MRB record group 331. Page 6: 'Relapsing Fever' "Dr. Fischer saw about 150 cases from North Africa... cases thought to be transmitted by ticks..."

(15) "THE HISTORY OF THE ROCKEFELLER INSTITUTE 1901-1953" G W. Corner, Rock. Inst. Press, NY 1964. Pages 388-389: cites Thomas Rivers' research use of vaccine reactions inducing MS in monkeys, and Russian Dr. Olitski's work on encephalitis. Page 463: cites "Thomas Rivers director of hospital 1937," collaboration with "Ralph Muckenfuss future director Naval Biological Laboratory Oakland, CA" and "Eugene Von Haagen, guest worker from Germany" in virus research.

CHAPTER 8

ON THE WATERFRONT

The Docking of the SS ELBRUS

Why were the peasants slaughtering their own livestock, millions of heads of cattle, sheep, ponies, and wild life? Was it infected with brucellosis, tularemia, Q Fever, typhus and Lyme disease? The following State Department files will substanciate this. Hence, there was nothing to eat, no leather for shoes, nor fur or wool for clothing. Welcome to the dead zone. On March 8th, 1949, the "New York Times" ran a curious little article on Russia's Amtorg Trading Company, based in New York City, purchasing hides from Argentina and wool through Australia. Boots and uniforms being a sign of military buildup, the journalist presumed the worst, assuming Russia was amassing a huge army. (1) The slaughtered animal's wool, furs and hides were railroaded to Vladivostok, Russia's fur-shipping center on the Pacific. With the devastating financial loss, Soyuzpushnina, the Soviet fur and textile industry, hoped for huge profits by selling to America. In pure gratitude, they hoisted the cargo upon the same Liberty ships we loaned Stalin to fight the Nazis, redirecting its fleet to Philadelphia, San Francisco, Portland, Los Angeles, and New York City. Pity the poor Koreans just south of Vladivostok's fur shipping center, their ports crawling with rats.

In 1939, when America decided to aid England in her declared war against Hitler, the Nazis began sinking our convoys like rubber duckies. The Maritime Commission used Henry Ford's assembly lines in its shipyards. From the Atlantic to the Pacific, the Great Lakes to the Gulf of Mexico, Rosie the Rivetter and her sisters cranked out a new Liberty Ship a day, faster than the Nazis could sink 'em. "Between 1939 and 1945 the Maritime Commission built 5777 cargo ships, 2770 of these were Liberties." (2) The European Allies got a few, the Chinese were sent 12, the British some 336, and the Soviets, 125. The particulars of this lend-lease

RACHEL VERDON_____ 195

deal were laid out before Congress by Merchant Marine Chief Admiral Smith, February 1947, Congress demanding to know why had the ships not been returned . (3) We had more than enough ships, many destined for the scrap yards. What was the rush? Was the United States under a Soviet biological warfare attack? .

Amongst the 125 lend-lease vessels made for the Soviet Union was a T-2 type oil tanker, christened the SS MUIR WOODS on March 22, 1945 in Portland's Kaiser Shipyards. Just months before the Reich's surrender, the SS MUIR WOODS would sail for Russia to be re-christened the SS ELBRUS after the highest peak in the Caucasus Mountains, the site of General Ewald Von Kleist's victorious retreat. (4) The ELBRUS's vessel status card and history 1945 - 1975 is housed in a small museum at the J. Porter Shaw Library on San Francisco's waterfront. Fortunately the material was retrieved by the author prior the 1989 earthquake with the kind assistance of an old Navy ship chandler, Bill Kooiman. The SS ELBRUS sailed into Philadelphia, January 6, 1946 with 426 tons of fur skins, and camel hair. (5)

Bill Kooiman is a real character, full of knowledge and sea stories. He explained that the ELBRUS, being a Type-2 oil tanker, would not be able to carry dry bulk cargo below deck. And, cargo above deck, would be uninsurable, therefore no ship record need be logged for content or condition. Soyuzpushnina's choice not to log or insure 426 tons of camel hair, and fur skins is highly suspicious. With 125 other lend-lease vessels to choose from, the Russians utilized an old oil tanker. Was the christening and the cargo a deliberate attempt at Soviet blackmail biological warfare? Were the Communists insinuating Eisenhower had been briefed on Beria's acquisition of Tabun at Katyn and the battle of Ordzhonikidze at the base of Mt. Elbrus, the whole history of I. G. Farben's treason bundled up into 426 tons of tick infested furs? The Russians knew that we knew Nazi Germany was allied with the Soviet Union all along. Eisenhower, Heusinger, and the Dulles gang were on the hot seat. And besides, why not destabilize America with a host of new infectious diseases? The following episodes of brand new tick borne epidemics plaguing American ports and livesstock are highly suggestive.

Brief mention of the lend-lease ships used for livestock transport, destination Vladivostok, was made in Sawyer and Mitchell's "The Liberty Ships" offering an explanation for the Lyme infestation at Port Arthur, Texas and the mouth of the Mississippi, entrance to the grain shipping centers of the Great Lakes. While America supplied the Russians with food and oil for the war effort, our allies repaid us with furs and rats. By 1948, the New York Port sanitary inspectors were battling it out with Amtorg, demanding fumigation of all Russian ships entering the harbor. (6)

Shortly after the ELBRUS docked in Philadelphia, Amtorg, at 261 - 5th Avenue, sold tons of furs to the their next door neighbor, Lampson, Fraser and Huth, a famous auction house in New York. After competing against each other for a decade, the three auction houses merged, their history easily traced in the 1930s editions of "Polk's Trow's Copartnership and Corporation Director of Manhattan and the Bronx." This made for an interesting partnership between the old German and Russian community in New York City. By the beginning of World War II, the US State Department was advising the British Embassy that Amtorg Trading Company was nothing but a Nazi pawn, funneling American secrets to the Fascists. (7) Was the 1939 Non-aggression Pact between Stalin and Hitler ever broken? Amtorg did not think so.

On January 6th, 1946, the SS ELBRUS pulled into Philadelphia, dumping its highly suspect cargo. Within a month, February 2nd, Lampson, Fraser and Huth auctioned off Amtorg's booty of 100,000 Persian lamb skins. (8) Suddenly, Amtorg pulled up stakes from 5th Avenue and moved into the luxurious Pratt Estate on Manhattan. Hoover advised Secretary of State, James F. Byrnes that "the Soviet representatives negotiating for the purchase of the Pratt Estate on Long Island insisted yesterday that a punitive cancellation clause be added to the contract of purchase calling for the payment of $10,000 by the Soviets in the event of "force majeur." " (9) Harold Pratt had managed the Rockefeller's Standard Oil Company, and was a millionaire in his own right. Many of America's wealthiest tycoons from the oil industry and Wall Street were members of the Council of Foreign Relations since its inception after World War One. This tightly knit organization of bankers and businessmen, lusted for greater foreign influence, with a track record of left-wing sympathies and affiliations, according to James Perloff's "Shadow of Power." Fidel Castro, Daniel Ortega, amongst many other Communist leaders have lectured or roomed at the Pratt Estate. Under Amtorg's occupancy, its fate was doomed.

The author FOIAed the FBI on Amtorg Trading Company and Lyme disease in 1990, and it has taken over a decade while they have dribbled out records, heavily censored, other files in joint custody with the Navy. Appeal after appeal was made as late as 1997, and by 2001, policy began to change. Thirty-seven pages were originally reviewed, and 13 released, most solidly blacked out, citing Ronald Reagan's executive order 12356 on national defense and foreign policy, (SS ELBRUS FBI file 65-35149-345). The next fourteen FBI files on the SS ELBRUS were also solidly blacked out, excepting the 'Character of the Case' listed is 'ESPIONAGE.' But little clues began to emerge on the ELBRUS's sister ship, the SS EMBA.

Out of 75 pages reviewed, 60 were released, again most blacked out. Seven Soviet tankers had tried to clear the Los Angeles breakwater in May 1946 and were denied access to the harbor; US Naval Intelligence issuing a 'stop order.' (10) Just a month prior, On April Fools Day, J. Edgar Hoover (the Joker), wrote the War Department's Assistant Chief of Intelligence, Hoyte S. Vandenberg, a 'personal and confidential' letter sent by special messenger regarding Russian shipping:

EMBA FBI file 100-343044-42, dated April 1, 1946

"Dear General Vandenberg: Reference is made to my letters of March 27, and 29, 1946, regarding Soviet ship movements... A check of the ports of New York, Newark, New Jersey; Boston, Massachusetts; Philadelphia, Pennsylvania; Norfolk, Virginia; Los Angeles, California, Portland, Oregon; Seattle, Washington; and Vancouver, British Columbia; has reflected the following activity of Soviet vessels during the last week of March, 1946... (Two paragraphs solidly blacked out, all ships listed but the ELBRUS, reason b7D) With apparent exception of the 'Tangus' in the Port of Philadelphia, repairs and loading of the above named vessels are proceeding in what appears to be a routine manner.

Sincerely yours, J. Edgar Hoover, Director"

Stymied and stonewalled, what's wrong with this picture - (blackout)? The FBI and Navy kept records of all Soviet ships entering US ports between 1946 and 1950, its destination, cargo, port of entry and departure. (11) Reflecting back on Chapter 6, Vandenberg died for his country, a patriot, caught in a vice "between the devil and the deep blue sea," (the Dulles gang and the FBI), to quote the Joker in "Batman." More would get snared in the same web of intrigue. The SS ELBRUS was not alone entering American ports with tons of furs. An old German freighter, the SS VILNIUS, seized as war booty by the Soviets, departed from Helsinki December 19th, 1945, sailing for New York with 750 tons of furs, woolen goods and pharmaceutical raw materials. The SS VILNIUS files are State Department files, the index cards running a summary of each topic, facilitating a researcher, even if files have been withdrawn. The ship was captained by Ilija Gavrilloff. Not long after, the SS SUCHAN hit San Pedro California with another 500 tons of furs and camel hair. (12) The American fur market was literally swamped.

The author's FOIA request to the FBI on the SS ELBRUS was originally made 5/21/89, case #316,824, receiving material 8/25/92. Appeals were filed 9/15/92, #92-2793 and 2/24/94, with further sparse declassification 5/13/98, posted to the author April 13, 2001, twelve years later.

See how long this takes? FBI file 100-138643-1364 subtitled "Government Purchasing Commission of the Soviet Union in the United States" "Internal Security-R" of January 1st, 1947, again, was 99% blacked out. One little paragraph appeared, "On December 3rd, (blackout) advised (blackout) that on December 7th the American Russian Lodge of the IWO would want a program with the purpose of collecting funds for the Minsk Hospital. The lodge wants a group of Soviet seamen to attend the program. (Blackout) will arrange to have four or five men from the ELBRUS". The previous pages and following pages were blacked out. A one liner mentioned six crewmen from the ELBRUS had made it ashore at Los Angeles, one of them "getting lost in the crowd." Brief mention was made of strikes impeding the unloading of Soviet ships at Los Angeles, diverting the ships to San Francisco in 1946, (FBI file "EMBA" 65-50883-38.) Pity the ELBRUS's crew.

As the Soviet ships lay in the Los Angeles breakwater, a fire broke out aboard the SS ELBRUS July 1947, (file 65-35149-345). The FBI had received information through its San Francisco SAC from the Soviet Consulate General regarding the condition of the SS ELBRUS and the SS APSHERON. The APSHERON had not been heard from in several days. Further broken discussion was made on ELBRUS repairs. Reference was made to the ELBRUS departure from Vladivostok October 17, 1945 "On board this ship were (whole paragraph blacked out). The San Francisco Office has been advised of this travel. (Blackout) advised that this individual's full name is (blackout). (Blackout) was also on board the "ELBRUS" and she left Los Angeles for Chicago and New York City on October 21, 1945. Both offices have previously been advised of this travel by teletype. No further action is contemplated by this office." Signed R. B. Hood, SAC. Even earlier, (ELBRUS file 100-138643505 April 13, 1945), the Portland SAC seized a box of bills of lading from the Government Purchasing Commission of the Soviet Union, which was "forwarded via Railway Express, under separate cover" to Hoover in the Washington Bureau. All the following pages were either withheld or solidly blacked out. Sailing the high seas aboard the SS ELBRUS with its cargo of furs and rats, no one would blame the crew for attempting mutiny, desertion, burning, or sinking the God damned ship.

The State Department files at the National Archives proved a more revealing source on the SS ELBRUS than the stonewalling FBI. On board the ELBRUS was a desperate soul. His name was Timofei Evstiney Gavrilov, possibly related to the captain of the SS VILNIUS? Gavrilov, meaning "sausage maker" in Polish, is a very common Slavic name, akin to "Smith" in English. Timofei Gavrilov jumped ship in Los Angeles, May

14, 1946 as the SS ELBRUS made its return voyage to Vladivostok. Was he sick? Boy, bet he had a tale to tell. Hoover would not help him. The FBI did everything possible to track down Gavrilov as a "spy"! God forbid this poor wretched soul talk. Perhaps the FBI had withheld its own files out of pure shame!

STATE DEPARTMENT FILE 861.865/8-2046 From Justice Department #310513, Russian Shipping Files of State Department, National Archives, Civil Reference Branch. US State Department of Justice Immigration & Naturalization Service, Franklin Trust Building, Philadelphia 2, PA August 20, 1946

To: The Honorable Secretary of State, Washington, DC

"My Dear Mr. Secretary: This acknowledges the receipt of your letter dated June 24, 1946, addressed to the Attorney General, your file 861.865/2846, enclosing a note from the Embassy of the Union of Soviet Socialist Republics regarding the case of Timofei Evtifievich Gavrilov, a Soviet seaman, who it is claimed, deserted from the tanker 'ELBRUS' on May 14, 1946 at Los Angeles, California. The Records of this office show that a warrant for the arrest of one Timofei Evstiney Gavrilov has been issued on the ground that after admission as a seaman at San Pedro, California via SS "Elbrus" on May 10, 1946, he remained in the United States for a longer time than permitted under the law and regulations governing his admission. A report regarding the status of his case is being requested of the appropriate field office of this Service. As soon as the requested information has been received you will be fully advised. Sincerely, Ugo Carusi, Commissioner."

It's all right there, in the State Department's Russian shipping files at the National Archives Civil Reference Branch. Gavrilov was not caught by the State Department's Immigration and Naturalization Service, despite Soviet demands he be turned over, trumping up charges of theft against him. Supposedly Gavrilov had stolen a suit and $50 from the cash-box. (13) The author went through the east and west coast DC Rom phone directory, calling every Gavriloff, Gavrilov, etc. in an exercise of futility, hoping for a witness to the condition of the SS ELBRUS.

Gavrilov was not alone in jumping ship. Leonid Georgiavich Degojnsky also ran for his life. His State Department file is marked with a 'Withdrawal Slip' on 3/23/76, by the FBI's Post 45. (14) More than this lone document on Degojnsky will vanish in 1976 under jurisdiction of the FBI's Post 45. At this particular time, the Ford Administration's new Vice President was Nelson Rockefeller, George Bush becoming CIA Director. How much did Nelson Rockefeller have to lose from exposure of the Soviet Union's shipping? We can only surmise. Were those KWI docs from Suchomi and Beketovka biting him in the butt? The plot will thicken as we discover oil tycoon Edwin Pauley, both George Bush's and Standard Oil's partner, chaired the WW II lend-lease shipping under Harold Ickes' Department of the Interior.

To help the reader understand the significance of the "withdrawal slips" in these State Department files at the National Archives regarding FBI correspondence, one must first understand its numerical file system. The State Department has a "subject list" which is assigned a corresponding number, like the Dewy-decimal system in the public library, followed by a slash and the date of the document. The subject code for Russian shipping assigned to the SS VILNIUS was "861.8591" so other index cards held under this number should be of significance to our research on Russian fur cargo. Instead of retrieving the documents listed upon the State Department index cards, the author received "withdrawal slips." The slips indicated the FBI had been the authority in 1976 responsible for the withdrawals. Hoping the FBI had duplicate copies, the author FOIAed the Justice Department on August 8th, 1994 and was stonewalled for four years. After much effort, two files were obtained through the intervention of Congressman Merrill Cook.

STATE DEPARTMENT file 861.8591/3-2746 from Acheson, St. Dept.

WITHDRAWAL NOTICE FBI/Post 45 4/14/76, withdrawal slip declassified 5/19/94, Nat. Arch CRB

"Memorandum of conversation between the Attorney General and Mr. Acheson regarding the "Loading of Russian Ships." The Item identified below has been withdrawn from this file: file designation 861-8591 Date March 27, 1946, From D. of State; To: Memo of Conver. In the review of this file this item was removed because access to it is restricted. Restriction on records in the National Archives are stated in general and specific record group restriction statements which are available for examination. the item identified above has been withdrawn because it contains: "Security Classified Information" Authority: FBI/Post 45 Date: 4/14/76. General Services Administration GSA from 7117 (2-72)"

[Four years later the FBI forwarded the withdrawn document.]

(Department of State Memorandum of Conversation March 27, 1946):

"This afternoon the Attorney General telephoned to me and read me the following: 'Information was received on March 27, 1946, from a confidential and reliable source that instructions have been issued by the Soviet Government that all Soviet ships in the United States ports are to be loaded immediately and clear the ports of the United States as quickly as possible." I asked the Attorney General whether the Army and Navy had been informed of this. He said that this had been done at twelve O'clock today through the Joint Intelligence Committee. I then asked the Attorney General to have the officer of the FBI familiar with this matter come to the State Department so that I could go over the report with him. I pointed out that it was impossible to evaluate the importance of this unless it could be ascertained how general this was, under what circumstances the information was obtained, by whom it was given and whether there were any circumstances which lead to connecting it with a desire to expedite ship turn-around. Subsequently the Attorney General telephoned me again and said that the information had been obtained from an agent in Philadelphia from a stevedoring firm where which had a contract with the Soviet Government for loading its ships....

Signed: Dean Acheson."

The second withdrawal slip and later retrieved document involved J. Edgar Hoover's reply, State Department file 861.8591/3-2746 to Secretary of State James F. Byrnes, again, withdrawal notice FBI/Post 45 on 4/14/76, "Information regarding instructions to Soviet ships in US ports" confirming Hoover's reception of Acheson's memo. It would not be long before Truman would remove Secretary of State Byrnes and replace him with former Secretary of War, George C. Marshall. Dean Acheson was the Undersecretary of State, and would soon replace Marshall. The musical chairs with all three men, members of the Council of Foreign Relations, were colleagues of the Wall Street financiers who backed the Bolshevik Revolution in World War I. Truman was like a babe in the woods, for Roosevelt had stacked the deck for four terms before him. (15)

The new Secretary of State, Dean Acheson, wrote his Foreign Service agent of the Division of Eastern European Affairs April Fools Day, 1946, (State Dept. file F#861.8591/4-146), he could not locate J. Edgar Hoover's letters of March 27th and March 29th regarding Soviet ship movements. "It is probable that these missing letters are not required for the purpose of the simple acknowledgement of Mr. Hoover's communication, April 1." Llewelyn E. Thompson replied to Acheson, (State Department file 861.8591/7-1646) "The only papers DC/R has been able to locate on this subject are attached. They reveal no grounds for the proposed change in customs examination of Soviet Vessels...." This goes beyond incompetence.

More State Department files would vanish in 1976, replaced by mysterious "withdrawal slips" under FBI/Post 45, the CIA, and British Intelligence. Who were they protecting? - Donald McClean and Kim Philby, responsible for importing "Paperclip" and "Dustbin" Nazi scientists from Soviet BW factories? With them vanished "Soviet vessels ordered to leave San Francisco Immediately" (file 861.8591/5-1646) and "Soviet Nationals and the US Custom Service Immigration & Nationalization Service" regarding deserter Degojhsky, (861.865/11-846) Again, courtesy of Congressman Cook, the FBI retrieved Leonid Georgievich Degojhsky's files. After deserting the Soviet freighter SS Denis Davidov, Degohjsky sought the assistance of Countess Alexandra Tolstoy in New York for political asylum. The Countess arranged an interview with the FBI. Degohjsky had witnessed millions of dollars of gold bars stored in the ship's hull. US Customs stumbled upon the cash by accident in a periodic search of incoming vessels. "The Federal Reserve Bank in New York received 41 boxes including 206 gold bars August 26, 1946, transferred to the Federal Reserve Bank from the SS Denis Davidov. The account of the State Bank of the USSR was credited in the amount of $2,725,600.00." The fur trade was very profitable indeed, but Amtorg had a few debts to pay off.

The American furriers knew the scoop. The Russians were dumping massive tons of furs upon the American market, forcing our own trappers into bankruptcy. Naturally, they approached their Congressmen. "The Fur Situation" unraveled. Mr. E. C. Ropes, Chief of the Russian Unit in the State Department was called to the stand to testify, detailing the organization of the Soviet fur industry and Soyuzpushnina, the "All Union Corporation of Furs." During the war, the United States sent seven "permanent agents" to Russia as buyers, only two remained after the war. The furs were then shipped to Amtorg Trading Company in New York. "The furs, therefore, come to us through the Soviet Government, are delivered to the purchasers if the contract has been made in Russia, or sold by the old auction firm of Lampson & Huth in New York, with furs from other countries." Accordingly, fur sales constituted 75% of all Soviet business deals in America. By 1946, $240 million worth of Soviet furs had been dumped upon the American market, American furriers had contributed only $125 million worth in skins. In the closing months of 1946, the prices of American furs had dropped between 25% and 30% of the previous year's catch. Congress accused the Russians of "dumping," the Russian catch including undressed pelts from their neighbors, Afghanistan, Persia, and China, bordering nations also overrun with Beria's rats and plagues. OACSI files detail the dissaster. The peasants were slaughtering anything and everything on four legs

As "The Fur Situation" hearings continued, Utah Congressman, Walter Granger, brought forth his witness, Joseph H. Francis, executive secretary of the National Board of Fur Farm Organizations. Francis had deeper insight into the real problems at hand, asking "How extensive a service does the Commerce Department have in the way of a foreign service to secure information in regard to the industry?... As a result, as an arm of the fur industry we are at a loss to know what the other counties are doing, and therefore cannot get our industry geared intelligently as to the production of furs." In response, he was told that "The State Department primarily has taken over that field during the war, and the particular agencies, such as Agriculture and Commerce, branches formerly interested in that foreign field service, have rather gone out of the picture." Granger was puzzled:

"HEARINGS BEFORE SPECIAL SUBCOMMITTEE ON FUR OF THE COMMITTEE ON AGRICULTURE" US House of Representatives "THE FUR SITUATION" Honorable Reid F. Murray (chairman) presiding, 88th Congress, 1st Session, (Y4.Ag8/1: F96 part 1)

MR. GRANGER: "I just want to comment on the record here that it is a strange situation where we have departments, the Department of Commerce, and the Department of Agriculture, who are skilled and trained and know the domestic industry, and yet they have very little, if anything, to say, or any knowledge of foreign markets. That is turned over to another department whose business primarily is to maintain peace in the world. It seems to me we are all mixed up on it."

MR. MURRAY: "That is what we are having hearings for. We think we will have the answer when we are done with the hearings...'

MR. FRANCIS: "Mr. Chairman, I might bring out this point, if I may. I think we should ask those people in commerce the relative aspect of importance of shipments of movements of fur articles. I think that will come into the whole program and picture. I know it does with imports and trade relations. Our merchant marine. That phase of it. Is it a very large item in this whole industry, the transportation, either by ship or rail or train, of furs?"

Page 55: MR. FRANCIS: The primary world market for fur products is the United States. At present the entire production of world fur is being dumped in our country.... fur farmers are being forced out of business.

Utah, mostly desert, was not a port, but a major railroad junction in the West. A great deal of cargo and livestock passed through Salt Lake City in those days before the building of interstate highways. A new wave of a previously unknown typhus, "rickettsialpox," would emerge in Salt Lake, along with brucellosis, which suddenly swept the country. The blame must be put squarely on the silence of the State Department, not the unsuspecting American businessmen. The State Department's Dulles gang had every angle covered. Joseph Francis suggested the Army and Navy open up their wilderness outpost in Alaska to compete with Soviet trappers. Next, the debate was passed to Hugh McPhee, Assistant Chief, Bureau of Animal Industry in the Department of Agriculture regarding animal parasites. This had previously been the responsibility of the Biological Survey within the Department of Agriculture, but the Survey was transferred to the Department of the Interior under Herold Ickes. Ickes was nicknamed "ratcatcher." From page 73-75 of the hearings, Mr. McPhee detailed the excessive monitoring of fur farming parasites in the American industry and its rigid controls to protect the product and public. It became clear that the American fur industry was in no way responsible for the Lyme epidemic at hand. Unfortunately, McPhee's field of investigation was limited to the American industry. Francis turned to his congressman and made a statement "off the record."

As "The Fur Situation" hearings continued into a second session, the fur auctioneers and manufacturers came forth in defense of "Dame Fashion," demanding more exotic wraps than the American fur industry could offer. In return, the American trappers speculated the auctioneers were price fixing, acting as both brokers and bankers. To clarify the debate, Frank G. Ashbrook of the Department of the Interior's Fish and Wildlife Service came forward. In his effort to explain away the economics of the whole situation, he unwittingly let the proverbial "cat out of the bag":

"THE FUR SITUATION" (page 99-100)
MR. ASHBROOK: "Mr. Henry Wallace's father, then Secretary of Agriculture, created the Division of Fur Resources in the Bureau of Biological Survey. When Mr. Darling came to the service as chief of the Bureau of Biological Survey he reorganized the Bureau. Then when the late President Roosevelt reorganized the Government, I think it was the second or third plan, biological Survey was transferred to Interior, and the Bureau of Fisheries was also transferred from Commerce to Interior, and about a year after that Mr. Ickes combines these bureaus as the Fish and Wild-life Service. A year after that we were decentralized and went to Chicago."

Hold it right there, folks. Who was Henry Wallace? Wallace was not only Roosevelt's Vice President, but future presidential candidate running against Harry Truman and Thomas E. Dewey in 1948, on the Communist Party ticket! Don't expect any help from him. Between Roosevelt's State Department and Fish and Wild-life Service, the deck was stacked. Surely Roosevelt was aware of the upsurge in brucellosis in 1937 when he chose Wallace as his running mate. With the poverty of the Great Depression at hand and brucellosis, was America being ripened for a Communist revolution? Coupled with the Council of Foreign Relations members' run on the banks, inducing the stock market crash of 1929, Roosevelt did more to destroy this country than any president on record.

It was the arrival of the SS SUCHAN on January 2, 1947, that provoked the American furriers into action again, this time approaching the FBI directly. Beautiful damsels dressed in fur coats waltzed across the inside pages of the news media in sale after sale. So did J. Edgar Hoover's "wife."

"SOVIET PENETRATION OF THE AMERICAN FUR INDUSTRY"

State Department file 8811.60/2.447, February 4, 1947, Subject: AMTORG.

To: Mr. Frederick B. Lyon, director Office of Controls, State Department

From: J. Edgar Hoover: Director FBI

"I have received through several sources in the Los Angeles, California area the expression of definite conviction that Russia, through its trading corporation, AMTORG, is endeavoring to break financially all of the retail and wholesale fur dealers in the United States and cause thereby unrest and unemployment... many facing bankruptcy... It has been learned that on two separate occasions prior to the Christmas holidays eighty tons of furs came into San Pedro, California, for delivery to AMTORG in New York City. On January 2, 1947, the Russian ship "Suchan" arrived at Los Angeles Harbor from Vladivostok with 500 tons of furs and camel hair aboard...."

[And then, at the end of this document is Hoover's reply, penned in by hand.]

"ITP - Mr. Wilcox - this sounds about as cockeyed as most FBI reports - but query, whether there is any evidence of Soviet fur sales not being governed by commercial considerations. I think it would be nice to be able to buy our wives cheap mink coats! EE. J.E. Hoover"

Suddenly, a strange new unheard of typhus named "Q Fever" broke out in cattle in southern California. Simultaneously, a brand new typhus "rickettsialpox" broke out in New York City's Kew Gardens, a low income housing development. Rickettsialpox was carried by the "house mouse mite", A. singuinus Hirst, indigenous to the Middle East. The first single specimen of the mite appeared in Washington, DC in 1909, not to be seen again till 1938, a rarity, a single rat from the Orient occasionally jumping ship. Suddenly, in 1946, it was found in large numbers at Kew Gardens. A detailed analysis of these two different typhus epidemics was published by Robert Heubner from the Health Department in the "Annals of Internal Medicine," (vol. 30, March 1949). Further investigation into the origin and symptoms of rickettsialpox appeared in Heubner's Public Health Reports noting its arrival in early spring, 1946, its symptoms similar to Lyme. Were there two diseases instead of one at hand here? Arachnid sleuths zeroed in on the foreign invader. (16)

Eventually, the Rockefeller Institute would join in the hunt, exposing Rickettsialpox in major American cities, New York, Washington DC, Philadelphia, Tucson, Indianapolis, Boston, West Hartford, and Salt Lake City. The parasite was tracked to the Middle East, South Africa, North Korea, and the Soviet Union. It was noted that the ixodes tick was also capable of carrying rickettsae bacteria. Who were the investigators?- Frank Horsfall and Thomas Rivers, Eugene Von Haagen's old virus partner. (17) Harry Plotz, the old Army typhus vaccine partner to Hans Zinsser, was put to task again for new vaccines. He died suddenly January 6th, 1947, one year to date after the docking of the SS ELBRUS in the same Walter Reed Hospital Hoyte Vandenberg perished. (18) Had Joker struck again? The medical journals today make brief mention of rickettsialpox as having declined but not disappeared since 1946, and consider it greatly overlooked. It can be chronic, but treatable, resistant to antibiotics, causing allergies. (19) Think of all the Pepto Bismol and Alkaseltzer guzzled by Americans with acid indigestion.

Just after the epidemics broke out in New York, a flurry of fleece between the State Department Byrnes and the American Embassy in Moscow arose over the organization of Soyuzpushnina, the Soviet fur and textile combine:

STATE DEPARTMENT file 861.60/10-2146 To Moscow, Airgram 359 10/21/46

"To: MAEMBASSYL, Moscow: Morrison of DRE urgently need of up-to-date information on the organization of the Soviet fur industry. Give names and duties of agencies, and the ministries controlling them, which deal with hunting, breeding, procurement, processing, domestic wholesale trade, imports and exports. Include the work of Glavsevtorg and

Zagotzhivayre. Show movement of fur from original source to market. Diagram would be helpful. To assist you, we are giving available data circa 1938 retaining the old nomenclature in nearly all cases... Internal Whole-sale - Council for Internal Trade (supervising agency not known) received finished furs... Soyuzpushnina, at present under Ministry of Foreign Trade, exports furs... also operated the Leningrad auctions..."

On January 14, 1947, the American Embassy in Moscow Airgramed (#59) a reply to Washington, State Department file 861.60/1-1447: "Soyuzpushnina is now believed to control entire fur trade except inter-nal distribution. Sources state that this organization controls numerous breeding farms throughout the country as well as fur collection points at Vladivostok, Irkutsk, Krasnoyarsk, Novosibirsk, Omsk, Sverdlovsk, Moscow, Leningrad and one in Dobas regions... Hunters are employed by the Soyuzpushnina agencies. The furs collected by Soyuzpushnina which are not scheduled for export (generally furs of poorer quality) are turned over to an agency, the name of which is not known to the American buy-ers...." Following this questionnaire were listed many division of the fur trade, export industry, and procurement agencies of furs from aboriginals. Soyuzzagotpushnina was run by the Commissariat for Agriculture Pro-duce Procurement agency in charge of individual hunters and fur breed-ing collectives. Soyuzkarskulvod was under the commissariat of karakul sheep collective farms. Glavsevtorg and Zagotshivshyre both procured furs from aboriginals. Soyuzmekhprom was under the Commissariat for Light Industry, responsible for sending raw furs to finishing factories onto the Council for Internal Trade and Soyuzpushnina for export. Soyuz-pushnina was under the Ministry of Foreign Trade, which also operated the Leningrad fur auctions. Foreign Service agent Smith from Moscow recommended the State Department contact American fur trader Rubin Papert of Papert-Strasburg Fur Brokers for a more details.

The following reshuffling of the deck in Soviet Finance Ministry result-ed in Alexi Kosygin, (future Secretary General of the Communist Party), taking over the Ministry of Finance, replacing A. G. Zverev, (State Depart-ment file 861.51/2-1848 and SECRET FILE 861.51 XR 861.002/2-2548 from Moscow). Important State Department correspondence regarding the Soviet intelligence apparatus' appointment of Alexi Kosygin to the Light & Textile Industry would vanish, no "Withdrawal" slip:

"STATE DEPARTMENT file 861.51 XR 861.002/12-2448, Tel. 3049 12/29/48

"Concerning decrees restoring A. George Zverev to Finance ministry

there and appointing Alexi Kosygin as head of new amalgamated ministry of Light & Textile Industry concerning Soviet industry and finance."
"MISSING" (index card only)

Volumes of State Department correspondence between Australia
and London over Soviet massive purchases of wool piled up. "USSR's
exceptionally large purchase of wool in Australia and New Zealand during
recent months raise question of actual extent of buying and of ultimate
destination of wool, as well as motives... Please advise Department in
most complete detail..." (St. Dpt. file 861.62222/7-1648m To Canberra,
Airgram 41 7/16/48). Further correspondence revealed "Soviet purchase
of sixteen million pounds in Australia and ten to twenty million from New
Zealand where it never bought previously," (St. Dpt. file 861.62222/7-
1948, Airgram 186). The reason for the massive purchases? "In a series
of republics, krais, and oblasts, and particularly in Turkmen, Uzbek, and
Azjerbadan SSR's Chelyabinsk, Gorki, Kalinin and other oblasts there is
still a significant waste and squandering of livestock on the farms... (due
to sickness of livestock)" (St. Dpt. file 861.6222/10-449). In the first half
of 1949, "only one third of the collective farms fulfilled the plan for the
increase in the number of collectivized cattle... More than half of the collective farms did not fulfill the sheep plan. The plan for increase of swine
is being carried out especially poorly... Poultry farming is in no better
position... the half year plan for milk output was not fulfilled" (St. Dpt
file 861.622/9-2149 Airgram 970 from Moscow). The Moscow Foreign
Service telegrammed Washington "Anti Brucellosis Work in the Livestock
Industry of the USSR" (State Department file 861.622/4-2949) that "The
USSR livestock industry according to official Soviet statements is the most
backward branch of agriculture." The Republic of Ajzerbadan had lost 25
million head of sheep during the war years, (St. Dpt file 861.6222/8-548,
airgram 79 from Wellington, New Zealand to Washington), just across
the border from Iran.

Along with rickettsialpox, other tick borne diseases arrived in New
York City. Mayor O'Dwyer took action. The rat wars began. Articles
flashed across the front pages of the "New York Times" "WAR ON RATS"
"RATS MUST GO" "RESTAURANTS HERE NOW FACE PADLOCK"
"SIX OFFICIALS MAP CITY WAR ON RATS." This precipitated new
action from New York's labor unions, "WASTE COLLECTORS GET
STRIKE ALERT" ("New York Times" Aug 28, 1946, page 28) involving
two thousand Teamsters, Unit 27, refusing to pick up commercial garbage
in Manhattan, Brooklyn and the Bronx. O'Dwyer offered a pay raise and
better hours, but that would not save the City. O'Dwyer formed a Rat

Control Commission with Dr. Harry S. Mustaard, New York City's Health Commissioner, also involving the New York City Police, Sanitation Commissioner, and Housing and Building Commissioner. Rats were blamed for destroying $45 million worth of property in New York City, alone. Philadelphia and Jersey City would follow suit, the Department of the Interior leading the charge. Across the front page, the "New York Times" continued its Rat Wars. "Typhus, trichinosia, bubonic plague, rat-bite fever and spirochetal jaundice were prevalent." (20) "Lyme Disease" had not been identified in 1946, but evidence of spirochetes was there.

To appease the labor unrest, Mayor O'Dwyer created a Business Advisory Council, made up of twenty-eight prominent businessmen and labor leaders. Assigned to clean up the city and its harbor, Nelson Rockefeller joined the bandwagon while the rest of the Rockefeller's funded KWI for Brain Research had hunkered down at Suchomi. Conveniently, Rockefeller was Assistant Secretary of State between 1946 and 1947, his illustrious career listed in "Who's Who." The State Department was on top of the situation. (21) Amongst O'Dwyer's select 28 were John Coleman, chairman of the board of the NY Stock Exchange and David Sarnoff, outstanding member of the Council of Foreign Relations, head of RCA and CBS, a member of the Industrial Advisory Commission of the U. S. Defense Communication Board in 1940. According to James Perloff's "Shadows of Power" Sarnoff had great financial backing from Kuhn, Loeb and Company who had financed Lenin's rise to power. The select advisors also included Gano Dunn, a representative of the J. G. White Engineering Corp, another heavy financier of the Bolshevik Revolution through a club of American industrialists at 120 Broadway, the American-Russian Industrial Syndicate, Inc. (22) Also a member of this American Russian Syndicate was William Boyce Thompson, who had organized the International Red Cross Mission to Russia, hiring future Air Force Surgeon General, Malcolm C. Grow and Hans Zinsser. O'Dwyer's Council definitely had a left-wing slant.

Basil Harris also joined O'Dwyer's select 28 playing a crucial role. Listed in "Who's Who in America," in his youth, he offered his shipping expertise to Norton Lilly & Company of New York, the Roosevelt Steamship Company, and the International Mercantile Marine Company. By 1941, Harris was senior Vice President of U.S. Lines. Just prior to WW II, Harris served as assistant to the US Secretary of the Treasury and Commerce of Customs. He knew the waterfront. John Reed Kilpatrick was a highly decorated Brigadier General in the US Army, Richard Lawrence was chairman of the YMCA, ex-president of the NY State Chamber of Commerce, and director of a string of insurance companies. By 1946,

Lawrence rose to the position of New York's zoning commissioner. Jerome K. Ohrbach's family owned Orhbach's Department Store, and Jack Strauss served as president for R. H. Macy & Company, and as Director of the Mutual Broadcasting System. One of Strauss' associates was Armand Hammer, also a member of the board of Mutual Broadcasting System and President of Allied American Fur Sales Agency, in business with the Soviets since the 1920s. Hammer did not sit amongst the Mayor's Council. David Tilly, also attending, was president of the NY Dock Company, serving with the State Warehousemen's Association of New York and director of the Brooklyn Chapter of the New York Red Cross.

On the labor side of O'Dwyer's Advisory Council sat Anna M. Rosenberg, Executive Commissioner to the United Seamen's Service and public labor relations consultant since 1924. Under Roosevelt, she became Regional Director of the Social Security Board and the Office of Defense Health & Welfare Service, and Regional Director of War Manpower Commission since 1942, serving as Roosevelt's personal representative to the European Theatre of War, reporting on problems of returning soldiers. Finally, Rosenberg was assigned to New York City's Industrial Relations Board and Labor Victory Board. Does this sound like a government cover-up yet?

Vice President of the AFL-CIO, David Dubinsky, a hard core Communist, joined the Mayor's Council. As the years passed under the McCarthy era, "Communism" became a dirty word, and Dubinsky dropped membership. His flamboyant autobiography "David Dubinsky: A Life with Labor" also highlights numerous others from the waterfront, including the Communist Party takeover of the AFL-CIO in the 1930s with the help of Communist Party president, William Z. Foster. Foster would eventually be put on trail for violation of the Smith Act, accused with eleven other cohorts, including Fur and Leather Union chief, Irving Potash, for trying to overthrow the US government by force and violence. Dubinsky had served as a delegate to the 1928 Profintern Congress in Moscow. (23) The original AFL, described by Dubinsky as "traditionally conservative and right-wing," was in the way of Wall Street and the Bolshevik Revolution!

Also attending were Joseph Curran, President of the National Maritime Union, Jacob Potofsky head of Amalgamated Clothing Workers Union, and Alex Rose, secretary to the Hatters Union. Martin Sweeny, who rose through the International Ladies Garment Workers Union, joined under the amalgamation of garment workers and craft unions including the Furriers, described in Dubinsky's autobiography. Was Martin Sweeny, born in the Bronx, related to current AFL-CIO president John Sweeny? According to Dubinsky, "The CIO and AFL unions worked together in politics, even though they were fighting like cats and dogs everywhere else" (page 263). David Dubinsky and General John Kilpatrick suddenly became benevolent. Just a few days prior the announcement of Mayor O'Dwyer's Business Advisory Council, the "New York Times" ran an article July 17, 1946 "$2,500,000 FUND TO BE SOUGHT FOR AR-THRITIS RESEARCH CENTER" listing the council members as gener-ous donors. Now those poor Lyme victims suffering arthritis in Harlem and the Bronx could seek comfort, that is, if they could afford the trip to Hot Springs, Arkansas! Surgeon General Thomas Parran attended its beneficiary luncheon, delivering a lecture, citing "three million persons were suffering from arthritis, and an addition four million from other rheumatoid diseases." Brucellosis is also known to induce arthritis. What was responsible for the sudden upsurge?

Mayor O'Dwyer was asked to testify before congress in "Investigation of Organized Crime in Interstate Commerce" (Y4 C86/2 C86/pk US Sen-ate 82nd Congress, 1st Session July - August, 1951) Indexed at the end of the hearings was a biography of his years in office. Special commendations were cited for ending a milk strike and cleaning up the harbor and Harlem, fighting racketeering in the garment industry, and booting out Commu-nists in City Hall. The whole Roosevelt Administration was full of them, a futile task. By just reviewing "Who's Who in America" for biographies on O'Dwyer's Business Advisory Council, it's obvious the City was doomed. Had they all taken a vow of silence? . By 1950, the Longshoremen of New York City were refusing to unload any Russian cargo. The "New York Times" business section flashed headlines "ARRIVAL IN PORT OF RUSSIAN FURS THREATENS NEW STEVEDORE ACTION" and 'LONGSHOREMEN FORCE RETURN OF SOVIET FUR" fol-lowed by "AIRPORT WORKERS BAR SOVIET CARGO." The word was out on the waterfront, and the Teamsters muscled their way into the labor scene. From previous FBI reports declassified on the SS ELBRUS, we know the West Coast longshoremen also went on strike. By the late 1940s, the AFL-CIO expelled the Teamsters for racketeering. Ironically, by 1944, Moscow labeled Dubinsky a Fascist for his protesting the fate of Jewish union organizers Henry Ehrlich and Victor Alter, executed in Poland! Dubinsky began to have his doubts. (24) The fur boycotts didn't last long. By December, 1949, a six million dollar fur deal in Soviet Trust contracts had been renewed, including "squirrel, marmot, marten, fox, sable, kolinsky, ermine, and muskrat" to grace America's "Dame Fashion." (25) Add it up: 80 tons of furs in San Pedro, followed by 500 tons off the SUCHAN, 750 tons from the VILNIUS, plus 426 tons from the ELBRUS; a total of 1,756 tons of furs on record. 1,756 x 2,000 pounds (a ton) =

3,512,000 pounds of furs, probably 1 to 2 million animals. Why wasn't the media demanding an explanation for the onslaught?

Congress had enough of this nonsense. American merchants were competing against the USSR, sailing our Liberty ships for free. "CONTROL OF MERCHANT SHIPS" Hearings before the Subcommittee on Ship Sales, Charters and Lay-ups of the Committee on Merchant Marine & Fisheries" began February 6th 1947. The State Department was petitioned to get them back. Out of the original 125 vessels, 95 remained in operation, only 26 returned! Congressman Weichel quizzed Admiral Smith of the Merchant Marine, "Do you know where the 95 ships are that the Russians have and what trades and routes they are being particularly operated on?" "I do not." Amongst them was the SS ELBRUS (page 106) with its 426 tons of fur skins, camel hairs. And then the fur began to fly! Russian shipping regulations had been secretly transferred to the State Department. What??? Weichel demanded: "But did the Maritime Commission transfer title or did the State Department transfer title [of the liberty ships to the USSR]"? Maritime counsel Skinner replied" "I can't answer that." Weichel pressed harder:

"CONTROL OF MERCHANT SHIPS" Congress Session: 80-1, 2/5-7/47

Page 137: MR. WEICHEL: "According to the testimony we have head here up to this time from the Maritime Commission, the Maritime Commission as an agent for the State Department did the dealing with the British in the open. With reference to the deal with the Russians concerning the use of ships, the Maritime Commission did not do it. They don't know anything about it. Everybody seems to be confused and know nothing about the deals with the Russians. Evidently that was made secretly by the State Department, and not by their agent, the Maritime Commission. That is what we want."

Under Secretary of State, William Clayton protested page after page that he had no authority to hand over the Russian response to returning the lend-lease ships. Alvin Weichel exploded:

Page 199: MR. WEICHEL: "I want to know what was said about the ships. I don't care what you said about horses, cows, and sheep, or anything else. What was said about the ships? That is what the inquiry is about."

"MR. CLAYTON: "Obviously the effort was to get ships back, but I haven't the note with me so I cannot give you the exact language in which it was couched."

Curious, the State Department had taken over the fur trade negotiations in "The Fur Situation" and lend-lease shipping with the Soviet Union in "Control of Merchant Ships," relieving the Maritime Commission, the Department of the Interior, and the Department of Commerce of all responsibilities. This sure looks like a cover-up.

On the ELBRUS's return to Vladivostok from Philadelphia, it docked in Miami, Florida, November 24th, 1946. An unusual focus of multiple sclerosis broke out on Key West, a few miles west of Miami, its huge garbage dump, nicknamed "Mount Trashmore," the suspected source. Had the ELBRUS bartered its garbage for a fresh pantry of local fruits and vegetables? The Key West Island had a local population of 26,000, with an unusually large number of its citizens infected with MS. The number of Mt. Trashmore's rat population could have easily competed with the number of the island's human population. (26) The ELBRUS would make numerous trips between Valdivostok and America, eventually sailing around the world, embarking at Hong Kong, Columbo, Sri Lanka, Abadan in the Shatt-al-Arab Way of Iran, and Odessa on the Black Sea, arriving at Trieste, November 7, 1948, the free city state contested between Yugoslavia and Italy under French, British and American protectorate. (27) Here, its Russian crew would transfer ship and title to Robert P. Joyce, trainer for the OPC's freedom fighters in the Balkans, under the State Department's Dulles gang. What a coincidence! The wake of misery behind the SS ELBRUS had only just begun. The SS ELBRUS would become the focus of the biggest espionage ring of Communists, terrorists, and Nazi drug peddlers in the Western Hemisphere.

CHAPTER 8 NOTES

(1) "800 INDUSTRIALISTS AID MOBILIZATION" "New York Times" 3/8/49 p. 37

(2) "SIMON & SCHUSTER ENCYCLOPEDIA OF WORLD WAR II" Simon & Schuster NY 1978, "Liberty Ship"

(3) "CONTROL OF MERCHANT SHIPS" Hearings before the Subcommittee on Ship Sales, Charters, and Lay-ups of the Committee on Merchant Marine & Fisheries. HR 80th Cong. 1st Ses. H. Cong. Res. 15 and H. J. Res. 113, February 5,6, and 7, 1947.
Page 109: ADMIRAL SMITH (Merchant Marine) Circumstances

relation to vessels transferred to the USSR. "In May 1943, President Roosevelt offered the Soviet Government a second protocol covering the flow of supplies from this country to the USSR during the period July 1, 1942 to June 30, 1943. Under terms of this protocol several vessels were requisitioned on the Pacific coast and then with the aid of lend-lease funds immediately delivered with change of flag to the Russians.... additional vessels were turned over... in all, 125 vessels... Twenty six of these vessels have been returned and four have been lost. There still remain with the Soviet government 95 vessels."

(4) "LLOYD'S REGISTER" 1946-1947, Lloyd's of London Press.

(5) "VESSEL STATUS CARD: MUIR WOODS FLAG" American: Type T2-SE-A1 Tanker. J. Porter Shaw Library, Fort Mason, San Francisco, CA.
"D.W.T. 16765a Gross; Hull No. 2411; built by Kaiser Co., Inc. (Swan Is.) at Portland, Ore.; Completed 3-22-45; Operator USSR (ELBRUZ); Port of Delivery Portland, Ore; Date delivered 3-22-45; Operator, Marine Transport Lines (American Export Lines) Berth Agent for Marine Transport Lines; Port of Delivery; Trieste Italy; Date 2-20-48; Operator, U. S. Navy-Reserve Fleet (Permanent Transfer); Port of Delivery, New York, NY; date 4-23-48; Reserve Fleet at James River 6-10-59; Operator, Luria Brothers & Co., Inc. (Scrap); Port of Delivery, James River; Date 12-2-75"
"US MARITIME COMMISSION MAIL & TITLES SECTION, #118-7, part 6, July 1, 1947, Subject: "Lend Lease Transfer of Vessels to the Soviet Union," Nat. Arch. CRB

(6) "THE LIBERTY SHIPS" L. A. Sawyer and W. H. Mitchell, Cornell Maritime Press, Inc. Centerville, MD
"THE LIBERTY SHIPS" John Gorley Bunker, Naval Institute Press, Annapolis, MD 1972. Lend -lease animal transport: Pages 47, 63, 69, 78, 113, 124-25, 133, 143, 153.

(7) "THE CAMBRIDGE SPIES" Verne W. Newton, Madison Books, Lanham, NY 1991
Pages 13-14: re. testimony of Soviet defector and spy, Walter Krivitsky "Soviet agents now in the United States or who may hereafter be sent there to operate either as individuals or through Amtorg will endeavor to acquire in the United States such material supply as the German government may desire." "And then from Brussels came "Positive proof that the German and Soviet governments are working together in matters of espionage and

sabotage." "footnoted: NA: 761362/09-2239" [US St. Dpt. files]

(8) "UNITED STATES MARITIME COMMISSION RESEARCH DIVISION Hugh D. Butler, Director UNION OF SOVIET SOCIALIST REPUBLICS LEND LEASE"

"'Status of Vessels Delivered Under Lend Lease to the USSR" 3/1/47, Nat. Arch. CRB

Page 2: "Tanker Vessels" "During the first eleven months of 1946, nine of the 20 tankers which were lend lease to the USSR engaged in trade with the United States..."

"Appendix III': "Employment of Tanker Vessels Under Lend Lease to USSR"

"The ELBRUS: Import $ value: $90,230: cargo tons 426 Fur skins and camel's hairs; Exports: cargo tons 61,753 dollar value $1,094,279; clearance with cargo: 4"

"NEW YORK MARITIME REGISTER" World's Maritime News Company, NY.

Shipping route and docking schedule of the SS ELBRUS using editions of January 23 & 30th 1946; July 3, 1946; September 18, 1946; October 8, 1947; March 3, 1948; April 7, 1948: "Arrive San Francisco, October 14, 1945. Arrives Petropavlovst March 6th 1946; Arrive Philadelphia January 6, 1946, Arrive Los Angeles February 15, 1946. Arrives Petropavlovst March 6th 1946; Sails from Vladivostok and arrives in Los Angeles May 9th, 1946; Sails from El Segundo May 30th 1946; Arrives in San Francisco July 30th, 1946; Arrives Los Angeles October 1946; Leaves Vladivostok and arrives in Los Angeles November 9th, 1946; Arrives in Miami November 24th 1946; Arrives in Hong Kong August 23rd 1947; Arrives Columbo September 1st, 1947; Sails for Odessa from Abadan January 16th 1948; Arrives in Trieste April 7th, 1948."

"AMTORG OFFERS PERSIAN LAMB" "New York Times" 2/2/46 P. 24, c. 5 "Business World" "Lampson, Fraser, & Huth, Inc. auction on February 14... 1000,000 Persian Lamb" [Reference to past sales in 1943 and 1944 included Persian lamb and silver fox.]

(9) STATE DEPARTMENT file 861.8591/3-2946 House letter to Sec. of St. James Byrnes [Amtorg moves to Pratt Estate]

(10) EMBA FBI file LA-65-4110 (FOIA request 316,825) "On May 5, 1946 an article appeared in the Los Angeles Examiner

stating that a Russian navy tanker had arrived at Los Angeles Harbor and was abruptly ordered to heave outside the breakwater and wait United States Naval Intelligence boarding party. The vessel is the TAGANROG. Navy officials declined to give any explanation... "

EMBA and ELBRUS FBI file 100-343044-37: "teletype" "Russian Merchant shipping information concerning attention Mr. Ladd" reference telephone call (blackout) Bureau to L. A. this date, EMBA, KRASNAIA ARMIA, APSHERON, ELBRUS" (page blackout)

(11) ELBRUS FBI file 65-63110-5 "Department of the Navy, Office of the Chief of Naval Operations, Washington, DC (date blacked out) from: Director of Naval Intelligence, to: Director FBI; Subject: Soviet merchant vessels calling at US ports..."

ELBRUS FBI file 100-343044-42, 30 March 1946, [Navy lists of all Soviet ships in US ports.]

(12) STATE DEPARTMENT file 861.8591/12-2045 from Helsinki, #1756, to Sec. St. Wash ., Tel. 786, US State Dpt files on Russian Shipping, Na. Arch CRB

"Soviet SS VILINUS [AKA VILNIUS] , Captain Ilija Gavriloff from Leningrad departed Helsinki December 19, direct for New York carrying cargoes of 750 tons of furs, woolen goods and pharmaceutical raw materials..."

STATE DEPARTMENT file 811.60/2-447 subject: AMTORG; 2/4/47 to St. Dept., from J. Edgar Hoover - re. SS SUCHAN in San Pedro, 500 tons furs & camel hairs.

(13) STATE DEPARTMENT file 865/8-2046 "ELBRUS" From Justice Dpt #310513; To: US St. Dpt of Immigration & Naturalization Service. Na. Arch. CRB St. Dpt files on Russian Shipping To: The Honorable Secretary of State, Washington DC:

"This acknowledges the receipt of your letter dated June 4, 1946, addressed to the Attorney General, your file 861.865/5-2846, enclosing a note from the Embassy of the USSR regarding the case of Timofei Evtifievich Gavrilov, a Soviet seaman who, it is claimed deserted from the tanker "ELBRUS" on May 14, 1946 at Los Angeles, California. The records of this office show that a warrant for the arrest of one Timofei Evstiney Gavrilov"

STATE DEPARTMENT file 861.865/6-1147 "ELBRUS" To US Just. Dpt. re. Gavrilov

STATE DEPARTMENT file 861.865/6/1147 "ELBRUS" from USSR

Embassy #107 re. Gavrilov deserter and theft.

(14) STATE DEPARTMENT file 861.865/11/846 From J. E. Hoover, re. Leonid Georgiavich Degojnsky, Soviet Seaman Deserter, "Russian Shipping" WITHDRAWAL NOTICE: Authority FBI/Post 45, 3/23/76 "Security Classified Information."

(15) "THE NEW AMERICAN" 2nd Edition Special Report "Conspiracy for Global Control" "Lengthening Shadows" Page 22.

(16) "Rickettsialpox A Newly Recognized Rickettsial Disease" Robert Heubner, William Jellison, Charles Pomerantz, Public Health Reports, #47, vol. 61, Nov. 22, 1946
"Q Fever A review of Current Knowledge" Robert Heubner, William Jellison, Dorothy Beck, 'Annals of Internal Medicine.' vol. 30 March 1949, no. 3 "In the United States since the Spring of 1946... 300 cases, 3 deaths, 4,000 cows infected... pasteurization... nearly 100% effective eliminating infection from milk."
"Rickettsialpox and Q Fever" by Robert Heubner "Symposium" vol. 14, 1950
"Manual of Parasitic Mites of Medical or Economic Importance" by E. W. Baker, R. M. Evans, D. J. Gould, W. B. Hull, H.L. Keegan, a technical publication of the National Pest Control Association, Inc. New York. Page 18: 'Allodermanyssus Sanguinus Hirst'
"Originally described as a parasite of rats in Egypt, it has since been found on house mice, as well as domestic rats in the United States.... Medical interest in sanguinus was aroused in 1946 with the recovery of Rickettsia akari, New York... vector of rickettsialpox."
"Medical Entomology: Arthropods and Human Disease" by William F. Horsfall, University of Illinois, The Ronald Press Company, NY 1962; Page 40: "Allodermanyssus sanguinus, the apartment mite...Rattus norvegicus is a factor in Russia... sylvatiac focus in Korea"
"Quarterly Bulletin" Dpt. Health, City NY vol. XIV, No. 3 Page 34: "A New Syndrome of Fever and Rash id Identified. The mysterious nonfatal fever which affected 92 residents of Kew Gardens has been identified as rickettsial disease never before recognized..."

(17) "VIRAL AND RICKETTSIAL INFECTIONS OF MAN" edited by Thomas Rivers, MD Rockefeller Institute, and Frank Horsfall, Jr. Physician in Chief, Rockefeller Institute Hospital. 3rd edition. J. B. Lippincott Company, Philadelphia. Pages 851-853: rickettsae, and ixodes

ticks. Pages 854-855: A. singuinus Hirst mite, worldwide, reference to Soviet journal, "Scientific Session Summaries" "Academy of Medical Science of the USSR and the Ministry of Public Health of the Uzbek SSR, 1954" "Scientific session on problems of regional pathology, Sept. 20-25"

(18) "The Journal of the American Medical Association" January-April 1947, vol. 133 'Deaths' "Harry Plotz" Page 879: "Harry Plotz, consultant to Secretary of War... chief virus and rickettsial diseases at the Army Medical School in Washington DC, died in Walter Reed General Hospital 1/6/47, age 56. WW I Siberia Red Cross Typhus Com."

(19) "Infectious Diseases and Medical Microbiology" 1986. "Rickettsialpox" p. 1253-54

(20) "RAT CONTROL GETS UNDER WAY IN 400 CITIES" New York Times 7/4/48, front page.

(21) "MAYOR INVITES 28 TO PROMOTE TRADE" "New York Times" 7/23/46 p.23

(22) "SHADOWS OF POWER" James Perloff, Western Islands 1988, Page 39, Kim Loeb, Page 181: Kuhn of NY Times, and David Sarnoff.

"WALL STREET AND THE BOLSHEVIK REVOLUTION Antony Sutton, Arlington House Publishers, NY 1974, Pages 136-137, 184. re. Gano Dunn.

(23) "DAVID DUBINSKY: A LIFE WITH LABOR" David Dubinsky and A. H. Raaskin, Simon & Schuster, NY 1977; Pages 102-103: ZIMMERMAN [of the International Ladies Garment Union] "In that period Foster advocated amalgamation of the craft unions... since unions are traditionally conservative and right-wing they would stand in the way of revolution. Therefore, it was our duty to break the reactionary unions and build new, revolutionary one that would help overthrow a dying capitalism."

(24) IBID. Page 273 re. Polish labor unions

25) "$6,000,000 FUR DEAL CLOSED BY RUSSIA: Trade Reports Soviet Trust Contracts With 5 Companies Here for 1949-1950 Season" "NY Times" 12/15/49 p. 59

(26) "Chilling Events on a Tropical Isle" Glen Carelik "Discover" May 1985, p. 65-66

(27) see note #5 for ELBRUS vessel status card and note #8 for New York Maritime Register listings of SS ELBRUS destinations.

CHAPTER 9

THE ARREST OF AMTORG

The Saga of James Forrestal, Fur and Fire

James Forrestal was a self made Wall Street financier, smart, savvy, good looking, and a work-aholic. In fact, the comic-book character, "Fearless Fosdick" from All Capp's "L'il Abner" was a sardonic caricature of James Forrestal. Roosevelt's Secretary of the Navy, Frank Knox, chose Forrestal for his Under Secretary in 1940 for his ability to secure Navy contracts and organize the massive war machine necessary to defeat the Axis Powers. It is not a sin to know money. Forrestal got the job done. Truman promoted Forrestal to full Secretary of the Navy after Roosevelt's death, and later, to Secretary of Defense. After the capitulation of the Nazis, Forrestal set about defeating the Communists with equal vigor. The Communist hated him, including the Communists inside the OPC. The Navy had just purchased the SS ELBRUS from the Marine Transport Lines, all scrubbed up, two months after the Soviets delivered it to Political Advisor, Robert P. Joyce in Trieste, the contested free city state between Yugoslavia and Italy. Forrestal was fully briefed.

As the War Department dissolved Bill Donovan's OSS, it eventually reorganized into the Office of Policy Coordination under another Wall Street banker, Frank Wisner, a rabid anti-Communist. Under Wisner worked the dubious Allen Dulles and his chameleons in the rogue Austrian CIC 430th unit alongside Robert P. Joyce's freedom fighters in Trieste. The OPC was also in the business of smuggling Stalin's old Nazi collaborators out of Russia. Frank Wisner would become an alcoholic and shoot himself in the head, upon learning his OPC had been penetrated with Soviet moles. Every freedom fighter trained in Trieste was identified and assassinated on setting foot upon their homeland behind the Iron Curtain. A good history of the OPC's failures was written by John Loftus, "The Belarus Secret" in 1982, Alfred Knopf, New York. Forrestal became very anxious over the OPC's failures.

American intelligence was in disarray after WW II. Every Department ran its own operation. Commerce had the Office of Scientific Research and Development "OSRD" confiscating Nazi patents as war booty for American industrialists. The State Department ran Donovan's OSS with its cult of ivy league dons in its Research and Analysis Branch "R&A." The Army had its Counter Intelligence Corps, "CIC." The Navy ran the largest organization of all, the Naval Technical Mission to Europe, "NavTecMisEu." On the home front was the FBI, under the dubious direction of a very vulnerable gay, J. Edgar Hoover. Truman and Congress realized the necessity to consolidate the competing intelligence agencies and proposed the Central Intelligence Group, "CIG," only to be reorganized 1947 as the Central Intelligence Agency, "CIA." The CIA created an Office of Scientific Intelligence under radar wizard, Isador Rabi, for the collation of technical data. Julius Robert Oppenheimer would be placed in charge of the Atomic Energy Commission, reporting to his old friend, Rabi. Forrestal demanded a new medical reporting system be organized within the OSI, for purpose of biological warfare defense. The CIA dragged its feet.

"ORGANIZATIONAL HISTORY OF THE CIA, 1950-1953" The DCI Historical Series, Chapter VI 'Problems of Scientific and Technical Intelligence,' HS-2 May 1957, approved for release 21 March 1989.

Page 35: "The subject then seems to have remained dormant until March 5, 1949, when Mr. James Forrestal, as Secretary of Defense, addressed a memorandum to the director of Central Intelligence on the subject of 'medical Intelligence' (footnote blacked out) in which he proposed that... "Each Service Intelligence Agencies assign a medical officer to CIA who would become part of the Office of Scientific Intelligence" Forrestal stated the case forcefully. He said that his action had been prompted by the recommendations of the "Hawley Committee" (footnote blacked out.)"

The UNRRA also addressed the increasing threat of Stalin's epidemics spreading in the Middle East and Africa, placing quarantines on international shipping:

"UNITED NATIONS RELIEF & REHABILITATION ADMINISTRATION HEALTH DIVISION EPIDEMIOLOGICAL INFORMATION BULLETIN" Washington DC vol. II 1946, chapter 'Relapsing Fever'

Page 931: "The sharp outbreak in the coastal area of Kenya occurred in November and December 1945... The outbreak which occurred in Ethiopia about the same time, had already been referred to... In Palestine,

relapsing fever notifications began to rise in November 1945 and continued up to August 1946. The data are not complete, but the peak seems
to have been about a hundred cases a week around 1 May. Transjordan,
too, had a small outbreak in spring 1946... Syria had small outbreaks in
1946, but the infection did not spread to any considerable extent. Iraq
was apparently not infected from the west because there were sporadic
cases of the louse borne type already in 1944. In 1945, 337 cases with
a seasonal maximum in February were reported. During the first half of
1946 there were 268 cases.

Iran, which suffered in 1943 and 1944 from the worst typhus
epidemic brought about by World War II, had an extensive outbreak
of relapsing fever which reached its peak in May 1946. From February,
when the record began, to 13 July, a total of 16,720 cases were reported
in the cities. Both Isphahan, Teheran and Abadan were infected. The case
mortality rate was low."

"EPIDEMICS ARE FEARED AFTER THE WAR" "The New York
Times" 4/1/45, (April Fools Day, Part 4, p. 9, c. 6) cited Dr. Frank G.
Boudreau's proclamation, former director of the Health Organization of
the League of Nations, that typhus, dysentery, cholera, relapsing fever,
diphtheria, plague, and smallpox were the most "immediate" of "post war
problems" demanding new international ship quarantines. The reason
for the Middle East's predicament will become increasingly evident as we
review State Department files on livestock slaughter in the Soviet republic
of Azjerbadan, just across Iran's border. The UNRRA report continued,
"Up to the time of the Russian occupation, Rumania contained Europe's
worst typhus focus in its entirety." One must keep in mind, that when
these records are read statistically, only an estimated one tenth of medical cases made it on the books. Between the rickettsae, spirochetes and
brucellosis eating up the spinal cords of these victims, the Middle East
and the Balkans became a basket case. Truman gave Stalin an ultimatum.
"Pull out of Iran, or be nuked."

In the meantime, the brucellosis rate in America skyrocketed. Dr.
Bennett T. Simms from the Bureau of Animal Industry rang the alarm in
"Defense Against Foreign Animal Diseases" now housed at the Department
of Agriculture's Library, citing "The possibility of attacks on our livestock
industry by agents of biological warfare is stressed in the booklet 'Health
Services and Special Weapons Defense' recently published by the Civil
Defense Administration" listing a host of new foreign diseases arriving
in America: foot-and-mouth disease, European fowl pests, and Asiatic
Newcastle Disease. Estimates ran between 6% and 10% of all livestock

"excreted the organism" brucellosis, and "38.4% of all dairy herds" in the United States were infected, with only "50% of the milk pasteurized." Worse, an estimated 10% of the population was infected, some twenty million Americans. The American prison system held a high percentage of brucellosis victims. (1) Had Nicolai's "Biology of War" been fulfilled under Joseph Stalin's dream for world revolution?

The United Nations organized an International Health Conference, June 19th - July 22, 1946, held in the Bronx at the Henry Hudson Hotel with the specific purpose of establishing a World Health Organization. Attending were members from the Rockefeller Foundation International Health Division, Drs. George Strode, Hugh Smith, Robert Lambert, John Grant, and Miss Elizabeth Smith. Other attendees included members from the UNRRA, UNESCO, World Federation of Trade Unions, vice president of the CIO, John Green and secretary Norman Dowd of the Canadian Congress of Labor. The United States was represented by Otis E. Mulliken, and Dr. Louis B. Williams of the Public Health Service, both from the Division of International Labor, Social and Health Affairs, US Department of State. Dr. Thomas Parran, US Surgeon General of the Public Health Service, attended with Dr. Michael B. Shimkin, Assistant Director Office of International Health Relations. Make a mental note of Shimkin.

Nations from all over the world sent representatives to the first WHO Conference, including Iran's Dr. Hefezi and Dr. Ghassem Ghani. Ghani, probably armed to the teeth with evidence against Azjerbadan's spreading epidemics, was detained by "auto-accident." In the name of saving the poor destitute children of the world, the Conference elected Dr. Fedor Krotkov, Deputy Minister of Public Health of the USSR, as the World Health Organization's first Secretary! (2) Dr. Hefezi, his records noted in the National Archives State Department correspondence files as "MISS-ING", later petitioned a visit to Dr. Willy Burdorfer's Rocky Mountain Laboratory, the same parasitologist who identified the Lyme spirochete, borrellia burgdorferi. Burgdorfer had accumulated a large collection of tick species from the Middle East through Dr. M. Baltazard of Teheran's Pasteur Institute. (3) Had the Communists strangled the UN into silence while Pavlovskii's Red Army with its Nazi accomplices perpetuated rats and plagues around the globe? The State Department voiced no complaints. The author could locate no reference to the SS ELBRUS or Soviet lend-lease shipping in the WHO records.

The State Department and the FBI were pursuing their own routes into medical espionage. Pharmaceutical giant, George Merck had headed the Biological Warfare Department under the War Department during WW and published a synopsis January 3rd, 1946, three days prior the docking of the SS ELBRUS in Philadelphia. The "Merck Report" portrayed our American wartime investigation into biological warfare as defensive and miniscule, for the "protection of troops" and "in the interest of efficiency, economy and secrecy... [it] remained a small organization. Extreme care was taken to protect the participating personnel from infection. Many new techniques were devised to prevent infection and proved highly successful... the safety record of our biological warfare program is truly remarkable." (4) In contrast, the leftwing medical community whipped up "The Rosebury Report" in 1942, announcing to the world that America was engaging in a gigantic BW program to eliminate all humanity. The "Rosebury Report" was a farce, republished May 1947 in the "Journal of Immunology," one of the prestigious magazine's editors was Rockefeller Institute's Thomas Rivers. Hoover kept track of every whisper of disease, filing derogatory comments on Dr. Rosebury and his American Society of Biologists, as well as Merck's motives.

"WAR COMMITTEE ON BACTERIOLOGY UNDER THE AUSPICES OF SOCIETY OF AMERICAN BIOLOGISTS" FBI file 100-93216-167

T: Director, FBI; From: Boston, 10/10/48. Subject: 'Bacteriological Warfare, aka Biological Warfare' BW, Internal Security-R [32 pages reviewed, 16 released.]

'Synopsis of Facts' "(line blacked out) have noted the extensive propaganda campaign on local, national and international levels, concerned with Bacteriological Warfare. (line blacked out) advise that the propaganda is misleading and inaccurate from scientific standpoint; that is apparently predicated upon ulterior motives. One ulterior motive would be to aid the Soviet Union, and another could be to increase War Department appropriations. Facts available tending to substantiate both theories recounted herein...

... The UN committee furnished a copy of the Rosebury report, carried in the Sunday New York Times... the last Sunday of July, 1947. Boston Herald for November 21, 1948, carried a news story detailed Paris, Nov. 20. (AP)... The text of these resolutions was released by UNESCO... quoted of Alexander Pavlov of the USSR made during debate on human rights in the UN Assembly Social Committee. Pavlov was quoted... "In the United States science serves the interest of militaristic classes. In America, the best intellectual forces are ordered to create the aggressive forms of weapons against all humanity, including women and children. One cannot read without ire and indignation that American scientists are seeking means of poisoning one hundred eighty million Russian people. I tell you we feel ire and indignation." The AP dispatch noted that PAVLOV did not quote the source of his material."

With Dr. Krotkov at the helm of the World Health Organization, UNESCO, the United Nations Education, Scientific and Cultural Organization, fingered America for instigating biological warfare! If we can believe the Hirsch Report, America did not have to attack Russia with BW, Lavrenti Beria, with his entourage of Nazi war criminals were doing a "bang up job" all on their own, not to make a pun of the pending world disaster. Perhaps the United Nations should be put on trial for war crimes for its complicity covering up Stalin's? Paying dues to this phony cult of environmentalists is literally peeing money down a rat hole.

Americans rushed to Russia's rescue! The FBI criticized Merck and his penicillin partner, Dr. Selman Waksman for their May 1946 debate "Town Hall Meeting," a broadcast promoted by the Westinghouse Research Foundation. Merck reassured the public that whatever the enemy dished out, antibiotics could cure. (5) Nobel prize winner, Selman Waksman, discoverer of streptomycin at Rutgers University Agricultural Research Lab, would save the world. Soon he would embark on mission to Moscow.

The Russians just couldn't get their penicillin formulas right. Amtorg was given the go-ahead to petition American pharmaceutical companies for "know-how" and approached Merck, Heyden Chemical and Technical Enterprises, Inc., insisting it needed a plant capable of serving 2,000,000 people! That should just about cover all the elite members of the Communist Party. The correspondence between these antibiotic manufacturers and the State Department express a good deal of skepticism over conducting business in such a hostile nation as the USSR. Could the State Department guarantee compensation if Stalin seized their factories and nationalized them? There were no guarantees. Merck declined the invitation, but someone else got the contract. (6) Most peculiar are the State Department file "withdrawal slips" under the Ford Administration:

STATE DEPARTMENT file 861.657/6-1548, To Commerce Department, 8/20/48, "Purchase of Penicillin Producing Plant by the USSR" "TOP SECRET" WITHDRAWAL NOTICE" authority, CIA, FBI/Post 45, BRIT/Intell, 4/14/76. Declassified 5/19/94

STATE DEPARTMENT file 861.657/6-1548, From Justice Department 6/15/48, "Russian Interest in Penicillin Plant" WITHDRAWAL NOTICE, authority, FBI/Post 45, declassified 5/19/94

STATE DEPARTMENT file 861.657/6-1548, From Justice Department, 6/23/48 "Russian Interest in Penicillin Plant" From Saltzman and SANPCC 386/6, To Att. Gen/copy #38. WITHDRAWAL NOTICE, authority, Justice/Post 45 FBI/Post 45, CIA, BRIT/INTELL Dated 4/14/76, declassified 5/19/94

Other State Department correspondence was "MISSING" pertaining to correspondence with the Department of Agriculture on tick-borne epidemics. The "Dragon Returnee" "Paperclip-Dustbin" smuggling operations of the British and Americans may have proved extremely embarrassing to the State Department. Here is a list of files the author was unable to retrieve from the National Archives Civil Reference Branch, the dates of withdrawals unknown. Who had been doing the selective housecleaning and when?:

MISSING STATE DEPARTMENT FILES.
800.24/5-134 Food in Poland, SECRET FILE
800.62222/5-29-47 Technical sub-committee abolished on wool
811.5018/5-1247 Bureau of Human Nutrition, Soviets in Berlin
800.24/1-1447 Revoking of lend-lease funds
022.857/11-2746 Public Health Reports [note: ELBRUS docked 1/6/46]
103.9132/4-947 Parker receives Indian ticks
811.4275 Ig S.E./1-2247 Bringing Dr. Toumanoff to US
811.42791/10-2246 Visit of Dr. Hefezi of Iran to Rocky Mt. Laboratory
865.61A/4/848 Dr. Max Adams McCall to Italy, Agr. Specialist SECRET
661.1115 Amtorg Trading Corp./5-1948 Regarding export activities
832.61a/2-747 From Agr. Dpt, shipment of household goods of Dr. Arthur G. Kevorkian being held in Havana Cuba, pending payment of freight charges [Is Arthur related to Jack Kevorkian? What's behind his MS executions?]

George Merck and Selman Waksman were like the odd couple; Merck, rather stiff, disciplined and polished, an industrial magnate; Waksman, a flamboyant and disheveled university intellectual. Waksman, with his discoveries in antibiotics, was sought after internationally, lecturing on the wonders of mold. During WW II, Waksman served on the War

Department's Scientific Committee on Bacteriology for Shipping while maintaining his post as chair of the US Department of Agriculture's Experimental Laboratory at Rutgers University. The profits from penicillin patents he turned back to the University. His son, Byron Waksman, helped establish the National Multiple Sclerosis Foundation in 1946, months after the docking of the SS ELBRUS, the same organization that hired Dr. Leo Alexander to make the largest MS survey in America. Byron Waksman settled down at Yale University as an esteemed immunologist.

The FBI's files on the National MS Hope Chest include a brochure on the Foundation's establishment, its objectives, and its solicitation of J. Edgar Hoover for assistance in a nation-wide fund raising campaign. Spirochetes and allergies were fingered as possible causes. Malmie Eisenhower had been elected chairwoman of the Hope Chest and William Buckley Public Relations man. Which Buckley? There are two of consequence, William F. Buckley, Jr., right wing commentator for "National Review" and "Firing Line" or William F. Buckley, Lebanon CIA station chief, tortured and executed by the Hezbulla, sacrificed by CIA director Bill Casey? Buckley is a common name. The MS Hope Chest proposed a "Suggested Radio Announcement" for Hoover to deliver:

"NATIONAL MULTIPLE SCLEROSIS/EPIDEMIOLOGICAL STUDIES"
FBI file 94-48410-6 MS Hope Chest letter to J. Edgar Hoover 3/14/57

Dear Mr. Hoover: ... 'Suggested Announcement'

"ANCHOR: Here is Mr. J. Edgar Hoover with a message from the National MS Society.

MR. HOOVER: As Director of the FBI for more than thirty years, I am proud of the reputation the men in the Bureau have built for our organization. The FBI functions as a team. We have learned through experience that although the identity of a criminal may be unknown when we start on a case, he can nearly always be tracked down if every single clue is properly and persistently pursued. In a way, doctors and scientists who are working with the National MS Society are conducting the same type of investigation. In their laboratories and hospitals they are trying to track down a mystery - the cause and cure of MS. They know that some day they'll solve this mystery, but they must have your help to do it. their research is supported by the dollars you drop into the MS Hope Chest. Work with them as a team. Give them the support they need - contribute to the MS Hope Chest today. (Time 59 seconds)"

Hoover politely declined the invitation. Does this sound like political blackmail to you? President Eisenhower had just appointed Nelson Rockefeller as Deputy Assistant to the Health Department, and Allen Dulles to direct the CIA! Malmie Eisenhower was chairing the Hope Chest! The MS Society's Leo Alexander went on to head the National Electro-shock Treatment Association, following Franz Jahnel's lead. The National MS Society was not alone in suspecting spirochetes as the cause of MS, research had been published in Germany and America since the 1930s. (7)

While stationed in Europe, serving in the US Army Medical Corps in July 1946, Dr. Byron Waksman made special arrangements for his father, Selman to travel to Moscow for a special conference on antibiotics. Reference to this trip is made in Selman Waksman's autobiography, "My Life With the Microbes" and the Army's OACSI files. The Army's interrogation of Waksman on his return voyage is most discerning; they found Selman aloof and uncooperative, with little light to shed on the Soviet biological warfare program. He could only recognize a few prominent scientists, identifying Professor Orbelli, director of the Pavlov Institute in Koltushi, secretary for Biological Sciences of the Academy. Eventually, Orbelli would be moved to a Soviet BW center at Valdivostok. After acquainting Waksman, Orbelli was demoted. (8)

Selman Waksman traveled and wrote prolifically, terrifying Hoover. In turn, the FBI built an enormous "ESPIONAGE' file against Selman, tracking his every move for decades. Waksman was guilty of nothing but naivete, caught in a vice between the State Department and their archenemy, Hoover. With Waksman's international circles and connections to everybody everywhere, pharmacologists, Soviet BW experts, government, industrial and university research assistants, himself such a gabby yak yak, Hoover feared he's spill the beans, somewhere, some time, some how. The FBI branded him an intellectual snob. Waksman literally drove the FBI nuts. If Waksman didn't hold classified material himself, most of his associates did, Hoover reasoned, presuming he'd be an unwitting target for Soviet espionage. Again, Hoover was barking up the wrong tree.

Waksman always got State Department backing for special passports on his missions to Moscow. The FBI dogged Selman incessantly, prying into every move and motive, their files extensive and much censored. The State Department's International Labor, Social and Health Affairs Division that attended the founding of WHO, established the American-Soviet Medical Society through the services of Michael B. Shimkin, Russian Ambassador Averill Harriman, Mr. Mulliken and Surgeon General Parran. Drs. V. V. Parin, Fedor Krotkov - WHO Secretary, and Drs Cayley and Roskin were on the exchange list planning a visit in the summer of

1947. (9) Selman Waksman was a long upstanding member of both the American-Soviet Medical Society and the Council of American Soviet Friendship, as was the Health Department's Dr. Michael Shimkin. By the time the McCarthy era rolled around, both organizations had been declared a Communist Front by Attorney General Clark.

Selman Waksman was born in Priluka, Russia in 1888, immigrating to America in 1910, citizenized by 1916. During these early years, he stayed with a friend of the family, Peter Mitnik, also from Russia. Selman married Peter's sister while Peter returned to Russia in 1917, enchanted by the upcoming Bolshevik Revolution. The family was very close. In the American tradition, Selman applied himself to old-fashioned hard work, paying his own way through college. His discovery of streptomycin made him an instant celebrity. One of Waksman's antibiotics was suspiciously similar to that of the Soviets' "albomycin" (FBI file 105-1551848). It would be worthwhile noting that other American pharmaceutical factories approached by Amtorg had taken up contracts to share know-how. Waksman's brother-in-law Peter Mitnik, "Peisi" became the center of an espionage controversy and vanished into the gulag for ten years. The FBI reasoned Peisi was held hostage to milk Waksman for all his worth:

SELMAN WAKSMAN FBI file 105-15518-50 April 19, 1957
To: SAC Newark (105-731)
"Note that a definite hostage situation exists in this case inasmuch as Mr. Waksman presently had three brothers residing in the Soviet Union. Waksman himself has stated that he is extremely close to his brother-in-law, Peisi, who is said to be working in Moscow as a consultant... Note that Waksman has stated that between 1947 and 1956, he did not hear from his brother-in-law. (Line blacked out) Your attention is invited to the fact that Waksman, an expert in the field of microbiology, has in the past spoken on germ warfare and may well be an expert in that field. Note that due to his prominence, it would be all probability be a simple matter for Waksman to come into possession of highly technical and classified material related to germ warfare and related fields, which information would be of great value to the Soviets..."

But through the hundreds of pages and decades of tracking Waksman, no incriminating evidence was ever discovered against him. Every associate interrogated testified to Waksman's loyalty to America. What was going on? Was Hoover retaliating against his enemies in the State Department who had been harassing him for his homosexuality, by harassing Waksman? Next, Hoover attacked Selman Waksman's lab assistant from the Institute at Rutgers who had taken up BW research at Fort Detrick. New espionage files on the "subject" were created. Almost all of the pages were withheld, (Selman Waksman FBI file 105-15518-69). We know from Waksman's autobiography "My Life with the Microbes," that Rene Dubos had been a former lab assistant to Waksman at Rutgers and went on to work for the Rockefeller Institute. But there is no way of confirming his identity, or the veracity of Hoover's accusations. No doubt the Communists wanted to know about the brand new diseases plaguing American cities and livestock, but Lyme statistics from the National MS Society were public knowledge, why bother Selman Waksman? "Nobody gets the dirt like Hoover, Nobody!" That's a fact, it's written right on the bottom of your vacuum cleaner. The author's letters to Ft. Detrick regarding possible experimentation with Lyme spirochetes received a curt, flat denial.

As new epidemics spread, after the docking of the ELBRUS, Truman began a game of musical managers, as did the Kremlin. During the war, Roosevelt felt oil tycoon, Edwin Pauley, merited the appointment to the Department of the Interior's Lend-lease program. Pauley had also chaired the Democratic Party's Campaign financing in the 1940s, heavily subsidized by oil contributions, and attempted to influence judicial rulings on the privatization of California's tidal oil fields. Harold Ickes, Secretary of the Interior, and Pauley's boss, sensed the onset of WW II, and pushed for Federal control and conservation of the tidal oil fields in the name of national security. Rockefeller's Standard Oil, a subsidiary of I. G. Farben, was Pauley's partner, had been arming Hitler through Amtorg. In turn, as a senator during WW II, Truman prosecuted the Alkali industries for collusion with I. G. Farben. To counter Ickes' efforts, Pauley offered a bribe of $300,000 contribution from the California oil companies to the Democratic National Campaign, hoping to sway President Roosevelt and his Attorney General for a favorable ruling. Campaign finance reform has been a hot topic for nearly a century.

When Truman nominated I. G. accomplice, Edwin Pauley for Under Secretary of the Navy, and God only knows why, just months after the docking of the lend-lease SS ELBRUS still under Pauley's control, old "rat killer" Harold Ickes blew the whistle. Such a scrap evolved between curmudgeon Ickes and Truman, that the old ratkiller resigned his office, making a grand exit speech before Congress, exposing Pauley's "raw deal" and destroying his nomination. Secretary of the Navy, James Forrestal, had been spared a scumbag for an assistant. (10)

Pauley had served Truman as US Industrial and Commercial Advisor to the Potsdam Conference with Stalin and Churchill, and later served Truman as US Representative on the Allied Commission on Reparations, carrying full rank of ambassador to Russia. His trip to Korea would result in severe illness and hospitalization. Pauley expanded his oil interests with the young George Bush, through family ties. It was years before Bush could rid himself of this barnacle. Bush, so fed up with his family's scandals and business ties to I. G. Farben, revolted and joined the Army Air Force, the youngest pilot to enlist in WW II. (11) Bush still makes parachute jumps re-iterating his WW II heroism and patriotism, much to the horror of his wife, Barbara.

Surely, if Edwin Pauley's files would not reveal anything on lend-lease and the SS ELBRUS, something might be gained from Amtorg's? On December 22, 2001, ten years after the author's original FOIA to the FBI on Amtorg, an additional 27 pages out of the withheld 260 arrived for Christmas. The reason for their release was astounding:

"Per the letter from the Department of Justice to you dated May 22, 1998, the sections noted above (FBI file 61-HQ-5381: 131, 132, 133) were remanded to the Department Review Committee for the review under Executive Order 12958, which sets the current guidelines for the proper classification of materials. With few exceptions the enclosed have been declassified."

Executive order 12958 was established by President Bill Clinton to release material on Nazi war criminals. The Justice Department set about compiling Amtorg's early history as it built a case against them for violation of the Foreign Agent's Registration Act. Did this case involve future Nazi war criminals in ARCOS, AMTORG's sister monopoly in the UK, put on trial by the British? Let's look at what has been recently released and what has been censored. Why would Amtorg refuse to register as a foreign business on American soil in the first place? Possibly Amtorg had too many dissatisfied customers and hoped to exempt itself from law suits under diplomatic immunity, insisting they were an executive branch of the Politburo, not a private business? The FBI files explain that at the end of the First World War, the United States did not recognize the newly formed Soviet Union, making direct trade between the two nations difficult. Nevertheless, several trade organizations sprang up to circumnavigate the US imposed boycott, using British and German middleman. The Products Exchange Corporation in America (PRODEX) made early ventures towards the Bolsheviks, as did the Anglo-American Incorporation extend contracts to the fledgling republic. By 1925, according to fur and oil tycoon Armand Hammer's autobiography, both AMTORG and ARCOS were established by the Soviets in America and England, respectively, to facilitate Communist prosperity through Capitalism. (12) Imagine Armand Hammer, America's leading fur trader, pitted against film star, William Hurt, the Soviet policeman, in "Gorky Park." Martin Cruz Smith's fiction ran a close parallel to fact.

First, to understand Amtorg, we must know Hammer. "Who's Who in America" lists this cunning and ruthless wheeler-dealer as a "petroleum company executive" and "art patron" writing "Quest of the Romanoff Treasures," later serving as treasure of L'Ermitage Galleries Incorporated. As personal financier to Nikolai Lenin, Hammer boasted he had introduced over thirty prominent American businessmen to the Communist dictator, establishing the Allied American Corporation. The Lenin museum today holds Hammer's gift of a bronze sculpture of a monkey contemplating a human skull. Nicolai and Einstein were not alone in their fears of "the invading Negro and Mongolian hordes destroying European culture." Racism IS the foundation of Communism. In 1923, a subdivision of the Allied American Corporation was established, Allied American Fur Sales, Inc. The FBI files on this firm go back as far as 1945, trailing Hammer in and out of Russia from his summer residence in Scarsdale New York. The files are categorized as "Internal Security-R"

"ALLIED AMERICAN FUR SALES AGENCY - ARMAND HAMMER" FBI file 100-60586 dated 7/7/45.

Page 17: "According to Hammer's "Quest of the Romanoff Treasures" he lunches with Henry Ford and "obtained the agency for all Ford products in Soviet Russia... and other American manufacturers... McCline Plow Company, U.S. Plywood Machinery Company, Berth Levi Company..."

Page 18: "... By 1923, the Hammer brothers were doing thriving business. They organized the Allied American Fur Sales Agency with Sutta and Fuchs, large New York fur merchants and jointly exported over a million dollars in furs. Hammer writes on page 174-176... "On July 14th we signed a contract with Mr. Frumkin, Acting Commissar of the Foreign Trade Monopoly Department. The Commissar, Mr. Krassin, had told me I could obtain this contract on condition that I guaranteed to export from Russia the equivalent of our annual imports from America.... In the two years of '23 and '24 we had a total turnover of twelve and a half million dollars. Our exports were principally furs, as we had established fur-collecting stations throughout Siberia, but also included a great variety of other products...." "

Hammer engineered American grain deals with the Russians from Lenin's reign until the fall of the "Evil Empire.". In spite of Hammer's efforts, Stalin succeeded in starving millions to death. The FBI files on Amtorg paint a more seedy side of the American businessmen's operations with the Soviets. Averill Harriman, a young American steel entrepreneur, looked to the new Soviet Union for cheap manganese:

"AMTORG ARREST OF OFFICIALS" FBI file 61-HQ-5381 Sect. 133

Page 19-20: "Because the Harrimans had an interest in the Hamburg-American Steamship Lines, the ships of that line were used by DERUTRA. Also, inasmuch as Harriman desired to develop an independent source of manganese ore, he was interested in establishing direct trade negotiations with the Russians (two lines blacked out) was unsuccessful because the Russians were then in the process of building trade relations with the British."

We can only guess why the FBI blacked out these two lines, if they pertain to the Harrimans, or if they pertain to someone from the UK, having something to do with the WW II Nazi spy case the British Government evoked against ARCOS. DERUTRA's sister company in Moscow was named SOVFRACHT and its American counterpart named AMDE-RUTRA. In the summer of 1923, the Bolsheviks sent Churgin Hoorgin to head DERUTRA in America:

"AMTORG/ARREST OF OFFICIALS FBI file 61-HQ-5381, Section 133

Page 20: "CHURGIN was interested in setting up an American Business trading company. His plan was to utilize the facilities of ARCOS which was an English-Russian trade organization and which had a branch in the United States, and the facilities of the Products Exchange Corporation (PRODEX), an American corporation, by effecting a merger of these two to form a new American corporation. Part of the plan was to have Russia import agricultural implements and to export to the United States furs, animal casings and ores."

In 1924, the two companies, AMDERUTRA and PRODEX merged, thus forming AMTORG Trading Corporation, over half of the monies from the Centrosoyuz Central Organization of Fur Cooperatives of Russia, putting the Soviets in control. Who was Averill Harriman? I. G. Farben's banker, Allen Dulles' partner, and George Bush's grandfather. Such a heritage. The child was destitute, later shunning both Communists and Fascists in his adult life. Further record of the Bush predicament is laid out in Mark Aaron's and John Lotus' "Secret War Against the Jews," (St. Martin Press, 1994, pages 363-365). According to the FBI files above, DE-RUTRA was located on Amtorg's premises of 210 Madison Avenue with a New York bank account as late as 1941. The Germans and the Soviets were indeed, partners in crime since the Bolshevik Revolution. The Bushes have struggled to right the wrongs of their in-laws and outlaws for nearly half a century. It is worth noting that the Anglo-American Fur Merchant Corporation brought suit against the US War Shipping Administration for damages ensued while rescuing 47 bales of Russian pony skins off their beached freighter at Archangel. (13) Gratitude!

The "Decennial Index" is full of court cases and lawsuits brought by and against Amtorg. By the end of WW II, Roosevelt's army of liberal judges was screwing the American textile merchants and rug dealers filing claims of "defective goods" and "breach of contract" against Amtorg. Attorney Jacob Pincus wrote the Secretary of State regarding Amtorg's immunity from law suits for "goods sold and delivered." His wife, who survived him twenty years, had no idea of what this case pertained to. The same question regarding Amtorg's status was raised by Barry, Treanor & Shandell, Counselors at Law, and Ynok Shegarian, Peter Doerflein, and John Buell, Persian rug dealers. (14) Fortunately, the Shegarian case was retrieved from the New York Court House for the author, courtesy of Mr. Elliot Moss, a legal researcher. Amtorg's Persian rugs were of "poor quality," delivered January 16th, 1946, just after the docking of the SS ELBRUS. The Shegarians wanted their money back, plain and simple. Papa Ynok had passed away many years ago, but one of his sons was kind enough to chat with the author. After Shegarian's father refused the Russian imports, his younger sister died of a mysterious illness no one could identify. Had these wool rugs sat on deck of the SS ELBRUS'? The Buell family was equally courteous, but could shed no light on their grandparent's business deals.

Camden Fiber Mills brought suit against Amtorg for defective goods. Camden, New Jersey, is just across the bay from Philadelphia. After the case went into appeals, the judge decided that Camden need to arbitrate inside Russian courts. (15) FBI files show that one of Camden's partners was Lush Cotton Products Company. Samuel Beryl Lush was a shady character, his early career as an attorney landed him in prison, convicted for fraud. Yet by the end of WW II, Lush had evolved into a multi-millionaire, brokering large shipments of cotton linters, used in ammunition, to the Soviet Union. On June 13, 1948, the FBI New York office issued an "URGENT TELETYPE" to the "DIRECTOR AND SACS" Washington Headquarters:

"LUSH COTTON PRODUCTS COMPANY" FBI file 100-356388

"SAMUEL BERYL LUSH, IS-R, REPHILATEL JUNE TWELVE LAST. NY INDICES SHOW LUSH A NINETEEN FORTY ONE MEMBER OF AMERICAN RUSSIAN INSTITUTE CONNECTED WITH LUSH COTTON PRODUCTS CO., FOUR HUNDRED CHESTNUT STREET PHILADELPHIA. NO OTHER INFORMA-TION STOP PLACED US CUSTOMS, NEW YORK... THOUGH APPARENTLY IN COTTON BUSINESS, SHOULD BE NOTED THAT IF HE HAS ANY INTEREST IN FURS SUCH FREQUENT TRIPS TO RUSSIA ARE COMMON IN THIS INDUSTRY... HAVE AGENT PRESENT DURING BAGGAGE SEARCH IF NOTIFIED BY CUSTOMS IN TIME. ALSO TO NOTE POSSIBLE CONTACTS AT AIRPORT..."

While other businessmen coveted trade with the Russians during the Cold War, Lush was able to obtain visas through assistance of the US State Department, scoring over twenty very profitable trips. Lush primarily dealt with Amtorg and the Exportljon textile combine in the USSR. Negotiat-ing a settlement through Soviet arbitration courts over Amtorg's defective goods could have easily landed many American businessmen in the Gulag as "spies." Was Lush acting as "broker," negotiating their release in a touchy situation for the State Department? We can only speculate. According to the FBI files, the Russians adored and trusted Lush. Hoover smelled a rat and ordered wire taps. And once again, we don't know if Lush was really the target, or more likely, Hoover's old nemesis, the State Department. One such conversation tapped on 8/8/49, includes Lush's comments, mostly "yeah" while his associate's conversation is censored:

"LUSH COTTON PRODUCTS COMPANY" FBI file 100-356388-31

'Office Memorandum of 8/8/49' To: Director, FBI, from SAC Phila-delphia

'Subject: Samuel B. Lush'

"(Blackout) Confidential Informant (blackout) advised of the fol-lowing conversation between SAMUEL B. LUSH (blackout) first name unknown, of Reynolds and Company...." (followed by twenty censored lines and "yeahs")

LUSH: "Well, I know, as a matter of fact, that they are holding meet-ings every day with the Russians in Washington." (line blacked out)

LUSH: "I know that the idea is to make a settlement on the Lend

Lease."

(line blacked out.)

LUSH: "Yeah. That's right. And, I think the intention is to make a settlement. Now, when the settlement is made and everything is clear and there's a certain amount of good relations restored, I think you still have a chance with your bonds." (line blacked out)

LUSH: "Yeah." (More line blacked out)

LUSH: "Well, I would... for the time being. You know that negotiations have been going on Lend Lease and on the ships and on the other stuff."

(Line blacked out)

LUSH: "I think so, that seven million dollars is still there." (Two lines blacked out)

LUSH: "Once the Lend Lease business is out of the way and all the other issues are out of the (two lines blacked out)

LUSH: "Well not, not right away. What I would do then, after the Lend Lease thing is settled, why then I would go over and I would talk to them and find out what the chances are and then I could make you a good report."

(Lush continued on regarding the value of bonds.)

The author made the original FOIA request #435846 on 12/2/91, and received a response ten years later, June 8, 2001. Again, the author appealed what seems an apparent cover-up of lend-lease shipping. Meanwhile, Lush took up the silk and cotton trade with Red China, hiring an old State Department spy as his agent, Jay Robinson (aka Jacob Rabinowitz) from the OSS Research and Analysis Far East Political Section. Hoover already had Robinson pegged as a Soviet spy, and the release of his files are still pending, (LUSH FBI file 100-33312). Hoover fully understood Robinson's significance. The OSS Research and Analysis Department ran a Political Section on Psychological Warfare named "Moral Operations" using international Labor Unions, German Spartans, and the Mafia. The operation was headed by future Kennedy Supreme Court Justice appointee and labor relations attorney, Arthur Goldberg. More on Goldberg's significance to follow in upcoming chapters. Hoover utilized every avenue available to launch his "counter attack" against the Dulles gang.

The "New York Times" ran further announcements on Amtorg's fur sales to the auctioneers, Lampson, Fraser & Huth, (11/28/48, page 46,) in the 'Business World' section involving "80,000 Persian Lamb, 106,000 muskrats, 1000,000 squirrel, 3,000 sables, 50,000 kolinsky and 60,000 marmots." Who was buying this stuff? The author browsed through "Davidson's Textile Blue Book" courtesy of the Windham Textile Museum in Connecticut, seeking possible participants in Amtorg's auctions. The Forte, Dupee Sawyer hair processing plant in Boston was a fairly large concern. Richard Forte, still operating their Woonsocket Rhode Island plant was most cordial, and referred the author to his Uncle Orville, the company's former vice president, now retired in Florida. Orville Forte is an extremely knowledgeable, informative, kindly, and patient gentleman. He wrote the author, detailing a history of the American-Russian-China fur trade during the war years and after. As the Communist rebellion progressed under Mao Tse Tung, they kept on shipping camel hair from the northern republics to Soviet brokers, who in turn, sold bales to America.

"Dear Rachel, Here is a little background material on the Cashmere and Camel hair trade. I am doing this all from memory and ask that you let me know if anything suggests to you that I should try to dig into it in more detail.

The best quality Cashmere (C) and Camel Hair (CH) come from the Mongolian Peoples Republic and China lesser qualities come from Iran and Afghanistan. Both fibers as they come from the goat and camel respectively are a co-mingled mass of fine under down and coarse outer or guard hair which must be separated by complicated special purpose machinery known as dehairing machinery.

Until about ten years ago Mongolian C and CH was gathered and packed in the MPR and bartered to other Communist block countries (principally the USSR) who sold it, still in the original packages, to de-hairers like out company (Forte Cashmere Company 148 Hamlet Ave, Woonsocket R. I.)

Until recently Chinese and CH was handled in the same way except that it was roughly sorted in China and then sold directly to overseas buyers.

Until just prior to World War II the only dehairing companies were located in England and Japan. In the late 1930s the Cashmere Corporation of America and its sister company Irie Dying and Processing Co. started a dehairing plant in Cleveland, Ohio. At Forte we developed dehairing process during World War II and started production in Needham Heights, Mass. just after the war. We later expanded to Norwood, Mass. And eventually closed these plants and bought a competitive plant in Woonsocket where we now operate.

From the mid 1940s to the mid 1950s several other dehairing plants were opened by different people. These plants were in Woonsocket, Danbury Conn., Bellingham Mass, and Charlotte N. C.

I just received in the mail this booklet on lyme disease and pass it on to you for whatever good it may be. I presume that with your knowledge you could write such a booklet.

Unfortunately, my computer tells me I have just gone to page two but that is all I have to say so page two is a short one.

Sincerely yours, Orville W. Forte"

Next, it seemed appropriate to write an FOIA to the FBI on Forte's referenced factories, and the FBI responded with more solidly blacked out files, (61-5381-402, and 65-28939-1810). Some of the Forte records had been withheld by the FBI, originating through the US Navy, which they later relinquished. The Fortes had received a large refund check from Amtorg for the sum of $15,675.00 reimbursing the factory for "merchandise of poor quality" (FBI file 105-11846 dated 3/10/55) subject "Forte, Dupee, Sawyer Company, IS-R Amtorg Trading Corporation IS-R. - citing an earlier SAC letter 10/22/52 "ESPIONAGE AND FOREIGN INTELLIGENCE INVESTIGATIONS-DOUBLE AGENT PROGRAM." Hoover, dressed in drag, waltzing around in Russian furs, portrayed the Fortes as villains, Communist conspirators! He was crazy, seeing a Communist under every bed while the State Department snooped under his own bed. Orville Forte as a double agent??? EEEE GADS! We really need a reality check here. Hoover couldn't think straight. Did Forte's re-imbursement come from Degojnsky's gold bars spotted on the SS DENIS DAVIDOV as he had reported to Countess Alexandra Tolstoy, (State Department file 861.865/11-846)? Most likely. The author wishes to thank the Fortes for their kind assistance and courage to persevere under both corrupt Soviet and American governments.

As the complaints piled up from the cheated American textile merchants, Amtorg played cat and mouse with the Justice Department. By 1947, a year after the docking of the SS ELBRUS, Amtorg refused to register as a foreign corporation, expecting diplomatic immunity? The Foreign Relations Registration Act was passed in 1938 but was ignored during the war years while lend-lease was under operation. The exemption expired September 30th, 1946 under Truman's executive order. Moscow pulled its personnel from New York, closed its Amtorg office at the Morgan Estate, (there were rumors of nude bathing) and proceeded to move into the Pratt House. Amtorg president, Michael Gulsov, was instructed to "resign" in November 1946 along with his chairman of the board. A strange series of events began to follow when the Kremlin sent the SS VOLGA to Jersey City and New York. The longshoremen refused to unload its cargo. The same fate was suffered by the SS VILNIUS a few weeks earlier. (16) The

State Department held "SECRET FILES" on the VOLGA, embarking on Moscow's orders to remove all Amtorg's gold in US banks! Suddenly, the Pratt Estate had a big fire:

STATE DEPARTMENT FILE 861.51/4-1448 "SECRET FILE"

Department of State European Affairs April 14, 1948, Nat. Arch. CRB

C-Mr. Bohien, U-Mr. Lovett

"FC has received information to the effect that on April 12 the Amtorg Trading Corporation of New York... informed the Federal Reserve Bank of New York that it had received instructions from the State Bank of the USSR in Moscow to withdraw 42 kgs of gold bullion valued at $4,491,000 which were being held by the Federal Reserve Bank of New York for Soviet account for resale... The bullion was delivered alongside the Soviet vessel VOLGA on the same afternoon, was personally loaded by the crew, and the vessel sailed for Leningrad at 6 p.m. on April 12. It is understood that this shipment represents all known Soviet gold holding in the United States.

FC has also received reports to the effect that records believed to come from Amtorg have recently been burned on the Pratt estate on Long Island. Additional Amtorg files have been crated and shipped back to the Soviet Union. The activities are believed to presage a drastic reduction or perhaps complete termination of Amtorg operations in the United States. This step was probably motivated by the new export control measures which are effectively limiting exports from the United States to the Soviet Union."

The US Navy sent a sub to track the VOLGA back to Odessa, so loaded down with gold, its speed reduced to 8 knots.(17) By July 29, 1948, the "New York Times" (pages 29 & 34) reported Amtorg shipping one hundred mysterious crates, labeled "refrigerators" back to Moscow. Do you think the "refrigerators" made it to Moscow, or did they sink to the bottom of the ocean with tons of infested furs and bills of lading? Along with the refrigerators went "a large number of employees" who may have been forced to walk the plank. Of course, Amtorg did not leave New York, only its staff, to be replaced by a whole new entourage. October 21st, 1948, Amtorg was indicted for violation of the Foreign Agents Registration Act, and the FBI's keystone cops followed.

A disgruntled insider, commercial counselor to Amtorg, J. Anthony Marcus, blew the whistle. Thoroughly disillusioned, he testified before a Senate Judiciary sub-committee in July 1949 on Amtorg's "commercial spying" insisting America abrogate its trade treaty with the Soviet Union:

"Communist Activities Among Aliens and National Groups" (US Senate 81st Cong., 1st Session, Y-4,189/2: C73/2/pt 1-3). Marcus became adamant, writing articles in "Plain Talk" on October 1949, accusing the Soviets for running an international monopoly: "A curious anomaly has arisen to plague America's economy at home and abroad." Hoover collected every newspaper scrap on Marcus' incessant protest. Marcus would die November 22, 1960 three years to the day before President Kennedy's assassination.

Finally, the Justice Department moved against "Gorky Park" in New York City and indicted Amtorg's top six officers October 21, 1949, targeting Alexander Alexandrovich Istchenko - expert on lend-lease. His underlings included, Nikita Vasiliovich Ermolov - director of Fur Department, Petr Vasilievich Kaftanov - Director of import-export, Sergei Nikolaevich Sosnin - Deputy Director of Fur Department, Elena Nikolaevna Svetlitskaia - Economist of Fur Department, Alexander Alexeevich Sasanov - Cargo Supervisor and Peter Ivenovich Titov - Specialist in charge of Miscellaneous Imports. The FBI cat fight with AMTORG had begun and the fur was flying.

The author's request of the AMTORG records (#353,796/190-IIQ-45770) were originally FOIAed to the FBI on 10/19/91, taking six years to be released after intervention of Congressman Merrill Cook. Out of 602 pages, only 145 pages were released, most solidly blacked out. The author's blood began to boil and claws began to grow at her fingertips, feeling like one of the innocent wild animals skinned by Soyuzpushnina. It's hard to type with claws. Again, the author appealed the FBI, #97,3041, Richard Huff, Co-director, responding May 22, 1998, that "I have decided to affirm the initial action in this case. The Amtorg Trading Corporation is the subject of one Headquarters main file entitled Treason." As of May, 2002, the FBI has promised more. Even from the few scraps the FBI was willing to release, a hilarious Fearless Fosdick comic-book caper began to emerge:

AMTORG TRADING CORPORATION - Office Memorandum 10/20/49

FBI file 61-5681-3726. To: Mr. Ladd, From H. G. Fletcher

"[SAC] Mr. Belmont was confident that at least three out of the five subjects could be placed at the Amtorg building tomorrow at one time. This was the figure orally mentioned by Mr. Ford and Mr. (blackout) as satisfactory for simultaneous arrests... I also read to Mr. Belmont the letter of the Department of October 20, 1949, addressed to Mr. McGohey. Mr. Belmont will try tonight to consult with Mr. McGohey...."

John F. X. McGohey was New York's prosecuting attorney, and bonds were set at fifteen thousand dollars each for the Amtorg officials, but there was concern that the Russians could not get to the banks in time. Penciled in at the bottom of the page was Fletchers' reply "See that there is no slip on our part. It makes me sick re. the solicitude for the international thugs. A night in jail would be good for them." At 2:55 p.m., FBI agents moved into the building, "immobilizing the two elevators," "instructing the receptionist and telephone operator...":

AMTORG TRADING CORPORATION Internal Security-R: Registration Act. FBI file 61-5381-3786, 11/29/49, Attention Mr. L. B. Nichols, To Director FBI, From: Edward Scheidt

"Supervisor (blackout) accompanied by Special Agents (blackout) proceeded immediately to the second floor where they located and apprehended SERGEI ANDREEVICH SHEVCHENKO and GENNAUDY N. OGLOBLIN without any difficulty. Agent (blackout) arrested OGLOBOLIN and Agent (blackout) arrested SHEVCHENKO... and took them to the U. S. Courthouse. The other apprehending party, consisting of SAC Edward Scheidty, ASAC Belmont and Special Agents (blackout) took the elevator from the lobby to the 8th floor... and proceeded to the office of ALEXANDER ALEXANDROVICH ISTCHENKO. In the office they found in addition to ISTCHENKO, one (blackout) and attorney ISIDORE G. NEEDLEMAN... ISTCHENKO advised that he was an official of the Soviet Government and would only go under protest. He accompanied Mr. Scheidt and Agent (blackout) willingly to the office of Mr. ALESKEI VASILIEVICH ZAKHAROV on the same floor."

As the roundup continued, the FBI agents moved down the hall into Zakharov's office, who picked up a chair, whirling it overhead, threatening the agents, then reconsidering, sat down while Mr. Tollokonnikov, "making vociferous protests," phoned the Russian Embassy.

AMTORG file 61-5381-3786 continues:

"ASAC Belmont turned from him to assist in the apprehension of ZAKHAROV, SAC Scheidt also returned immediately from the elevator. However, special Agent (blackout) needed no assistance. The Bureau may recall that Agent (blackout) formerly played three seasons of professional football with the Jersey City Giants. He stands about 6'4" and weighs approximately 235 pounds. He merely stooped down and applied an arm lock to ZAKHAROV, who was sitting in his chair, whereupon ZAKHAROV arose promptly and tip-toed out of the office as though he were walking on eggs. In the elevator, ZAKHAROV was asked by ASAC Belmont whether it was necessary for Agent (blackout) to continue to hold him and ZAKHAROV replied that it was: that he wanted it understood that he was going under protest."

On November 2, 1949, five of the Amtorg officials appeared before US Commissioner Edward McDonald for arraignment. But the sixth suspect, Vasili Petrovich Rebrov, beat it back to Moscow. Only months earlier, Amtorg's vice president, Rebrov received orders from the Kremlin to serve as Commercial Counselor to the Soviet Mission in Bogota, Columbia. In the upcoming chapters, we shall see that both the Soviets, Amtorg and their mercurial band of Nazis had operatives working the South American drug cartels. After a few nights in jail, Zakharov decided to register Amtorg with the US Justice Department. They paid a $10,000 fine, sentence suspended, a slap on the wrist.

Amtorg then concocted a slick legal move, listing all its agencies and trading combines as separate sub-contractors, forcing the American businessmen to arbitrate cases inside the Russian courts against these individual firms, releasing Amtorg of all responsibility. Mr. Ermolov, heading Amtorg's fur department, delivered the necessary lists of Amtorg's "foreign principals," the Soviet trade combines and corporations. These included the different shipping lines such as the Black Sea State Steamship Line of the Ministry of the Maritime Fleet, "acting as an independent financial basis, enjoying the rights of a juridical person, acting in accordance with this charter on the basis of economic self-sufficiency... not responsible for debts of the Government, nor was the Government responsible for debts of the steamship line... etc." Likewise were the cases of the Far Eastern State Steamship Line, the Northern State Steamship Line, the Baltic State Steamship Line, Soviet Vsesojuznoe Objedinenie Sovfracht, Soyuzpushnina (fur and textiles) and Exportljon, (FBI file 61-5381-3770 and 3780). Eventually, Hoover began to comprehend the Communist crisis. Writing in the FBI's weekly newsletter "Counterattack":

"THE COMMUNIST TRAIL IN AMERICA" Jacob Spolansky, Macmillan Co. NY 1951, Page 13: quoting "Counterattack"
"God help America or any other country if the Communist Party ever gets strong enough to control labor and politics... I feel that, once public opinion is throughout aroused as it is today, the fight against Communism is well on its way. Victory will be assured once Communists are identified and exposed, because the public will take the first step of quarantining them

so they can do no harm. Communism, in reality is not a political party. It is a way of life - an evil and malignant way of life. It reveals a condition akin to a disease that spreads like an epidemic, and like an epidemic, a quarantine is necessary to keep it from infecting the nation."

Finally, Truman took action. The New York Times ran articles "REDS, ORBIT TO LOSE U.S. TARIFF FAVORS" (July 7, 1951 page 5) and "PRESIDENT TRUMAN FORMALLY PROCLAIMS BAN ON RUSSIAN AND CHINESE IMPORTS" (August 2, 1951 page 1). Secretary of Defense James Forrestal, was appalled and infuriated that the public heard nothing on biological warfare. Everybody kept advising him to take a vacation. The Navy having purchased the SS ELBRUS after its return in Trieste to OPC freedom fighter training center, Forrestal began to take a hard look at Wisner and Dulles' rogue operation. Every freedom fighter was assassinated upon return to their native lands, all identified by an inside mole. He watched the OPC smuggled the double dealing Nazi BW agents out of Beketovka and Suchomi. Forrestal listened to Eisenhower direct a campaign of silence over virtually all mention of biological warfare, simultaneously, Americans got sicker and sicker. For the US Navy's victory at sea, it seemed we had won the battle and lost the war. Boldly, Forrestal approached the "New York Times" and attacked Eisenhower in the press for silencing the Merck Report and censoring any talk on biological warfare, aids promising "security would be cast aside and treatment would be made available to the public." Flashed across its Sunday March 13th, 1949 edition, the "New York Times" front page blasted: "FORRESTAL SCOUTS GERM WAR AS ARMY SAYS U.S. IS READY"

Forrestal had just signed his own death warrant. Ike had presidential ambitions. He would make I. G. Farben's patent lawyer, Allen Dulles, Director of the CIA, brother John Foster Dulles would be appointed Secretary of State. Nelson Rockefeller, owner of Standard Oil, (I. G.'s subsidiary), would become Deputy Assistant to the Health Department as well as CIA intelligence operative for South America, overseeing ratline resettlements. Senator Richard Nixon, having collated Naval Intelligence files, his political career backed by Allen Dulles, would rise to the Vice Presidency.(18) Later, Eisenhower appointed I. G. Farben's mentor and protector, OKH chief Adolf Heusinger, to chair NATO and lead the Western nations in an alliance against Communism! Farce! Under NATO and Heusinger, America would nearly enter WW III in the Cuban Missile Crisis. The Republican Party had been infiltrated by Roosevelt's most infamous left-wing moles. Was Forrestal about to expose them all for treason, recruiting Stalin's Nazis as "advisors" after perpetrating, what appeared to be the most devastaing biological warfare attack upon America, while the Nazis served in Soviet BW factories?

On March 26th, 1949, James Forrestal resigned as Secretary of Defense and was sent to Bethesda Naval Hospital for a rest. According to biographer Arnold Rogow, Forrestal had "anxiety about the presence of Communists, or Communist influence in the White House, the Defense Establishment, and other agencies of the government... and convinced that he had been chosen as their Number One target for liquidation as a consequence of his efforts to alert Americans to the Communist menace." (19) By May 22, 1949, just three months later, Forrestal was dead. A more conservative author, James Perloff, described the "suicide" more accurately, noting his "explosive" diaries had been "confiscated by the White House":

"THE SHADOWS OF POWER" James Perloff, Western Islands, Appleton, WI, 1998, Page 98: "On May 22, 1949, Forrestal was scheduled for discharge. But at 2 AM that morning, he fell from a window near his sixteenth-floor room. His bathrobe cord was found knotted around his neck. The death was declared suicide. Forrestal's brother Henry called it murder."

Even more peculiar is the striking parallel between James Forrestal's "suicide" and cartoon strip "L'il Abner in Lower Slobovia" by Al Capp. Fearless Fosdick looked more and more like Forrestal. In this cartoon within a cartoon, police detective, Fearless Fosdick, portrayed as a lifeguard on the beach, battles the world's most notorious criminal, "Any Face." L'il Abner himself, a caricature of his creator, Al Capp, professed his complete love and loyalty to Fearless Fosdick. "Any Face" takes on the image of Fosdick's police chief, and later his girl. Fosdick goes crazy trying to solve the mystery. The illustrator for L'il Abner's favorite comic strip, "Fearless Fosdick," ends up in an insane asylum, executing his own character while his newspaper editor jumps out a window. Was Al Capp, famous for his right wing politics, trying to warn Forrestal of impending disaster in the 1947 comic strip? We will never know.

Forrestal had played an enormous role in defeating the Nazis and the Communists, allied from the start. It is hard to imagine him an anti-Semetic, yet left-wing historians insist he opposed the creation of Israel out of bigotry. Perhaps, being a businessman by profession, he would have preferred a deal brokered between Arabs and Jews on their own terms, avoiding the traps set by the United Nation. Both Jews and Arabs have a wealth of history, faith, and beauty to offer the world. One day they will recognize their common enemy, the Communist-Fascist alliance, still in

244 —————————— Lyme Disease and the SS Elbrus

progress since the Bolshivik Revolution.

Al Capp's "L'il Abner" ran one of the most biting conservative commentaries of our times. As noted by his brother's introduction to volume 15 of the Kitchen Sink edition "L'il Abner Adventures in Lower Slobovia," Al Capp, too, would suffer a tragic end, dying of an auto-immune disease similar to lupus, while residing along the coast of Connecticut. Did he have Lyme disease which attacks the immune system? Was this another attempt at murder by madness, a fate like his hero, James Forrestal? His brother professed his astonishment when Al requested their mother's menorah be lit at his funeral services. Al Capp remains an American hero, as does his cop, "Fearless Fosdick." With James Forrestal gone, America was left adrift.

CHAPTER 9 NOTES

(1) "Brucellosis in the United States" Alice Evans, Am. J. Pub. Health & the Nation's Health, vol. 37, no. 2, Feb. 1947, pages 139 - 151

"The Status of Abortus Infections in the United States" Harry J. Schmidt. Presented at the Inter-American Congress for the Study of Brucellosis, Mexico City, October 28 - November 2, 1946, pages 552-554.

(2) "Official Records of the World Health Organization" No. 2 'Summary report on the Proceedings Minutes and Final Acts of the International Health Conference' Held in New York from 19 June to 22 July 1946, Published by the World Health Organization Interim Commission, 350 Fifth Avenue, NY June 1948.

"United National Relief & Rehabilitation Administration Health Division Epidemiological Information Bulletin" Washington DC vol. II 1946 'Relapsing Fever' Page 422

(3) "Experimental Infection of the African Relapsing Fever Tick, Onithodoros Moubata Murray, with Borrelia Latychevi (Sofiev)" Willy Burgdorfer and Gordon E. Davis, The Journal of Parasitology, 1950 vol. 11, pages 456-460

(4) "BIOLOGICAL WARFARE" report to the Secretary of War by Mr. George Merck For Release at 7:30 PM, EST, January 3, 1946. Pages 1-2.

(5) "A Challenge to the World: The Westinghouse Centennial Forum"

May 16-17 & 18, 1946, Sponsored by the Westinghouse Educational Foundation, Pittsburgh, Penn, McGraw Hill Book Co., Inc. New York, London. "Peacetime Implications of Biological Warfare" by George Merck, President and Director Merck & Company, Inc.

(6) State Department file 661.1115 AMTORG TRADING COR-PORATION/10-2847, From Carl Anderson, Executive Assistant to the President, Merck & Co., To: Richard Davis, Division of Eastern European Affairs, Dept. of St., Wa. DC., Nat. Arch CRB

"PENICILLIN FACTORY AT KIYEV" OACSI file MIS 664653, Nat. Arch MRB

"Information date March 1949 by William Pakalaka S/A source of information: HECKMANN, Werner, returned POW, Card No. 55501"

Page 1: "Subject factory was located in the center of the town of Kiyev... during 1948 and 1949, this damaged factor was entirely rebuilt and converted into a penicillin factory..."

State Department file 861.657/11-147, AMTORG From Technical Enterprises Inc., To: Mr. Francis C. Stevens, Russian Desk, State Department, Wa. DC, Nat. Arch CRB

State Department file 861.657/10-1647, AMTORG From State Dept. East. European Affairs, Stevens, re: Technical Enterprises, Inc. Nat. Arch. CRB

'Memorandum of Action' October 16, 1947: "Mr. Stevens, EE, called to request MD to determine the views of the Services on the proposed construction of a penicillin plant in the Soviet Union. Lt. Colonel Houston, Intelligence division, department of the Army, informed me that the Army has no interest in the proposed plant from the point of view of military security. He pointed out, however, that the medical department of the Army would be very much interested in having the United States firm keep the Army fully posted at every stage of the negotiations and construction, so that this Government could be kept fully informed of possible BW implications or developments in the USSR."

Signed: Col. Harry H. Mole, ID, Army. [P.S. The moles were in the State Dept.]

State Department file 861.657/11/1447, AMTORG "Memo from State Dept. East. Eur. Affairs Div. Subject: Soviet Desire to Purchase Penicillin Plant." Nat. Arch. CRB

(7) "RESEARCH ON MULTIPLE SCLEROSIS" Third Edition, Byron H. Waksman, MD, Stephen C. Reingold, PhD, William E. Reynolds, MD; Department of Research and Medical Programs, National Multiple Sclerosis Society, NY, NY, Demos Publications, NY, NY 1987.

(8) "MY LIFE WITH THE MICROBES" Selman Waksman, Simon & Schuster, NY 1954, Pages 246-247 re: 1946 trip to Moscow, Orbelli. Page 199: S. Waksman as president of Society of American Bacteriologists, 1941 and chairman of War Committee on Bacteriology.

"Microbiology in the USSR in 1946" Selman Waksman, Agricultural Experimental Studies, New Brunswick, NJ 'Scientific Monthly' vol. 64 April 1947. "It has been said that the "germs know no international boundaries." One might paraphrase this truth thus: the search for germs and their role in human health and human diseases knows no national affiliations. This was brought home to me very forcefully during the summer of 1946 when I had an opportunity to look into the progress made in the Soviet Union during the war years in the field of microbiology..." Page 294: "several institutes in the Academy of Sciences are interested in antibiotics..."

"The Microbe-Friend and Enemy of Man" Selman Waksman, 'Chemical & Engineering News' May 26, 1946. Page 1372, re. typhus WW I in Russia & Serbia

"INDIVIDUAL SCIENTIFIC PERSONALITIES" OACSI file MIS 328571, Nat Arch. MRB, record group 319. Page 2: "From 30 July 1946 to 6 October 1946, Source [Selman Waksman] gave a series of lectures on scientific subjects and attended several scientific conferences in Russia, Sweden, Denmark, France, Holland and Belgium. While in Russia, Source gave three lectures on Microbiology at the Academy of Science in Moscow... {son arranges trip] Byron H. Waksman, was recently released from the US Army active service after having served as a Captain in the Army Medical Corps for over two years... now a physician at the Mayo Clinic... attached photos show: Professor Orbelli, Director of the Pavlov Institute in Leningrad..."

"USSR - POLICY - RESEARCH & DEVELOPMENT IN THE PACIFIC" OACSI file MIS 337894 Serial 140-16, Nat. Arch. MRB, record group 319, box 2221. (filed under NA bid system BW-USSR 'N') Office of Chief of Naval Operation, Navy Department Intelligence report, From: US Naval Attaché of Moscow, USSR date 5 November

1946, source: Magazine VESTNIK AKADEMII NAUR SSSR #2-46
Evaluation B-2. Page 1:

"Plans are discussed for coordinating research and exploration in the
Pacific adjacent areas. Biological and geological exploration of the Far East
will require the establishment of several bases: Jagadan, Petropavlovsk, and
Vladivostok are proposed.... comments by Academician L. A. Orbelli..."

(9) State Department file 032/3-746 (233622) from Federal Security
Agency, Invitation to Parin in Moscow to visit USA.

State Department file 811.42761/7-1346 (316820) from Federal Security Agency Public Health Service US July 13, 1946: "Seeks information
whether there may be any funds available... from State Department to help
support the activities of the American-Soviet Medical Society"

State Department file 811.42761/2-2746 from St. Dpt. International
Labor, Social and Health Affairs Division, Public Health and Medical
Information on Interchange between USA and USSR. Participants: Ambassador Smith, Mr. Harriman, Surgeon General Parran, Mr. Mulliken,
and Doctors Williams, Hyde and Shimkin.

(10) "HAROLD ICKES OF THE NEW DEAL" Graham White
and John Maze, Harvard U. Press, Cambridge., MA 1985 Page 3: re Ickes
resignation, Truman and Pauley. Page 230: re Pauley and tidelands oil,
chief fundraiser Democratic National Committee.

"Text of Secretary Ickes' Letter of Resignation to the President Ending
13 Years in Office" "New York Times" 2/14/46, p. 21

(11) "THE SECRET WAR AGAINST THE JEWS" John Loftus
and Mark Aarons, St. Martin's Press, NY 1994, Pages 362-363: re Pauley,
George Bush's Mexican oil partner, and petroleum coordinator of Lend
Lease supplies to Russia and England, WW II.

"INTERNATIONAL WHO'S WHO" 1978-1979 'Edwin Pauley'

"Marshall's Team for Moscow: the Players Don't Know the Line-Up"
"Newsweek" v. 29, 3/3/47. Page 36: "Secretary Marshal's asked Edwin W.
Pauley to accompany him to Moscow as Reparations Advisor..."

"New York Times" "Obituaries" 'Edwin Pauley' July 29, 1981, p.
19, c. 1

(12) "HAMMER" by Armand Hammer, G. P. Putnam's Sons, NY
1987. Pages 138, 160, 184 re Allied American Corporation.

"ARMAND HAMMER: the Untold Story" Steve Weinberg, Little
Brown & Co. p. 52.

"FEDERAL SUPPLEMENT" vol. 47, "Amtorg Trading Corp. v. Standard Oil Co. of California. "district court, S.D. New York, August 7, 1942. Page 467 re. "American tank vessel "J.C. Fitzsimmons" to transport gasoline to Vladivostok..."

(13) "FEDERAL SUPPLEMENT" vol. 77, Page 1000 "Anglo-American Fur Merchant Corporation v. United States et al." District Court, S.D. New York Feb. 2, 1945, John F. X. McGohey, US Attorney of NY.

(14) State Department file 661.111/7-148, AMTORG From Jacob. J. Pincus, Counselor at Law, 14 Glen St. Glen cove, NY. To secretary of State, Wa. DC
"Dear sir: Will you kindly advise me now whether the Amtorg Trading Corporations subject to any type of immunity to suit for goods sold and delivered, or whether an action therefore can be prosecuted in the State courts... Very Truly Yours, Jay Pincus."
State Department reply from Stanley D. Metzger, Assistant to the Legal Adviser: August 6, 1948: "My Dear Mr. Pincus: Reference is made to your letter of July 21, 1948 inquiring whether Amtorg Trading corporation is entitled to the privilege of sovereign immunity from suit in New York. It is the understanding of this Department that Amtorg Trading Corporation, which is incorporated under the laws of the State of New York, may sue and be sued in New York courts.... citing court case 'Amtorg v. US' '71 F (2n) 524 (1934)."

State Department file 661.111/3-1849 AMTORG Barry, Treanor & Shandell, Counselors at law, 41 Park Row, NY 7, NY. Nat. Arch CRB March 18, 1949 letter to Dpt. St.
"Gentlemen: Will you kindly advise us whether or not the State Department has recognized the Amtorg Trading Corporation as a public agency or instrumentality of the government of Russia... We have particularly in mind whether or not that corporation is immune from civil suit in the course of the State of New York." St. Dpt. replies "Yes" on 4/8/49, citing same case above, 'Amtorg v. US" in 1934.
"SUPREME COURT OF THE STATE OF NEW YORK, COUNTY OF NEW YORK" Amtorg Trading company Plaintiff against Ynok Shegerian, Peter L. Doerflein, and 'John' Buell, defendants August. 26, 1946. "On or about the 16th day of January 1946 New York city, plaintiff and defendants entered into an agreement thereby the plaintiff agreed to sell and the defendants agreed to purchase 51 bales of rugs consisting of 466 pieces... The defendants refused to take delivery or accept said rugs or to pay..."

(15) CAMDEN FIBER MILLS, INC. plaintiff, against AMTROG TRADING CORPORATION, defendant, 1949-1952. June 12, 1949, Supreme Court of the State of New York, County of New York. Documents retrieved by court reporter, Elliot Moss.

Court Appeals of NY, as listed in the "North Eastern Reporter" 2nd Series, v. 109 p. 606

(16) "Amtorg President Returns to Russia to Resign His Post" "New York Times" 11/16/46 p.1

"Amtorg Keeps Its Office" "New York Times" 7/29/48 ps. 29 & 34. re refrigerators.

"Russia Orders All Ships in US Ports to Leave at Once" San Francisco Examiner 2/29/48

"SS VOLGA" FBI file 94-1-24549-35 "March 30, 1948 "US Customs advised that veterans commenced picketing of the SS Volga, Russian Vessel, at Claremont Terminal, Jersey city... Longshoremen have refused to cross picket line up to present time..."

"Office Memorandum 3/6/48 FBI file 100-343044-272 re SS VILNIUS leaving Clairmont Terminal, Jersey City. (four paragraphs blacked out)

(17) VOLGA FBI file 100-34044-300 letter from At. Gen. to Director, FBI 4/14/48

and file 100-343044-317 re. Navy following Volga gold.

(18) "THE SECRET WAR AGAINST THE JEWS" John Loftus & Mark Aarons, St Martin's Press 1994, p. 221 re. Nixon collating naval intelligence at Brooklyn Navy Yard

(19) "JAMES FORRESTAL" Arnold A. Rogow. Macmillan Co. NY 1963 Page. 6

CHAPTER 10

THE STATE OF THE UNION

The Communists, the OPC,
and the International Labor Organizations

The 12th National Convention of the Industrial Union of Marine and Shipbuilding Workers of America, headed by a Scotsman, John Green, convened September 23 - 28, 1948 at Saratoga Springs, upstate, New York. Here he blasted "There is no difference between Fascism and Communism... both of them are totalitarianism," the IUMSWA constitution banning Fascist, Communist, the KKK, and anyone else trying to overthrow the US Government by force and violence. James Forrestal sent his "greetings" to the convention as did Lilyn Moscowitz from the Barbers & Beauty Culturists Union of America. Guest speakers included Jacob Potofsky of the Ladies Garment Workers Union from Mayor O'Dwyer's Business Advisory Council, and Secretary General of the World Confederation of Labor, Louis Sailant, applauded with standing ovation. Sailant also headed the Confederation of Labor of France, and ran the French Underground's labor effort to overthrow the Nazis. His speech demanded American labor accept world socialism, citing the membership of the World Confederation of Labor included the Soviet Union, China, Italy, Holland, Mexico, France, Great Britain, and America. All along, according to Roy Medvedev's "Let History Judge," Stalin was sending labor unionists to the Gulag.

"Proceedings of the 12th National Convention of the Industrial Union of Marine & Shipbuilding Workers Union of America-CIO" September 23-28, 1948

Page 8: John Green: "Insecure and hungry men become easy victims of medicine men who, by some hocus pocus, promise a cure for every economic and social evil"

Pages 223-225: Louis Sailant: "We must declare that a Third World

War can be prevented by people of good will. We must see that the spirit of international cooperation replaces the spirit of imperialism and its supporters. Second, it is necessary that each nation, each political democracy, be supplemented by democratic and social democracy... A campaign of hostility against America, which we might have in Europe, would be detrimental to the cause of peace. For the same reasons, the campaign of hostility against the Soviet Union would not bring us nearer to peace, either."

Sailant's speech directly contradicted John Green's leadership, and soon, with the excess number of Liberty ships for sale on the world market, the Shipbuilders Union went under. John Green, having attended the WHO founding conference, fully briefed on the catastrophe at hand, was the last voice of reason in the CIO for years to come. Sailant's French Underground will evolve into a murky cult of Fascists and Communist spies.

Earl Browder, had been leader of the American Communist Party during the Great Depression, and suddenly departed in 1946, to be replaced by William Z. Foster, (FBI file 100-25693). Browder had been convicted in 1939 for violation of the Smith Act, trying to overthrow the US Government by force and violence, Roosevelt releasing him during the war, fearing labor unrest. Browder spent many years inside of China with lengthy stays in Shanghai, detailed in the thousands of pages held by the FBI, (file 40-3798-756 dated 12/13/36). Browder became the perfect patsy for all the ACP woes, and beat it out of the country after the docking of the SS ELBRUS, making a special trip to the Soviet Union. Were the Communist moles hidden high in the State Department sacrificing the lowlife in the CIO? Upon Browder's return to America, as an "illegal alien," he was hauled before the New York Southern District Court's new judge October 20, 1952, John F. X. McGohey, all too familiar with the fur situation, (Earl Browder FBI file 100-25693).

As Browder sat before Judge McGohey, he took the Fifth, refusing to testify on grounds of self incrimination. Even with William Z. Foster replacing Browder as Secretary General of the American Communist Party, the ACP was not immune. By 1947, the top twelve members of the ACP were hauled into McGohey's court. The "trail of the century," "William Z. Foster et al versus the United States Government," went all the way to the Supreme Court in appeals, convicting the dirty dozen for violation of the Smith Act, its secret grand jury testimony still kept under wraps to this day. Chief Justice Vinson wrote "Their conspiracy to organize the Communist Party and to teach and advocate the overthrow of the Government of the

United States by force and violence created a 'clear and present danger"..."
while dissenting justices, Black and Douglas wrote "No matter how it is
worded, this is a virulent form of prior censorship of speech and press,
which I believe the First Amendment forbids." (1)

"Virulent censorship?" We know from James Forrestal's expose in the
"New York Times" of Eisenhower's censorship on the discussion of "biological warfare" and can presume the rest of the Government followed. But
the "Daily Worker" was not interested in exploring the possibility that the
Soviet Union was dumping tons of infested furs upon American shores.
Instead, they fingered the newly imported Nazi, Dr. Walter Schreiber,
(fresh out of Moscow's KGB school of sabotage), for aiding the US Air
Force in orchestrating BW attacks upon North Korea! The charges were
totally bogus!:

WALTER P. SCHREIBER FBI file 105-15549-3
page 53: "Alleged American Use of Germ Warfare"
"March 4, 1952, stated that there had been an official Peking-Korean
charge that germ warfare is being waged against the blood-soaked Korean
people. The editorial stated that, "Morally speaking, the kind of warfare
being waged against the Asian peoples - both in Korea and traditionally
against all the colonial peoples - has been of such merciless cruelty that
the use of germ warfare to spread mass disease, is not surprising..." An
article appearing in the "Daily Worker" March 13, 1952, page 1, column
2, states that new light has been cast upon the charge that bacteriological
warfare has been exercised in Korea by developments of the information
that the U.S. Air Force has employed Dr. Walter P. Schreiber... Schreiber
was brought to the United States because the air corps had dropped germ
cultures on civilian populations, a subject on which Schreiber is reputed
to have extensive knowledge."

Of course Schreiber had "extensive knowledge" of biological warfare,
he had just left the Soviet Union, waging an extensive campaign against its
own citizens. The Russians were also making a massive effort to aid North
Korea in constructing BW factories of its own. Coincidentally, Dr. Leo
Alexander noted Schreiber's arrival in the US when Schreiber published
an article in a popular medical journal. Raising the alarm, Alexander approached the press, resulting in Schreiber's hasty exit to Argentina. (2)

China and Russia were interested in securing Korea into the Communist block. Battle lines were drawn about the 38th parallel, cutting Korea
in half. The ensuing Korean "war" theoretically began in 1950 under the
auspices of a United Nations "peace keeping mission." Eight captured

American pilots and Marines had been forced into "confession" to US Air Force BW activities. After sleep deprivation and torture, they signed confessions, submitted to the United Nations by the Soviet Union, the stage set for future accusations against Plum Island. America's ambassador to the UN, Henry Cabot Lodge, Jr. made a meek protest against the false accusations while the newly elected WHO secretary, Dr. Fedor Krotkov, laughed like hell. (3)

General Douglas MacArthur, having won the war in the Pacific against Japan, returned to lead our troops against the Communist in North Korea. Truman would soon fire MacArthur, citing his military ambitions to defeat both the North Koreans and Red Chinese too ambitious. MacArthur's intelligence team led by G-2 chief Charles Willoughby, had a more accurate picture of the BW scenario through captured Chinese intelligence files:

"MAC ARTHUR: 1941-1951" Major Charles Willoughby and John Chamberlain, McGraw Hill Book company, NY 1954

Page 412: "After our withdrawal from North Korea, General Mac Arthur feared the potential of epidemics of smallpox, typhus and typhoid fevers. The foci of infection were already smoldering. We doubted that the Communists were able to control epidemics. Their vaccines made under Russian supervision, were found to be practically worthless... The following document, dated March 8, 1951, was received by ATIS on April 5... "An NKA hospital is located in the vicinity of our Medical Section.... the number of patients has increased to over four hundred. Most cases are typhoid and recurrent fever [brucellosis]..."

The Chinese intelligence report was signed: "Med. Sec. Regt. Hq." The Pentagon's OACSI files held more deadly secrets, the Russians were deeply involved in Korea. A vile of live plague, camouflaged as a "vaccine" was intercepted and shipped back to Washington for analysis, the instructions for "vaccination" between the back shoulder blades almost barbaric. (4) Soon, the US troops would move into Pyongyang, North Korea, and cease its biological warfare factory, most of its members had fled to Manchuria, China, the remaining were interrogated:

"BACTERIAL INSTITUTE OF NORTH KOREA" - OACSI file 737427

date of report 30 November 1950 concerning PYONGYANG

"(2) On 20 October 1950, Colonel Leach, Commanding Officer of the 171th Evacuation Hospital, who was consulted, informed the 51st Cml TID verbally of a bacteriology research laboratory in the PYONG-

YANG, North Korea Area. An investigation was then undertaken to find and evaluate the laboratory."

Page 4: "... Kim stated that in 1949 there was a Japanese B. Encephalitis epidemic in North Korea and the Soviets sent four women doctors and three Army Medical Officers to the institute."

The "Bacterial Institute of North Korea" went under another name "The Communicable Disease Institute of North Korea," probably more like a "roach motel" where once you check in, you don't check out. Dr. Yang Chang Fah ran the livestock research laboratories, experimenting with Japanese Encephalitis B virus, his other three remaining associates were Chun Chong Ho, Kim Sung Hyu and Won Byong Hi, chief of the "pestis" (plague) department. Others who escaped to Manchuria were Won Byong Hi (Research Pests), Chun Chong Ho (Epidemiology), Kim Sung Hyu (Tuberculosis) and Han (Experimental Animals), Chai Hyung Koo and Kim Young Sup. Yang Chang Fah testified that the Russian doctors had taken the Japanese Encephalitis virus back to the Soviet Union while Karakena Nikoiai stayed on with Pyongyang working on plague for further study (pages 6-9) of the above report. The grounds were quite extensive, housing rooms of rat crates along with 800 preserved specimens, some forwarded on to Chemical Officer, GHQ-FEC APO 500, October 6th, 1950, for further evaluation. Bottles of fleas had also been located on site, but had to be destroyed. To sum things up, the Communist charges, prompted by the presence of Schreiber, against the United States, were a farce.

American intelligence sat in silence, fully aware of the Soviet facilitated BW factories in the Orient. Meanwhile, the ACP was put on trial, while our Communist infiltrated State Department looked on in amusement. Foster's cohorts included John Gates, editor of the "Daily Worker," the ACP propaganda machine, and Irving Potash, leader of the International Furriers and Leather Workers Union. Potash was allowed to travel about the country, addressing labor issues in Atlanta City May 21, 1947 and vacationing at Bolton Landing on Lake George, up-state New York, July 1950. (5) The author's family knows Lake George very well, Bolton Landing, merely a dock and gas station, is adjacent Tongue Mountain and Roger's Rock, a granite cliff that plunges several hundred feet deep into the crystal clear waters. On the northern side of Rogers Rock stood the grand hotel of the Roger's Rock Club before its catastrophic fire, a resort for the rich and famous. The grounds still sport cottages, clubhouse, and boating facilities.

FBI files on Irving Potash make a curious note on an attempt of the ACP to infiltrate the Teamsters Union, this internal friction may explain the disappearance of Jimmy Hoffa, the man who knew too much, his longshoremen on the waterfront having boycotted the unloading of Soviet ships. Hoffa's wife, Josephine, had been infected with brucellosis from drinking un-pasteurized milk. James Hoffa became adamant in his anti-Communism, calling them "screwballs and nuts." (6) (Enter Batman's nemesis, James Riddle Hoffa, "The Riddler.") Hoffa, convicted July 26, 1964 under LBJ's Administration, on one count of conspiracy and three counts of mail and wire fraud involving union funds, was sentenced to prison, until released under Richard Nixon, when he mysteriously vanished, July 30th, 1975. His IBT having been infiltrated by the pink squad, leaving him to alone take the heat for the missing funds, raised serious questions on the fairness of the judicial system. Reference to Potash and Gold's Furrier's Joint Council having served on Amtorg's board were discovered in 26 note books "Secured by SAs of the NY office on 7/11/50." (7)

On 6/1/50, the CIO president Philip Murray expelled the OFLWU and the FJC from the Union. Soon, Potash would sign a "peace plea" for the Korean War in the "Daily Worker" with a host of other top labor officials. The Immigration and Naturalization Service finally deported to Poland as an illegal alien, March 4, 1955. Ironically, Lech Walesa's "Solidarity" in the Polish shipyards was fighting the Soviets, tooth and nail. Potash was odd man out. What became of Irving Potash? The FBI holds 3,377 pages available for disclosure to the public on Irving Potash, with an additional "correlation summary" created by the FBI on May 20th, 1965, totaling an additional 128 pages. Potash left Poland, toured the Soviet Union, and headed for China, later returning to America, was booted out again! Visiting China he returned "home" to stay. (8)

Congress would lead the charge where the courts left off. The Southern District Court of New York, with its garment district, had been plagued with union troubles since the 1930s. Ben Gold, President of the International Furriers and Leather Workers Union, was hauled into testify regarding union brutality, "CIS 80-H1222-5 "Investigation of Communist Infiltration Into the Fur Industry." Irving Potash, his assistant, was facing a prison sentence for violation of the Smith Act. Amongst the investigating committee on Education and Labor were senators Richard M. Nixon and John F. Kennedy, future presidential contenders. Gold played the persecuted saint, detailing his union's efforts to secure health insurance for his own members, the dirty fur shop owners contracting out to non-union labor were perpetrating the "unsanitary conditions." No specific mention was made of Russian infested furs. What emerged was a sordid history of union violence between the anti-Communist AFL and their takeover by the CIO, witnesses speculated the CIO was out to destroy small shops that were hard to organize. Lloyd Graff, Executive director and Joseph Katcher, Labor Relations director of the Fur Dressers and Fur Dyers Association cited New York alone had between 10 and 12 thousand employees doing $25 million worth business annually.

One of the largest in the fur dressers and dyers industry was A. Hollander & Son, Louis Hollander sat on Mayor O'Dwyer's Business Advisory Council. On page 97 of these hearings, Mr. Albert Feldman testified regarding Hollander's negotiations with Ben Gold and the Furriers Union. When Senator Graham asked "Have you experienced any difficulties with this union which would tend to demonstrate that it is a control of the leadership by the Communists?" Feldman replied "None whatsoever." Some three hundred pages later, Ben Gold was insisting the non-union shops were "sweatshops, dirty, filthy shops. They compete with the wages of the workers in the legitimate shops... they have kickback rackets... They are pirates, parasites and after 20 years we came to the conclusion that it is impossible to live with this evil in a responsible industry..." When asked "How many of your international officers, to your knowledge are Communists?" Gold replied "Do you call this intimidation or an investigation?"

Every session in the House of Un-American Activities grilled its suspects with "Are you a Communist? Are you a member of the Communist Party? Have you ever been a member of the Communist Party? Do you know any others who are members of the Communist Party?," making the inquisitions a spectacle and a circus. Basically, Gold's hearing achieved nothing, he took the Fifth. The Taft-Hartly Act was passed, banning labor leaders' membership in the Communist Party while using the services of the National Labor Relations Board. Next, Ben Gold would quit the Party. Somehow the courts did not take Gold's resignation from the ACP seriously, and sentenced him to five years in prison. But there was a problem, Some of the witnesses were federal employees, and the Supreme Court, ordered a retrial. Eventually, the case was dropped, Eisenhower's Warren Court set Gold free. (9)

There may be a motivating factor behind Senator Joseph McCarthy's radical right wing House of Un American Activities investigations in the William Z. Foster trail of top leading Communists in the ACP. A young politically conservative homosexual, Roy Cohn, served as an assistant to the prosecutor on the staff of Attorney John F. X. McGohey, privy to all the Grand Jury Testimony against the ACP's efforts to overthrow the US Government by force and violence. Cohn and another young attorney, Robert Kennedy, would next join McCarthy's staff, most likely tipping off congress's radical crusader against the Communist threat. Bootlegging

Joseph Kennedy, JFK's dad, had financed McCarthy's rise to power. The two Irish families held close ties. McCarthy would propose to marry JFK's oldest sister, Pat, before her fatal car crash. President Eisenhower with the recommendation of the Majority Leader, Senator Lyndon B. Johnson, moved to silence McCarthy before his investigations progressed too far, using Utah Senators Arthur Watkins and William Bennett to head an inquiry into McCarthy's personal behavior. (10) McCarthy died a miserable alcoholic, another victim of murder by madness?

According to hearings before the Senate, published in a seventeen volume series, the Mafia had infiltrated the unions on the waterfront. Mayor O'Dwyer had hired retired navy officer Charles R. Haffenden to watch the waterfront as New York's Commissioner of Marine and Aviation in 1946. Haffenden was too honest, a miss match, and O'Dwyer fired him after six months. Hauled before Congress to testify on the Mafia's Waterfront activities, he exposed an alarming alliance:

"INVESTIGATION OF ORGANIZED CRIME IN INTERSTATE COMMERCE" Hearings before the Special Committee to Investigate Organized Crime in Interstate Commerce, US Senate 81st Congress, 2nd Session, 1st Session Part 7 New York - New Jersey. Pages 1187-1198:
MR. HAFFENDEN: "Well, I know very little about the parole... I can tell you how Luciano came into my jurisdiction as an informant: is that what you mean?"
MR. HALLEY: "Tell me what ever you can about the matter."
MR. HAFFENDEN: "Well, I had headed an investigation in the third Naval District from, I would say, 1941 or 1940 it might have been, and some time during 1942, as I recall, Murray Gurfein... was connected with the district attorney... and suggested that an informant from the waterfront would be desirable; an informant..."

Added to the list of Mafia informants on the waterfront with Lucky Luciano was Sacks Lanza. Officer Haffenden next admitted he had been severely "roughed up and hospitalized," coerced into writing New York Governor Dewey about Lucy Luciano's great wartime service resulting in his 1945 parole. Dewey would contest Truman for the Presidency in 1948, the Mafia nearly had their man in the White House. Haffenden explained his intelligence gathering operation passed out tips on sabotage threats to the Army, Navy, and FBI. Halley insisted Haffenden must have been dealings with the waterfront labor unions. Obviously, the Navyman had to manage them too? Haffenden skirted the question. But according to J. Edgar Hoover's biographer Anthony Summers, the waterfront Mafia had two bosses, Haffenden and the State Department's OSS, Hoover's "feud with the OSS chief William Donovan" resulted in both espionage sleuths digging deep for sexual dirt on their political foes. The FBI scored nothing on Donovan, but the OSS, through Godfather Meyer Lansky, discovered Mafia photos of Hoover in bed with his homosexual partner, Clyde Tolson, compromising all FBI inquisitions into organized crime:

"OFFICIAL AND CONFIDENTIAL: The Secret Life of J. Edgar Hoover"

Anthony Summers, G. P. Putnam & Sons, NY 1993

Page 245: "It may be significant, too, that compromising pictures are reported as having been in the hands of both the OSS and Meyer Lansky. The OSS and Naval Intelligence had extensive contacts with the Mafia during World War II, enlisting the help of criminals in projects including the hiring of burglars and assassins, experimentation with drugs, the protection of American ports from Nazi agents and the invasion of Sicily. Lansky helped personally with the latter two operations, meeting with Murray Gurfein, New York Assistant District Attorney who later became one of Donovan's most trusted OSS officers."

The Mafia being the Mafia, could be bought off by anyone, or any government, including Mussolini's, Hitler's or the KGB's. What was the point? The OSS had actually helped facilitate an international import-export racket in the name of national defense! The battles for control over these rackets amongst the Mafia's crime families are notorious, with greed the driving force, their professed patriotism was of little significance. Once the OSS was dissolved by Truman and reorganized into the OPC, its shenanigans didn't stop there. As the SS ELBRUS sailed the globe, Congress demanded the Soviet Union return our liberty ships. Out of the remaining 95 ships engaged in commerce under Soviet flag, eight more came home. They were not returned directly to American ports. Stalin preferred to send the SS ELBRUS back to the OPC in Trieste, engaged in training freedom fighters to topple his own government. The OPC was also engaged in ratlining "Dragon Returnees," Nazi chemical and biological warfare specialists from Beketovka and Shuchomi. These Nazis were a hot commodity. One of the most damaging State Department files on Stalin's Nazis vanished under the Ford Administration days before the inauguration of President Jimmy Carter. Carter would soon establish the Justice Department's Nazi hunting unit, the Office of Special Investigations, "OSI.".

STATE DEPARTMENT file 740.00119 Control (Germany)/12-446,

Disp #7959, 4/12/46 from Berlin. WITHDRAWAL NOTICE from
Health, to Sec. State, authority, Army/Secret, 3 January 1977
"Transmittal of Top Secret Report on Soviet mass deportation of Ger-
man Scientists and Technicians Oct. 21-22nd"

The vanishing of State Department files on these Nazi war criminals
can imply several things. Either America was protecting the Nazi war
criminals inside Russia, or the Communists were protecting their Nazi
double agents inside of America. These dudes were so mercurial, no one
knew whose side they were on. More important, whose side was our
State Department on? During WW II, Allen Dulles ran the Italian Desk
of the OSS, arranging the surrender of the Nazis on the Italian Front.
(11) Most of the OSS boys in the Dulles gang merged into the OPC and
subsequently, the CIA.

Yale and Harvard Universities were stomping grounds for recruiting
the Government's top spies. Robin Winks' "Cloak and Gown," a Yale
graduate himself, gives the inside scoop on the farce in progress with the
OSS. During WW II, the defeat of the Nazis involved recruiting their
"enemy," the Communists, including those amongst the French Under
ground, the German Spartans and a host of international labor unions,
and the Mafia. Not only was the OSS's Research and Analysis "R&A"
Group staffed with left wing radicals like Jay Robinson of Lush Cotton,
one of the R&A sub-divisions, the Morale Operations Project, "MO,"
engaged in psychological warfare against the enemy. The MO desk was
headed by Arthur Goldberg, who had served as counselor to the CIO in
the 1940s.

Born in Chicago, 1908, Arthur Goldberg rose in power and influence
to become a Supreme Court Justice under the Kennedy Administration. He
would chair the American Jewish Committee, a nationwide human rights
organization. Of Course, J. Edgar Hoover kept secret files on Goldberg,
targeting him for "custodial detention" along with thousands of other
left-wing Americans on file during WW II, the facts finally surfaced from
a 1990 FOIA request, exposed in "USA TODAY" (Monday April 8th,
1996, page 3A). It wouldn't be surprising if half the State Department were
listed in Hoover's files. It was Goldberg's ability to negotiate the merger of
the AFL and CIO in 1955 that led to the expulsion of Communists and
racketeers from the unions. After the Kennedy assassination, President
Johnson appealed to Goldberg's sense of patriotism and asked him to resign
the high court and become ambassador to the United Nations in 1968 in
an effort to negotiate a settlement to the Vietnam War, which Goldberg
deeply regretted taking in his later years. Getting Goldberg off Chief Jus-

tice Earl Warren's Court and away from the pending Warren Commission investigation into the Kennedy assassination would save LBJ's and Allen Dulles' butts. Goldberg had the inside scoop on Dulles from his OSS days, the "New York Times" "obituaries" published a lengthy biography of his lifetime achievements, January 20th, 1990. (12)

Goldberg's involvement in the OSS's Morale Operations surfaced in Robin Winks' "Cloak & Gown" where Lieutenant Colonel Heber Blankenhorn in the OSS psychological warfare department "convinced Donovan to organize a special labor unit to contact European trade unions, which he felt could become the center of anti-Nazi resistance groups." The futility of this operation will become apparent, for Goldberg did not know of the alliance between I. G. Farben, Adolf Heusinger and the Soviet Union at that time. MO organized "Soldiers Committees" to disrupt the moral of the German soldiers within the ranks, under the pretense of establishing a "4th Reich" to replace the 3rd. The Soldiers Committees purpose was to "undermine confidence in the German High Command," leading to "disobedience" inciting "withdrawals" "Mutiny" and "insurrection." (13) The Soldiers Committees had been patterned after a similar success during WW I, incorporating German Spartans.

"SOLDIERS COMMITTEES: HISTORY OF THE MO PROJECT 1944-1945" by Heber Blankenhorn, OSS Report, Washington, MO PRO-7, National Archives, Washington, DC Folder 2288, Box 172, Entry 139.

Page 3: "The French Forces of the Interior had been carrying on a limited effort to prod such Soldiers Committees underground since 1943... since distribution is the key to any large scale MO activity, the plan urged full cooperation with the French underground.

Page 6: The Independent Labor Party, headed by Haase, known to the anti-war Socialists, became the chief source of spreading the committees.

Page 7: The Trade Union groups in Germany clandestinely helped them spread, seeing the Army Committees a natural replica of trade union members, mostly Social Democrats. The Spartikists were then so weak that they do not seem to have contributed much to Soldiers Committees as a whole, though they were responsible for several which became best known during the revolution in November 1918, notably the Soldiers Committees from Kiel...

Page 8: French Communists, of course, became an integral part of the FFI [French Forces of the Interior], but the underground newspapers and leaflets showed no Communist content, though giving an extensive pronouncements of the Free Germany Committee of Moscow; which pronouncements were of a military-defeatist character, and noticeably eschewed Communist propaganda."

It is of great significance that OKH chief, Adolf Heusinger on the Eastern Front with Field Marshal Von Paulus under his command, was responsible for the defeat at Stalingrad, the turning point of the war. Kleist's separation from Von Paulus on a separate mission to the Baku, greatly contributed to this defeat. Upon Soviet capture, Von Paulus became head of the Free Germany Committee in Moscow. As noted in the above Blankenhorn Report, the French underground, who joined in with the French Communists, were now allied with the Free German Committee, orchestrated by Von Paulus from Moscow. Next, the FFI would incorporate the German and French "Todt organization." The foundation was laid for an enormous American intelligence fiasco. The Blankenhorn report continues:

"SOLDIERS COMMITTEES"
Page 13: "The search for a suitable cooperative organization was shortened by the discovery of a leaflet, unlabelled by Allied intelligence, which I traced to the Commission de Prisoners de Guerre, Refuges et Departees. This organization headed by Captain Warisse was essentially along military lines. It extended not only into the French prisoner of war camps in Germany, but into the departed labor units. Most important it had members in, and current connections with, the Todt organization. In other words its espionage, and its propaganda, facilities reached right into the German garrisons of the Atlantic Wall as well as among the reserves in Germany. It had members on the railway lines of France and Germany.
Page 23:... Since the tightening of the battle line at the German borders, what connections survive between the French underground and its members inside Germany? Do their undergrounds maintain live contacts there: does the French Commission for Prisoners of War, Refugees and Departees maintain its contacts, particularly with its members in the Todt Organization?"

Nazi occupied Vichy France assigned Lyon's Gestapo Chief, Klaus Barbie, to interrogate the French Underground. His brutalities would earn him the nickname "the Butcher of Lyon," often beating his victims to death with his bare hands. There was an incident where a French underground railway agent, Rene Hardy, was "turned" by Barbie, after a brutal interrogation. After the war, Hardy was tried for treason, the French

Government seeking Klaus Barbie as a witness for the prosecution. The French had a problem, Barbie was in the employ of the US Army's CIC, so the French interrogated him there. Eventually, Barbie's war crimes surfaced. Responsible for exporting a whole Jewish orphanage of children to Auschwitz, Barbie vanished.

Beate Klarsfeld, a German national married to a French Jew, tracked down Klaus Barbie, aka Klaus Altman, in La Paz, Bolivia, finally resulting in his extradition to France where he was tried for war crimes in the early 1980s, triggering a panic in the American intelligence community. The US Justice Department under William French Smith, whose former law partner, Paul Ziffrin, was a Mafia lawyer, hired the new OSI chief, Alan Ryan, to publish a tell-all expose of Barbie's relation with the CIC. (14) They didn't tell everything. The Mafia ties to the film and music industry were exposed in Dan Moldea's "Dark Victory: Ronald Reagan, MCA and the Mob." Meyer Lansky's crowd included Chicago mobster, Willie Bioff, who, as far back as 1931, had attached himself to George Browne, head of the Chicago local union of the International Alliance of Theatrical Stage Employees (IATSE). Moldea's expose on the Mafia's shakedowns of the actors' unions and film industry, opens the possibility there may have been an ulterior motive for attorney general William French Smith in ordering the Klaus Barbie investigation. Did Barbie have ties to the American Mafia through the OPC? Did William French Smith pre-empt a deeper investigation into the Barbie affair? We must consider the Barbie documents that were not included in the Justice Department's report.

"DARK VICTORY: Ronald Reagan, MCA and the Mob" Viking Penguin Inc. NY 1986, Page 26: "While the Mafia was playing ball with both the unions and the studios... By 1937, (Willie) Bioff and the Chicago Mafia had started shaking down the major film studios, including Twentieth Century, Paramount, MGM, and Warner Brothers, for $50,000 a year and the smaller studios - like RKO and Harry Cohn's eleven-year-old Columbia Pictures - for $25,000. ... the payoffs simply ensured that motion picture productions came off on schedule without problems from the 12,000 IATSE members, who were assessed two percent of their earnings by Bioff and Browne for no particular reason for forty-three weeks, beginning in December 1935. The total skim from the IATSE membership alone was over $1.5 million."

Ronald Reagan, heading the Screen Actors Guild, was called before Attorney General Robert Kennedy to testify on Mob infiltration of the Hollywood industry, Moldea supplying his complete testimony gained by freedom of information request. Suddenly, Reagan "couldn't remember," an early onset of Alzheimer's? Reagan, was also called upon by the OPC to help fund the Freedom Fighters in Trieste through Radio Free Liberty's Crusade for Freedom, the center of the real action and the return of the SS ELBRUS. (15) Reagan's career became a sad testimony of a patriot used and abused.

As we uncover Barbie's role in the OPC history, we need ask the question, not only whose side was Rene Hardy on, but whose side was Klaus Barbie on, something the William French Smith Justice Department and Alan Ryan in its OSI completely overlooked? Hardy insisted in his trial that he was innocent of treason, Barbie had not killed him, nor "turned him." (16) Instead, the Justice Department report exposed Barbie as an agent of the French Underground:

"KLAUS BARBIE AND THE UNITED STATES GOVERN-MENT" Allan Ryan, Jr., and the US Department of Justice, University Publications of America, Frederick, MD 1984. Page 351: TAB 55 Doc. 1: "CIC Ln Officer - please sent to Col. Erskine: the following is pertinent to our telephone conversation this morning:

a. Public Information division this Headquarters requested information, for transmission to Mr. Louis DeRoche, French Correspondent, as to whether KLAUS BARBIER was a CIC agent and whether he was living in Munich. PID stated that inquiry arose from story in "Figaro" relative to Hardy trial in Paris. It was stated that Barbier is a principal witness and was described as a "former member" of the French underground, later a member of the Gestapo and now an agent for the CIC in Munich."

b. The intelligence division reply was "no comment."

c. Subsequently, PID advised that the statement had been passed to DeRoche and intimated that "the statement is bound to result in a derogatory story in the French press, slanted to the effect that by "no comment" statement we have admitted allegation..." PID further recommended giving DeRoche an off-the-record briefing."

If "Figaro" reports were true, we can now connect Klaus Barbie to the French Underground, Hardy's Todt railway organization, and Arthur Goldberg's OSS Labor Desk and Moral Operation. The Soldiers Committees of the MO held ties to the Moscow's Free Germany Committee, the German Communist Party, Walter Schreiber, Von Paulus, and Ewald Von Kleist, not to mention the rest of the old German Spartan Party. Would this lead to future ties between the OSS's Mafia on the American waterfront, Klaus Barbie's drug and arms cartels in Bolivia and the KGB in Russia? Yes. For a detailed answer, we must follow Klaus Barbie and the OPC to Trieste, the training ground for the Balkan freedom fighters. As Congress demanded Russia return all the lend-lease vessels after the war, the State Department made a rash desperate move to snatch the SS ELBRUS out of the hands of Soyuzpushnina.

STATE DEPARTMENT file 861.852/2-948 Dpt. St. outgoing Telegram, Tokyo, #39, control 1713, February 9, 1948 6 p.m. Nat. Arch CRB
"The USSR has agreed to return to US eight Lend-lease merchant vessels. Soviet desire return ships on the following schedule at following places: 1) Tanker KRASNAYA ARMIYA in Hong Kong... 2) Tanker EL-BRUS in Trieste between Feb. 10 and 15. 3) Remaining six vessels in one of ports of South Korea on following dates: Later transmitted: "No logistic support or billets are available for transfer of the six vessels."

The six other liberties were re-routed to Yokohama, Japan, while Russian Captain Pomerintz sailed the SS ELBRUS from the Black Sea port of Odessa to Trieste, delivering it into the hands of Robert P. Joyce, American "Political Advisor" to the contested free city state, training the OPC freedom fighters to overthrow the countries behind the Iron Curtain. Joyce had earlier served under George Kennan in the State Department as his assistant for Eastern Europe. Kennan, former ambassador to Moscow, had helped arrange the exchange visits between the American-Soviet Medical Society members, Krotkov and Shimkin. (17)

STATE DEPARTMENT file 123 JOYCE, ROBERT P. Incoming telegram. 74 February 17, 1948, 'Restricted' from Trieste, To: Secretary State, From JOYCE.
T-2 Tanker ELBRUS docked Trieste February 10. Inventory stores and equipment (REDEPTEL 54, February 10) proceeding favorably."

STATE DEPARTMENT file 195.2/2-2648 TRIESTE Russian Shipping
Page 1: "On February 25, 1948, Captain Pomerints and his crew departed from Trieste by train for Yugoslavia. Captain Pomerints made it quite clear that his entire stay in Trieste that he had no intention of either engaging in political activities or allowing members of his crew to do so...
Page 3: A G-2 report on the activities of the Russian crew states: "The sailors from the Russian ship handed over to the United States have been

going around the town. The only people they spoke to were White Russians, owners of stalls in the closed market, and then they only discussed the weather, prices of vegetable and the town in general." It is believed that the local faithful (staging pro-Russian rallies) were bitterly disappointed that Captain Pomerints and his crew declined to cooperate. Signed: respectfully yours, Robert P Joyce, US Political Advisor"

The chit chat between Joyce and the Washington State Department went on for months, describing not only the scrubbed up condition of the SS ELBRUS as most acceptable, but the huge epidemics raging in Trieste and the need for more medical supplies. Who would notice one more infected rat off an old liberty tanker? If this wasn't collusion between the US State Department and the Soviet Union to disguise the source of the Russian epidemics, what was? The Soviets obligingly silenced the leftwing press upon the arrival of the SS ELBRUS. The whole OPC should have been arrested for treason. Trieste and Yugoslavia had been a medical disaster during the war, the Communist resistance fighter Draja Mikhailovitch put on trial by the Soviets, who accused him of treason and initiating BW attacks upon the citizens. The huge show trial was a farce, since Suchomi, Tomka and Beketovka had been running full steam ahead since the 1930s. Brucellosis expert, Dr. Wesley Spink, suggested the huge brucellosis infestation in Yugoslavia and Trieste originated from infected Italian sheep being driven across the Alps during the war. The Russians must have loved Spink. (18)

According to the Vessel Status Card of the SS ELBRUS at the J. Porter Shaw Library in San Francisco, the tanker was turned over to the American Transport Lines in Trieste on February 20th, 1948, the American Export Lines were the Berth Agent for Marine Transport Lines. From there the ship went to the US Navy in New York City on April 23rd, 1948 and went to the Reserve Fleet at James River on June 10th, 1959. Luria Brothers & Company purchased it for scrap, December 2, 1975, coincidentally, the same time Lyme disease was recognized by Yale doctors, the OPC's old stomping grounds.

Lieutenant Colonel Lewis Perry was a special case for scrutiny. To further facilitate the Soviets in removing their hot potato Nazis, OPC ratlines were established. Donovan assigned Frank Wisner, a former Wall Street banker, to oversee the freedom fighters in Trieste, the National Security Council directive 10/2 giving Wisner "carte blanche" to overthrow the Soviet Union. Before its merging with the CIA, the OPC employed over four thousand field operatives, including Ronald Reagan, its fund raiser, and Bill Casey, who welcomed "Dragon Returnees" into the port of New York, through the OPC's International Rescue Committee. (19) The fire-breathing dragon was the symbol for Chemical Warfare. First, we need investigate Joyce's role in the death of BW-CW Waffen Pruf 9 chief, Walter Hirsch in the hands of "Agent Barber" and last, we need consider whom Joyce hired in Trieste to train his freedom fighters. There are many clues as to why the OPC was a complete flop, all the freedom fighters identified and assassinated.

Waffen Pruf 9 chief, Walter Hirsch, beat it to Russia along with the rest of the I. G. Farben CW experts. Once his usefulness was up, realizing his days were numbered, he beat it back out. The US Army Intelligence and Security Command at Fort Meade hold in their DCII indexes some of Hirsch's files, indicating Hirsch had escaped his "captors" and made it back to the British Zone of occupied Germany. From there, he landed in the hands of the CIC 430th Unit under Lewis Perry, the rogue unit attached to Allen Dulles' (OSS - DDU - WDD - DAD - OPC). Ordered to write for FIAT, (Field Intelligence Agency Technical) the famed Hirsch Report, "Soviet BW & CW Preparations and Capabilities," he would expose every bastard, East and West.

Watching the Russian ratlines of Nazi doctors was Dmitri Boris Shimkin for the War Department and FBI. His brother, Dr. Michael Shimkin, serving the Soviet American Medical Exchange program, and WHO, was a cancer research specialist for the US Department of Health. Brother, Dmitri, was an anthropologist, working for the Department of Commerce's Office of Scientific Research and Development and also re-porting to Hoover's FBI. The FBI holds extensive files on both Shimkin brothers, Michael's files only recently released in 2001, days after George Bush's inauguration. Both brothers share biographies in "American Men of Science" 8th edition, 1949.

The Shimkins were born in Russia and became naturalized US citizens in the mid 1930s, perfect pickings for Roosevelt's intelligence agencies. Michael had been appointed to the US Department of Health medical liaison to lend-lease matters with the USSR on March 9th, 1943 through the OSRD and edited "The American Review of Soviet Medicine" for the American-Soviet Medical Society between 1943 and 1948. He would accompany Dr. Baird Hastings from Harvard on a Medical Research Mission to the Soviet Union" in 1943, later written up in "Science" a month before the first WHO conference would adjourn. Once New York was plagued with epidemics, Michael Shimkin would escort Soviet doctors around the country. (20)

Michael Shimkin needed numerous security clearances for the State Department's Civil Service Commission and missions to the United

Nations and abroad. The CSC asked the FBI and the New York Police Department's "BOSSI" (Bureau of Special Services and Investigations) to conduct the clearances, which Shimkin passed in flying colors. By the mid 1960s, Michael was on the hot seat, having raised defense funds for a Philadelphia's underground Communist party leader, Dr. Jeremiah Stamler, through Chicago's Committee for Preserving Constitutional Rights. Stamler refused to testify before the House of Un-American Activities Comity, (HAUC) and was eventually sentenced to prison after appealing the case all the way to the Supreme Court. Shimkin's involvement in no way impeded his security clearances, the last granted for President Johnson in 1968 for another UN mission. (21)

Brother Dmitri Boris Shimkin was far the more dangerous of the two, as listed in his brother's FBI files, Dmirtri was a Communist Party organizer on the UC Berkeley campus in his youth. He fit right into the ivy league community at Harvard, proving the "missing link" in more ways than one. Dmitri Boris Shimkin was assigned to the Russian O/B (Order of Battle) Military Branch of the War Department's Military Intelligence Division in the Pentagon, tracking Nazi scientists in and out of Russia, including Walter Hirsch.

WALTER HIRSCH FBI file 105-8090-17 "SECRET" Office Memorandum, June 12, 1946 to Director FBI, From Guy Hottel, SAC, Washington Field Office, Subject: Russian Activities - Internal Security - R

"Attention: (Blackout) The following four documents which are projects of the Russian O/B Section, Military Branch, MID the War Department, was supplied to Special Agent (Blackout) of this office by Miss Mary Terry, secretary to Lieutenant Colonel D. B. Shimkin, chief of that Section. They are classified secret and are for permanent Bureau possession. (Three paragraphs blacked out.) The document E-2, undated, consists of two parts. It contains brief biographical data concerning a number of German scientists and attempts to give their whereabouts.... Dr. Walter Hirsch: Colonel, "Chief OKH, Wa Pruf 9" last seen in latter part of 1944 in Berlin. Now probably at Munsterlager..."

Detained in Salzburg by the CIC 430th unit, Hirsch was stationed with Klaus Barbie, who also worked under Lewis Perry. "Operation Headache/Boathill," the CIC 430th Unit's Nazi smuggling ratline, took a serious interest in the Hirsch report. Perry and his OPC superiors, Allen Dulles and Frank Wisner, placed super mole, White Russian Prince Anton Turkul in charge of the ratlines. This is the same Anton Turkul who held Connecticut's "reverse radish," Anatase Vonsiatsky, as his subordinate. A very detailed history of Barbie, Perry, Turkul and the Dulles gang running the ratlines of Headache/Boathill is exposed in Mark Aaron's and John Loftus' "Unholy Trinity" (22) Their thorough research published in 1990 did not include the FBI Walter Hirsch files involving "Agent Barber" released to this author May 5, 1993. Of more significance, is the fact that the following Hirsch files detail other Army CIC reports on "Agent BARBER" which did not appear in Allan Ryan and William French Smith's 1983 publication "Klaus Barbie and the United States Government," Ryan was an employee of the Justice Department with access to both FBI files and Army reports. It is increasingly evident to this author that "Agent BARBER" was Klaus Barbie.

The following FBI file on Walter Hirsch, covers his sudden death, which reads as if he had been beaten to death, suffering "kidney failure" in the hands of "Agent BARBER." Keep in mind, the myriad of Klaus Barbie files spell "Barbie" as "Barbier," but no others came to light under "BARBER." Is "Agent Barber" Klaus Barbie from Perry's CIC 430th Unit? The first section of the FBI Walter Hirsch files below involves Army G-2 intelligence attempting to analyze a series of events in Austria, an attempted kidnapping by the Soviets of a severed CIC agent "HOETTL," (possibly Guy Hottel, the FBI's SAC?) and his failed rendezvous with other CIC agents and "BARBER" at Salzburg, Austria. The second section covers the death of Walter Hirsch and the ensuing mad dash to grab the Hirsch Report between competing intelligence agencies. Robert P. Joyce from the OPC in Trieste and "Agent Barber" suspected of being a Soviet or Israeli mole in Lewis Perry's rogue CIC 430th Unit, were all scrambling for the goodies. G-2 Intelligence in Washington was in a panic, fearing "Agent Barber" would turn the files over to Headache/Boathill, or worse, the Russians. To complicate things, the Nazis and the Jewish refugees were using the same ratlines to escape Europe, and the Jews were bartering with Moscow for information on the Arab situation. The Hirsch Report was valuable to many for many different reasons. It would take several more years for the sophistication of the Mossad to grow, their Jewish contacts inside the Soviet Union would elucidate them on the nature of the Nazi-Soviet alliance. The Communist purges inside Russia, facilitated by the Nazis, would prove equal to the holocaust.

WALTER HIRSCH FBI file 65-58841-53, Originating from Army, case number 1247F-92, US Army Intelligence and Security Command, Ft. G. Meade, ND. Admissions United States Forces in Austria Deputy Assistant Chief of Staff, G-2 APO 777-A US Army March 22, 1950. HEADACHE SUBJECT: BOATHILL.

"To: G-2, USUSA, Department of the Army Washington D.C...

1. Enclosed are the following reports and memoranda, in triplicate:

a. CIC Vienna Progress Report #38, dated 2 Mar 50

b. CIC Vienna Progress Report #39, dated 7 Mar 50

c. CIC Vienna Progress Report #40, dated 15 Mar 50

d. Operation Freedom, Report #14, 28 Jan 50

e. Operation freedom, Progress Report #15, 15 Mar 50

f. Memorandum for the Record, dated 21 Feb 50

g. Memorandum for the Record, dated 21 Mar 50

h. Memorandum for the Record, dated 22 Mar 50

2. In reference to para 5 of Vienna Progress Report #40, which records ARCHER's request for information on plans for the evacuation of Vienna in case of emergency, the identity of the C-3 informant who reported on HONNER's possession of an evacuation order is being procured from Vienna files; available background information and the informant's identity will be forwarded in the near future. Investigation of this entire matter, which involves another rather vague report that an American colonel has been in touch with the Soviets, is continuing and results will be reported/ (Blackout).

3. In reference to para 10 of Vienna Progress Report #40, which recounts SIMPSON's recent activities in connection with O'BRIEN, we conjecture as follows:

a. If one assumes that ARCHER [pencilled over the top - Otto Verber] and O'BRIEN [pencilled in over the top - Curt Ponger] are parts of an operation directed by the MVD, then O'BRIEN's approach to SIMPSON [pencilled in over the top - Peter H. Miller] can be explained as an attempt on the part of the Soviets to learn more about the whereabouts and activities of HOETTL, whom the Soviets are known to have attempted to abduct. It is noted that the severance of HOETTL by CIC in the fall of 1949 has been on the intelligence grapevine for several months largely because HOETTL himself has industriously put rumors on the grapevine and has tried by many means to obtain the re-employment of the whole, as well as of portions, of his organization.

b. If we assume that ARCHER and O'BRIEN are members of a group directed by the Israeli intelligence service, then O'BRIEN's interest in HOETTL may be explained as an attempt to acquire information which is known through the grapevine to be of interest to the Soviets and which can therefore be used in bartering with the Soviet Services for information on the Arab States and for favors to the Israeli underground in their ratline activity.

c. If we assume that ARCHER and O'BRIEN are members of KPO

or Communist free lance operation, then O'BRIEN's approach can be explained as an attempt to acquire information which is known through the grapevine to be of interest to the Soviets and which can therefore be used to acquire official backing for the independent organization.

d. If we assume that HOETTL is already in touch with the service which operates ARCHER and O'BRIEN, then O'BRIEN's approach may be a rather unsubtle attempt to penetrate CIC via HOETTL. It is to be noted that surveillance on 8 March 1950 established that ARCHER and O'BRIEN left Salzburg driving in the direction of St. Gilgen. At that time it was concluded that, having missed BARBER in Salzburg, they had arranged a meeting at some point between Salzburg and Linz. Surveillance in Gunden, the logical place for such a meeting, failed to uncover the vehicle in which they were moving. In the light of Progress Report #40, it should be noted that HOETTL's main base of operation is in Strobl on Wolfgangsee, which lies midway between Salzburg and Gunden, east of St. Gilgen. No action in pursuit of this lead is contemplated here for the present. It has been decided not to contact O'BRIEN directly nor to indicate further interest in SIMPSON.

4. In reference to HARDY's report (Salzburg Progress Report #14) and the Memorandum for the Record, dated 21 February 50 "discussion in Salzburg", HARDY has reported verbally that BARBER's interest in the NEUMANN case continues to be intense. NEUMANN has been instructed by SEDA to meet her on 1 April 50 and to proceed with her via Vienna to Gund in the Soviet Zone, where they are to cross the border and meet two Czechs, one allegedly named HANUS (fnu) and the other NU. It has been decided here to forbid NEUMANN to make this meeting.

5. In reference to Operation Freedom Progress report #15, the HIRSCH case is summarized in Memorandum for the record, dated 22 Mar 50, for the Assistant Chief of Staff, G-2.

MEMORANDUM FOR THE RECORD SD 21150, March 22, 1950 SUBJECT: HIRSCH CASE

1. On 28 February 1950, Dr. Walter HIRSCH, who will appear in Washington traces as a correspondent of BARBER, died of a kidney ailment in Linz.

2. Dr. HIRSCH who, during the war, was a ranking expert in chemical warfare research for the German Army had, during the two years previous to his death, been exploited by IB-5 (Technical Intelligence Section) of ODI, USFA. As a source both on Soviet chemical warfare and on German war-time research.

3. Dr. HIRSCH had in his possession a large quantity of documents, some of them captured by the Germans from the Russians during combat,

others containing the results of German war-time research. BARBER was the interrogator who handled and paid HIRSCH.

4. When the report of HIRSCH's death was received, it was immediately decided for very obvious reasons that the documents remaining should be take over by CIC and that BARBER should be kept out of the negotiations with Mrs. HIRSCH. Accordingly, JOYCE was dispatched from Linz to make contact with the widow who stated that she would release some of the documents, but that others she intended to burn in accordance with her husband's dying wish. JOYCE left two agents to guard the documents and drove to Salzburg for instructions. It was decided to send a deputation of high ranking American officers in full regalia in a staff car to confiscate the documents in proper Prussian style. this was accordingly done, the CO of CIC Linz and his subordinates taking the part of the high ranking Americans, and the documents were transferred secretly to a safe in CIC Salzburg. there they were inventoried by Mr. Hermann JACOB, a former German-document specialist. Copy of the inventory is attached to this memorandum. The documents were transmitted to Washington in crates on 22 March 1950.

[Author's note, the inventory list was not in this FBI file.]

5. Meanwhile, however, the news of HIRSCH's death became known to IB-5 and to BARBER. It appears impossible to determine whether BARBER learned of HIRSCII's death through a phone call from IB-5 or whether he heard the story around CIC Linz. In any case, Major TOWNSLEY of IB-5 immediately proposed sending BARBER to get the documents from Mrs. HIRSCH and expressed a strong desire to examine and screen these documents before they were sent to Washington. Since it was considered inadvisable for the documents to be left with IB-5 while BARBER still had access to IB-5's files and personnel, Major TOWNSLEY was instructed by Henry LOGAN, and subsequently by each of his superior officers in turn, that the matter of the HIRSCH documents had been taken away from IB-5 and that further discussion was not desirable. Major TOWNSLEY then stated that he was expecting a visit from Lt. Col. WILLIAMSON, officer of the Chief of the Chemical Corps, Washington, and Lt. Col. LOUCKS. Technical Intelligence Section, ID, EUCOM, and that these two officers would be extremely interested in examining the documents themselves. Major TOWNSLEY was again instructed that the documents had passed out of the jurisdiction of IB-5 and would be forwarded to Washington, where Lt. Col. WILLIAMSON could see them if he wished. Major TOWNSLEY also stated that included among these documents were two "musty old notebooks" which were the most valuable items in the HIRSCH collection and that he doubted the ability

of non-technical personnel to distinguish these notebooks from the other material. Upon being questioned as to the source of his knowledge of the existence of the two musty notebooks, Major TOWNSLEY stated that he had learned this from BARBER, that he himself had never seen the notebooks. BARBER had never reported the existence of these notebooks to the G-2 staff.

6. On 16 March 1950, Lt. Col. LOUCKS, who had just arrived in Salzburg, mentioned to Major YEAGER, chief of IB and Major TOWNSLEY's superior, that he had on the previous day, 15 March 1950, encountered BARBER in Heidelberg, that BARBER had stated that he was in EUCOM on several days "informal leave". (NOTE: It has been ascertained that BARBER took three days' annual leave from 15 through 17 March 1950 with the permission of the Administrative Officer of the MIS Detachment in Linz to which BARBER is currently attached.) Major YEAGER is not briefed on BOATHILL, but, being dimly aware of the fact that some sort of counter intelligence existed in Operations for BARBER, he reported the conversation with Lt. Col. LOUCKS to Mr. WOLF. It is believed here that BARBER, never having been officially instructed to concern himself with the case of HIRSCH's death, on his own initiative intercepted Lt. Col. WILLIAMSON and Lt. Col. LOUCKS in Heidelberg and gave them his version of the way in which the HIRSCH case had been handled. BARBER knew of Lt. Col. WILLIAMSON's visit since he had access to the cable announcing this forthcoming visit to USFA. The colonels stated that they knew that CIC, using MP's and employing physical force against Mrs. HIRSCH, had rudely and clumsily seized the documents and had behaved in such a way that Mrs. HIRSCH was currently suffering a nervous breakdown. This information is entirely incorrect.

7. It is to be pointed out that the two musty documents are known to us only through BARBER's statement to Major TOWNSLEY after HIRSCH's death. It is further pointed out that perhaps the deftest maneuver which BARBER could use to explain the disappearance of two sensitive documents after an unexpected event such as the death of HIRSCH would be to assert that they had been lost or destroyed through the ineptness of CIC. If there is any basis for our conjecture that on one occasion ARCHER and O'BRIEN were taken by BARBER to interview HIRSCH, and if there is any basis to believe that the two musty documents ever existed, and if they are not among those listed in the attached inventory, then it is possible to conjecture that at some time in the winter of 1949/1950 the documents passed from HIRSCH's possession to that of our opponents in BOATHILL.

8. Request that particular note be made of para 6 and 7 above in the

event Lt. Col. WILLIAMSON registers a complaint with G-2, D/A reference the alleged two musty old documents.

Signed: WALTER WOLF"

What on earth do we have here? Lewis Perry's 430th CIC is running amuck with Soviet moles. Whose side is "Agent BARBER" on? Is "Guy Hottel" "HOETTL"? Hoover's informants, the Shimkin brothers, seem to be in bad company. Most of the 9 chapters of the Hirsch Report vanish, along with his two musty notebooks, just as the original Van Vleit report and Walter Flotho's black book had vanished. Were they burned by BARBER, and did the Russians get the musty old notebooks? If "Agent BARBER" was Klaus Barbie, the Butcher of Lyon, did he murder Walter Hirsch with his bare hands, causing "kidney failure" and thus induce Mrs. Hirsch's "nervous breakdown"? Other references to Germans fearing assassination from being placed under Barbie's care surfaced in Allan Ryan's "Klaus Barbie and the United States Government," in a CIC report from Bad Nauheim, February 20, 1947. This Justice Department publication further expose Barbie's ties to the "Peterson Net" of the CIC 66th unit, which had replaced the CIC 970th. Barbie had joined this operation in 1947 and roamed all over Europe till 1949, prior to his assignment with Lewis Perry's CIC 430th. The Peterson Net, under Kurt Merk, a former Abwehr operative stationed in France during the war, was dissolved in late 1949 because of Merk' failing health. Now that the French were pursuing Barbie as a witness for Rene Hardy's trial, Barbie moved on to more sinister covert operations with Dulles' rogue 430th CIC. (23)

At this point, the US Government report on Barbie dropped the ball, ignoring Lewis Perry's 430th CIC affiliation with Dulles' OPC, employing Nazi war criminals instead of hunting them down. Where Allan Ryan dropped off, Loftus and Aarons picked up the trail of Klaus Barbie in "Unholy Trinity" chapter 11, "Klaus Barbie and the American Ratlines." The Defense Department was reorganized after WW II, and the intelligence networks in Germany and Austria were permanently severed. The CIC 970th Nazi hunters and the CIC 430th Nazi recruiters were put under separate command. Next, the CIC 430th mysteriously vanished from Army supervision altogether, and re-emerged under Allen Dulles' OPC. Colonel Lewis Perry, Klaus Barbie, Anton Turkul and Operation Headache/Boathill went with it. Loftus and Aarons explain that the CIC 430th Unit and the Austrian, Italian and Trieste commands were placed directly under Colonel Lewis Perry in Salzburg. Every three years, the intelligence files of this band of bandits were purged from DDU-OPC records "for unexplained security reasons." (24) Under the newly re-organized Defense Department, after

James Forrestal's "suicide", Hirsch didn't stand a chance.

In Fort Meade's CIC 430th Unit detachment report on Walter Hirsch, questions are raised regarding the effectiveness of biological warfare during WW II and the possibilities of BW implementation by the Communists after the war. Contrary to Hirsch's expressed concerns over an enormous, extensive Russian BW threat in his report, the CIC insisted Hirsch viewed the threat as insignificant. Was the CIC 430th Unit lying, anticipating his death and destruction of the Hirsch Report? Joyce had just received the SS ELBRUS at Trieste, all scrubbed up, spick and span, from Captain Pomerints. Is this why Hirsch was placed under Agent BARBER'S command?

COUNTER INTELLIGENCE CORPS 430th DET. USFA Land Upper Austria Sub Detachment APO 174 U.S. Army Special Projects Branch 3, 20 April 1949, Case No. SP-24 Subject: HIRSCH, Dr. Walter N. CW Expert. Fort G. Meade, US Army Intelligence & Security Command, RE: Evaluation Report

1. "Reference is made to IRS from ODI (IB-5) dated 8 March 1949, with file number (?) TIN 99. The following report is submitted in compliance with requests contained in this IRS.

2. Part 1 of cited IRS requests evaluation and comment by Dr. HIRSCH on sections of a BW report obtained from Dr. VIA-WALTER who was formerly in the medical department of the German Army on the eastern front and (line illegible). Dr. HIRSCH states that nothing contained in this excerpt contradicted information and impressions he has had, and that it appeared to be very good and interesting material. The Doctor stated that bacteriological maters were a "secondary" field for him, since during his service with the German Army, he did not specifically occupy himself with such problems until given the assignment in addition to his chemical warfare duties.

[Hirsch continued on citing British and American failed attempts on a BW attack upon Germany with Texas Fever and potato bugs.]

BW generally, as a weapon of war, will never be a major threat, according to the doctor among the Western nations standards of sanitation are such as to check any widespread advance; among the Soviet peoples, on the other hand, their present high rate of infant and childhood mortality has resulted in a sort of super-health by means of "natural selection", and many diseases which might prove an annoyance elsewhere, apparently do not constitute a health threat in the Soviet Union..."

This certainly contradicts the OACSI reports on returning German POWs from Russia as well as the Hirsch Report's chapter 2, the direction of this report is highly suspicious. By the summer of 1950, the Klaus Barbie affair, with the French in hot pursuit, had caused such a stink, that Barbie beat it to Rome and made his exit via the Vatican's ratlines, organized under the help of Anton Turkul. Turkul, in turn, was under command of the Soviet MVD (Military intelligence of the Red Orchestra) all along. Pope Pius would become the OPC's patsy for all of its failures.

Trieste was an international den of intrigue. The Jews were in a terrible predicament. The Socialist Europeans did not want the survivors; anti-Semitism, driven by greed, ran deep. The Soviet Union had branded all religions as "the opiate of the people" and had been conducting pogroms against Christians, Moslems, Buddhists, and Jews alike. The Jews could go neither East nor West. A rogue British Israeli unit reorganized after the war and began smuggling refugees to Israel. The same US State Department files on the SS ELBRUS, holds files on the SS Exodus' history. In the beginning, the young intelligence operatives of the future Israeli Army did not understand that their Nazi collaborators in the ratlines were Soviet moles, all the more dangerous, with ulterior motives. They learned quickly. While the OPC ratlined the Nazi war criminals out of Russia to South America, the Mossad began tracking them down and executing them. Adolf Eichman of Hitler's High Command, who orchestrated the Final Solution, was kidnapped in Argentina and tried for war crimes in Israel. But to win votes in United Nations approval for the formation of the State of Israel, the Jews made a deal with the devil and dropped their hunt to appease American intelligence. The Mossad's efforts are valiantly documented in Simon Wiesenthal's "The Murders Among Us" and John Loftus and Mark Aaron's "Secret War Against the Jews," St. Martin's Press, NY 1994. More intrigue surfaced in the US State Department files.

Joyce's' freedom fighters were being smuggled in and out of Yugoslavia through a network of local fishermen in Trieste and the Soviets began boarding Italian vessels bound for Trieste "seizing the catch of the day." Worse, the Iron Curtain Communists were seizing Catholic Priest, torturing them and assassinating them, prompting Pope Pius to create a "Black Orchestra" to counter the Red Orchestra's activities. Unfortunately, Pius relied on advice of the OPC to utilize Turkul's double agents, working for both Reds and Blacks, compromising the fate of the Balkan Catholics. (25) The money for Joyce's freedom fighters in Trieste came from Uncle Ronnie, "the Gipper" soliciting funds for the OPC. Did Hollywood become the OPC's cash cow? Ronald Reagan was just as much a babe in the woods as the Jews fleeing Europe.

The British political advisors in Trieste began to witness a bizarre phenomenon and posed questions to Robert P. Joyce in a letter to the State Department, 1/6/48, "subject: Paramount Pictures." Accordingly, Captain

Pello Levi of the PWB Film section (US Army), director of Paramount in Italy, had hope to offer 30 million lire to the American Joint Defense Committee in the free territory of Trieste through Mr. White, Director of Finance & Economics, who was absent from his post. Levi was referred to White's British counterpart in the Allied Military Government, upsetting Levi, the British suspecting the AJDC was "siphoning funds into the Zionist movement." (26) Had Ronald Reagan facilitated their escape? Was the Jewish underground collaborating with Joyce's OPC? Could this explain how "Henry Tolkmith" escaped the Soviet Union with the aide of his Russian Jewess wife Valentine, "Xena, the Warrior Princess"? How long has "McGyver" been in operation? Again, we can only speculate. Hollywood supported Ronald Reagan's rise to the governorship in California and welcomed a friend in the White House, but once again, Reagan' naivete would cause him to blunder, choosing old OPC buddy Bill Casey to direct the CIA.

CHAPTER 10 NOTES

(1) "West's Federal Practice Digest" 2nd, vol. 86 M-Z "Potash - US DCNY, 332 FSupp 730; "Federal Supplement" vo. 81, page 281, "United States v. Foster et al."

"Federal Supplement" vol. 83 West Publishing co. 1949, St. Paul, Minn. Page 197 United States v. Foster et al, US District Court, S.D. New York, March 4, 1949.

"HIGH COURT UPHOLDS GUILT OF 11 TOP COMMUNISTS: OTHER PROSECUTIONS ARE SET" "New York Times" 6/5/51 p. 1

(2) DR WALTER P. SCHREIBER (DRAGON RETURNEE PROGRAM) FBI file 105-15549-10: "Subject has arrived in the US with his family on September 18, 1951... destined to Randolph Field Air Base, San Antonio, Texas... employed in the Department of Global Preventive Medicine, US AF, School of Aviation medicine for 6 months from Sept 1951 through February, 1952 on a contract basis.... departed on May 22, 1952... destination was Argentina..."

WALTER P. SCHREIBER FBI file 123-15258-10 Page 5 'WFO 123-14076'

"On December 9, 1951, the Boston Globe newspaper dated April 9, 1951, under heading "Ex Nazi High Post with United States Air Force says Medical Man Here...Plans for a formal protest heightened after Doctor LEO ALEXANDER... identified the doctor in question as the Wehrmacht's

#2 Medical Chief who condoned the experiments which took the life of thousands of prisoners... Doctor ALEXANDER said... "the man was smart enough to beat it to the Russians and escape... twenty years in prison.""

WALTER P. SCHREIBER FBI file 100-13-27-132 PHOENIX ARIZONA 7/16/52 INTERNAL SECURITY - C "International Commission Testifies' Korea, charges of germ warfare... unknown in Korea have been found the last weeks in many districts..."

(3) "Statement by U. S. Officers Transmitted to United Nations" US delegation press release 10/26/53 US Dpt. State, Bulletin, vol. 29, page 648 "The Question of Impartial Investigation of Charges of Use by United Nations Forces of Bacterial Warfare"

(4) 'PLAGUE VACCINE OF RUSSIAN MANUFACTURE OACSI file MIS 741838, report no. 1415-50, from T/I, G-2, GHQ, FSC. Reference; D/A ltr 3550.0913, dated 24 Oct 50 date of report 13 Dec 50, incl two, prepared by MISD, G-2 GHQ, FEC.

(5) "FUR UNION BACKS DISSENT" "New York Times" 6/6/51 p. 23 c. 2
"3 REDS WIN RIGHT TO QUIT THE CITY" "New York Times" p. 28 c. 7

(6) IRVING POTASH FBI file SERIAL 195, 234, 248, 297, 321, 341, 344 - Supplementary correlation Summary , Page 93: "The following references in the file captioned "Cominfil of the International Brotherhood of Teamsters, Chauffeurs Warehousemen and Helpers of America" (IBT), file 100-13124, contain information pertaining to the CP activities of Irving Potash relative to the IBT. During the approximate period of September, 1961, through May, 1962, Potash attended CP meetings to various localities, including Newark, NYC, Chicago, Detroit, Baltimore and Fall River, Mass., at which he discussed the trade union activities with the CP. Potash as CP Labor Secretary took an active part in the formation of a Teamsters Commission in the CP (whole paragraph blacked out.)
"HOFFA" Arthur A. Sloane, The MIT Press, Cambridge, MA 1991, Pages 20, 27

(7) IRVING POTASH FBI file 61-5381-3912; Page 93: "This reference set out the verbatim contents of six stenographic notebooks of the 26 books recovered upon their abandonment when the Amtorg Trading Corporation (61-5381) moved from 210 Madison Ave, New York. These

278 _____ LYME DISEASE AND THE SS ELBRUS

books were secured by SAC of the NY office on 7/11/50 (three lines blacked out) The book appeared to be the records of an interviewer at the Soviet Government Purchasing Commission at Washington, DC of job applicants. Book No. 11, which covered the dates from 12/11/44 to 12/28/44, contained information concerning (line blacked out). The information noted that she was "Russian-English Secretary - Furriers Joint Council, 250 W. 26th St., New York City." and among other things, stated "Referred to us by (blackout) Irving Potash. (lines blacked out) New York City."

IRVING POTASH FBI file 100-52010-21 Page 3, (on page 29 of FBI Supplemental Correlation Summary.) re. Potash and OFLWU and FJC expulsion from CIO

IRVING POTASH FBI file 62-31615-905 (Supplementary Correlation Summary - p. 50) and FBI file 65-57493-43, (Supplementary Correlation page 36)

(8) IRVING POTASH FBI file 100-23165-154 , pages 38-40, 58, 121 in China, USA

IRVING POTASH FBI file 100-46808-575.(travels in Poland & USSR), file 61-330816 and 100-400646-5548; (Supplementary Correlation page 59, Potash in China.); file 100-23165, Potash returns home to USA in 1957.

(9) "Gold Guilty of T-H Lie, Faces 5 Years" "New York Times" 4/3/54

"Million Transcripts to Expose Ben Gold Frameup" "The Daily Worker" 5/5/54 p. 3

"It Could Happen There" "The New York Daily News" 1/30/57

"Investigation of Communist Infiltration Into the Fur Industry" CIS no. 80 H1222-5 September 8-10, 13-16, 1948, SUDOC: Y4.Ed8/1:F96. Page 316: Gold testifies.

(10) "MCCARTHY" Roy Cohn, New American Library, NY 1968 Page 22

"ENOUGH ROPE" Arthur V. Watkins, Prentice Hall, Inc. & The University of Utah Press, Salt Lake City, UT. Page 2

(11) "The Historical Background of the Central Intelligence Agency" Office of General Counsel, CIA, August 25, 1960.

(12) "THE NEW ENCYCLOPEDIA BRITANNICA" Golden Press, 1986, 15th Edition

'Arthur Joseph Goldberg' re. counsel for (CIO) and the United Steelworkers of America, AFL-CIO 1955 merger, expels Communist and racketeers.

"New York Times" 'Obituaries' January 20, 1990 Sec. 1, p. 1, c. 5. "Arthur Goldberg"

(13) "CLOAK AND GOWN: Scholars in the Secret War, 1939-1961" Robin Winks, William Morrow & Co. Inc. 1987. Pages 44-45: re. Blankenhorn, OSS MO, Goldberg

(14) "UNHEALED WOUNDS" Erna Paris, Grove Press, Inc. NY 1985

"THE BUTCHER OF LYON" Brendan Murphy, Empire Books, NY 1983.

"DARK VICTORY: Ronald Reagan, MCA and the Mob" Dan Moldea, Viking Penguin, Inc. NY 1986. Page 8: "(Sidney) Korshak('s) [attorney to Chicago Mafia boss, Bioff who later penetrated the Hollywood movie industry]... close associate, Democrat Paul Ziffren, became a law partner of William French Smith... Reagan's attorney general."

(15) "THE BELARUS SECRET" John Loftus, Alfred Knopf, NY 1982, Page 107, 141

(16) "KLAUS BARBIE AND THE UNITED STATES GOVERN-MENT" Allan Ryan, Jr., US Dpt. of Just., University Publications of America, Frederick, MD 1984, Pages 348-349: re. TAB 24: newspaper clippings "Lawyer Assails US Army At Hardy's Trial on Treason" and "Ex-Resistance Leader Contests Statements on Role in Occupation" Page 351: TAB 55 Klaus Barbier as CIC agent in Munich.

(17) U. S. Maritime Commission file No. 118-7, Part 6, July 1, 1948. Bureau of Operations, February 18, 1948 "Russian Vessels Being Delivered from Lend Lease"

State Department file 861.852/2-1648, No. CITE 45, from Army Dept Yokohama, Incoming Telegram, control 4621, Rec'd Feb 16, 1948 6:52 a.m.

"THE BELARUS SECRET" John Loftus, Alfred Knopf, NY 1982. Page 68: re. "George Kennan, chief State Department's Policy and Planning staff, and Robert P. Joyce, Kennan's assistant for Eastern Europe." Page 70: re. Joyce as OPC's liaison officer & OSS guerrilla warfare in Yugoslavia. Kennan USSR ambassador, 1939-41

STATE DEPARTMENT file 811.42761/2-2746, from St. Dpt Internal Labor, Social and Health Affairs Division, exchange program in medicine. Nat. Arch. CRB "Memorandum of Conversation" St. Dpt. 2/2746. Subject: Public Health and Medical Information on Interchange between USA and USSR. Participants: Ambassador Smith, Mr. Harriman, Surgeon General Parran, Mr. Mulliken, and doctors Williams, Hyde and Shimkin."

(18) STATE DEPARTMENT files TRIESTE 800.48 FRP/11-2647, Incoming Telegram #187, November 26, 1947 To Secretary of State, From JOYCE in Trieste. "No word of received here re arrival programmed medical supplies. Please cable status."

STATE DEPARTMENT file 800.480FRP/3-1948, Incoming Tel. #145, March 19, PAR 50, 1948, RE HAP 39 To Sec. St.., From JOYCE. "Please continue your efforts ship medical supplies soonest. Impossible predict whether April 30 deadline satisfactory - no indication here which supplies will be shipped first. Urge earlier shipping date if possible."

STATE DEPARTMENT file 800.48 FRP/5-148 Incoming Telegram 253

"US AIDE, BRITON ACCUSED AS MIKHAILOVITCH CASE OPENS" "New York Times" 6/11/46, p. 1 & 8

"MURDERING DENIED BY MIKHAILOVITCH" "New York Times" 6/17/46 p5 c1

"The Nature of Brucellosis" Wesley Spink, MD D. Sc. The University of Minnesota Press, Minneapolis, MN 1956 Page xi.

STATE DEPARTMENT file 195.2/2-2048 Incoming Tel. #84 'Confidential' February 20, REMYTEL #75, Feb. 18, 1948. to: Secretary of State, From JOYCE

"Kelly and McKenny state ship in perfect condition and all equipment maintained in first class shape. Soviet master most cooperative and friendly. Neither master nor crew have shown any indication of interest in political activity here and have maintained complete reserve vis-a-vis local Communist organizations...."

(19) "THE BELARUS SECRET" John Loftus, Alfred Knopf, NY 1982. Pages 9, 81-84

"UNHOLY TRINITY: The Vatican, The Nazis, and Soviet Intelligence" Mark Aarons & John Loftus, St. Martin's Press, NY 1990 Page 271: re. Reagan & Casey in OPC

(20) MICHAEL BORIS SHIMKIN FBI file 121-HQ-4389 re. Mis-

sion to Moscow, OSRD

(21) MICHAEL BORIS SHIMKIN FBI file 138-HQ-4947 and 121-HQ-4389, re Jeremiah Stamler and BOSSI clearances.

(22) "UNHOLY TRINITY" Mark Aarons and John Loftus, St. Martin's Press, NY 1990, page 254, Barbie with CIC, pages 240-241: Lewis Perry and "Operation Headache/Boathill and the CIC 430th Unit as part of Dulles' DDU - (OPC).

(23) "KLAUS BARBIE AND THE UNITED STATES GOVERN MENT" Allen Ryan, Jr., U. S. Department of Justice, University Publications of America 1984, Frederick, MD. Page 109-110, Germans afraid of Barbie - report from Bad Nauheim. Page 365: "TAB 58 (Doc 2) Hdqtr. Intelligence Corps detachment US Army, Europe APO 178 11 May 1950 Memorandum to the Commanding Officer, Subject: BARBIE"

(24) "UNHOLY TRINITY" Mark Aarons and John Loftus, St. Martin's Press, NY 1990, Page 243: re. reorganization of the CIC 430th.

(25) STATE DEPARTMENT file 865.628/3-2648 "Yugoslav Inter ference With Vessels" US Political Advisor to the Commander, British US Zone, from free Territory of Trieste. Nat. Arch CRB "Yugoslav patrol vessels are... making a practice of machine-gunning and seizing Italian fishing vessels en route to Trieste... a "deliberate plan of the Yugoslavs to frighten fishermen from the markets of the British/United States Zones of the Free Territory. There have to date been eight recorded instances during March, 1948."
STATE DEPARTMENT file 860S.404/10-647, dispatch No. 17, October 6, 1947, US Political Advisor Allied Forces Headquarters. Nat. Arch CRB "Religious Persecution in Yugoslav Administered Territory." To: Secretary of State - From: Robert P, Joyce
"MURDER OF 230 PRIESTS REPORTED IN YUGOSLAV ANTI-CHURCH TERROR" "New York Times" 7/24/46, Page 1 & 8 by Camille M. Cianfarra
"UNHOLY TRINITY" Mark Aarons & John Loftus, St. Martin's Press, NY 1990. Pages 162-172, 214, 262-263, 280-281.

(26) State Department files "TRIESTE" 867N.01/6-1548 "Confidential" United States Political Advisor to the Commander British US Zone, No. 143 Subject: Paramount Pictures and the American Joint Distribution Committee Trieste.

CHAPTER 11

THE ASSASSINATION OF PRESIDENT KENNEDY

The Treason of I. G. Farben and the Dulles Gang

You can't be so stupid as to believe that the Jews were responsible for the death of Walter Hirsch, nor involved in the assassinations of Trieste's freedom fighters. Nor can you believe that Pope Pius was allied with the Nazis and responsible for the OPC's ratlines. Yet the picked over files from the State Department insinuate these possibilities, as did the FBI's Walter Wolf report on Headache/Boathill and the death of Walter Hirsch in the hands of "AGENT BARBER." You have to ask yourself, not only what is possible, but what is probable. The desperate Jews needed the ratlines to escape Europe as much as the Nazis and were not about to undermine the system. It is far more logical that "AGENT BARBER" was responsible for the death of Walter Hirsch serving the interest of the German Spartans, I. G. Farben and Turkul's Red Army. How is it that we have retained these insinuating files, but all the goodies on I. G. Farben's Nazis inside the Soviet Union are "missing" or "withdrawn"? I. G. Farben had much to fear from exposure of its treason against the Third Reich, a far greater motive to knock off Hirsch who was ratting on everyone.

So far, we have only circumstantial evidence on a Soviet biological warfare attack upon the United States through infested furs, and we need a witness who served inside the Soviet Union's biological warfare factories to testify. This was why it was so important to have Henry Tolkmith step forward, but he is dead. If someone could identify this man as Josef Mengele, would that help substantiate the author's theories? Who are and where are the other "dragon returnees" who could testify to the Soviet Union's BW program? Is Bernhard Von Bock still alive in Germany? Could he identify the real Henry Tolkmith?

Furthermore, the preponderance of "missing" and "withdrawn" documents regarding Soviet BW and CW collaboration that vanished just after the Kennedy assassination and Watergate may also help substantiate the author's theories. As bizarre as it sounds, we have to build our case on lack of evidence. We have the summaries on the State Department's purport cards, some withdrawal slips, index titles to the missing and destroyed OACSI files, and hidden copies of "destroyed" classified documents tucked away in public libraries, pointing to a mole and his counter mole at the very top of the intelligence community. Let's go back to the existing file on Paramount Pictures with Pello Levi in Trieste. There it sat, for all to see, its purport card and files accessible to all in the National Archives. Yet, coincidentally, other files the author sought on TRIESTE and its freedom fighters were missing, only the purport card summaries remain:

STATE DEPARTMENT file 860S.50/1-3048, telegram #46, "Regarding Survey Certain Project" January 30, 1948.
STATE DEPARTMENT file 861.8598/5-2548, telegram #132, "Mercantile Marine relations Between Yugoslavs and Russians." May 25, 1948.
STATE DEPARTMENT file 860S.1561/6-2348, telegram #366, "Shipping Trieste Port"

During the Nixon-Watergate resignation, newly appointed President Ford assigned his hand picked Vice President, Nelson Rockefeller, the task of reviewing campaign finance abuses in the CIA and Mexican banks. The Rockefeller Commission recruited old OPC hands to finger through the files, a farce. Other indexes to intelligence files simply vanished through internal agency reorganizations, according to John Loftus in "The Belarus Secret": "As a result, each American intelligence agency carefully maintains acres and acres of cavernous vaults under heavy guard without the remotest idea of their contents." (1) Had Rockefeller's crew also gone through State Department records on OPC history in Trieste, pulling out incriminating evidence of the OPC's Communist infiltration by Anton Turkul, deliberately implicating the Jews for its flop? Klaus Barbie was a Communist, but so were his handlers.

When Barbie moved to Bolivia, he took up the drug and illegal arms industry, financing Israel with weapons in the early years, until the Jews realized Barbie was also arming all of their terrorist enemies, triggering Beate Klarsfeld's hunt to extradite him back to France for trial as a war criminal. ODESSA, an organization of old Nazi war criminals in South America, had been heavily penetrated by Turkul's Headache/Boathill double agents, something Allan Ryan's book "Quite Neighbors" acknowledged with out mentioning Turkul's role. (2) The intelligence files that vanished after the Kennedy assassination have a direct connection to Allen Dulles, I. G.

Farben and Klaus Barbie.

The Kennedy family posed an enormous threat to Roosevelt's camou-flaged Republicans, Eisenhower, Rockefeller, and Dulles. Robert Kennedy and attorney Roy Cohn had served as assistants to Senator Joseph McCarthy on the Un-American Activities hearings, Cohn also serving as assistant prosecuting attorney in the William Z. Foster trial including furrier union chief, Irving Potash. As discussed in the previous chapter on the labor unions, Roy Cohn's biography on McCarthy cites Robert and Jack's father, Joseph, as having financed the ultra right wing McCarthy's political career. Joseph Kennedy had actually planned to run against President Roosevelt during the Great Depression, but in a slick move, Roosevelt appointed the senior Kennedy as ambassador to Great Britain, eliminating his opposition. This close knit cult of Irish Catholics was adamantly anti-Communist! Jack Kennedy had also attended the Congressional hearings along with Richard Nixon on the "Investigation of Communist Infiltration into the Fur Industry." It would be a logical conclusion to assume the Kennedys were privy to Amtorg's fur trade.

When the two presidential contenders, JFK and Nixon faced off, the Kennedys commandeered Texas Senator Lyndon Baines Johnson to carry the Southern states. This was a fatal alliance, for Johnson's political career had been financed by oil tycoon, Edwin Pauley, former lend-lease chief of the SS ELBRUS.(3) Pauley was also Standard Oil's business partner, Standard Oil, a subsidiary of I. G. Farben. By the time the Kennedy Administration took over, former President Eisenhower had already stacked the deck against JFK. Allen Dulles, I. G. Farben's patent lawyer, was directing the CIA's Bay of Pigs foiled invasion of Cuba and Adolf Heusinger, I. G. Farben's poison gas mentor and protector, was heading NATO. With the Cuban missile crisis around the corner, imagine America's fate under the Command of Heusinger! Did Kennedy know of I. G. Farben's secret gas alliance with the Soviet Union? He very well may have, once we examine the stack of destroyed and missing OACSI files, and establish a motive for murder. JFK fired CIA director, Allen Dulles. In retaliation, did Heusinger order the execution of JFK?

Jack Kennedy had more pressing problems than just concealing his entourage of illicit girl friends from his wife, Jackie. His health was quite poor. Raised on Cape Cod, between Boston and Old Lyme's fur and woolen textile industries, he developed "back problems." He hired the best physician available, someone he could trust, Dr. William Randolph Lovelace, Air Force intelligence officer from the Heidelberg Medical Center and NATO advisor. Lovelace was privy to the Luftwaffe medical experiments and Richard Kuhn's SOMAN gas research for I. G. Farben, serving as an

Army Air Force Intelligence officer after the war at Heidelberg's Medical Center.

The FBI and Air Force hold files on Lovelace. Here was an American hero who had served his country with great honor. Hoover searched high and low, seeking gossip to smudge Lovelace's reputation and credibility, and finally scored; one of Lovelace's classmates from the Mayo Clinic was a Communist! Nevertheless, Hoover had to clear Lovelace for White House service. FBI files include the Air Force Lovelace resume, his WW II service record, and post war employment. In 1947, Dr. Lovelace had served with the US Public Health Service Quarantine Division, surely privy to incoming ships. By 1950, Lovelace joined the New Mexico chapter of the Arthritis & Rheumatism Foundation, serving as a member on the board until his appointment to the White House. With Lyme disease and brucellosis both inducing arthritis, running rampant on Cape Cod, Lovelace was a perfect choice for JFK's back ailments as well as being appointed his "science and technical advisor." (4)

Leaving Heidelberg, Lovelace attended the Military Surgeon's Conference in Detroit with Air Force Surgeon Malcolm C. Grow; the topic of discussion being tropical diseases. (5) Even though the Dulles gang had destroyed the CIA's OPC index files, Lovelace would have known where to look on Nazi-Soviet collaboration in chemical and biological warfare through his NATO intelligence connections. Unfortunately for Hoover, Lovelace was not only very well informed, he was squeaky clean. Recall in this book's "Introduction" mention of Dr. Allen Steere's article in "Principles and Practice of Infectious Diseases" 2n Edition, (John Wiley and Sons Inc., 1985), citing the first case of Lyme disease reported in 1962, and the second in 1965 at Old Lyme. Who was this first case, and how did this spirochete become distinguished from Newcastle's disease? Recall Steere was an investigator for the CDC's epidemiology department. Did someone in the Kennedy family on Cape Cod have Lyme disease, and could Lovelace be trusted not to talk? Again, we can only speculate, but the turn of events strongly supports this hypothesis.

I. G. Farben had not given up on its quest to conquer the world if Hitler failed, nor had they ended their secret alliance with the Soviet Union. During WW II, after Senator Truman's Congressional inquiry into the alkali monopoly, the Department of the Treasury seized the stock of I. G. Farben's American subsidiary, Aniline Film Corporation. Even after the onset of the Cold War, when Germany became our new ally against the Red threat, the Department of the Treasury refused to return I. G.'s stock, fearing the re-organization of this monstrous cartel into a new international octopus, initiating World War III. Unabashed, I. G. Farben approached

President Kennedy through their new representative, Prince Radziwill, Jackie's brother-in-law, to have the stock returned. "Absolutely not." was the President's reply. Keeping in mind that one of the Radziwill princes, and we don't know which one, with his family, had served inside the elite Soviet POW camp along with BW expert Walter P. Schreiber and German Communist Party leader, General Von Paulus, we need ask ourselves if some of Jackie's in-laws were KGB operatives, trained to overthrow the US Government. (6)

On November 22, 1963, President Kennedy was assassinated, theoretically by lone gunman, Lee Harvey Oswald, suspected to be a double agent in the employ of Castro and the Communists. Robert Kennedy, next serving as President Johnson's Attorney General, said "Yes" to I. G. Farben's demands; the Aniline Film Company stocks were auctioned off to the highest bidder, Blyth & Company Syndicate, for $329,141,926.49. Was this a final victory for Bosch, Ilgner, Krauch, Ipatieff, Frossard, and the Soviet Union? (7)

Many authors have speculated upon the assassination of President Kennedy. The last place anyone would turn would be the "National Enquirer," November 22, 1983 twentieth anniversary edition on our national tragedy. A very lengthy debate ensued over a shadowy figure on the grassy knoll. No one takes this hyped up rag seriously, but this time, they may have got it right. Jeane Rene Souetre, a well known French terrorist and soldier of fortune, having once contemplated assassinating President deGaulle for granting independence to its colony, Algeria, coincidentally appeared in Dallas, Texas that fateful day and was on his way back to France just two days later. The "National Enquirer" interviewed Souetre, who cited another French criminal, Michael Mertz in Dallas that day. The "National Enquirer" also noted Washington attorney Bernard Fensterward Jr. unsuccessfully sued both the FBI and CIA for material on Jeane Rene Souetre. (8) Could NATO chief Adolf Heusinger have hired this French assassin to regain I. G.'s stocks?

Others have inadvertently implicated Souetre, such as Anthony Summers in "Official and Confidential: The Secret Life of J. Edgar Hoover." The Mafia's ties to pre-Castro Cuba and the OSS on the New York waterfront are public knowledge and have often been implicated in the assassination, but Klaus Barbie's ties are far less publicized. Castro had seized the very profitable gambling casinos and nationalized other American businesses in Havana under the revolution. Summers implicated the Mafia, a long standing target of the Kennedy Administration, as possible accomplices to "lone gunman," Lee Harvey Oswald, in the assassination. But Summers also unearthed the history of Oswald's associates, Guy Banister and

David Ferrie, who held ties to Allen Dulles' Anti-Castro operatives and to Barbie's Latin American drug cartel.

Banister, a "senior member of an Anti-Castro group," known as the "Friends of Democratic Cuba," was truly a sick man, suffering brain damage from an operation. Banister, a 20 year veteran of the FBI, retired in 1955, and joined the CIA, next setting up a detective agency in New Orleans on 531 Lafayette Street, its back door around the corner on 544 Camp Street. Le Harvey Oswald, in an attempt to penetrate the pro-Castro movement, published leaflets out of Banister's office, which included the Camp Street address on the back.

David Ferrie, a former Eastern Airlines pilot, appears in a photo with other Latin American drug smugglers, exposed in Al Martin's "The Conspirators," available through the internet, ALMARTINRAW.COM. Ferrie was a close personal friend to Banister since their CIA Anti-Castro days in the 60s. After the JFK assassination, Ferrie made a mad dash to retrieve his library card earlier lent to Oswald, fearing guilt by association. J. Edgar Hoover's biographer, Summers, reported Banister had met with a group of French terrorists plotting the assassination of President de Gaulle, and one can't but help wonder if this group included Jean Rene Souetre mentioned In "The National Enquirer." Banister would soon die of a heart attack after a lurid confrontation with private investigator, Jack Martin, where Banister beat Martin over the head with a .357 Magnum revolver. "The fracas started, according to Martin, when he asked Banister: "What are you going to do, kill me like you all did Kennedy?" Ferrie would later commit suicide in 1967, "after New Orleans District Attorney Jim Garrison had re-opened the case and was about to call him before a grand jury." (9)

Banister's cult to overthrow Castro had been organized through the CIA under Allen Dulles, who had extensive ties to Klaus Barbie's money laundering banks and drug trade through out the Caribbean. None of this will come to light until we uncover Richard Nixon's campaign financing scandals during Watergate. During the Nazi occupation of France, the Pouderie National du Bouchet was shot down and research confiscated on CW.(10) If ever there were a "French connection" in the Kennedy assassination case involving Jeane Rene Souetre, it would not have been directed through its government, but more likely through I. G. Farben's tentacles, Heusinger and the Dulles gang. The French Government and the Jews had a strong motive to capture Barbie in Bolivia who knew all the players. The French and the Jews weren't going to be left holding the bag on this one. France does not allow the death penalty, and the Israelis were perfectly willing to go along with his sentence of life imprisonment.

Big mouth Barbie was their trump card.

When President Johnson assembled the Warren Commission to investigate the Kennedy assassination, key material was overlooked regarding Guy Banister and Ferrie's relation to Lee Harvey Oswald.(11) LBJ had made a special point of selecting just the right members to sit in on the Commission, headed by Chief Justice Earl Warren, his Supreme Court now rid of Arthur Goldberg, the last surviving witness to the OSS's ties to the French underground. Amongst Warren's investigators were Senators Richard Russell and John Sherman Cooper; Representatives Gerald Ford and Hale Boggs; also former CIA director Allen Dulles; and former High Commissioner to Germany, John J. McCloy, the Rockefeller's former bank president. Rockefeller's Standard Oil was also a subsidiary of I. G. Farben. (12) Nixon would appoint Ford to be his second Vice President, when Spiro Agnew was forced to resign because of tax fraud. After Nixon's Watergate resignation, Ford would be appointed President of the United States. Ford had ascended to the highest levels of government without ever being elected. An insider to the Warren Commission, Ford was a safe bet. Smell like a cover-up yet? I. G. Farben had all its bases covered.

Just three months into the new year after the Kennedy assassination, Adolf Heusinger resigned NATO and most of his top generals resigned the West German government. A tiny itsy bitsy blurb, tucked away on the inside pages of the "New York Times," acknowledge the coup d'etat on March 29th, 1964, page 3, column 1: "Bonn is Retiring Older Generals." God forbid the truth leak out and undermine NATO, the backbone of our Western alliance against the Soviet Union! No one was following these generals all the way back to Moscow, or, almost no one. David Rockefeller made a special vacation trip just after the assassination that was most out of the ordinary:

"NONE DARE CALL IT CONSPIRACY" Gary Allen & Larry Abraham, Concord Press, Rossmore, CA 1971 - Chapter 6 "The Rockefellers and the Reds"

"David Rockefeller, president of the Chase Manhattan Bank and chairman of the board of the Council of Foreign Relations, took a vacation in the Soviet Union. This is a peculiar place for the "world's greatest imperialist" to take his vacation since much of Communist propaganda deals with taking all of David's wealth away from him and distributing it to "the people." A few days after Rockefeller ended his "vacation" in the Kremlin, Nakita Khruschev was recalled from a vacation at a Black Sea resort to hear that he had been fired... did David Rockefeller journey to the Soviet Union to fire an employee?"

Or, to the contrary, did David Rockefeller journey to the USSR to facilitate the installment of his employees, the new Secretary General of the Communist Party, Leonid Brezhnev, who survived Beria's gassings at Suchomi and Taupse, and President Alexi Kosygin, former Minister of Soyuzpushnina's textile industry? Suddenly, voices of opposition to the Soviet Union's biological warfare program began to vanish at an alarming rate. The "New York Times" "Obituaries" reported General Douglas MacArthur's death April 6th, 1964 at the Walter Reed Army Medical Center, the same hospital where General Hoyte Vandenberg had parished a decade before him. Kennedy's physician, Dr. Lovelace would soon follow. As the Kennedy assassination investigation expanded, the Air Force requested the Johnson White House for permission to release the FBI's clearance files on Lovelace:

WILLIAM RANDOLPH LOVELACE, II FBI file 161-1637-39, Nov. 15, 1965
4D 36 14 887:8 November 1965
William Randolph Lovelace, II
DOB· 30 December 1907
SPECIAL REQUEST
Honorable Marvin Watson
Special Assistant to the President
Attention· Mrs. Mildred Stegall
The White House, Washington, D.C.

"Dear Mr. Watson:
1. A security investigation is being conducted by the Air force on the above individual. Officials of the FBI have advised that background investigations were conducted by the FBI and a summary of the investigations were furnished to the White House in October 1961. These officials have referred us to your office for authority to release the reports of investigation to the Air Force.
2. Your cooperation in authorizing the FBI to release the reports of investigation to this District Office will be appreciated."
FOR THE COMMANDER
Signed: E. F. Swint, Chief, National Agency, Checks Division

Just a few weeks after the Air Force letter to the White House, William Randolph Lovelace was dead. His small plane crashed just outside Aspen Colorado while returning from a ski trip with his wife, Mary, and pilot, Milton Brown. High in the Rockies, uninjured, they froze to death, rescue teams unable to reach them in time. (13) This was an eery, coincidence, for the new head of the US Air Force Medical Center, Hubertus Strughold, had previously experimented on live humans in the concentration camps, freezing them to death, as reported in Leo Alexander's CIOS report "Treatment of Shock From Extreme Exposure to Cold, Including Electroencephalography." Strughold had been assigned to collate the Luftwaffe medical research at the Heidelberg Medical Center just after the war under Air Force Surgeon General, Malcolm C. Grow where Lovelace was also employed as an intelligence officer. Strughold then immigrated to America to assist the Air Force in its new Aero-Medical Center, Lovelace becoming Air Force intelligence liaison to NATO.

With Lovelace's death vanished an incredible number of OACSI files, the remains accessioned to the National Archives in 1967, four years after the assassination of President Kennedy, and four years after the expiration dates of their withdrawal slips for TOP SECRET classified documents. The author has attempted to list these "missing" or "destroyed" files, totaling over forty, dealing in Soviet and German chemical and biological warfare, only a few of which still remain classified, (see APPENDIX). If Dr. Lovelace supplied these reports to President Kennedy regarding I. G. Farben's history when it requested the return of its stocks, also unlocking the history of Kennedy's personal health, then who destroyed the OACSI files? It is easy to see why Lovelace's death would follow in the wake of the hundreds of others after JFK's assassination.

How extensive was the Spartans' network in ordering assassination of the Communist Party's arch enemies, such as Robert Kennedy and Pope John Paul II? East Germany's Secret Police ran the Grey Wolves, an assemblage of Arab youths totally oblivious to the WW II atrocities that Stalin and Beria had committed against their own people. This cult of hooligans was used to counter any pro-western movements in the Soviet Union's Central Asian Republics, a cult indoctrinated on the propaganda of "redistribution of the wealth," the "worker's paradise," and all the rest of Marxists' baloney used to trick the poor and destitute into selling themselves back into slavery. Did the Spartans have operatives assisting them in the United States? Was President Carter's Justice Department's Office of Special Investigations intended to prosecute these chameleons? After all, how does one distinguish a "little turnip" from a "big turnip" or a "reverse radish" from a "real radish"?

After the assassination of John Fitzgerald Kennedy, Lyndon Johnson ascended to the presidency, one of America's leading hypocrites of all time. Johnson's political career rising from Texas senator to the vice presidency had been financed by the slime factor, oil tycoon Edwin Pauley, the same man in charge of lend-lease shipping when the SS ELBRUS docked in Philadelphia with 426 tons of Soviet furs. Pauley's influence over LBJ is only speculative, although FBI holdings on Pauley shed some light. The author was able to secure the "lost" "100" Pauley file and others. President Johnson had requested an FBI clearance for Pauley's appointment to the United Nations in 1967. Pauley's ties to I. G. Farben through the Rockefeller's Standard Oil during WW II, as well as his Mexican oil ventures surfaced in the FBI investigation, but nothing impeded his appointment. His health was poor, suffering arthritis in his back just as former President Kennedy had suffered. Drinking three martinis at lunch and often falling asleep at meetings, some of Pauley's associates felt he was not up to the job. Yet his friends and associates vouched for his shrewd business prowess and patriotism and clearance was granted in flying colors. (14) His meteoric rise to the top in the oil industry as noted in the FBI's "100" file is highly questionable, one former acquaintance testified:

EDWIN WENDELL PAULEY FBI file 100-57068 July 19, 1945
Page 1: "(Blackout) recalled that contrary to news releases, Mr. Pauley was not a successful businessman and oil executive... On the contrary, Pauley, who ran the Petrol Oil Company, was "unable to pay his rent" and only through the machinations of the Standard Oil Company who bought up a group of oil wells belonging to Pauley's company at "five times their market value" was Pauley able to meet his current obligations. (Blackout) went on to say that under the auspices of STANDARD OIL COMPANY, PAULEY spent a million dollars in Sacramento lobbying certain legislation which had to do with oil companies. The bill in question was known as the "Atkinson Bill." At the time PAULEY was soliciting funds for the Democratic Party..."

On page 3 of this above "100" file report, it was noted that Pauley, as Democratic National Committeeman, "wiped out the $750,000 deficient in 1942... and he will probably slide into the Navy's secretaryship when Secretary of the Navy Forrestal resigns." According to FBI files 100-57068 and 161-4895, Pauley had befriended J. Edgar Hoover in the 1940s. But most peculiar is the suspect attempt of the Communist Party's propaganda machine, "The Daily Worker" to threaten Pauley's health with Newcastle disease just after the docking of the SS ELBRUS:

EDWIN WENDELL PAULEY FBI file 100-57068-A DECLASSI-
FIED 10/20/97

"This is a clipping from page 7 of "THE DAILY WORKER" dated 2-10-46 clipped at the seat of Government." "Oily Smell is Pauley" by Travis K. Hedrick

WASHINGTON - Oil has always been able to ruffle the neck feathers of the political chickens in Washington and the petroleum is pouring at the capitol as the senate naval affairs committee wades into the nomination of Edwin W. Pauley for Undersecretary of the Navy..."

Communist pride themselves on their linguistic skills, "reciprocal altruism through language," their left-dominant sided brains elevating them to racial superiority in this "human" art of communication. One need not be a poet laureate to see this as Bolshevik blackmail. It would not be long before President Johnson would send Dr. Michael Boris Shimkin to the United Nations, requesting FBI clearance and New York City's Police Department BOSSI clearance. Between Pauley and Shimkin, Roosevelt's old pawns were still securely in place under Johnson. No one could track Kennedy's assailants back to I. G. Farben.

We need to take a closer look at Johnson's "Great Society" Here was a man who publicly preached civil rights and privately sneered at racial equality. To continue segregation without appearing to advocate it, Johnson created an enormous welfare state trapping blacks in the ghetto, unedu-cated, propertyless, and crowded into government subsidized tenements for generations to follow, in a game of survival of the fittest, "Social Darwin-ism." Socialism is like being a roach trapped in a garbage bag, guaranteed food for life with no control over the situation. Johnson attempted to create a huge new voting block using these mascots for misery. Fed up with the Democrat's hypocrisy, blacks would emerge on the radical right in the next generation.

To balance the inequities of slum life, psychiatrist Dr. Fredric Wertham marched to Washington as an advocate for school bussing, further inducing white flight! You remember Wertham from Franz Jahnel's Spirochete and Serology Department at the Kaiser Wilhelm Institute for Brain Research, studying chicken brains? With 44% of all America's Lyme cases residing in New York City, Wertham was perfectly situated to keep score of the city's increasing madness and potential race riots. First, Wertham headed the massive sprawling Bellevue Insane Asylum, but his work did not end there. Next he moved on to direct the psychiatric services at Queens General and became chief resident psychiatrist at John Hopkins. The clincher of his compassion culminated in setting up Lafarge Clinic for the blacks in Harlem. To help with Johnson's hype in creating a welfare state, devoid of private property, Fredric Wertham published:

"A SIGN FOR CAIN, AN EXPLORATION OF HUMAN VIO-
LENCE"

Fredric Wertham, Macmillan Co., NY 1966; 'Climates for Violence'

Page 92: "Ghettos are monuments to racism... In New York City,
people used to go slumming in Harlem ghettos, in night clubs located in
blocks where the inhabitants lived in tenements infested by rats, which bit
sleeping children... Outbreaks of violence in a ghetto are like bouts of fever
in the course of a chronic disease... race riots are most important violent
social phenomenon... Every major race riot is an abortive revolution...

Page 93: The recent riots in Harlem, Brooklyn, Rochester, Elizabeth,
and Philadelphia were especially instructive. Almost a year before the most
destructive race riot in the United States history, in the Watts district of
Los Angeles, I wrote in the British magazine "XXth Century": "They were
predicted and predictable, just as we can now predict that there will be
further riots. Their violence has remained unresolved."

Page 95: If a man in Harlem sees his infant child being bitten by the
descendants of the same rats that bit him when he was a child, it is hard
for him to have a firm belief in nonviolence..."

"A Sigh for Cain"? Who, Bob Cane, illustrator of Batman and Alfred, the butler? Was this the voice of another Spartan, advocating the
destruction of America from within? Fredric Wertham ranted and raved
against the violence in the media, including Bob Cane's comic books.
Would Wertham expose the collaboration between the KWI for Brain
Research doctors in Berlin and Moscow? No. Would he uncover the
history of Amtorg's fur auctions in New York? No. What was behind all
of these neurological manifestations? Dr. Leo Alexander's CIOS report
"Neuropathology and Neurophysiology" cited Franz Jahnel's research on
spirochete infected soldiers going crazy from diphtheria vaccinations. Are
our vaccines inducing madness? The controversy over mandatory vaccination and its ramifications is well documented in Barbara Lee Fisher's "Shot
in the Dark" published by "The Next City" summer edition of 1999. Her
long crusade to protect Americans from adverse reactions to vaccinations
established the National Vaccine Information Center. She asked "Does
the state have the moral authority to command that citizens give their
lives against their will for what the state has determined to be the greater
good?... If the state cannot determine which individuals are genetically
or otherwise at high risk for being injured or dying from vaccines, does
state-forced vaccination translate into a de facto medical experiment and

an immoral application of utilitarianism?"

One Sunday night in the fall, a local Salt Lake City TV news station broadcast from the Delta Center a news blip. One-hundred-forty-two patients had died between 1988 and 1998 in Connecticut insane asylums; the state was investigating. How many of these victims had Lyme disease? It would be worth noting that Connecticut's State Insane Asylum at Norwich was headed by an East German psychiatrist, Hans Langhammer, who at first was repeatedly denied entrance to America because of his Communist party activities. How many died under his care, we only speculate, for the oldest records have been destroyed. How many died at the Lafarge Clinic under Fredric Wertham? How many old Spartans had infiltrated the American medical community while Nelson Rockefeller served as Deputy Chief of the Health Department?

Were America's Lyme victims being slowly and deliberately exterminated by allergic reactions to vaccinations, being finished off in the state insane asylums? Was this the same "murder by madness" that had plagued Frank Wisner, Joseph McCarthy, James Forrestal and Al Capp? Were all true conservative voices being systematically silenced by a radical left-wing medical community? Were the mad students at Littleton Colorado's Columbine High School the medical communities' latest victims? Was there a deliberate attempt to incite violence through vaccination amongst our youth in an attempt to frighten Americans into disarmament and a total gun ban? Had America raised questions over the origin of Lyme disease and the effects of vaccination, would the rest of the Soviet block have raised questions too, tracing its troubles back to Suchomi and Beketovka? We can only speculate, but the author can assure you, human will can triumph over socialist "science."

Just what was Watergate all about? The slime and fur factor passed from one presidential administration to the next. Martin Cruz Smith's "Gorky Park" touching on Watergate, involved fictional characters as well as real ones. "Arkady" personified the fur dealing Armand Hammer, one of Richard Nixon's biggest illegal campaign contributors as well as the fictional detective "Kirwill" cast as Richard Nixon's real-life body guard, John Caulfield. Nixon's private eye, Tony Ulasewicz is Tony Ulasewicz. (15) Ulasewicz, the son of Russian immigrants, had served on New York Police department's "Red Squad," an anti-Communist riot control elite guard since the 1940s, attending the William Z. Foster Trial et al with furrier Irving Potash. The Red Squad became BOSSI, the Bureau of Special Services Investigations, the same organization that cleared Shimkin and Pauley for President Johnson's assignments to the UN.

Tony Ulasewicz would publish his own account of his Watergate venture, "The President's Private Eye," documenting his days as Nixon's bag man and detective. Nixon's White House attorney, John Dean, with ties to illegal gambling and prostitution rings through his wife, Kathy Dieter, ordered the bugging of the Democrat's National Campaign headquarters at the Watergate Hotel. Ex-FBI agent Gordon Liddy, and past CIA operatives, James McCord, Bernard Barker, Virgilio Gonzalez, Eugenio Martinez, and Frank Sturgis were instructed to execute the clumsy break-in. Gonzalez and Martinez were Cuban nationals, left overs from Dulles' botched Bay of Pigs invasion.

There is much more in Ulasewicz's book than just Watergate. Ulasewicz's previous investigation into the kidnapping and murder of Jesus de Galindez, an anti-Castro FBI informant and Columbia University professor who had published a book against dictator Rafael Trujillo of the Dominican Republic, should have forewarned Nixon not to use the Latin American banks to launder illegal campaign contributions. Galindez had also informed the FBI on the history of the OSS in hiring Communist Spanish Basque separatists to facilitate the French Underground's efforts to defeat the Nazis. (16) What did Galindez know about Klaus Barbie's early days in the French underground? Ulasewicz is dead, so we don't know, but Turkul's drug triangle stretched from the Soviet Union's Red Army GRU to Barbie in Bolivia, and the Dulles gang in America, embezzling everything our crooked politicians were depositing.

One need only pick up Len Colodny and Robert Gettlin's "Silent Coup: the Removal of a President" for a full history of Nixon's dastardly deeds. Caulfield and Ulasewicz were tied to Nixon, as was John Dean's gang of money launderers and illegal gambling racketeers. Congress passed new campaign finance legislation and instigated Nixon's impeachment. Here we are, some thirty years later, back at square one. Phil Bailley, an insider to Dean's gambling exploits, would be dragged into St. Elizabeth's insane asylum under false accusations of sexual perversion, only to emerge weeks later, virtually destroyed, a discredited witness against Watergate. But Colodny and Gettlin go much further exposing the extent of Nixon's corruption and his money laundering of illegal campaign contributions through Mexican banks. The FBI had actually seized cancelled checks from Mexican banks, and knew who the other depositors were, putting the CIA on the hot seat. The committee to Re-Elect the President "CREEP" was in deep dodo. (17) Recall that famous Nixon line "I am not a crook?"

The FBI was hot on the CIA's tail, for the old Dulles gang set Nixon up to be impeached out of naivete. J. Edgar Hoover sent a special mission to La Paz to investigate Klaus Barbie and help the French with their cause. Back in the early 1970s, with his drug rings from ODESSA, Barbie began to make secret escapades to North America under the alias of Klaus Altman. Up till now, Barbie had basked under the protection of Bolivian President Suarez, who refused to extradite the old weasel to France.

Back in 1984, the author asked the FBI for holdings on Julius Robert Oppenheimer to see what inside knowledge he held on Nazi war criminals and the State Department's ratlines. The FBI holdings ran into thousands of pages, and agent G. R. Schweickhardt offered the Klaus Barbie files for a starter on Nazi war criminals. After receiving these Barbie files, totally clueless as to their significance, the author forwarded them on to retired OSI agent, John Loftus who had been recently interviewed on a "60 Minutes" documentary, "The Nazi Connection." Loftus had expressed quite an interest in the Barbie files and was just about ready to give secret Congressional testimony on the Iran-Contra Affair. Only years later did the author realize their significance when Loftus asked for a duplicate copy, having lost his secretary and the files. The FBI forwarded a new copy of the Barbie files to the author in 1998. These files, not included in the Justice Department's report: "Klaus Barbie and the United States Government," are now available to the public over the FBI's web site. Barbie's trips to the United States between 1969 and 1970, included New Orleans, San Francisco, Houston, and Galveston, Texas. A Canadian ex-convict, Robert G. Wilson, attempting a biography on Barbie, had actually made a tape recording of his interviews with his subject. (18)

Only until a change in Bolivian politics, in 1983, with President Suarez being ousted by a more liberal Siles Zuarzo, could Beate Klarsfeld and the French Government's request for Barbie's extradition be fulfilled. This sent the Republican Party into panic. Clues emerge in a series of FBI Barbie files excluded from the William French Smith's Justice Department report "Klaus Barbie and the United States Government" that Agent G. R. Schweickhardt had offered the author in 1984. In 1972, the FBI's Washington headquarters contacted its San Francisco Branch to acquire Russian and Lithuanian newspaper articles regarding Barbie's whereabouts. San Francisco supported a large White Russian emigre community resettled from the Bolshevik Revolution. One article in "Voice of the Homeland" published the location of Klaus Barbie; the FBI approached a San Franciscan Supervisor to locate a copy:

KLAUS BARBIE FBI file 105-221892-16, dated 3/28/83. "This document is classified "Secret" in its entirety unless otherwise noted."

"Reference is made to the letter of William J. Anderson, director General Government Division, General Accounting Office (GAO), Washington, DC dated March 2, 1986 to the Honorable William H. Webster, director, FBI... [regarding] review of documents concerning Gestapo chief Klaus Barbie who was recently extradited from Bolivia to France. The central files of this bureau reveal the following information, which may relate to the subject of your inquiry...

On September 28, 1972, our San Francisco, California, Office requested that current issues of Lithuanian and Russian language publication "Voice of the Homeland" published by the Soviet Committee on Cultural Relations with Compatriots Abroad be translated from Russian into English. The translation of these Russian publications was completed. On page 7 of one of these Russian publications was a report by V. Vesensky from Lima, Peru, which dealt with the many "Faces of the Butcher of Lyon," Klaus Hartmann-Barbie who was hiding out from justice in South America. 100-341862-2597.

On July 18, 1973, Radio Panamerica, La Paz, Bolivia, announced that the Bolivian Supreme Court had approved the extradition of Altmann to Peru. (Whole paragraph blacked out.) On 9/28/72, our San Francisco Office requested that current issues of Lithuanian and Russian language publications "Voice of the Homeland" be translated into English, which was done and returned to San Francisco on 11/22/72.

On 2/25/83, Supervisor (Blackout) San Francisco, advised that a search of their file concerning these publications failed to locate them. On 2/28/83, Supervisor (Blackout) secretary advised that the publications, one of which contains an article regarding Klaus Hartmann-Barbie, had not been found (u) 100-341862-2597. The GAO representative referred to in the memorandum is Mr. John Tipton."

Who was the San Francisco Supervisor who could shed light on this story? We can only guess. Harvey Milk, the gay Supervisor, along with Mayor Mosconi would soon be assassinated by Supervisor Dan White. Dan White, a former policeman, was declared mentally ill, stoned on a diet of junk food, and sentenced to just four years in prison. White's case became known as the famous "Twinkie Defense." Once released from prison, Dan White committed suicide. Only in San Francisco, only in San Francisco! Those next in line for the mayorship were the top vote getters, the popular Supervisors Quentin Kopp and Diane Feinstein. There were numerous others also serving on the city's council. The above files, continued with the history of the FBI's La Paz office in Bolivia, maintained between 1971 and 1974, then shut down, its personnel transferred to Buenos Aires in Argentina. The Barbie hunt came to a close with the death of FBI Director, J. Edgar Hoover, his biographer Anthony Summers speculating Hoover had been poisoned. Barbie FBI file (105-221892-12), amongst the collection of Agent Schweickhard's material, noted that the Nazi hunters in pursuit of Barbie turned their attention to Josef Mengele. A "Jewish avenger squad" had tracked the "doctor of death" to a small Paraguayan town, later found with "their throats cut from ear to ear, floating down the Parama River" in the style of Colombian drug lord executions. Another investigator attempting a biography on Barbie was a young Californian, Mary Moon, who was killed after receiving FBI files on her subject. Mary Moon's mother returned her documents to FBI headquarters.

Was there a connection between this "Josef Mengele" and Klaus Barbie? Yes, this author is convinced. This particular Brazilian "Mengele," whom this author suspects to be Karl Mengele, Josef's brother, may very well be the ellusive Dr. Engeles of Sao Paulo, Henry Tolkmith's espionage contact to the Soviet Union. The Brazilian "Mengele" is exposed by his biographers, Gerald Posner and John Ware as Barbie's drug partner in ODESSA. The old German flying ace, Hans Rudel, was the missing link between the two war criminals, having arranged accommodations for Mengele in Brazil. (19) The Mengele family in Germany had made arrangements through ODESSA connections to house their fugitive son. The Justice Department report further corroborates Hans Rudel assisting "Mengele" but stops short of introducing Hans Rudel's ties to Klaus Barbie. Perhaps they weren't looking very hard since other authors and reporters were able to uncover the connection in La Paz:

"IN THE MATTER OF JOSEF MENGELE" OSI report to Attorney General, by Neal Sher and Eli Rosembaum, 1992.

Page 130-131: "Following the 1985 discovery of Mengele's body, it became clear that, while in Brazil, he had benefited from the assistance of several people in addition to his family in Guenzburg. Most important of these was Wolfgang Gerhard, an Austrian who had settled in Brazil in 1948. Hans Rudel apparently introduced Mengele to Gerhard, who in turn, introduced him to two families, the Stammers and Bosserts. These families provided Mengele with companionship and a place to live in the Sao Paulo area. Wolfgang Gerhard and Hans Sedlmaier then the General manager of the Mengele family business served as mediators when conflicts arose between Mengele and his protectors. Gerhard also gave Mengele his identity card, and as will be discussed below, Mengele was ultimately buried under Gerhard's name in a grave which had been purchased by Gerhard, supposedly for his own use."

Murphy's "Butcher of Lyon" cites the famed Nazi hunter, Simon Weisenthal's history of ODESSA, the Kamerandenwerk organization's involvement with Klaus Barbie and Hans Ulrich Rudel in La Paz running arms smuggling operations through the Transmaritima Corporation. This was most peculiar in Bolivia, a land locked nation. (20) Klaus Barbie's drug connections are also detailed in "Inside the League" by Scott and Jon Anderson. These two apprentice reporters under the famed columnist, Jack Anderson, ventured to Latin America to document the Communist infiltration of WACL, the World Anti-Communist League. WACL was founded by South Koreans and Taiwanese to counter the Communist threat from China, North Korea, and the Soviet Union. This international band of soldiers of fortune and freedom fighters, including the Moonies, a religious cult headed by Reverend Sun Moon in the munitions manufacturing business, blundered by picking up Barbie's bandits in ODESSA which had joined "CAL."

The Latin American Anti-Communist Confederation "CAL," WACL's subsidiary, held its annual conference in Buenos Aires including "several celebrities among the audience, including John Carbaugh, an aide to North Carolina Senator Jesse Helms, and Stefano delle Chiaie, an Italian terrorist wanted for countless murders and bombings throughout Europe. Chiaie had made the journey from his asylum in Bolivia, where he was allegedly in a cocaine smuggling partnership with Klaus Barbie..." (21) According to the Anderson brothers, some of WACL's double agent membership evolved into agent provocateurs, torturing neutral peasants into becoming radical left wing radicals.

As far back as the Mexican revolution of 1910, a counter-revolutionary force, the "Tecos" was formed by wealthy land lords. Early Mexico was virtually a feudalistic country, like Europe two hundred years ago before our American revolution. Mexico's revolutionaries' mistake was to chose Communism over democracy and oust their feudalistic land-lords. The Catholic Church has been caught in the middle, advocating strong land reform but taking an adamant stand against Communism. The Tecos made the tragic flaw of linking up with Barbie and ODESSA, the old Nazis' only ambition was to embezzle funds for Turkul's Red Army GRU and perpetuate war, economic turmoil, and disease till millions died for the cause. Whose cause was insignificant, as long as they died. Nicolai's "Biology of War" was in full swing as he watched from the side lines in Chile. Brucellosis and madness were rampant in South America. Coincidentally, the Soviets had also been dealing in animal hides for decades as shown in the US State Department files on Russian shipping. The post WW II State Department files cross-referenced with US Health Department correspondence include numerous Latin American conferences on brucellosis.

Tecos' contemporary political front began in the 1950s, renaming itself FEMACO (Mexican Anti-Communist Federation), using Raimundo Guerro to organize its new recruits on Mexican University campuses. The Anderson brothers saga on WACL's penetration continues: "Operating under the front group FEMACO, the Tecos' power within the League became enormous," making Guerrero executive board member, "with little or no review by the League's Asian godfathers" eventually taking over CAL leadership. (22) WACL, CAL, and the Tecos' had been hijacked by the Soviet Union's double dealing Nazi war criminals. But how could they know? Turkul's and Barbie's history with the OPC's Headache/Boathill was classified information.

Brendan Murphy's "The Butcher of Lyon" not only exposes Barbie's drug cartel inside ODESSA, but also their intelligence gathering on Communist subversion for Bolivia's right wing dictators. In turn, Bolivian intelligence passed this same information on to the US Army and CIA. Were Roaxer and Engeles, (Henry Tolkmith's contacts), also ODESSA agents, feeding intelligence to the Russians? ODESSA appears to have been a revolving door for all parties interested. Anton Turkul's Russian ratlines had stacked the deck. Biographer Brendan Murphy obtained his material on Barbie from interviews with journalist Peter McFarren, an American correspondent for the Associated Press in La Paz. The AP reporter fingered Bolivia's Ministry of Interior as the intelligence community's missing link. Amazingly, the US Justice Department seemed oblivious, insisting Barbie had been dropped after his CIC escapades:

"THE BUTCHER OF LYON" Brendan Murphy, Empire Books, NY 1983
Page 293: "Allan Ryan's Justice Department report categorically denies that Barbie worked for the CIA in South America. The report is probably accurate in that Barbie never met or spoke with the CIA, but some observers in La Paz believe that the CIA connection was made indirectly through the Bolivian government."
Page 294: "He [the Bolivian Minister of the Interior] gave them [the American Embassy] regular reports on what Barbie was feeding them.... They wanted to have more of it. They knew the source was Barbie. He's absolutely certain of that."

Murphy further indicated former Bolivian President Rene Barreintos Ortuno's "government was working in conjunction with the CIA and anti-Castro Cuban exiles" responsible for the execution of Che Guevara and ousting his guerrilla insurgency when Hugo Banzar Suarez deposed

Ortuno by military coup. (23) Now we have established a connection between the CIA, Bolivian intelligence, Klaus Barbie, and anti-Castro Cuban exiles. Were Nixon's Cuban Nationals facilitating the Watergate break-in for CREEP also tied to Nixon's money laundering in Mexican banks and Barbie in Bolivia? Where do Banister and Ferrie fit into this picture of Anti-Castro rebels and Barbie's bandits? Were the remnants of the old Dulles gang setting up Tricky Dick for the assassination of Kennedy, exempting Heusinger and Brezhnev from the plot? Dulles was a wizard at implicating others, the Jews, the Pope, the Mafia, etc., etc. and so forth.

Nixon's detective, Tony Ulasewicz, leery of the looming Mexican banking scandal, may have saved our Treasury Department from further embarrassment. He began to investigate Nixon's nomination of Mrs. Romana Banuelos for Secretary of the Treasury, eventually foiled when the press uncovered her hiring illegal aliens for her own private business along the California-Mexican border. Accordingly, the "illegal aliens were giving Nixon a headache." As in Operation Headache/Boathill? (24) The ex-New York BOSSI cop had the inside scoop on the friction between the FBI monitoring Dulles' gambling casinos and banks throughout the Caribbean. Nixon used Ulasewicz and then hung him out to dry. Were CREEP's Latin American and Asian contributions into Mexican banks being embezzled by Barbie's bandits in ODESSA? Where did the money go from there? Russia? Red China? Castro's Cuba? International terrorists? Greed has no boundaries. Tony Ulasewicz's co-author, Stuart McKeever, is writing a second, more detailed account his friend's investigation of the Jesus de Galindez kidnapping and the Caribbean banking scandal. Hopefully, McKeever may shed further light on the Dulles gang's connection to the Kennedy assassination and Watergate and Klaus Barbie.

The whole reputation of the CIA was at stake after Watergate. Newly appointed President Ford assigned Edwin Pauley's old oil partner, George Bush, to rescue the CIA. After assuming the directorship in 1976 with only a few months to go before a change in administrations, Bush discovered another insidious plot in the making. Dulles' CIA was brimming with horror stories. James Jesus Angleton, formerly assigned to the State Department's Italian desk during WW II, had later collated the Vatican's "Vessel Files" for Dulles' CIA. As more and more Nazis were proving to be Soviet double agents, Angleton conceived a plot to frame Pope Pius for the OPC's failures. The OPC's "dragon returnees" smuggled out of Russia would be added into previous "Vessel files" regarding Pope Pius' Black Orchestra. The Pope proved a better patsy than Paramount Pictures for the failures at Trieste and future atrocities in Latin America. Next, Angleton was appointed to the CIA's Israeli desk, which he severely mis-managed during the Israeli-Arab war, leaving the Israelis to fend for themselves. The plot to frame the Pope with Angleton's bogus additions was uncovered by a Catholic historian, Father Robert Graham while writing Freedom of Information requests to the CIA. While comparing original Vatican records to Angleton's records, the additions became obvious. Newly appointed CIA Director, George Bush, acting upon former director James Schlesinger's wishes, ordered Angleton to clean out his desk and vamoose. (25)

After snuffing out the CIA's little faux pas, Bush would be confronted with an even bigger disaster. The Iran Contra Affair was looming upon the horizon. And once again, Klaus Barbie's bandits were in the middle of it. Worse, in between Republican Presidents, the Democrat's Jimmy Carter scored an election in 1976. His first move was to create the Justice Department's Office of Special Investigations to track down Nazi war criminals in America and extradite them to their homelands for prosecution. Having trained the Israelis in weapon technology as a young Army intelligence officer, John Loftus joined Carter's OSI for its first four years, hoping to rid America of its war criminals and double agents alike. Carter was forced out of office by the Iranian hostage crisis, and the Republicans seized the opportunity to placate the irate Ayatollah whose revolution established the Moslem Fundamentalists securely in power. The first thing the Ayatollah Khomeini did when Rockefeller's backed Shah was removed, was hang ten thousand Communists.

The day Reagan was inaugurated, Khomeini released the hostages. With the arms for hostages deals in the making, John Loftus resigned the OSI, while his co-worker Allan Ryan moved into the directorship. Loftus published a history of the OPC's flop in 1982 in his "Belarus Secret" and his efforts to prosecute Belorussian Nazi war criminals allied with both the Nazis and the Soviet Union. Next, he would make secret Congressional testimony, initiating the Iran Contra investigation.

WACL's CAL had been hired to train the Contras against General Ortega's Communist coup in Nicaragua. The Contras desperately needed money. The profits raised from arms sold to Iran in hopes of releasing the hostages, would be diverted to the Contras, irregardless that this prompted Hezbulah to snatch even more American hostages. This was a harebrained plot from the beginning. Reagan's National Security Council appointed an old Green Beret, Oliver North, to be the Contra's fund raiser, just as the OPC had hired the young Ronald Reagan to solicit funds for its freedom fighters in Trieste. Thousands of patriotic Americans would deposit their hard earned savings into the Contras' account, only for the money to vanish. Nothing had been learned from the escapades of Nixon's CREEP.

Barbie worked for ODESSA, ODESSA, in turn, worked for CAL,

and CAL worked for WACL training the Contras. Barbie was a Communists, ODESSA was full of Communist, and CAL and WACL had been penetrated. To put it simply, the Contras had been penetrated. Consequently, the Contras never got their money. WACL President, General John Singlaub, exposed the embezzlement in his autobiography, "Hazardous Duty," citing 48 million dollars had been collected in proceeds from the Iranian financier, Hakim, through arms sales, and an additional 18 million dollar profit from Hawk surface-to-air missile sales, totaling $66,000,000.00. Yet the Contras only received 5 million dollars out of the 66 million. No one could account for the missing money! Oliver North pointed a finger at WACL, and Singlaub pointed his finger at Olly's Swiss bank accounts. (26) Neither understood ODESSA had been penetrated by the Soviet Union.

President Reagan appointed Bill Casey, his old OPC partner, to direct the CIA. Despite the fact that Congress had forbidden funding the Contras by passing the Boland Amendment, CIA Director, Bill Casey, along with National Security Council chair, Robert McFarlane and George Bush, heading the Special Situation Group under the National Security Council went about circumnavigating the Constitution. Aarons and Loftus in their "Secret War Against the Jews," hold George Bush, Senior fully accountable for the debacle. (27) But this author disagrees in part; George Bush, Senior had only served as CIA Director in 1976 for just a few months before a change in administrations, hardly enough time to be briefed on Anton Turkul's penetration of ODESSA. The full extent of Allen Dulles' damage to the CIA through Anton Turkul had yet to be fully assessed. Bush Senior may have been over zealous in administering the new SSG, "White House within the White House," as Loftus and Aaron's accuse, breaking the law in an attempt to confront terrorism, but he was not guilty of treason, just stupidity. President Reagan should have been impeached for treason, but as history unravels, we now know the old Gipper was losing his wits from Alzheimer's. Dr. Allan Macdonald of Southampton Hospital, Long Island, adjacent Plum Island, has speculated Alzheimer's disease to be caused by the Lyme spirochete, adding to the irony of our tale of the SS ELBRUS. (28)

On the other hand, old OPC operative, Bill Casey, who ushered in the newly released "dragon returnees" straight from Russia with love, must have fully understood Turkul's penetration of the OPC, CIA, ODESSA, WACL and the Contras. President Reagan, living in his Hollywood dream world of Rambo, had placed the last of the Dulles gang's moles in his Cabinet to direct the CIA! The night before Bill Casey was called to testify before Congress on the Iran Contra Affair, he mysteriously died of a "brain tumor," most likely a lead one, by his own hand, afraid to face charges of treason. Several summaries of the lengthy Tower Commission investigation were published by the "New York Times," available to the public for scholarly review. (29)

A side show on the Iran Contra Affair arose in Nebraska, where Vietnam veteran and attorney, John DeCamp, began investigating a case of child molestation. He soon uncovered an underground organization of pedophiles, financed by Larry King, President of the Franklin Credit Union. King's bank was suspect in money laundering for Contra contributions and drug money. Larry King's ties to the local police, FBI agents, and underworld extended to prominent men in Omaha's elite business community and both the Republican and Democrat Parties. Elected to the Nebraska Senate, John DeCamp took on the case of the child victims, unfortunately, the jury convicted the children for perjury, and the cases were never solved. His attempts to uncover the truth were stymied. (30)

In the meantime, Reagan's Justice Department was racing to cover its butt, first publishing "Klaus Barbie and the United States Government" as we have seen, leaving out key documents implicating Barbie's ties to the Communists. And next, "In the Matter of Josef Mengele" was crafted, emphatically denying any connection between the Barbie case, where Barbie had been employed by the US Government and that of Josef Mengele, a man who had "nothing to offer," and was never "used nor protected by US authorities":

"IN THE MATTER OF JOSEF MENGELE" Report to the Attorney General of the United States, October 1992, prepared by OSI Criminal division, Neal M. Sher, Director, and Eli M. Rosenbaum, Principal Deputy Director:

Page 119: "Whereas Barbie, a career intelligence officer, had skills and information of obvious value to broker for his protection, it was suggested that Mengele bartered the results of his medical experiments. As in the Barbie investigation, OSI approached this question with no preconceived notions and devoted considerable resources to determine the facts.

...However, in the Barbie case, detailed records of his use by the CIC and his sponsored exit were found easily under his name. If there were any basis for the comparison with Barbie, one could expect to find records to document it. However, OSI discovered no documentation whatsoever even to suggest a relationship between Josef Mengele and the United States. However, to be satisfied with the correctness of this answer, OSI had to be fully confident in the thoroughness of the search for relevant records. With significant assistance from the Department of the Army, OSI undertook an unprecedented effort to find any indication of U. S. assistance to Mengele; an account of this search can be found in the introduction to this report and is an integral part of the answer to the question. The absence of even a scintilla of evidence that Mengele was involved with U. S. operation or personnel, along with the information unearthed by OSI concerning Mengele's actual postwar whereabouts and activities, leads OSI to the firm conclusion that Mengele was neither used nor protected by U. S. authorities. Thus, there can fairly be no comparison to the Barbie case."

Hocus Pocus! Switched at birth, switched at death! With the "doctor of death" discovered in the Brazilian Sao Paulo grave, Barbie's drug smuggling partner had been silenced. Or had he, if they had the right Mengele? Can anyone step forward and identify the photos in Henry Tolkmith's Army dossier? Tolkmith himself, had insisted they were not of him. Had Tolkmith still been alive, real or impostor, he could have solved a lot of mysteries; I. G. Farben's poison gas history, the assassination of President Kennedy, Klaus Barbie's ties to Watergate, the vanishing Contra funds, the whole history of the Soviet Union's BW program and the mystery of Lyme disease and the SS ELBRUS. Was Amtorg Trading Company involved in a Soviet biological warfare attack upon America?

Further questions arise on the history of I. G. Farben and its operatives, like patent lawyer, Allen Dulles. Newly declassified files from the National Security Agency involving decoded Soviet messages titled the "VENONA" files, implicate a mole deep inside the State Department. Most historians presume this to be a mid level employee, Alger Hiss, exposed by his fellow conspirator, Whittaker Chambers, a former "Time" magazine editor, was hauled before the House of Un-American Activities Committee and pressed hard by Congressman Richard Nixon's grand standing in 1948. Chambers, who had left the Communist Party, citing it a hoax of false promises, fingered four Communist moles passing information to the Soviets in New York: Nathan Witt, John Abt, Lee Pressman, all Labor counselors, and State Department official, Alger Hiss. The VENONA files in 1945 spoke of a high ranking operative in the State Department with access to military logistics, under the code name "ALES." This acronym does not fit "Alger Hiss" letter for letter, nor his career including "responsibility for organizing the Dumbarton Oaks world monetary conferences, the U. S. side of the Yalta conference, and the meeting at San Francisco where the UN charter was written and adopted." Ales matches perfectly with the two beginning and two last letters of Allen Dulles' name. (31) Once again, the high life was sacrificing the lower life. Alger Hiss, a left wing dingbat, (it is not against the law to be a left wing dingbat), protested his innocence to his death.

Would it not follow that if Allen Dulles, I. G. Farben's patent lawyer was a Soviet mole, I. G. Farben, Adolf Heusinger, Anton Turkul, and Klaus Barbie were also Soviet operatives? The intelligence communities never admit to their blunders, but this time, it may have cost us more than our pride. Certainly the American, German, and Israeli intelligence services have failed their citizens with this entourage of international terrorist, pedophiles, arms and drug dealers, precipitates of Turkul's triangle of phony Fascists, hot potatoes, big turnips and reverse radishes. There's just too many worms and spirochetes in the garden, boys. Would any of these government employees like to step forward and fess up to the cover-up? Nazism is synonymous with Communism. Get rid of one, and you get rid of the other.

CHAPTER 11 NOTES

(1) "THE BELARUS SECRET" John Loftus, Alfred A. Knopf, NY 1982

Pages 140-141: re. intelligence agencies unable to retrieve its own files; Rockefeller Commission "a whitewash effort to divert further investigation."

"THE SECRET WAR AGAINST THE JEWS" John Loftus & Mark Aarons, St. Martin's Press, NY 1994, Page 217: re. James Jesus Angleton sanitizing CIA files on OPC

(2) "QUIET NEIGHBORS" Allen Ryan Jr., Harcourt Brace Jovanovich, NY, 1984

Page 312: re. ODESSA, Klaus Barbie, Bolivian Transmaritima Shipping Co. and Israeli arms transfer on the high seas during Arab-Israeli war.

"UNHEALED WOUNDS" Erna Paris, Grove Press, Inc. NY 1985, Pages 125-129

(3) EDWIN WENDELL PAULEY FBI file 161,4895; see note #14 for text.

(4) WILLIAM RANDOLPH LOVELACE FBI file 161-1637 "The White House, Office of the Special Assistant for Science and Technology September 12, 1961, Memorandum for (blackout) FBI, technical assistant.

Subject: Transmittal SF-86 for William Randolph Lovelace... purpose of obtaining a White House clearance.... Membership organizations..."

WILLIAM RANDOLPH LOVELACE FBI file 116-50241, BALTI-MORE "Files of G-2 reviewed without locating any derogatory information concerning the captioned individual"

(5) "Conference for Military Surgeons of the United States: Detroit, 9-10-11 Oct 1946" OACSI file MIS 284797, Nat. Arch. MRB BID 7502, BW USA. "Oct. 11, 1946: Tropical Diseases & Aviation Medicine and Nursing; persons attending convention... Lt. Col. William Lovelace II, Dr. Williams, US Public Health Service; General Hawley, Veterans Administration; Brig Gen. Malcolm C. Grow, Air Surgeon, Foreign Delegates Attending Convention... Surgeon Capt. A. McCallum, Medical Director, Royal Canadian Army and four others, whose names are unknown."

"Medical Conference for Military Surgeons of the United States to be held at Detroit 9-10-11 October 1946" OACSI file MIS 311230 and 306727, Nat. Arch. MRB

(6) "THE CRIME AND PUNISHMENT OF I. G. FARBEN" Joseph Borkin, The Free Press, division of Macmillan Publishing Co, NY 1978. Pages 212-213: re I. G's stock, and Prince Radziwill, brother-in-law to JFK.

"Individuals in Soviet PW Specialist Camp" OACSI file 661866, Page 15: Prince Radziwill serving in Soviet POW camp 7027/x with his family.

(7) IBID. Pages 221 - 222: "On March 9, 1965 the General Aniline Film stock was sold... Once again, the wartime confiscation and peacetime recapture of I. G. Farben property has completed its cycle."

(8) "NEW SUSPECT IN JFK SLAYING - A FRENCH TERROR-IST" "The National Enquirer" November 22, 1983, Page 30: "Is This the Man Who Killed JFK?"

(9) "OFFICIAL AND CONFIDENTIAL: The Secret Life of J. Edgar Hoover" Anthony Summers, G. P. Putnam's Sons, NY 1993. Page 322 - 324: re. Guy Banister, Lee Harvey Oswald, David Ferrie, Anti-Castro group.

(10) "GERMAN CW ACTIVITIES IN PARIS AREA" Dept. of Commerce Board of Publication #160 Library of Congress

(11) see note #9

(12) "JOHNSON NAMES A 7-MAN PANEL TO INVESTIGATE ASSASSINATION: CHIEF JUSTICE WARREN HEADS IT" "New York Times" Nov. 30, 1963, pg.. 1-2

(13) "SPACE AIDE'S DEATH IN CRASH IS LAID TO COLD, NOT INJURIES" "New York Times" 12/18/65, p. 16 c. 6 Aspen Co, December 17 (AP)
"LOVELACE, DR. W. RANDOLPH 2nd": 'Missing' 12/14/65, p. 86 c. 4; 'Search' 12/15/65 p.22 c. 7; 'Found dead' 12/16/65 p. 42 c. 1

(14) EDWIN PAULEY SENIOR FBI file 161-4895, inclusive of San Francisco FBI Office file 161-1084: Special Inquiry; unclassified 4/12/83: Standard Oil company, California, stated PAULEY was one of the principal financial backers of JOHNSON when he was Vice President candidate in 1960. Acquaintances all consider PAULEY to be a person of good moral character, and there is no reason to question his loyalty or reputation. He was described as a capable and astute business executive.
EDWIN PAULEY sub-file la 161-1136 FBI letter 2/23/67 to Marvin Watson, Special Assistant to the President, The White House: "Dear Mr. Watson: In accordance with a request received from Mrs. Mildred Stegall on February 1, 1967, an investigation has been conducted regarding Mr. Edwin Wendell Pauley... Here within is a summary memorandum containing the results of this investigation..."
"Professional Acquaintances in the Oil Industry"
Page 24: "(Blackout) commented that in regard to Mr. PAULEY's health, he appears to be somewhat arthritic... walks quite slowly, undoubtedly the result of an old back injury. He looks older than his age... three martinis before lunch on business days..."
EDWIN PAULEY FBI file 161-1136 Page 56-57: "In 1941 he was special representative of President Roosevelt to formulate plans for Coordinator of Petroleum Industry... later that year... Petroleum Coordinator for War... dealt with petroleum lend-lease supplies for Russia and England..."

(15) "GORKY PARK" Martin Cruz Smith, Random House, NY 1981; p. 299: re. Nixon

(16) "THE PRESIDENT'S PRIVATE EYE" Tony Ulasewicz & Stuart

A. McKeever, MACSAM Publishing Co., Westport, CT 1990; p. 39: re. work for BOSSI, p. 83: OSS hires Communist Basque Spanish Loyalist to work against Nazis, tied to French underground - Basque professor Jesus de Galindez and kidnapping. p. 107-108: re. Galindez as informant to FBI on Communist in Caribbean, Castro plans to topple Samoza with help of Dulles' CIA.

(17) "SILENT COUP: THE REMOVAL OF A PRESIDENT" Len Colodney & Robert Gettlin, St. Martin's Press, NY 1991. Pages 229-232: re. Phil Bailley. Page 196: re. Mexican banks and FBI.

(18) KLAUS BARBIE FBI files 62-118313-122, FOIA/PA request #224,962 1/16/84, re-initiated 11/16/98, request #411,663. "U.S. Is Reported to Have Evidence That Barbie Visited in '69 and '70" by Ralph Blumenthal (FBI collection of newspaper clippings)

(19) "MENGELE: THE COMPLETE STORY" Gerald Posner & John Ware, McGraw Hill, NY 1986. Page 159: re. Hans Rudel and Wolfgang Gerhard making housing arrangements for Mengele. Page 222: "During one explosive period in 1969, Hans Rudel suggested to Gerhard that Klaus Barbie, the "Butcher of Lyons," who was hiding in Bolivia, was willing to provide refuge for Mengele. But Mengele balked at the idea. He did not want to move again." Page 301: re 1972 CIA reports Mengele as Henrique Wollman, "heavily involved in narcotics traffic..." and re. November 1979 CIA-DEA contract on Mengele.

(20) "THE BUTCHER OF LYON" Brendan Murphy, Empire Books, NY 1983. Pages 272-273: re. Barbie, Hans Rudel, and ODESSA

(21) "INSIDE THE LEAGUE" Scott Anderson & Jon Lee Anderson, Dodd Meade & co., NY 1986. Page 147: re Barbie & cocaine trade.

(22) IBID. Page 79: re FEMACO and the Tecos.

(23) "THE BUTCHER OF LYON" Brendan Murphy, Empire Books, NY 1983: Page 296

(24) "THE PRESIDENT'S PRIVATE EYE" Tony Ulasewicz & Stuart McKeever, MACSAM Publishing, Westport, CT 1990. Page 231: re Mrs. Ramona Banuelos

(25) "THE SECRET WAR AGAINST THE JEWS" John Loftus & Mark Aarons, St. Martin's Press, NY 1994. Pages 372-374: re. Father Graham and Vessel files.

(26) "HAZARDOUS DUTY: an American Soldier in the Twentieth Century" Major General John Singlaub, U.S. Army (retired) with Malcolm McConnell, Summit Books, Simon & Schuster, NY 1991. Page 509: re. Contra's money loss.

(27) "THE SECRET WAR AGAINST THE JEWS" John Loftus & Mark Aarons, St. Martin's Press, NY 1994, Page 407 re. Bush and the NSDD #3, creating the SSG

(28) "THE CONNECTION OF LYME DISEASE TO ALZHEIMER'S AND MULTIPLE SCLEROSIS" by Alex Wood, "Journal Inquirer" Manchester, CT 8/3/87

(29) "REPORT OF THE CONGRESSIONAL COMMITTEES INVESTIGATING THE IRAN-CONTRA AFFAIR WITH THE MINORITY VIEW" abridged Edition, "Times Books" by Random House, NY 1988
"THE TOWER COMMISSION REPORT" The New York Times, NY 1987

(30) "THE FRANKLIN COVER-UP" John DeCamp, AWT Inc. Lincoln, NE 68501
Page 59: re Larry King of Franklin community Federal Credit Union funding Contras, "guns and money transfers to Nicaragua."

(31) "THE ARROGANCE OF POWER" Anthony Summers with Robbyn Swan, Viking, NY 2000. Page 79: re. Alger Hiss as "ALES" in VENONA files. Page 493: copy of VENONA files from NSA.
"SIX CRISES" Richard M. Nixon, Warner Books, NY 1972. Page 4: re. Alger Hiss

EPILOGUE

Communism has been selling Utopia to the duped and the doped for a long time. America's sin has been sitting back in silence, not challenging the hoax. Economically, redistribution of existing wealth could never keep pace with the expanding world population. The issue is not planning, but who is doing the planning. Economic planning is essential, but the "centralized planning" of socialism does not work. The Communist know it, the racists know it, deliberately deluding the desperate with false promises, pitting poor against the rich. Communism is a flawed theory concocted by university dons in ivory towers, geeks that couldn't get the girl, calculating how to lessen the competition. Racism was the founding principle of Marx's Communism brutally exposed in "The Biology of War," plotting the massacre of mutants, technically obsolete, and useless eaters. Somehow, the Communists never saw themselves in the same picture.

Is inheritance a random occurrence, as Mendel postulated, opposed to prolonged nutrition being the dominant influence on gene passage? Wealth cannot be "redistributed," it simply runs out. Wealth has to be built and created. The wealth of a nation is derived from the wealth of ideas that flow from a free people. Free people solve problems better than dictators and slaves, they just have a better attitude. Genetics is not random, Mendel fudged his own data to conform to a neat, calculable outcome. There are outside influences. There will always be weak, sick, and mutated, but there should be less if people are free to provide three square meals a day for their families. With fewer minds involved in problem solving, the pool of knowledge diminishes, hence, a greater generation of degenerates. Mutants do not beget more mutants, dictators beget mutants. After all, look at the odds, all you ego maniacs, which would you rather have: six billion morons making their own decisions, or one moron making all the decisions? There is a curious little anonymous poem in a recent publication mocking Mendel's flawed research on genetics that suits this author's politics very well:

"BETRAYERS OF THE TRUTH: Fraud and Deceit in the Halls of Science" William Broad & Nicholas Wade, Touchstone Press, Simon & Schuster, NY 1982

Page 33: "Peas on Earth" "In the beginning there was Mendel, thinking his lonely thoughts alone. And he said: 'Let there be peas,' and there were peas and it was good. And he put the peas in the garden saying unto them 'Increase and multiply, segregate and assort yourselves independently,' and they did and it was good. And now it came to pass that when Mendel gathered up his peas, he divided them into round and wrinkled, and called the round dominant and the wrinkled recessive, and it was good. But now Mendel saw that there were 450 round peas and 102 wrinkled ones; this was not good. For the law stateth that there should be only 3 round for every wrinkled. And Mendel said unto himself 'Gott in Himmel, and enemy has done this, he has sown bad peas in my garden under the cover of night.' And Mendel smote the table in righteous wrath, saying 'Depart from me, you cursed and evil peas, into the outer darkness where thou shalt be devoured by the rats and mice,' and lo it was done and there remained 300 round peas and 100 wrinkled peas, and it was good. It was very, very good. and Mendel published."

The easiest way to cure the world of disease and poverty will be to wipe out Communism for ever, which, ironically, would eliminate their accomplices, the Nazis. Killing people will not solve the problem, the theory of Communism itself must be destroyed. Exposure is the weapon. Truth is the biggest weapon in a world of liars, murderers and thieves. The call for a new "Marshall Plan" for the Third World cannot be ushered in by governments and more money, but a renewal in faiths that believe in the dignity of man and the gift of life. The true Moslems, Christians, Jews, Buddhists and Hindus, not their impostors hiding under the facade of nationalism, must form a new alliance against Communism, fascism, and racism. Humans were given the gift of free will, genetics nor health can not pose as an alibi for behavior. Perhaps the Buddhists, very knowledgeable in nutrition as well as philosophy, could shed some enlightenment upon the world in the benefits of vegetarianism. Blood parasites feed upon meat as well as greed, envy, and destitution. Faith, knowledge and freedom to solve problems is worth more than all the mis-directed money the socialists have thrown into the wind.

Buying into socialized medicine from this cult of death doctors who have either participated in biological warfare or sat in silence for decades is like buying insurance from the Mafia. Enough of these high tech cannibals. The preventative medicine of three square meals a day and the freedom to choose will save many more lives than their legal or illegal drug industries. Vaccinating the hell out of newborns and inducing a lifetime of unnatural allergic reactions is not the solution either. The whole process and timing in developing immunology needs further investigation. This "treatment by neglect" and callus indifference toward our neighbors is the wrong path, leading us into a world cataclysm with no survivors. The Communist dictators of the world should step down now; their egotism and sadism has failed humanity. These bastards have no shame. Banish them from the kingdom, extradite them to the astroid belt, or better yet, send them to jail.

How many Americans have suffered from Lyme disease, arthritis, Alzheimer's and multiple sclerosis? Do we write them off as necessary losses for the good of the state? Do we say "everybody's got to get stoned" and "go kill yourselves"? How do we solve this Communist plot to destroy America from within, using diseases of the nervous system and the illegal drug trade to put its victims out of their misery? If your answer is socialized medicine, then we shall next elect David Duke for president with Jack Kevorkian running the Health Department, establishing a medical police state to institutionalize, shock, and drug its population into submission. How many more Phil Bailleys are out there? George Orwell saw it coming. Maybe it's already here. The time has come to put an end to this corruption.

Numerous others have sought a witness to the Nazi-Communist collaboration. Personal conversations between the author and John Loftus revealed that his Nazi hunter partner, Mark Aarons, requested permission from Russia's Mikhail Gorbachev to interview Kim Philby. Philby, the British mole who defected to Moscow, with Donald McClean of MI6, had run the Nazi ratlines of Paperclip and Dustbin. Gorbachev granted permission to Aarons to videotape an interview, but soon after Philby was murdered. To this day, the Communists have closely guarded their secret alliance with the Nazis, the Dulles gang, and I.G. Farben.

We end, where we began, looking for a witness to the origin of Lyme disease, to testify against I. G. Farben, the Nazi doctors, and their Soviet collaborators in crimes of the holocaust, which extended not only across Europe, but to Asia, the Middle East, and finally reaching the shores of America. Who can substantiate the author's theories here? Who will come forward and identify the face on the cover of this book? Is this man the key to an international plot to destroy democracies from within, using drugs and disease? Who can solve the mystery of Lyme disease and the SS ELBRUS?

2005 UPDATE

SmithKline Beecham removed its Lymerix vaccine from the market in 2003. Instead of just a dose of preventative medicine, one third of the world's citizens carrying the genetic marker HLA-DR4+ would be chronically maimed with rheumatoid arthritis after receiving Lymerix whether or not they encountered Lyme disease. The vaccine induced these people's antibodies into attacking their own cartilage, their white blood corpuscles unable to distinguish between the Lyme bacteria's outside protein coating and the human protein. According to a July 1, 2003 news flash from ABCNEWS.COM, SmithKline Beecham was aware of this allergic reaction induced by the vaccine prior introducing Lymerix on the market.

But there is a much greater significance behind this report than mentioned in the ABC News briefing. Brucellosis, far more globally prevalent than the Lyme parasite also induces arthritis amongst many of its victims, and therefore, one must presume the bacteria has the same protein coating as the Lyme spirochete. Both parasites attack the nervous system. One third of the world could become chronically infected with Lyme or brucellosis, an enormous potential market for cocaine, heroin, hemp, LSD, and ecstasy. With these statistics in hand, would our justice system bother to combat this trillion-dollar global narcotics racket or just cash in, rendering it a taxable revenue? Recent developments expose the awful truth, and may shed some light on the terrorists' attack on America, September 11, 2001.

Let us review this book's second chapter, "Connecticut Caddy Shack" and the Lottery. James Blain Lewis ran not only the Connecticut State Lottery, but also the North American Association of State and Provincial Lotteries for the USA and Canada. Connecticut profits skyrocketed starting with a $30 million revenue in sales in 1972 systematically rising to $525 million by 1988. Lottery revenues went toward supplementing school and property taxes, and citizens were equally willing to gamble with their children's education and the economy as well as their purse. Connecticut schools reaped a windfall in cash from the Lottery while taxpayers got relief. The Teacher's Unions must have been thrilled. This was phenomenal for such a small state with a population of barely 3 million and its surrounding states offering competing lotteries, border hopping surely did not play a roll in increasing profits before Powerball was introduced. Corruption was suspected, instigating a special State Police Administrative Investigation involving both Gtech and General Instrument's gaming contracts but none was found; instead, Lewis was fired because of his "attitude."

But no investigation was made of the origin of lottery profits itself. In January 1988, General Instruments won the CT Lottery gaming contract regardless of its previous track record of failures in other states. A convenient patsy, GI's annual lotto sales systematically declined year by year starting with the advent of the new Bush administration during 1988, totaling $382,628,795 in losses by 1995. This is all publicly documented in Tina Lewis's biography on her husband, Blaine, "Justice Denied: Politics, Perjury and Prejudice in the Lottery" Appendix, page 178. Meanwhile, the stock market began a feeding frenzy of "irrational exuberance" to quote Allan Greenspan, chairman of the Federal Reserve up until the close of the Clinton Administration. Where had the money come from, and to where did it vanish? Did CIA directors, Bill Casey, William Webster, and George Tenent at the helm sanction this money laundering dope through the lottery and the stock market? Was Arthur Andersen money laundering dope through its clients 401K plans in the Fortune Five Hundred, creating a new taxable revenue to balance Ronald Reagan's $5½ trillion national debt? Was enriching everyone's 401K plans more just than the shady distribution of Lottery winnings? How could senior citizens retire on the profits from peddling poison to their children? Is this how 1/3 of the human race ends carrying the HLA-DR4+ genetic marker?

How could the State of Connecticut consent to Arthur Andersen auditing GI's off track betting accounts? How did the Canadians hire Arthur Andersen to audit their lottery? How did the sovereign Indian Nations hire Arthur Andersen to audit their casinos? What would be the ramifications? Arthur Andersen had already accrued an incredible criminal track record for cooking the books on Wall Street by 1972. How could people be so damned greedy and ruthless with their own children's lives? Peddling poison to children to balance the budget and promote democracy? What lunacy! Who was crazy? And who were Arthur Andersen's next victims - Nicaragua, Columbia, Afghanistan, Enron, Global Crossing, World. Com, Tycos, ZCMI, The May Company, Yukos, Russia, Azerbaijan, and Red China? Heads up, planet! Was this the Fourth Reich in action?

Between 1968 and 1969, originating under the Johnson Administration, General Dynamics and its accountants, Arthur Andersen, were taken to court by there stock holders for fraud, inflating company profits. Soon to follow, by 1972, the same scenario would follow with the Four Seasons Nursing Home chain and the Walston Construction Company, sparking the biggest fraud case in Wall Street history. With Johnson ushering in his Great Society signing Medicare into law, hospitals, nursing homes and daycare centers jumped at the investment opportunity. Chains sprung up everywhere, known as the "fevered fifty" and the stock market flush with funding even before the foundations had been laid. Upon appeal, Arthur Andersen walked away scot free, leaving Four Seasons and Walston Construction holding the bag. This was front-page news, not top secret and began a long precedent of convictions overturned upon appeal after appeal. Opening a new branch in Moscow to usher in Richard Nixon's "Détente" with the Soviet Union, Andersen had a new beginning with a global market.

Under Détente, Arthur Andersen International became America's economic advisor to the Soviet State Commission on Science and Technology under the Ministry of Economics, headed by Prime Minister Kosygin's son-in-law, Dzhermen Gvishiani. Now the seeds of crime had been sewn in the Kremlin. Keep in mind that Kosygin had formerly been in charge of Russia's textile industry and Soyuzpushnina, fur shipping to Amtorg Trading Company in New York. On March 19th 1974, the ghoulish portraits of Gvishiani and Harvey Kapnick, Andersen's CEO, were plastered across the front page of the New York Times business section, ushering in Détente with the Soviet Union. Soon to follow Secretary General Leonid Breshnev's invasion of Afghanistan. A thirty-year civil war would ensue. Andersen's biggest partner in crime was Occidental Petroleum, hoping to win a multi billion dollar oil pipeline concession from Kosygin but Oxy was out of cash. Who owned Occidental Petroleum? Russia's biggest fur trader, Armand Hammer, previously having introduced Wall Street to Lenin and the Bolshevik Revolution now re- establishing ties to the Soviet Union. The Hammers had installed Amtorg Trading Company in New York City half a century ago by secretly selling the family business, Allied Chemical, to the KGB. Through the Hammers, the KGB recruited top members of the American Communist Party to be installed in the American Labor Unions. It was all so cozy. Were there still ties between the labor unions, the ACP, the Hammers and Arthur Andersen in the late 20th Century? The Justice Department officially banned the ACP under the McCarthy era. Who was facilitating Arthur Andersen's massive expansion in corporate takeovers and acquisitions, Labor Salts and saboteurs? Certainly, the Justice Department will never look into this, for you will soon see, any potential evidence has vanished.

The CIA ran an article on its FOIA web-site, "SOVIET ECONOMIC

AND TECHNOLOGICAL BENEFITS FROM DÉTENTE (ER IR 74-2)" listing several dozen Fortune Five Hundred firms making a beeline to this financial bonanza, concluding we were virtually arming our enemy to the teeth with military technology and industrial know-how. Arthur Andersen and Occidental Petroleum led the charge, followed by General Dynamics, DOW Chemical, (was Tolkmith on the payroll then?), Aramco International, Singer, BASF, Monsanto, Union Carbide, Hewlett-Packard, Litton, IT&T, General Electric, Kaiser Industries, Lockheed, Control Data Corporation, and Food Machinery Corporation (which bought out Westvaco Chlorine.) Ring any bells? The Import-Export Bank, chaired by Bill Casey, was called upon to help finance the Soviet deals going down under Hammer's Occidental Petroleum. The bank needed presidential approval from Richard Nixon to subsidize a Communist enemy. Once the loan cleared, the USSR and Hammer announced to the London Times that the deal of the century had gone down, Oxy stock soaring through the roof, over a million shares traded in one day prompting more US businesses to jump on the band wagon. In return for the economic windfall, Hammer was obliged to bankroll the Watergate break-in goon squad with Oxy slush funds hidden in a Swiss bank, passing unmarked hundred dollar bills through Nixon's bagman, retired NYPD BOSSI cop, Toni Ulascewitz. Was Hammer's accountant, Arthur Andersen, privy to the slush fund? Was Armand Hammer privy to Arthur Andersen's ties to the lottery? What kind of slush was in the funds? President George Bush eventually pardoned Hammer's roll in Watergate in 1989. The Trans-Siberian pipeline was never built, and as always, Arthur Andersen and Wall Street slipped under the radar.

Meanwhile, the Bush Administration declared this author's claim with the Vaccine Compensation Act involving a severe allergic reaction to passport vaccines on top of a Lyme infection as fraudulent! I had only asked for back wages lost during hospitalization at Norwich under the care of a monster, Dr. Hans Langhammer. There at Norwich, a series of seventeen shock treatments was administered, followed by another series of five under Dr. Brian Heath, nearly rendering the author a human vegetable for months after. Tied to beds, wrapped in icy sheets, hooked up to a catheter tube and choked into passing out, Norwich was hell on earth. Langhammer became Connecticut's official legal advocate for compulsive gambling disorders, the Lafferty case is posted on the Internet. Coincidentally, Hans Langhammer's elderly nurse was Ruby Ziegler, nicknamed Ziggy. Ruby was Ron Ziegler's mother, as listed in his New York Times obituary just a few months after of the publication of this book. Had I been dragged off to Norwich during Watergate to be questioned regarding Arthur Andersen and illegal campaign funds and money laundering? Was Ron Ziegler Deep Throat? Now, Woodward and Bernstein are fingering the recently deceased FBI agent, Mark Felt as their informant. Is the left wing media still covering for Ziegler, or Arthur Andersen? We will never know.

Connecticut State Senator, Joseph Lieberman, documented 142 deaths in asylums between 1988 and 1998 in his address to Congress. Senator Lieberman had been Attorney General during Blain Lewis' dismissal at the Lottery and would become a future vice presidential contender with Al Gore in the upcoming 2000 election. But Blain's dismissal had actually been conducted in Lieberman's absence under the Deputy Attorney General, Richard Sheridan; and there had been an attorney Sheridan that signed this author's admittance to Norwich during Watergate with out my personal appearance before the judge's hearings. Had this man been promoted due to the destruction of my health? This was gulag style politics at its worst. Gore's family fortune was derived from Occidental Petroleum stock. Did we have a political alliance made out of the embarrassment of riches on the Democrat ticket or a new wave of crime headed to the White House?

When reading this history of Hammer in 2005, the wind was virtually knocked out of me. I had missed the full significance of this major player. But my puny little life circumstances were nothing compared to what was to follow. I wasn't alone. Not only had Phil Bailley suffered destruction in an asylum under the Nixon Administration, clued into John Dean's wife's gambling background, Professor John Nash would slide into madness, the Noble Prize winning economist portrayed in the film "A Beautiful Mind." Having taught at MIT in Boston, heavily infested with Lyme in the 1960s, Nash was invited to lecture in Paris needing passport vaccinations. He returned to America in chains, a madman and subjected to shock treatments. Nash published his "Non-Cooperative Game Theory," in 1949 using vectors to calculate winnings and losses amongst "closed and open games" in gambling, economics, genetics, Wall Street and the stock market. Nash was hired by the Rand Corporation, think-tank to the Pentagon. With Nash's game theory, the collapse of Communism was publicly predictable; Russia and China would have a harder sales pitch to the Third World to sell itself back into the slavery of socialism. Arthur Andersen now had new tools to orchestrate the stock market, the world's biggest gambling casino. Was it more important to shelter Arthur Andersen, this I. G. Farben re-incarnate, than allot simple protection and justice to American citizens? It's quite obvious the Communists decided to destroy Nash's credibility. Armand Hammer had long been on the payroll of the KGB since the 1920s, but were his accountants also working for the Evil

Empire? We need to follow Arthur Andersen's progress.

Back in 1965, to further solidify Occidental's economic footing in Moscow (President Brezhnev and Hammer plotted a new chemical fertilizer factory), Hammer bribed Libya's King Idris into granting the largest oil concession on the continent of Africa. Occidental was bought by Hammer in 1956 using his second wife's fortune for collateral; Arthur Andersen LLC put on the payroll. By 1966, Andersen announced King Idris's biggest Libyan oil concession to Wall Street. Occidental's stock soared to $100 per share even though Hammer was $700 million in debt. Hammer was not a Capitalist, but a die hard Communist, an ideologist, wedded to the cause. Using King Idris's adopted son-in-law, Sheik Shelhi, Hammer had his foot in the door to negotiate. Shelhi's business associates Hans Albert Kunz of Switzerland, Kemal Zeinal Zade (of both Azerbaijan and Chechnya heritage) who held business ties to Chechnya's KGB chief Geidar Aliyev, furthered Hammer's inroads to negotiating Libyan oil concessions with King Idris. Hammer, also paying huge bribes and promising royalties to Kunz and Zade, opened doors to every terrorist network across the Middle East and the Central Asian Republics.

In 1970, Muammar Kaddafi led a military coup against King Idris and his son Shelhi, threatening them with death penalties if they returned to Libya. With a new Libyan chief in power, Oxy cancelled all debts to Kunz and Zade, sewing more seeds of bitterness between East and West. Kunz filed suit in Washington Federal District Court to recover the overdue royalties: "Hans-Albert Kunz, plaintiff v. OCCIDENTAL PETROLEUM INTERNATIONAL, INC. et al, Defendants" CIV.A. No. 88-1169LFO, July 12, 1988, only to be put on a legal merry-go-round. Presiding Judge Oberdorfer dismissed the case, citing the main action between Occidental and the plaintiffs, Kunz and Zade, took place in Switzerland, not America and Zade, a major party to the deal, was not even present. The seeds of malcontent had once again been sewn by Occidental Petroleum. Special note is made that Arthur Andersen had no knowledge to these "royalties." Edward Jay Epstein's biography on Hammer, "Dossier: the Secret History of Armand Hammer" Random House, 1996, covers this new perspective on Hammer and Occidental Petroleum, derived from personal interviews with Sheik Shelhi, many of Hammer's family and business associates as well as recently declassified KGB files. Three bigger questions remain. Was KGB Chief, Geidar Aliyev also in on the bribe? Was Arthur Andersen privy to the deal even though Epstein emphatically states they were out of the picture? Did someone high up in the Justice Department influence Judge Oberdorfer's decision to defer the plaintiffs to Switzerland and keep Arthur Andersen out of the loop? The Israelis took a dim view of

Hammer's cohorting with terrorists.

Aliyev would rise to become Deputy Prime Minister of the Kremlin, and later, after the fall of Communism, first Prime Minister of Azerbaijan. The newly freed nation of Azerbaijan would sink into corruption instead of profiting from freedom and its oil reserves. America offered Azerbaijan military protection in exchange for lucrative oil contracts as noted in "The Journal of the Third World Studies." The plight of this nation's sad decline, virtually taken over by the Russian Mafia, forcing millions of Azeri citizens to flee to Moscow and Turkey, is documented in Alec Rasizade's report below:

"Azerbaijan Descending Into the Third World After a Decade of Independence" published in the "Journal of Third World Studies" volume XXI, No. 1, 2004, pages 198-199.

"But all this malfeasance pales in comparison with the oil smuggling scheme being perpetrated on a national scale by the presidential family, which hold virtual monopoly on the export, as well as domestic distribution, of petroleum production. President Aliev's [Aliyev's] brother Jalal Aliev owns the national gas-stations cartel called Azpetrol, Ilham Aliev, whom his father appointed vice president of SOCAR (State Oil company of Azerbaijan Republic), controls every shipment of crude oil produced by the national monopoly. According to Georgian government statistics, every year SOCAR exports via the Georgian Black Sea ports of Batumi and Poti about 6.5 million tons more crude oil than is officially reported by Azeri government. These unreported shipments bring into the pockets of presidential clan around $1 billion annually.

Just how much of this money fell into the hands of the Chechnya rebels and terrorists? Even after the collapse of Communism, Arthur Andersen, still Oxy's accountant, was counseling the Russian Economic Ministry in oil. The plight of Capitalism, itself, was on the chopping block. Was Andersen in Russia to destroy Communism or to destroy Capitalism or both and establish a New World Order under the Fourth Reich? Hammer, Lenin, and Amtorg had been as racists as Hell from the start, having armed Hitler uptil operation Barbarosa in WW II. SOCAR was nothing but a payback present to Aliyev, Kunz and Zade for Oxy's long overdue royalties in winning the Libyan oil concession.

All the clues to the mystery of the SS Elbrus lay with Hammer, Amtorg, and Arthur Andersen with its international web of 50 thousand clients home and abroad. Arthur Andersen, with its tentacles in every nation, mirrored I. G. Farben's octopus. In the 1980s, Armand Hammer, who had hired Arthur Andersen in 1956 as Occidental Petroleum's accountant, began a curious series of freedom of information requests on himself, hoping to purge FBI files of his Communist past. The Hammer family business of Allied Chemical, transformed into Amtorg Trading Company by a deal with Lenin, was just the beginning of his troubles. After the Kremlin established Amtorg in New York to circumvent the American embargo on the Bolsheviks, they created ARCOS in London and WESTORG in Berlin. As we have seen, ARCOS was arrested for treason by the Brits for collaborating with the Nazis, mention made Chapter 9 "The Arrest of Amtorg." By the 1960s, the CIA's top agent, James Jesus Angleton, had assigned himself to Operation Dinosaur, hoping to identify an elusive Soviet mole posing as an American capitalist implicated by Soviet defectors. The dinosaur was possibly embedded within the CIA itself, but Angleton fingered Averill Harriman, George Bush's great grandfather, not Armand Hammer or Angleton's former boss, Allen Dulles.

The FBI too, had a mole; did Armand Hammer know him? Quite possibly. Deep inside the Bureau slept this mole, Robert Hanssen, hired by FBI Chief, William Webster under the Carter Administration. He would worm his way to the top. Raised in Chicago, hometown to crooked cops, the Mafia, and the headquarters of Arthur Andersen LLC, Hanssen ascended America's most trusted police force emerging as head of the FBI's Soviet Counter-Intelligence desk. Here, Hanssen was appointed to Project Pocketwatch, overseeing Amtorg Trading Company's American business transactions, which of course, would have included Hammer's fur deals, Kosygin and Soyuzpushnina. Were later records on Kosygin and Hammer's accountant, Arthur Andersen also to be found in Amtorg files? According to Hanssen's biographer, Adrian Havill ("The Spy Who Stayed Out in the Cold," St. Martin's Press 2001) the files on Pocketwatch vanished. Meanwhile, my FOIA's on Amtorg were stonewalled for over a decade until release after President George W. Bush's inauguration in 2001. Other State Department files vanishing all together. One might note the State Department Kosygin telegram #861.51 XR 861.002/12-2448, Tel3049 12/29/48 vanished with no withdrawal slip in its folder, only the purport card remained describing Kosygin when he headed the Soviet textile industry and fur trade. (See the previous Chapter 8 "On the Waterfront" page 207-208 in this book.)

Simultaneously, Edward Jay Epstein was FOIAing the FBI on Armand Hammer and Amtorg. Just how much material was withheld, confiscated, or outright destroyed by Robert Hanssen because of Hammer's, Epstein's and Verdon's FOIA requests remains a mystery. Hanssen forked over 60,000 pages, many original documents, to his handlers in the Soviet

Embassy in New York until reeled in by FBI director William Freeh February 17th, 2001. Epstein, in turn, relied heavily on KGB declassified documents on Armand Hammer and personal interviews with Hammer's family and business associates to write his biography. Sheik Shelhi had probably offered greater insight to Hammer and the Communists' mode of operations than any files held by our government. Watergate was the real "Gorky Park." If only I knew then what I know now. Or would I have been turned into a human vegetable like Phil Bailley?

Just prior Christmas 2004, the author, now more skilled on the Internet, uncovered the CIA's Freedom of Information web page and keyed in "Arthur Andersen" to their search engine, retrieving the Détente report mentioned above. By January, 2005, the author FOIAed the CIA for further material on Arthur Andersen, and to great dismay, they responded that because Arthur Andersen's activities were not government sponsored, the CIA could not offer a waiver exemption for research fees, nor did they expect to find anything else. Wasn't the Nixon Administration, its Executive Branch, then responsible for Détente? How about the State Department under Henry Kissinger? Who sent Arthur Andersen to Moscow? Surely Kissinger would not have removed Kosygin's files while leaving the purport cards intact at the National Archives after the files had been accessioned. Their removal must have occurred later, hastily, by someone unfamiliar with the National Archives filing system. Locating records on Arthur Andersen became a giant shell game, but instead of Shell Oil, it was Oxy Oil.

On the day after Christmas, December 26th, 2004, the author FOIAed the Security and Exchange Commission for material on Arthur Andersen and its dealings with Four Seasons Nursing Home, Enron in Afghanistan and al Qaeda on its payroll, the Lottery, and more. The SEC replied they had NOTHING! They had no withdrawal slips, nor any accession records either. On the other side of the globe, that same day after Christmas, Indonesia, with a ring of other nations encircling the Indian Ocean, was devastated by a powerful Tsunami.

Curiously, only a month after the inauguration of George W. Bush, just after the arrest of FBI mole, Robert Hanssen, the Bureau was suffering a list of humiliating embarrassments. The false arrests of Wen Ho Lee and Richard Jule posed an embarrassment to the Bureau. The FBI's failure at Ruby Ridge, Waco, and the withholding of over 1300 pertinent pages of evidence on Timothy McVeigh by 36 FBI stations were a humiliating demonstration of incompetence. The antiquated Bureau couldn't even communicate and collate data between its own branches. Two FBI agents from Las Vegas were arrested for passing secrets to the Mafia. The list of screw-ups by this dysfunctional agency went on and on. Bush's newly appointed Attorney General John Ashcroft demanded an overhaul of the decrepit Justice Department. Here was a former senator, one of the few Republicans, who would not co-sponsor any of the National Right to Work Act legislation fighting organized crime in the Labor Unions now leading the Justice Department? Out of all Republicans, the Bush Administration nominated Ashcroft for Attorney General. Who was counseling him on this one? The Mafia, the AFL-CIO, Global Crossing and Arthur Andersen went hand in hand. Did John Sweeney, AFL-CIO president, have a protector high up in the Justice Department? The FBI did not even have a computer system to collate its data. Hence, the Strategic Management Council was formed, headed by no less than Arthur Andersen! Andersen could pick up where Hanssen left off. The Tyrannosaurus was back in the chicken coup again. On July 21, 2001 "Federal Computer Week" made an announcement to its technocrat patrons that under Ashcroft's recommendation, "information technology, personnel, crisis management and other issues" were on Arthur Andersen and the Strategic Management Council's agenda. Arthur Andersen swept in and cleaned house. Is it any wonder that Hannsen's reports on Project Pocketwatch vanished? How many Hammer, Amtorg, Kosygin, Aliyev, Chechen Rebels, al Qaeda Enron and Arthur Andersen files vanished????? Two months later, the Pentagon and New York's World Trade Center were under attack on 9/11.

Next, the Wall Street giants would crash: Enron, World.com, Global Crossing, Tyco and finally, their accountant, Arthur Andersen. The stock market plummeted. Doug Perry, columnist to "Organized Labor" wrote on 8/9/2002 that the Arthur Andersen scandal on Wall Street involving Enron, World.com and Global Crossing had driven President Bush to sign the Sarbanes-Oxley Act creating the Accounting Oversight Board and the Truth in Accounting Act. The stock market's loss, Perry estimated, was $4.78 TRILLION "much of it attributed to corporate fraud." The AFL-CIO's pension funds were heavily invested in Global Crossing, their accounts overseen by Arthur Andersen. Top labor CEOs cashed in just before the bottom fell out, Global stock dropping from $64.00/share to 8 cents per share. Is it any wonder why labor membership since WW II has dropped from 80% of the American work force to less than 20%? The extended history of big labor's infestation with the Mafia is exposed in an 80 page indictment culminating with the Clinton Administration, is posted on the World Wide Web: "Union Corruption in America: Still a Growth Industry" by Carl F. Horowitz. It is worthwhile reading for all labor union members, an incentive to throw the bums out. Was it worth exporting the seeds of Arthur Andersen's slippery wheeling and dealing across the globe while sacrificing justice in America? The Odd Couple, George Bush Senior and Bill Clinton, walked hand in hand down the rubble of Indonesia's beaches leveled by one of the worst tidal waves in world history, calling upon American charity for donations. What did these two stooges have in common?

John Loftus, who had corresponded with this author for nearly 20 years, posted a curious tale on his web-site, "What Congress Does Not Know About Enron and 9/11." Enron had been in Afghanistan building a gas pipeline with al Qaeda on its payroll, subsidizing the very terrorists that would later attack America. Did Enron's accountant, Arthur Andersen know about this? Former FBI counter-terrorist chief, John O'Neil, approached both the Clinton Administration officials and later, the newly elected vice president, Dick Cheney with the secret transcripts. No one listened. In disgust, O'Neil quit the FBI and was hired by the World Trade Center as chief of security. The first day on the job, 9/11/2001, O'Neil would die trying to rescue his fellow employees in the burning rubble. The Enron/al Qaeda transcripts were passed on to Loftus. Was Arthur Andersen money laundering Afghanistan poppy filled profits through the Fortune Five Hundred's 401K plans? Had similar activity occurred in the Lottery profits? Who would know? New York Stock Exchange president Richard Grasso? Federal Reserve Chief Alan Greenspan deploring the market's "irrational exuberance," the Connecticut State Gaming Board, Occidental Petroleum CEO's, Sheik Shelhi? Further incriminating evidence on the Taliban, al Qaeda, and Osama Bin Laden being on Enron's Afghan pipeline payroll was cited in a lengthy article by Jeffrey Steinberg (editor of the 'Executive Intelligence Review') interview with "The National Enquirer" March 4, 2002, "ENRON GAVE TALIBAN $MILLIONS." Had Clinton and his CIA Director, George Tenent, pulled the plug on Wall Street's feeding frenzy, fearing either party in the upcoming 2000 election would not sanction this racketeering? Did al Qaeda stage a purple snit? Was 9/11 a terrorist attempt to blackmail the next presidency into continuing business as usual? Fortunately, Baby Bush had higher values than his father or Clinton. Next, Harvey Pitt commandeered William Webster to clean house at the Security and Exchange Commission. A public uproar went out, Webster already under investigation for stock fraud at U. S. Technologies. The two conspirators resigned the SEC together. Ah, yes, the Devil and William Webster; was he our biggest mole?

In the aftermath of 9/11 emerged a tangled web of oil and gas pipeline concessions across Russia's newly freed Central Asian Republics involving Enron, al Qaeda, Arthur Andersen, Afghanistan, Aliyev, SOCOR, YUKOS Oil with Dick Cheney and Halliburton in the middle. Under the former

Soviet Union, major industries were operated by the State, including oil. As the Soviet Union dissolved after the fall of the Berlin Wall, privatization of State industry and land was a necessity if the newly freed citizens were to succeed under capitalism. Arthur Andersen took it upon itself to advise both the Americans and the Russians on economics, hoping to expand its web of power. The world's fifth largest accounting firm had approached the Security and Exchange Commission early on to loosen laws for corporate mergers, most advantageous to Arthur Andersen's clients' expansion. (See the New York Times 10/19/71 page 64). Later, Andersen consulted the Russian Ministry of Economics on price manipulation in oil noted in "Izvestia": "Andersen's Fairytales" quoting Arthur Andersen's letter to Russian Deputy Prime Minister Viktor Khristenko, 01/31/2002. It was right that Russia's first freely elected leader, Boris Yeltsin, auction off state industries, including oil, but to whom, Mikhail Khodorkovsky, his biggest campaign financier? YUKOS Oil was born. The Russian Mafia grew by leaps and bounds.

Russia's black gold stretched across the steps of Central Asia, between Chechnya, the Baku, and Kadzakistan. Khodorkovsky emerged as Russia's wealthiest businessman. Yeltsin was an innocent in a pool of prehistoric sharks. Imagine the Tar Pits of La Brea, where old dinosaur bones kept resurfacing, bubbling up in the black ooze. Russia's next President, Vladimir Putin, would re-nationalize YUKOS, charging Khodorkovsky for tax evasion and racketeering. YUKOS next declared bankruptcy, attempting a merger with Exxon/Mobile, filing in a Texas court, only to be booted out. "Fortune" magazine's issue (4/16/2001 volume 143 page 148) ran an article "Oil, Oil, Everywhere" noting "Exxon Mobile is terrific at taking something complex, simulating it, standardizing it on a global basis, and then rolling out on a massive scale," says John Burke, a partner in the energy practice of Accenture, formerly Andersen Consulting." It is speculated that YUKOS's attempts to go global forced Putin's hand into nationalizing Russia's largest oil and gas company. YUKOS attempted a merger with another Russian giant, Apatit, a large chemical fertilizer concern. Was Apatit a foster child of Occidental Petroleum? Khodorkovsky's vice president, Platon Lebedev, was also on the hot seat, having attempted to merge with an insecticide research institute NIUIF. Pesticides and poison gases? (See "The Fate of Mikhail Khodorkovsky" in "Business Week Online" 5/17/2005) Any relation to Serge Lebedev and his buna rubber escapades with I. G. Farben? Earlier, in 1997, China and Russia signed the Kovyktinskoye gas field project with intent to build a pipeline from Lake Baikal to Jiangsu Province. Korea joined the project. By 2000, YUKOS Oil, Transneft, and the China National United Oil Corp. plotted a new pipe to extend from Irkusk to Beijing. China made a bank bid to buy out YUKOS but as CEO Khodorkovsky's misfortunes mounted, China backed off. The Japanese offered financing, all parties hoping to have the pipeline extended eastward to their thirsty economies. Lesser YUKOS oil executives fled Russia, seeking sanctuary in America! The terrorists had turned Chechnya into a war zone, and Putin, a former KGB chief, had every right to suspect Arthur Andersen and Armand Hammer as the source of its troubles.

Everything in the 2002 publication of "Lyme Disease and the SS Elbrus" on biological and chemical warfare had been public knowledge since the late 1980s, much since the 1940s, the patented formulas for Tabun and Sarin gas listed in the dictionary! There was no reason for the clamp down on radio talk show interviews or the book's sale, but everything came to an abrupt halt. This book was not a source for terrorists, but most evidently, a tool to identify their financiers. Yet the Wall Street Journal on 4/8/2002 published a most curious article: "Can the Risk of Terrorism Be Calculated By Insurers? Game Theory Might Do It" by Dr. Gordon Woo, an economic consultant to the post 9/11 insurance companies. Woo insinuated that the terrorists behaved like "insect swarms and German U-boat fleets" arguing terrorists who were suicidal would delay firing as opposed to duelist, expecting to win. Was this Chinese consultant implicating my book as inciting terrorism, instead of Wall Street having money laundering their dope pipeline for the past decade? It would be worth further investigating Armand Hammer, Arthur Andersen, Occidental Petroleum and YUKOS Oil's ties to Red China and the terrorists.

Better yet, investigate Oxy's coal concession in Red China as a motive to re-direct the blame for inciting terrorism, seeing how "Lyme Disease and the SS Elbrus" was published November, 2002, long after 9/11. Hammer, himself, published a lengthy article "On A Vast China Market" in "The Journal of International Affairs" (1986 Winter edition, volume 39, Issue 2, page 19-26.) in his self-grandizing style, expounding on his partnership with Red China in the An Tai Bao Coal Mine. Arthur Andersen International was still Oxy's accountant. Armand Hammer died December 10th, 1990, weeks before his planned bar mitzfa! Having armed every terrorist against Israel, an avowed atheist and Card Carrying Communist, the Jews hated him. Perhaps, there is a God, after all. By June 12th, 2005 on the Fox News Network, John Loftus' program "Top Secret" announced Red China had dispersed nuclear weapons to every known terrorist in the Middle East, and China was the prime source of arms and funding for al Qaeda. How did American intelligence discover this? Kaddafi told them so, handing over nuclear secrets from Pakistan and Red China. Kaddafi vowed to give up its own weapons of mass destruction in return for an end of economic sanctions. In the meantime, Occidental Petroleum has opened a new gas pipeline through Columbia, costing Americans millions of dollars to protect against Communist rebels. "Here we go again." to quote Ronald Reagan. Let Red China's house of cards, built on half a century of lies to its own people, come crashing down. The world can be cured of brucellosis, Lyme disease and drug addiction, but can it ever be cured of the greed and arrogance of Communism and Fascism? Let's hope so.

June 1st, 2005 Arthur Andersen's appeal to overturn its 6/15/2002 conviction for fraud went to the highest court in the land, and ALL MEMBERS OF THE SUPREME COURT UNINIMOUSLY CLEARED ARTHUR ANDERSEN OF ANY WRONG DOING! They had no idea their clients were cooking the books and shredding documents. How could they be held accountable? On the other hand, Enron officials were convicted June 15, 2005 for fraud and destruction of documents, CEO Ken Lay sentenced to prison. Enron Broadband is also on the chopping block for stock fraud and money laundering. Bernard Ebbers, CEO of World.com, shorted $11 billion in stock fraud, was sentenced to 25 years in prison on Thursday, July 14, 2005. Other Arthur Andersen clients would follow suit and individual fools, listed in the Sacramento Bee, page D7, on June 14th, 2005: Tyco, Credit Suisse First Boston, Healthsouth, Martha Stewart, Aldelphia Communications and of course Global Crossing, which the Bee forgot to mention. The liberal press fingered corporate greed behind Wall Street's fraud, avoiding the AFL-CIO/Global Crossing scandal and Arthur Andersen and its left wing affiliates through Armand Hammer and Moscow and China.

Meanwhile, back at the ranch, Occidental Petroleum began building a gas pipeline through Columbia, and once again, Congress has an excuse to rush to democracy's aide and provide protection to right wing death squads and leftwing rebels both peddling dope to America. It is now rumored that al Qaeda has partnered up with the Communist rebels, MS13 and other drug gangs in Latin America, making it a snap for terrorists to illegally cross the Mexican/American border. "Here we go again" to quote Ronald Reagan. Both the Russians and the Americans are going to have to put their heads together to investigate Red China, Occidental Petroleum and Arthur Andersen and there suspect roll in funding terrorism. Perhaps Arthur Andersen is not guilty of paper shredding at Enron, but why not begin looking at Andersen's escapades in the FBI with the Strategic Management Council and possible destruction of incriminating evidence on Robert Hanssen, Amtorg, Armand Hammer, Occidental Petroleum, al

Qaeda, the Chechen rebels and even Arthur Andersen itself? This would constitute treason on the highest order.

APPENDIX

Author's FOIA request to National Archives Military Reference Branch on OACSI file holdings for CW and BW, Germany and Russia, listed as "Missing" or "Destroyed." This material was removed prior to their accession to the National Archives in 1967, according to NA MRB personnel. (Note "S.D." means "Sensitive Document" and "MIS" means "Military Intelligence Service." An "*" indicates the document remains classified, (only a few on this list.)

OACSI file #,TITLE
(FOIA Request made July 13, 1987)
S.D. 27403Clandestine Attack on Crops and Animals Overall Survey
S.D. 32636Clandestine Attack on Crops and Animals, 15 May 1951
S.D. 22772Clandestine Attack on Crops and Animals

(FOIA Request July 192 1987)
S.D. 17847Chemical Warfare (Germany), Report based on Interrogation of Jurgen E. Von KLENCK
National Archives Military Reference Branch response L87-2324-WL, and L87-2358-WL: August 17, 1987
"Dear Ms. Verdon: This is in response to your letters of July 13, and 19. I have surveyed records in our custody and have determined that documents bearing SD numbers 17847, 22772, 27403, and 32636 were destroyed by the Department of the Army prior to the Intelligence Document files being accessioned by the National Archives...
Sincerely, William G. Lewis". (these numbers were clarified

10/7/87.)

Author's note: According to William G. Lewis' conversations with the author, these OACSI files were accessioned to the National Archives in 1967. With a long enough passage in time to remove the "withdrawal slips," a three year requirement for "secret" files and four year requirement on "Top Secret" files, any intelligence officer who borrowed the files in 1963 during the Kennedy assassination would become unidentifiable.

(FOIA Request December 17, 1987)

S.D. 17482Chemical Warfare Sub-Committee Liaison with the US & Canada

S.D. 18908CW Sub-Committee 4th Meeting, Minutes, Meeting, Ministry of Defense, 1 Nov. 1949

S.D. 19033CW Sub-Committee 5th meeting, Minutes of Meeting held in Conference Room 'F', Ministry of Defense

S.D. 19508CW Sub-Committee (19) 6th Meeting Minutes of Meeting Held Ministry of Defense on Friday, 9 December 1949

S.D. 22372CW Sub-Committee Chiefs of Staff Committee, Minutes of Meeting held in Conference Room 'F', Ministry of Defense Tuesday, 16 May 50

S.D. 28127CW Sib-Committee Chiefs of Staff Committee, Minutes, Conference Room 'D', Ministry of Defense, Friday, December 8, 1950, 5th Meeting

S.D. 28127CW Sub-Committee 4th Meeting August 28, 1950

S.D. 20556CW Sub Committee Minutes of Meeting 10 February 1950

S.D. 21467SW Sub-Committee Minutes of Meeting 22 March 1950

S.D. 18412CW Sub-Committee (49) 3rd Meeting 29 Sept, 1949

S.D. 16816CW Sub-Committee (49) 1st Meeting Tuesday 14, June 1949

S.D. 29898CW Sub-Committee Assistance in Research by Commonwealth Countries, CW (51) 6

No./3Chemical Warfare Projects/2 Canadian Monthly Progress Report/1

No./3Chemical Warfare laboratories/1 Development Section Report/2

Review #4, LD files - Chemical Warfare, Indications of Biological and files as Scientific Intelligence Review #4 LD Files

Vegyi Harc/1Chemical Warfare Hungary 1944/3, Hungary/2

Military Reference Branch, National Archives response to author January 27, 1988, reply L88-0694-HHW. "Dear Ms. Verdon: I am enclosing a copy of the 21 Army Group report of interest to you, number 15, on your list (excluded from list above)... documents(your list numbers) 1 and 5-12 were destroyed according to the numerical card list of the "SD" documents. We were unable to locate numbers 2-4, 13-14, and 16-17 among the "SD" and related files in our custody. Sincerely Howard H. Wehmann, Assistant Chief, Military Field Branch."

(FOIA Request May 7, 1988)
S.D. 19306CW Sub-Committee Research and Development Policy in Relation to Intelligence on Russian CW (49) 26
S.D.CW Sub-Committee CW (49) 20 (Draft) Research and Development Policy in Relation to Intelligence on Russian Development
S.D. 19034CW Sub-Committee (49) 20 (Second Draft) Research and Development Policy to Intelligence on Russian Development
S.D. 19034CW (49) (Final) also D.R.P. (49) 133, Research and Development Policy in Relation to Intelligence on Russian Development
S.D. 19178CW Sub-Committee (49) 14, Russian CW-Nerve Gas-3C3
S.D. 18589CW Sub-Committee (49) 18 Research and Development Policy in Relation to Intelligence on Russian Development
S.D. 18950CW Sub-Committee (49) 19, CW-Foreign Progress and Capabilities
Project No. 6090 - MI 950050 CW-Soviet Capabilities for Intelligence Staff Study March 19, 1951
S.D. 17483CW Sub-Committee 1949 Report CW 'The Enemy Threat' CW (49) 7

Military Reference Branch, National Archives reply L88-2002-HW, May 25, 11988 from Elaine C. Everly. "Dear Ms. Verdon: We are unable to locate any of the other items (above) of interest to you in the relevant record series."

(FOIA Request July 25, 1988)
S.D. 225427CW Sub-Committee CW (50) 23 Release of Information to India and Pakistan
S.D. 2159CW The Enemy Threat JICM - 956 J.I.C. (50) 35
ONI/1 Translation/2
A-406/3CW Agents and Defense Against Them Czechoslovakia
(no number)CW 3/CINCPAC CINCPOA/1 INDEX CAPTURED

DOCUMENTS/2 VOL./4

Military Reference Branch, National Archives reply L88-2812-WL. August 25, 1988
"Dear Ms. Verdon: We have been unable to locate the documents described (above).
Sincerely, Elaine Everly, Chief Military Field Branch"

(FOIA Request January 20th, 1990)
MIS 244726Russia Research and Development (Who's Who Scientist & Medicine)
MIS 270277Russia Dr. Zellner of German Chemical Rocket Service
MIS 203971Germany - Detention Camp, Dustbin Periodic State Report #18
MIS 221262CW Installations in the Munsterlager Area CIOS xxxi-86
(Author's note: this title was located at the National Library of Medicine, unclassified, through the Library of Congress NUC Pre-1956 Index)
MIS 329097Development of New Insecticides & Chemical Warfare Agents BIOS

Military Reference Branch, National Archives Reply NN90-076 February 15, 1990
"Dear Ms. Verdon: ... document numbers listed above could not be located.
Sincerely, John Butler, Chief Suitland Reference Branch"

(FOIA Request January 20th 1990)
MIS 744587*Russia Military Medical Academy Purges 20 Dec. 1950
(classified per NA MRB letters 5/11/90 and Dec. 1993)
MIS 436505Interrogation of Dr. Gerhard Schrader on Nerve Gases 6 Jan 48
MIS 549086German Nerve Gases Interrogation Dip. Ing. Anton Schmahl dated Aug 47, BIOS 814
(FOIA Request April 30, 1990)
MIS SD26043Return of Technicians from USSR, Oct 19, 1950
MIS 67628*Soviet BW Research Center June 12, 1950 (Classified, 5/11/90, 12/93)

MIS 923862Microbiology USSR 1950

MIS 6822922* Dr. Von Bock USSR June 28, 1950 (classified)

MIS 716489*RE Von Bock Sept. 8, 1950 (note: Von Bock = Tolkmith's partner)

MIS 925919Germans CW USSR July 28, 1950

MIS 924435List of German Scientists & Engineers Employed USSR Sep 26, 1947

(reviewed under appeal and released to author, biography of 800+ men)

MIS SD12169 Info. on German CW & BW Activity & Scientists USSR Se 24, 1950

MIS 924162*Schmidt on Tabun March 28, 1949 (classified)

Military Reference Branch, National Archives Reply NN90-339m May 11, 1990

"Dear Ms. Verdon: this is in response to your FOIA request of Feb. 11, 1990 and April 16, and 30, 1990... documents (not starred above) are missing from the file, and (documents starred * above) are classified. all classified records have been submitted to our declassification unit for review... Sincerely, John Butler, chief Suitland Ref. Br."

(FOIA Request February 18, 1990)

MIS 822502*Return of Chemist to Germany from USSR June 19, 1951 (classified)

MIS SD31540Return of Chemist from the USSR June 22, 1951

MIS SD15016Top Secret Series Intelligence Paper No. 1/49 Russian BW project No. B.M./4820 B March 28, 1949

National Archives Suitland Reference Branch Reply NN90-168, March 12, 1990

"Dear Ms. Verdon: We have located one of the three classified documents you requested (MIS 822502), from Record Group 319, and have submitted it to our declassification unit for review. The other two documents MIS SD 31540 and MIS SD15016 were not in the files. Cards in the Numerical index indicate that these documents were destroyed.

Sincerely, John Butler, Chief, Suitland Reference Branch"

National Archives Suitland Reference Branch Reply NN90-168, December 20, 1991

"Dear Ms. Verdon: This is in further response to your FOIA request of February 18, 1990... One document (SD 82502) {authors note: should read 822502] has been denied in full from box S806, Intelligence Document file, Assistant Chief of Staff, Intelligence, Record Group 319. The denial is pursuant to 5 U.S.C. 522 (b)(1). The Department of the Army (case number 1870F91) and (NND 901555) is the denial authority. You may appeal this denial by writing, within 60 days of the date of this letter...

Sincerely, Trudy Huskamp Peterson, Assistant Archivist for the National Archives"

(FOIA Request July 2, 1990)
MIS SD7108Document materials Dec. 29, 1947
MIS SD7088"no title" Dec. 15, 1947
MIS SD6586"no title" Oct. 23, 1947
MIS SD7184Anti Gas Personnel Decontamination Dec. 19, 1947

National Archives Suitland Reference Branch Reply NN90-450, July 19, 1990

"Dear Ms. Verdon: We regret that numbers (listed above) were inadvertently omitted from our letter of June 26, 1990. All four numbers were among those we were unable to locate. Sincerely, John Butler, Chief Suitland Reference Branch, Textual Reference Div."

(FOIA Request December 26, 1991)
MIS 377163Epidemics in Far Eastern USSR 6/20/47
MIS SD6770Content and Use of Tri-Vaccine 11/12/47
MIS 824536Increase Manufactures of Vaccines/Rubber Works 7/11/51
MIS 195597Public & Medical Affairs Monthly Report of Military 8/20/45

National Archives Suitland Reference Branch Reply NN92-10, January 31, 1992

"Dear Ms. Verdon: Out of the 24 intelligence document files requested, seven were located and are offered to you on the enclosed NATF Form 72, four were not located (list above) and the other remaining 13 documents are still classified. The classified documents have been submitted to our declassification unit for review...

Sincerely, John Butler, Chief Suitland Reference Branch, Textual Reference Division"

(FOIA Request May 2, 1992)

MIS 68617Canalization Sewerage (Sociological Health & Sanitation Disease Control, USSR)

MIS 729562Hygiene & Sanitation (Sociological Health & Sanitation Disease Control, USSR)

National Archives Suitland Reference Branch Reply NN92-359, May 20, 1992

"Dear Ms. Verdon: We located 30 of the 32 intelligence documents you requested. We did not locate items 686171 and 729562. (list above) Twelve of the documents are declassified. We have submitted your request for declassification of the remaining eighteen documents to our declassification unit for review. As soon as the review is completed, we will notify you."

(FOIA Request March 15, 1993)

MIS SD3244Special Study BW Activities & Capabilities of Foreign Nations

National Archives Suitland Reference Branch Reply NN93-285, March 22, 1993

"Dear Ms. Verdon: The fifth report described as SD 3244 (961415) Special Study Biological Warfare Activities and Capabilities of Foreign Nations, March 30, 1946, was not located. The index card was annotated to show that it was destroyed.

Sincerely, John Butler, Chief Suitland Reference Branch (NNRR)"

GLOSSARY OF MILITARY, INTELLIGENCE & POLICE ORGANIZATIONS

Abwehr	German Intelligence Bureau under OKW (Wehrmacht – Ordnance)
ALSOS	Spy mission to uncover Nazi atomic bomb (US Army, WW II)
BIOS	British Intelligence Objectives Sub-Committee (British Forces, WW II)
BOSSI	Bureau of Special Services & Intelligence (New York City Police Dept.)
CIA	Central Intelligence Agency
CIC	Counter Intelligence Corps (US Army)
CIG	Central Intelligence Group
CIOS	Combined Intelligence Objectives Sub-Committee (Allied Forces, WW II)
CWS	Chemical Warfare Service (US Army)
DDU	War Dept. Document Disposal Unit (US) precursor to OPC
Dustbin	British Nazi smuggling operation
ETOUSA	European Theater of Operations, USA
FIAT	Field Intelligence Agency Technical (Allied Forces, WW II)
FBI	Federal Bureau of Investigations (US Justice Dept.)
FBI SAC	FBI Special Agent in Charge
FOP	Fraternal Organization of Police
G-2	US Army Intelligence
Gestapo	German Secret Police under NAZIs
GRU	Red Army Intelligence (USSR)
Gulag Archipelago	
	Chain of prisons across Soviet Union
HICOG	High Commisioner to Germany (US State Dept.)
JIOA	Joint Intelligence Objectives Agency (Allied Forces, WW II)
Kempie	Japanese police (Manchuria 1930s &

	1940s)
KGB	Soviet Secret Police (USSR - 1940s through 1980s) see: OGPU & NKVD
Luftwaffe	German Air Force
MID - O/B	War Dept. Military Intelligence Division, Order of Battle, US
MI5 & MI6	British Secret Services
MRB	National Archives Military Reference Branch, Suitland, MD
NATO	Northern Atlantic Treaty Organization
NAZI	National Socialist Party of Germany
Nav/Tech/Mis/Eur	US Naval Technical Mission to Europe
NKVD	Soviet Secret Police (USSR - 1930s - 1940s) see: KGB & OGPU
NTS	Narodny Trudovoi Soyuz (White Russian National Toiler's Alliance)
OACSI	Office of Army Chief of Staff of Intelligence (US Army)
OGPU	Soviet Secret Police (USSR 1920s - 1930s) see: KGB & NKVD
OKH	Oberkommando des Heeres (German High Command of Operations)
OKW	Oberkommando der Wehrmacht (German High Command Armed Forces)
ONI	Office of Naval Intelligence, US
OPC	Office of Policy Coordination (US State Dept.)
OSI	Office of Scientific Intelligence (CIA)
OSI	Office of Special Investigations (US Justice Dept.)
OSRD	Office of Scientific Research and Development (Dept. of Commerce)
OSS	Office of Strategic Services (State Dept)
Paperclip	American Nazi smuggling operation
SHAEF	Supreme Headquarters Allied European Forces
SOE	Special Operations Executive (British intelligence - guerilla warfare)
SS	Schutzstaffel, Security Service of the German Army
SSU	War Dept. Strategic Services Unit (US)
Waffen Pruf 9	

	OKW - Wehrmacht Ordnance Chemical and Biological Warfare Unit
Wehrmacht	German War Ministry
WDD	War Dept. Defense Detachment unit (US) precursor to OPC

INDEX

Josef Mengele aka Henry Tolkmith ?

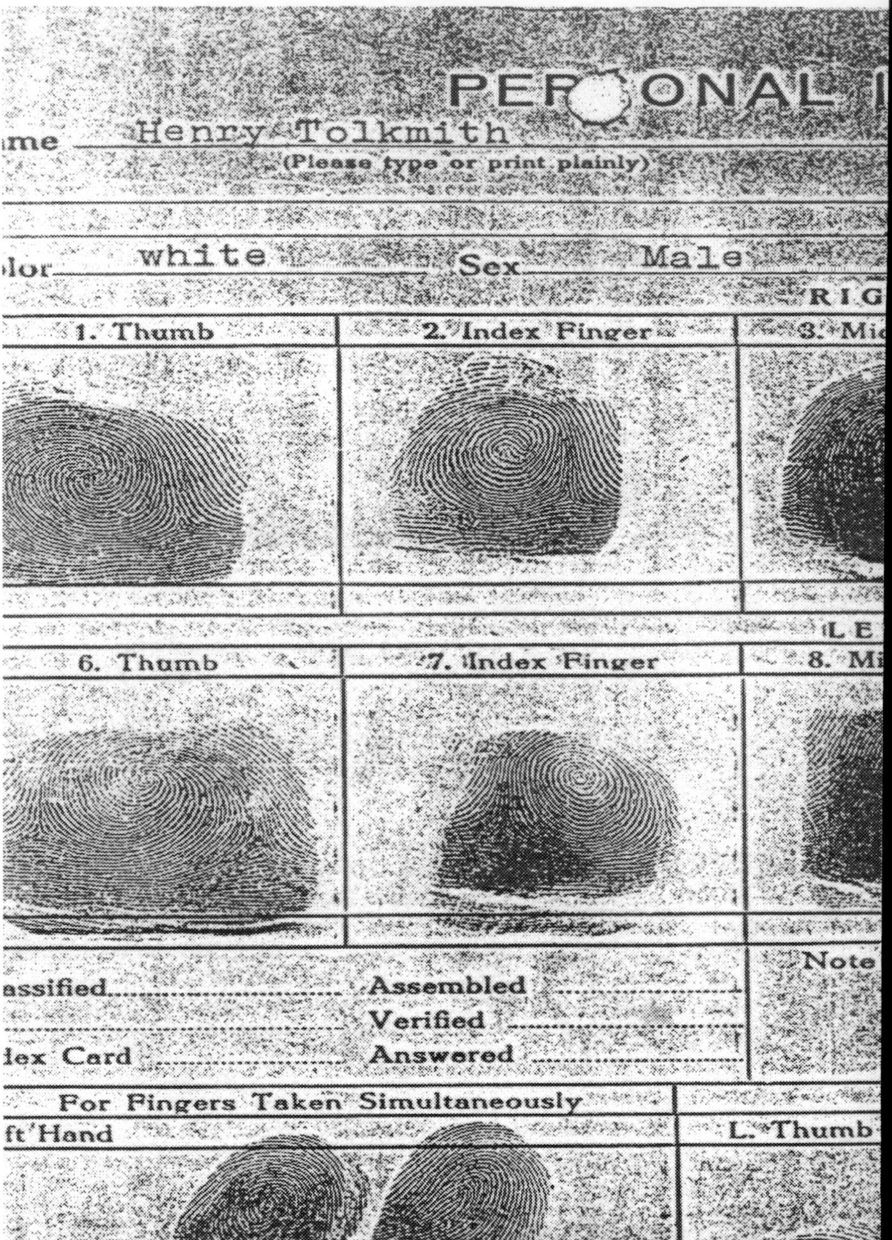
PER ONAL I

...me Henry Tolkmith
(Please type or print plainly)

...lor white Sex Male

RIG...

1. Thumb	2. Index Finger	3. Mi...

LE...

6. Thumb	7. Index Finger	8. Mi...

...assified .... Assembled ....
.... Verified ....
...dex Card .... Answered ....

Note ...

For Fingers Taken Simultaneously

...ft Hand

L. Thumb

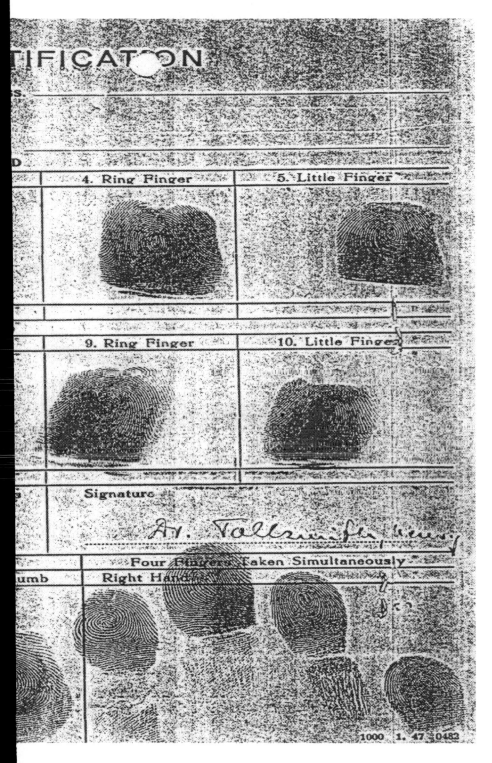

[Henry Tolkmith's fingerprint card]

Printed in the United States
79102LV00003B/37

9 781932 762624